STUDY GUIDE TO ACCOMPANY PINCHES: ESSENTIALS OF FINANCIAL MANAGEMENT

Third Edition

David C. Ketcham
University of Tennessee

George E. Pinches
University of Kansas

HarperCollinsPublishers

Study Guide to accompany Essentials of Financial Management

Copyright © 1990 by HarperCollins

All rights reserved. Printed in the United States of America. No part of this book may be used or reproduced in any manner whatsoever without written permission, except in the case of brief quotations embodied in critical articles and reviews. For information address HarperCollins
    10 East 53rd Street, New York, NY 10022.

ISBN: 06-045167X

90 91 92 93 94   9 8 7 6 5 4 3 2

CONTENTS

Essential Ideas in Financial Management .... Inside Front Cover
To the Student v

PART ONE   THE FINANCIAL MANAGEMENT ENVIRONMENT
- Chapter 1   Why Financial Management Matters 1
- Chapter 2   The Financial System, Interest Rates, and Taxes .. 8

PART TWO   FINANCIAL ANALYSIS
- Chapter 3   Analyzing Financial Statements 28
- Chapter 4   The Emphasis on Cash Flows 43

PART THREE   FUNDAMENTAL CONCEPTS FOR FINANCIAL MANAGEMENT
- Chapter 5   The Time Value of Money 68
- Chapter 6   Bond and Stock Valuation 85
- Chapter 7   Risk and Return 101

PART FOUR   LONG-TERM INVESTMENT DECISIONS
- Chapter 8   Capital Budgeting Techniques 126
- Chapter 9   Replacement Decisions, Cash Flows, and Capital Rationing 149
- Chapter 10   Risk and Capital Budgeting 166
- Chapter 11   Options and Investment Decisions 180

PART FIVE   LONG-TERM FINANCING DECISIONS
- Chapter 12   Obtaining Long-Term Financing and Common Stock ... 198
- Chapter 13   Liability Management 216
- Chapter 14   Required Returns for Companies and Projects 238
- Chapter 15   Capital Structure 254
- Chapter 16   Dividend Policy and Internal Financing 279
- Chapter 17   Leasing 293

PART SIX   WORKING CAPITAL MANAGEMENT
- Chapter 18   Working Capital Policy 306
- Chapter 19   Cash and Marketable Securities 322
- Chapter 20   Accounts Receivable and Inventory 336
- Chapter 21   Short-Term Financing 351

PART SEVEN   FINANCIAL STRATEGY
- Chapter 22   Mergers and Corporate Restructuring 372
- Chapter 23   Financial Planning and Strategy 392
- Chapter 24   International Financial Management 407

TO THE STUDENT

The study of financial management is challenging and interesting; however, it can also be the source of difficulty, anxiety and frustration. The purpose of this STUDY GUIDE is to promote your effective mastery of the material presented in ESSENTIALS OF FINANCIAL MANAGEMENT by George Pinches. It does this by presenting concisely, and in a different format, the key ideas covered in ESSENTIALS OF FINANCIAL MANAGEMENT. By applying yourself and using the STUDY GUIDE in addition to the text, you will gain a solid grasp of the financial concepts, terms, and applications that are so much a part of our daily lives.

The STUDY GUIDE is designed to assist in this process. It does this by presenting the following material for each chapter in which it is needed:

1. How This Chapter Relates to the Rest of the Text
2. Topical Outline
3. Formulas
4. What to Look For
5. Completion Questions
6. Problems
7. Answers to Completion Questions
8. Solutions to Problems

Before turning to this STUDY GUIDE, it is beneficial to read first the appropriate chapter in ESSENTIALS OF FINANCIAL MANAGEMENT. (Often it is useful to begin by skimming the chapter; once you have observed its key features, you can then read it in depth.) The first four elements of this STUDY GUIDE can be reviewed in order to expand upon the material in the chapter. The completion questions in this STUDY GUIDE are designed to reinforce key concepts by covering the main points in each chapter. Finally, the problems in this STUDY GUIDE are designed to supplement those in the book. By working these additional problems you will improve your mastery of the relevant concepts and gain understanding and confidence so you can master the problems in the book. The STUDY GUIDE also lets you verify immediately whether your answer is correct and see a step-by-step solution to the problem.

Inside the front and back cover of this STUDY GUIDE is an outline summarizing the essential ideas in financial management. This summary is useful early in your studies to point the way and emphasize key concepts, and it is also a helpful review of the essential ideas later in the course. If you don't understand the "Essential Ideas in Financial Management" by the end of your studies, you: (1) didn't study the material sufficiently after it was assigned; (2) understood the material when you studied it but have forgotten it now; or (3) never were assigned the material. Let's hope only the last of these applies to you.

Most of the material in this STUDY GUIDE has been revised from a prior edition and a number of people have contributed to its completion. Students at both the University of Kansas and the University of Tennessee (gleefully) made us aware of errors in earlier additions. Philip Baird (University of Tennessee) checked numerical solutions to all problems, proofread much of the text, and provided several suggestions; the result of his efforts is a much clearer product. Cynthia Ketcham did an outstanding job in typing, editing, formatting and proofreading this STUDY GUIDE; without her efforts the STUDY GUIDE might never have been completed. We of course are responsible for any errors and inconsistencies.

We would appreciate hearing comments from both students and instructors concerning the clarity of this STUDY GUIDE, any problems you might have or errors you may have discovered, and any suggestions for improvement you may wish to make. Good luck; we hope you find the study of financial management as interesting and as informative as we do.

David C. Ketcham
School of Business Administration
434 Stokely Management Center
University of Tennessee
Knoxville, TN 37996-0540
(615) 974-1726

George E. Pinches
School of Business
University of Kansas
Lawrence, Kansas 66045
(913) 864-3536

CHAPTER 1

THE FINANCIAL MANAGEMENT ENVIRONMENT

HOW THIS CHAPTER RELATES TO THE REST OF THE TEXT

Chapter 1 provides a preview of the structure of the text, defines financial management, and enumerates the goal of the firm. Financial management is the acquisition, management, and financing of resources for corporations by means of money. Good financial management results in achieving the goal of the firm; maximization of stock price. Since the firm can be thought of as a collection of assets, decisions affecting asset value will affect stock price. Value is a function of the size of cash flows, their timing, and riskiness. Through the course of the text, each of these components and how financial decisions affect them are analyzed. The chapter also discusses the financial structure of a typical corporation.

TOPICAL OUTLINE

I. Why is financial management important?
   A. Increasing world-wide competition, deregulation, and slower growth in the American economy have boosted the importance of good financial management.
   B. Stockholders, employees, and managers benefit from good management and suffer from poor decisions.
II. What is financial management?
   A. The acquisition, management, and financing of resources for corporations by means of money.
   B. The primary concern of financial management is the firm and its operations.
III. The primary objective of the firm: Maximizing stockholder wealth.
   A. How effectively resources are used is determined by how much someone is willing to pay for claims on those resources in the financial marketplace.
      1. The total value of the firm (V) is equal to the value of the claims of the stockholders (S) plus bondholders (B); ie. V = S + B.

2. Maximizing V can be accomplished by maximizing S; this is equivalent to maximizing the price per share of common stock.
B. Constraints: Stockholders versus management.
1. If you are the owner of a small business, it is obvious that you should act to maximize your own wealth.
2. In large corporations, there is a separation between ownership (stockholders) and management; managers act as agents on behalf of the stockholders.
3. To insure that management acts in the best interests of the stockholders, the firm incurs agency costs such as reporting requirements, outside audits, bonuses, or stock options for the managers.
4. Management performance is judged in the financial marketplace and is reflected in stock prices.
C. Constraints: Shareholders versus creditors.
1. Stockholders can expropriate wealth from creditors by increasing the risk of bankruptcy.
2. Creditors constrain stockholders by limiting dividends, additional debt, or asset sales.
3. Other stakeholders include employees, customers, suppliers, and the community at large. Because of possible conflicts between the firm's goal and stakeholders, other constraints may exist.
D. Maximizing stockholders' wealth in practice.
1. The goal of shareholder wealth maximization is theoretically correct.
2. It is limited by constraints.
3. It provides a standard of comparison to evaluate management.

IV. Achieving the objective.
A. The value of the firm or an asset is a function of the magnitude, timing, and riskiness of the future cash flows.
1. Cash flows are the actual cash received or paid.
2. Timing is the point at which cash is actually received or disbursed, since we must consider the time value of money.
3. Risk is the possibility of an undesirable outcome.

4. Valuation is the process of determining the worth of an asset based on expected returns and risks.
   B. Only those management actions that positively affect the magnitude, timing, and riskiness of the future cash flows are desirable.
V. The finance function.
   A. Financial managers in a firm are numerous, including the financial vice-president and anyone else who makes or influences financial decisions.
   B. Financial management involves the acquisition, financing, and management of resources.
VI. International Financial Management
   A. American business participates in a world-wide economy; approximately 25% of the assets of U. S.-based manufacturing firms are located outside the country.
   B. Japan and the European Common Market are major participants in the international economy.
   C. Most firms need to think globally in terms of markets and competition.

WHAT TO LOOK FOR

Each year, hundreds of thousands of new businesses are incorporated and thousands fail. Effective financial management might have saved some of these firms.

Financial Management: Acquisition, Financing, and Management of Resources

Financial management is the acquisition, financing, and management of resources for corporations by means of money. The goal of financial management is to maximize stockholder wealth or share price.

A business enterprise can be viewed as a pie. Like a pie, several ingredients go into its making. These include the firm's investments and acquisitions, how the firm's resources are managed, and how the firm's needs are financed. How much the firm is worth is determined in the financial markets and this value changes as the market's assessment of the effectiveness of the firm's ingredients change. The value determined in the market is simply the sum of the value of the firm's stocks (S) and bonds (B).

Corporate resources can be classified as short-term assets, such as inventories and accounts receivable, or long-term assets, such as plant and equipment. Corporations acquire both types of assets in the course of doing business. While you might think that financial management will be difficult because of the variety of assets available, it is relatively straightforward. The value of any asset is based on the asset's cash flow, its timing, and its riskiness.

With this simple rule in mind, the book first discusses the financial marketplace (Chapter 2) and interest rates. Chapters 3 and 4 describe financial statements and examine the similarities and differences between accounting earnings and cash flows. Chapter 5 examines timing of cash flows and its effect on value, and Chapter 7 discusses risk. The valuation concepts are critical to an understanding of financial management; they are used in capital budgeting (Chapters 8 through 10), leasing (Chapter 17) and mergers and corporate restructuring (Chapter 22). These tools are also used for managing a firm's short-term assets (Chapters 18 through 21).

Acquisitions require that a firm either generate funds internally or go to the financial markets. Again, financial decisions are based on value. We will discuss how firms raise money through using short-term debt (Chapter 21), long-term debt (Chapter 13), and common stock (Chapter 12). The mix of debt and equity, the firm's capital structure (Chapter 15), affects the cost of funds (Chapter 14). This is the minimum rate of return the firm needs to earn in order to benefit stockholders. Resources must produce a return for their investment to be worthwhile. Short-term and long-term assets, if carefully managed, will produce increased cash flows for the firm and a return to its stockholders. This return will come from the cash cycle. However, short-term and long-term financing are not free. In Chapters 2, 12, and 21, we consider the cost of borrowing money--interest--and factors like risk that can increase this financing cost. To be successful, firms must consistently manage their finances well. Chapter 23 discusses financial planning and strategy, and points out some serious consequences of poor financial management.

Three Fundamental Concepts

Three fundamental concepts--time value of money, risk and return, and valuation--help us understand the theory and practice of financial management. As you will note from the discussions below, these concepts all relate to cash flow and will be common themes throughout the text.

Cash flow

The timing, magnitude, and riskiness of a firm's future after-tax cash flows are critical. A shortage of cash can require a firm to seek additional and increasingly costly debt or equity, or can push the firm toward bankruptcy. Net income, as presented in GAAP financial statements, does not give a clear picture of the firm's cash position. In addition, the financial markets determine the firm's value according to its expected future cash flow. Therefore, we will use cash flows rather than net income when evaluating the firm's financial management. Chapters 4 and 8 discuss cash flow.

Time value of money

The cost of financing is the opportunity cost of money or interest. When a firm invests money in resources, the return must exceed this financing cost. Chapter 5 helps us learn to calculate both the future and the present values of investments. We will use time values throughout the text.

Risk and return

As the riskiness of a firm's future cash flow increases, so must its return. The return must compensate investors for bearing this additional risk. Bondholders' interest payments come from pre-tax cash flows, while preferred and common stockholders' cash dividends come from after-tax cash flows. If investors fear for this interest or dividend payment stream, they will demand a higher required rate of return. In Chapters 6 and 7, we work through these dynamics.

Valuation

The required rate of return and the expected cash flow from an investment determines its value. In valuation, we use the cash flow ideas from Chapter 4 and the time value of money concept from Chapter 5. We will learn how to value debt, common stock, and preferred stock in Chapters 6, 13, and 14. In Chapters 8 through 10, we learn to value capital investment projects. In Chapter 17, we learn to value leases. Valuation of short-term assets and liabilities is covered in Chapters 19 through 21. In Chapter 22 we apply valuation concepts for making merger decisions.

The Ultimate Goal of Financial Management

You will find that the goals of many individuals ultimately determine the kinds of decisions managers make. The stockholder's goal is to maximize wealth. Since common stockholders are the residual owners of the firm, they want to maximize their cash dividend and capital gains return from their shares of the firm. As we noted earlier, the price or value of common stock depends on the magnitude, timing, and riskiness of the firm's cash flows. Therefore, in order to boost market price, the stockholder hopes for high positive cash flows which are frequent and of low risk. This leads to increases in the value of the firm's stock and/or the payment of higher cash dividends.

Preferred stockholders, like common stockholders, have a claim on assets, although their cash dividend stream is generally fixed. Preferred stockholders, in order to ensure their dividend payments, hope for predictable, positive cash flows. The bondholders' or creditors' goal is to receive their interest payments and principal repayments on schedule. To the extent that payment is questionable, creditors will require a higher rate of return to compensate for this uncertainty.

As you see, there are many parties with stakes in the firm. The stockholders, as owners, hire managers who act as agents for them. But, the stockholders must insure that these managers act in the shareholder's interests, not the manager's, and maximize the firm's stock price. Possible conflicts between managers and stockholders may result in constraints being placed on the managers and result in agency costs. There are other possible conflicts as well. Bondholders want the firm to remain safe so that they can be paid back. Stockholders, on the other hand, may want the firm to invest in more risky projects with promises of higher returns. Bondholders may put constraints on the actions of the stockholders to insure that the firm can pay them back. The goal of stockholder wealth maximization, subject to the constraints of the various stakeholders, is the appropriate goal for the firm.

The financial market's purpose is the efficient transfer of money from borrowers to lenders. In the market, interest rates help allocate the scarce loanable funds. Chapter 2 discusses this mechanism. Managers must understand the workings of financial markets in order to plan the future financing needs or surpluses. The timing of these needs or surpluses can be critical, since the cost of funds can change drastically over the course of a year or two.

COMPLETION QUESTIONS

1.1 _____ involves the _____, management, and financing of resources for corporations by means of money, but with due regard for the prices in external economic markets.

1.2 The financial manager's interest is in maximizing the _____ in the financial marketplace, not its book value.

1.3 The investor determines the value of the firm by estimating the magnitude, timing, and riskiness of the firm's _____, rather than looking at the firm's _____.

1.4 When we consider the timing of cash flows, we mean when the cash is _____.

1.5 Investors individually estimate the magnitude, timing, and riskiness of a firm's cash flows. Their resulting aggregate demand for the firm's common stock versus the supply of that stock will determine the stock's _____.

1.6 The _____ of a firm is deeply involved in financial policymaking, as well as in corporate or strategic planning.

1.7 Stockholders, as owners of the firm, hire managers who act as _____ for them.

1.8 To ensure that management acts in their interest, stockholders use various incentives and monitoring devices; one such incentive which is tied in with the value of the firm is a _____ plan.

1.9 To insure that management acts in the best interests of the stockholders, the firm must incur _____ such as reporting requirements, bonuses, or salary plans tied to stock performance.

ANSWERS TO COMPLETION QUESTIONS

1.1 Financial management; acquisition
1.2 stock price
1.3 cash flows; earnings (or net income)
1.4 actually received or disbursed
1.5 market price

1.6 financial vice-president (or chief financial officer)
1.7 agents
1.8 stock option
1.9 agency costs

CHAPTER 2

THE FINANCIAL SYSTEM, INTEREST RATES, AND TAXES

HOW THIS CHAPTER RELATES TO THE REST OF THE TEXT

Financial managers do not make decisions in a vacuum. The decisions they make and the results are dependent upon the structure and operation of the financial marketplace in which firms operate. The U.S. financial system provides for the orderly transfer of funds from suppliers to demanders. The financial system consists of institutions such as commercial banks and markets such as the New York Stock Exchange.

Value (Chapter 6) is determined in the financial markets. An important component of value are the interest rates, which are a function of the supply and of the demand for loanable funds, expected inflation, and risk. While the later chapters, most notably Chapter 6, examine the relationship between value and rates of return, this chapter discusses the various components of interest rates.

TOPICAL OUTLINE

I. The American financial system.
   A. The goal of the financial system is to aid in the transferring of funds from suppliers to demanders.
      1. Suppliers are individuals, business, and government.
      2. Financial institutions help channel the funds from suppliers to demanders of funds.
      3. Demanders of funds--individuals, business, and government-- invest the funds in productive resources or services.
      4. Financial markets--the money market and the capital market-- facilitate the issuance of financial assets.
   B. The transfer of funds creates financial assets for suppliers of funds and financial liabilities for demanders of funds.
      1. Money is a medium of exchange used to acquire goods and services or to pay debt.
      2. Debt is a promise to pay back a certain amount on a specified future date.

3. Stock is an ownership in a business.
    a. Common stock has a residual ownership in a business.
    b. Preferred stock has a prior but limited claim on the assets and cash flows of the firm.

C. Financial institutions.
  1. Bring suppliers and demanders of funds together in order to
     a. Provide liquidity and flexibility.
     b. Provide convenience.
     c. Provide expertise.
     d. Spread risks.
  2. Types of financial institutions.
     a. Commercial banks are the traditional financial department store.
     b. Insurance companies and pension funds are also important.
     c. Investment companies include mutual funds, which allow individual investors to pool their funds. These funds invest in stocks, bonds, and recently money market instruments.
     d. Thrift institutions include savings and loans, credit unions, and mutual savings banks, which accept deposits and make loans and investments.
     e. Other types of financial institutions include finance companies, mortgage companies, and real estate investment trusts, which are specialized loan sources.
  3. Financial institutions are currently undergoing substantial restructuring.
     a. Deregulation of interest rates allows financial institutions to broaden services.
     b. Interstate banking.
     c. Increased competition from other firms offering financial services.
  4. Chief providers of funds are listed in Table 2.1.
  5. Investment bankers provide assistance to firms raising funds (by issuing new stocks or bonds) in the financial markets.

6. Institutions help demanders indirectly meet suppliers in the financial markets.

D. Financial markets.
1. Money market securities mature in less than one year.
   a. U.S. Treasury bills
   b. Short-term government agencies
   c. Federal funds
   d. Certificates of deposit
   e. Commercial paper
   f. Bankers' acceptances
   g. Repurchase agreements
   h. Eurodollars
2. Capital market securities mature in more than one year.
   a. Long-term U.S. government bonds or notes
   b. Long-term government agency issues
   c. Debt issued by firms
   d. Common and preferred stock
3. Primary market: Market for selling newly issued securities. This market is operated through investment bankers who provide assistance and advice to firms raising funds.
4. Secondary market: Market for buying and selling seasoned securities.
   a. Provides a ready market for investors wishing to liquidate holdings.
   b. Provides a market in which issues trade when they have become seasoned.
   c. Transactions occur on the organized exchanges (NYSE, AMEX, for example) or in the over-the-counter (OTC) market.

II. The government's role.
A. The U.S. government provides regulation and support through government agencies such as the Securities and Exchange Commission, the Comptroller of the Currency, and the Federal Deposit Insurance Corporation.

B. The Federal Reserve System: Tools to influence the operation of commercial banks:
   1. Change the reserve requirement.
   2. Change the discount rate.
   3. Open market operations: If the Fed sells (buys) U.S. government securities, the Fed will contract (expand) money supply and increase (decrease) interest rates.
C. Fiscal Policies are government policies dealing with taxation, investment tax credits, capital gains taxes, or other issues. These may positively or adversely affect the business climate.
   1. Increased deficits increase the demand for money and push up interest rates.
   2. Large amounts of government debt "crowd out" corporate borrowers because not enough supply is available to meet their needs after the demands of the government are met.

III. Why is the financial system important?
A. The financial system provides an efficient means of bringing together suppliers and demanders of funds.
B. The financial system, through the secondary markets, provides liquidity to investors and enhances the capital raising ability of firms.
C. The evolution of the financial system affords new opportunities to raise capital to astute firms.
D. Value is determined in the financial marketplace.

IV. Interest rates and the required rate of return.
A. What are interest rates?
   1. Interest rates are the prices paid when an individual, firm, or governmental unit borrows funds.
   2. Interest rates are costs or benefits, depending whether you are a borrower or lender.
   3. Interest rates are usually stated on a percentage per year basis.
   4. The amount borrowed is called the principal.

B. The real rate of interest.
1. In a world with no expected inflation or risk, the real rate of interest would be the cost of funds.
2. The real rate is determined solely by the supply of and the demand for loanable funds.
C. Inflation and its impact.
1. As the purchasing power of the dollar is eroded by inflation, investors must be compensated by a higher rate of return to preserve their purchasing power.
2. Fisher effect: The real rate of interest (between 1 and 2 percent) plus the expected rate of inflation equals the observed risk-free rate of interest.
    a. Those who borrow at fixed rates when interest rates are low benefit at the expense of lenders when rates rise with unexpected inflation.
    b. Higher inflation causes an increase in the cost of all funds available to firms.
D. Maturity premium.
1. The maturity premium is an additional return required by investors because long-term bonds are more sensitive to interest rate changes and thus more risky.
2. Graphs of the yield to maturity and term to maturity of securities of the same level of default risk are called yield curves and show the "term structure of interest rates."
E. Default premium.
1. The default premium is an additional return required to compensate investors for the risk that the firm will not be able to pay interest or the principal or both.
2. Corporate bonds are rated by quality from AAA (very safe) to C and below.
3. The higher the bond rating, the lower the default premium and hence the lower its nominal interest rate.
F. The "risk premium."
1. The risk premium is composed of the maturity premium, the default premium, a liquidity premium, and an issue-specific

premium.
   2. A liquidity premium arises if the market for the security is not active.
   3. An issue-specific premium arises from the type of security and its provisions.
   4. The required return on an asset equals the nominal risk-free rate plus the risk premium.
   5. The higher the risk, the higher the risk premium and the required return.
 G. Required rates of return, business decisions, and stock prices.
   1. A downward-sloping term structure indicates long-term debt is cheaper than short-term debt.
   2. As inflation falls, the term structure generally shifts downward.
   3. Interest rates tend to fall in recessions.
   4. Interest expense is tax deductible for a firm.
   5. Common stock is more risky and thus is more expensive than debt financing.
   6. Stock prices are affected by changes in interest rates and changes in the firm's cash flow or risk.

V. Risk, return, and market efficiency.
 A. Risk and required return.
   1. Historically, there is a positive relationship between risk and return; assets with the best performance generally have more variable returns.
   2. It is important to remember that there is no such thing as a "free lunch." Increases in risk cause increases in required returns, and hence costs.
 B. Market efficiency.
   1. An efficient market is one in which security prices adjust rapidly and accurately to the announcement of new information. Characteristics that lead to efficient markets are:
     a. Many profit-maximizing individuals who analyze and value securities and who act independently.
     b. New information arriving randomly.

c. Investors reacting quickly to new information, causing prices to change to reflect that new information.
d. In an efficient market, the price of an asset is an unbiased estimate of its actual worth.

2. Event tests are used to analyze the impact of a news announcement on stock prices.
   a. An abnormal return is the difference between actual and expected returns.
   b. In an efficient market, new relevant news should be immediately reflected in stock prices; abnormal returns should be positive (or negative) only on the day before and on the announcement day, and zero thereafter.
   c. Most studies conclude that the financial markets are reasonably efficient.

3. Implications of efficient markets for financial managers.
   a. Since security prices are unbiased estimates of firm value, they provide assessments of the performance of the firm.
   b. Trying to influence investors with lavish reports or campaigns to "sell" the company are, in the long run, ineffective. Rational, intelligent investors will see through these cosmetic efforts.

VI. Individual and corporate taxes.
   A. Taxes are an important consideration since individuals and corporations are interested in usable cash flow--cash flow after taxes are paid.
   B. Federal taxes are progressive; the higher the taxable income, the higher the tax rate.
   C. There is a difference between marginal tax rates (what you pay on your last dollar of income) and average tax rates.
   D. Individual tax details.
      1. Individual tax rates vary from 0% to 33%.
      2. Dividend and interest income is taxed as ordinary income.
      3. Prior to 1986, only 60% of a long-term capital gain was taxable income. Today, capital gains and dividends are

taxed at the same rate as income.
- E. Corporate tax details.
    1. Corporate taxes are progressive and the structure is much like that of personal taxes. Marginal rates range from 15% to 34%.
    2. All interest received by the firm is taxed as ordinary income.
    3. 80% of dividend income is excluded for tax purposes if the firm owns 20% or more of the outstanding stock; otherwise, the exclusion is 70%.
    4. Losses are carried back and then carried forward.
    5. Firms can treat part of the cost of a piece of equipment as a yearly expense over a period of time (depreciation). Depreciation reduces taxable income and hence taxes. We focus on depreciation specified in the tax code rather than accounting depreciations.
    6. Firms accruing 80% or more of another corporation can consolidate income and file one return.
    7. Corporations pay estimated taxes quarterly.
    8. Subchapter S corporations can escape double taxation of dividends.
    9. Multinational corporations are subject to taxation in other countries as well.

FORMULAS

Fisher Effect

Observed (nominal) risk-free interest rate = real rate of interest + expected rate of inflation

Required return = risk-free rate + risk premium

WHAT TO LOOK FOR

Central to financial management are the financial markets. Chapter 2 introduces us to the financial markets and to their participants. Today's effective managers have learned their lessons about the financial markets and sometimes attempt to time their participation accordingly.

Briefly, financial markets bring borrowers of funds together with lenders of funds. Depending on the supply and demand of loanable funds, money can be relatively cheap or relatively expensive. That is, real interest rates rise and fall according to the supply and demand for loanable funds. Also, inflation expectations will cause nominal rates to fluctuate. Managers who want to minimize their costs will attempt to time their financing accordingly. In the following section, we will review the financial markets, the securities traded in them, the participants, and the cost of borrowing.

Financial Markets and Their Respective Securities

The financial markets can be split into short-term and long-term markets.

The money market

In the short-term or money market, such instruments as commercial paper, U.S. Treasury bills, certificates of deposit, bankers' acceptances, and federal funds are traded. A firm might invest in commercial paper, Treasury bills, or certificates of deposit if it has excess cash over a short period. If a firm has an adequate credit rating, it may issue commercial paper for its own short-term credit needs. Import or export firms employ bankers' acceptances, which become another type of money market security. Federal funds are traded between the Federal Reserve and commercial banks that are members of the Federal Reserve system. These loans adjust the banks' reserve position. Banks borrow federal funds overnight or over the weekend.

The capital market: Long term

Long-term financing for a firm occurs in the capital market. This financing can be in the form of debt or equity. Debt issues can be unsecured (debentures), or they can be secured with land, equipment, or some other collateral.

Firms can also issue debt with warrants, or debt that is convertible into common stock. Warrants and the conversion feature sweeten the bond issue to induce investors to buy debt yielding a relatively low rate of interest. Warrants and convertibles allow investors to exchange the firm's fixed-income security for its common stock, at a specific exchange rate for a specified period of time. Thus, the conversion feature and warrants allow investors a chance to share in potential capital gains as the firm prospers.

Rather than issuing more debt, managers may decide to issue stock. Two types of stock--preferred and common stock. Preferred stockholders have a prior but limited claim to the income and the assets of the firm. Common stockholders, however, share in both the losses and the gains of the firm.

The primary market: Issuing financial securities

In order to issue financial securities, firms must use the primary market, since the secondary markets are reserved for securities which have been previously traded. This issuance can take two forms.

To place a debt issue privately, a firm or its investment banker might ask several insurance companies to buy the entire issue. Insurance companies would probably hold the issue until maturity. In recent years, roughly one-fourth of all debt issues are privately placed. (Common stock is seldom sold this way.)

New securities not privately placed will generally be sold through an investment banker. The managing investment banker and the other investment bankers underwriting the issue will plan the sale and distribution of the new issue. Depending upon the size and attractiveness of the issue, the underwriting syndicate will agree to sell the entire issue itself or to bring investment bankers into the selling syndicate. If you open any issue of the Wall Street Journal, you will observe public announcements of new security issues. These announcements list the investment bankers who are in the selling syndicate, and from whom you might get information about the new issue.

The secondary market: Trading seasoned securities

The secondary markets are designed for trading in outstanding securities. These markets include the organized exchanges and the over-the-counter market. The organized exchanges include the New York Stock Exchange, the American Stock Exchange, and various regional stock exchanges. Companies who meet the guidelines can list their stock for trading on one or more of these exchanges. Unlisted stocks trade in the over-the-counter market, an informal network of security brokers who buy and sell stock. Bonds trade either on the New York Exchange or in the over-the-counter market. The secondary markets provide liquidity to the holders of securities.

Financial Intermediaries

Financial institutions play the important role of bringing borrowers and lenders together. They gather lenders' deposits of varying maturities in order to match the borrowers desired loan maturity. In addition, they combine many small deposits in order to make larger loans.

Each financial institution tends to specialize in specific types of lending. Savings and loans provide most of the real estate mortgage loans. Commercial banks primarily make commercial loans. Insurance companies, as we noted before, buy large blocks of new corporate debt, and through various types of business insurance, bear some risk for corporations. Credit unions make consumer loans. As the text notes, financial institutions are going through rapid changes that are making them financial supermarkets. Fairly soon, there may be little difference among the various financial institutions.

Interest Rates and Forces That Determine Their Level

Interest rates are the prices paid by investors to borrow funds. The required rate of interest on an investment depends upon several factors.

Time and interest rates

Money has a time value, as Chapter 5 will show you. Seldom can you borrow money without paying the lender some rate of return. If conditions in the economy are stable and your credit is flawless, the rate of interest on the loan should be a riskless or risk-free rate--the rate paid on U.S. Treasury securities. The U.S. Treasury bill rate is the proxy for the riskless rate, since the repayment of these bills is virtually certain.

The economy is not stable, however. The riskless rate rises and falls as a result of supply and demand conditions. Facing a deficit, the U.S. Treasury may decide to issue new government debt. This fiscal action will increase the demand for money and will push interest rates upward. The Federal Reserve (the Fed), in its role of stablizing the economy, may decide to counteract inflationary forces by selling U.S. government securities in the open market. The resulting contraction of the money supply makes money more costly, pushing interest rates upwards. On the other hand, if the Fed buys U.S. government securities, interest rates will fall in the short run, but the inflation that follows from money supply expansion often pushes interest rates up in the long run, as discussed below. As you can see, interest rates are a complex subject. The Fed can also raise interest rates by increasing the reserve requirements for member banks, or by increasing the discount rate, the rate at which it loans federal funds.

The real rate of interest

Interest rates are the prices paid when an individual, firm, or governmental unit borrows money. These rates are usually stated as an annual percentage of the amount borrowed. In a world without risk or expected inflation, investors would expect to pay the real rate of interest, which is determined by the supply of and the demand for loanable funds.

Inflation and interest rates

Over time, the price level in the economy changes. We call an upward change in the price level inflation. If inflation exists, investors demand compensation for this upward change in the price level, since they want to achieve a certain rate of return, net of inflation. A useful way of looking at this net rate of return is with the Fisher effect. The Fisher effect shows the relationship between the expected rate of inflation and the observed or nominal rate of interest. The real rate of interest for a riskless investment (net of inflation) is about 1 or 2 percent. The equation for the observed rate of interest is below:

$$\text{Observed or nominal rate of interest} = \text{Real rate of interest} + \text{Expected rate of inflation}$$

Generally, the Treasury bill rate is the measure of the observed or nominal rate of interest and is the base for the term structure of interest rates. We next look at risk, which causes interest rates to increase above the riskless rate.

Risk and interest rates

The interest rates on most bonds have components other than the real rate of interest and an inflation premium. These components are called risk premiums and are designed to compensate investors for specific forms of risk associated with bonds.

Among these premiums are the maturity premium, an additional return that compensates investors because long-term bonds are more sensitive to changes in interest rates than short-term bonds. A useful tool in analyzing maturity premiums and interest rates is the yield curve, which shows the term structure of interest rates.

Corporate bonds will also contain a default premium, which compensates investors for the risk that the issuer will be unable to pay interest or principal on the bonds. Corporate bonds are rated from AAA (very safe) to C and below. The higher the rating, the lower the default risk premium.

Other premiums include the liquidity premium, which arises if the market for the security is not very active, and an issue-specific premium, which compensates investors for risks associated with specific attributes of the security.

The required, or expected, return on an asset is the sum of two components. The first is the nominal (observed) risk-free rate of interest which, according to the Fisher effect, is equal to the real rate of interest plus expected inflation. The second is the risk premium, which is the sum of maturity, default, liquidity, and issue-specific premiums. There is a positive relationship between risk and return; the higher the risk, the higher the required return. Understanding interest rates and their effects on asset values is an important tool in financial management.

Market Efficiency

An efficient market is one in which prices rapidly and correctly adjust to reflect new information. In order for a market to be efficient, there must be large numbers of value maximizing participants, random arrival of new information, and investors who react quickly to new information.

An efficient market has many properties that are important to financial managers. First, the markets are forward looking; they have no memory. Second, market prices reflect the true value of the firm. Management should consider the impact of decisions on security prices. Third, the market cannot be fooled by creative accounting. Fourth, in an efficient market, individuals can duplicate any financial decisions made by the firm. Finally, the law of one price holds; assets with the same risk return characteristics sell for the same price.

Taxes

An important aspect of the financial system is the tax code. The value of any financial asset is a function of the usable cash flows after taxes are paid. In the U.S., marginal tax rates are progressive; the proportion of income paid in taxes increases as taxable income increases. For individuals, the 1989 marginal tax rates are:

Individual Taxable Income Increment	Marginal Tax Rate
First $18,550	15%
$17,851 - $44,900	28%
Over $44,990	33%

Suppose that when you graduate, you are offered a job paying $50,000 (net of deductions). You also have $2,000 in dividend and capital gain income from stocks and $1,000 in interest income from bonds. What can you expect to pay in taxes?

Since investment income is fully taxable, your taxable income is $50,000 + $2,000 + $1,000 = $53,000. According to the marginal tax rates above, your tax liability is:

(0.15)($17,850) + (0.28)($43,150 - $17,850) + (0.33)($53,000 - $43,150)
= $2,677.50 + $7,084.00 + $3,250.50
= $13,012.00

Note that while additional income will be taxed at 33% (the marginal tax rate), your average tax rate is 13,012/53,000 = 0.2455 or 24.55%.

The tax structure is similar for corporations. The marginal tax rates are:

Firm's Taxable Income Increment	Marginal Tax Rate
First $50,000	15%
Next $25,000	25%
Over $75,000	34%

As for individuals, interest income is taxable, but dividends are treated specially. Firms are allowed to exclude a portion of dividend income, depending on the percent of the dividend paying firm they own, for tax purposes. This provision in the tax code encourages U.S. corporations to invest in other businesses.

There are two other aspects of the corporate tax code that should be mentioned. First, expense (for instance, the interest a firm pays on its bonds) is tax deductible, but dividend payments are not. Thus, debt has advantages not available to common or preferred stock. Second, firms can treat depreciation as an expense. The specifics of depreciation are discussed in Appendix 8A, but it is important to note that while depreciation lowers taxable income and taxes, it actually increases usable cash flow after-tax.

Although the tax code is complicated, it is extremely important. Since taxes affect usable after-tax cash flows, they affect value. Sound financial management requires careful consideration of the tax impacts of any financial decision.

COMPLETION QUESTIONS

2.1 An _____ is used to measure the reaction of a stock's price to new information; an abnormal return is defined as the difference between the stock's _____ return and its _____ return.

2.2 The efficient market theory says a security's price reflects all readily available information and is an unbiased indicator of _____. Therefore, the security price also provides an unbiased assessment of the _____.

2.3 According to the efficient market theory, a large number of profit-maximizing investors independently value securities, process any new information, and react to the information quickly. Thus, security prices _____ as they reflect _____.

2.4 During periods of inflation, interest rates _____ in order to compensate lenders for the loss in _____ they experience by being paid back with dollars of lower value.

2.5 The Fisher effect states that the observed rate of interest is the sum of a real rate of interest plus _____. The real rate of interest is about _____.

2.6 _____ refers to a promise to repay a certain amount on a certain date, often with a stated rate of interest.

2.7 Common stock represents _____ ownership in the business, while preferred stock signifies a prior but _____ on the assets and cash flows of the firm.

2.8 _____ often come between suppliers and demanders of funds to accept deposits and make loans or investments.

2.9 _____ is the process of directly selling a new stock or bond issue to a financial institution rather than having the investment banking syndicate sell the issue.

2.10 A well-developed _____ allows investors to easily add or to liquidate their security holdings.

2.11 Any security that is not listed with an exchange will trade in the _____.

2.12 When the Federal Reserve conducts open market operations to purchase U.S. government securities, the money supply _____; in response, interest rates will _____.

2.13 When budget deficits are funded with additional government borrowing, interest rates _____.

2.14 Marginal tax rates for individuals range from ____ to ____ while marginal tax rates for corporations range from ____ to ____.

2.15 _____ is the deduction of a portion of the cost of new equipment annually over a specified time period.

2.16 Corporations are allowed to exclude a portion of _____ _____ for tax purposes, depending on the proportion of the firm they own.

PROBLEMS

2.1 Recently, an economist forecast the following rates of inflation:

Year	Expected Inflation
1990	6.2%
1991	6.8
1992	5.4
1993	4.0

What should be the nominal risk-free rate of interest in each of the above years assuming a real rate of interest of 2 percent?

2.2 Suppose the real rate of interest is 2 percent and inflation is expected to be 6 percent per year over the next 15 years. All bonds have a maturity premium of 0.3 percent per year (that is, 0.3% for a 1-year bond, 0.6% on a 2-year bond, etc.). Corporate AAA Bonds have a default premium of 2.5 percent, a liquidity premium of 0.8 percent, and an issue specific premium of 2 percent. Calculate the interest rates for 1-, 5-, 10-, and 15-year government bonds and AAA corporate bonds.

2.3 Kandel Manufacturing and Durrough Industries are two firms with common stock trading on a major exchange. Premiums associated with each stock are as follows:

	Kandel	Durrough
Maturity premium	none	none
Default premium	4.0%	3.5%
Liquidity premium	3.1%	5.2%
Issue-specific premium	2.0%	2.5%

Which of the two securities has the highest level of risk?

2.4 Kenneth Costello, an accountant, had a salary of $55,000 over the past year. He also had $1,000 in interest income and received $500 in dividends. What is Mr. Costello's tax liability?

2.5 Intertel Corp. had earnings before tax (EBT) of $300,000, interest income of $50,000, and dividend income of $100,000. What is the company's tax liability?

2.6 Maryann Roseman has a part-time job paying $5,000 per year. At the end of the year when she graduates, she will take a job paying $25,000. How will her average and marginal tax rates be affected?

ANSWERS TO COMPLETION QUESTIONS

2.1 event test; actual; expected
2.2 the security's value; performance of the firm's managers
2.3 change; new information
2.4 rise; purchasing power
2.5 the expected rate of inflation; 1 to 2 percent
2.6 Debt
2.7 residual; limited claim
2.8 Financial institutions (or intermediaries)
2.9 Private Placement
2.10 secondary market
2.11 over-the-counter market
2.12 increases; fall
2.13 rise
2.14 15%; 33%; 15%; 34%
2.15 Depreciation
2.16 dividend income

SOLUTIONS TO PROBLEMS

2.1

According to the Fisher effect:

Nominal rate of interest = real rate of interest + expected rate of inflation

Year	Real Rate of Interest	+	Expected Rate of Inflation	=	Nominal Rate of Interest
1990	2.0%		6.2%		8.2%
1991	2.0		6.8		8.8
1992	2.0		5.4		7.4
1993	2.0		4.0		6.0

2.2

Step 1. Government Bonds

	Year			
	1	5	10	15
Real Rate of Interest	2.0%	2.0%	2.0%	2.0%
+				
Inflation Premium	6.0	6.0	6.0	6.0
+				
Maturity Premium	(.3%)(1)= 0.3	(.3%)(5)=1.5	(.3%)(10)=3.0	(.3%)(15)=4.5
Interest	8.3%	9.5%	11.0%	12.5%

2.5

(100-70)

300,000
50,000
30,000
―――――――
380,000 Tax.Inc.

(50,000)(.15) = 7,500
(25,000)(.25) = 6,250
(380-75)(.34) = 103,700
―――――――
$117,450 taxes

2.6 In her $5000 job her Marg.tax rate is 15%   2782.50
     "   " 25,000   "   " Marg.tax rate 28%   1806.00

Her marg. tax rate goes up to midbracket.   avg tax is 15%
                                                to 18%

Step 2. AAA Corporate Bonds

	Year			
	1	5	10	15
Real Rate of Interest	2.0%	2.0%	2.0%	2.0%
+				
Expected Rate of Inflation	6.0	6.0	6.0	6.0
+				
Maturity Premium	0.3	1.5	3.0	4.5
+				
Default Premium	2.5	2.5	2.5	2.5
+				
Liquidity Premium	0.8	0.8	0.8	0.8
+				
Issue-Specific Premium	2.0	2.0	2.0	2.0
Interest Rate	13.6%	14.8%	16.3%	17.8%

2.3

Step 1. Risk premium = $\frac{\text{maturity}}{\text{premium}} + \frac{\text{default}}{\text{premium}} + \frac{\text{liquidity}}{\text{premium}} + \frac{\text{issue specific}}{\text{premium}}$

Kandel: Risk premium = 0% + 4.0% + 3.1% + 2.0% = 9.1%

Durrough: Risk premium = 0% + 3.5% + 5.2% + 2.5% = 11.2%

Since Durrough Industries has a higher risk premium than Kandel Manufacturing, it is more risky.

2.4

Step 1.

Salary		$55,000
Interest income	$1,000	
Dividend income	500	
Total dividend + interest		1,500
Taxable income		$56,500

Step 2. According to Table 2A.1, the tax liability is

$0.15(\$18,550) + 0.28(\$44,900 - \$18,550) + 0.33(\$56,500 - \$44,900)$

$= \$2,782.50 + \$7,378.00 + \$3,828.00 = \$13,988.50$

2.5

Step 1.

EBT		$300,000
Interest income		50,000
Dividend income	$100,000	
Less 70% exclusion	70,000	
Taxable dividend income		30,000
Taxable income		$380,000

Step 2.

	Income	Marginal Tax Rate	Tax
1st	$50,000	15%	$ 7,500
2nd	25,000	25	6,250
Remainder ($380,000 - 75,000)		34	103,700
Tax Liability			$117,450

2.6

Step 1.

Tax on $5,000 = $5,000(0.15) = $750.00

Marginal Rate = 15%

Average Rate = $\dfrac{\text{Tax}}{\text{Income}} \times 100\% = \dfrac{\$750.00}{\$5,000} \times 100\% = 15.0\%$

Step 2. Tax on $25,000 = 0.15($18,550) + 0.28($25,000 - $18,550)

$= \$2,782.50 + 0.28(\$6,450.00)$

$= \$2,782.50 + \$1,806.00 = \$4,588.50$

Marginal Rate = 28%

Average Rate = $4,588.50/$25,000 = 18.35%

CHAPTER 3

ANALYZING FINANCIAL STATEMENTS

HOW THIS CHAPTER RELATES TO THE REST OF THE TEXT

Accounting is the language of finance. The analysis of financial statements prepared under generally accepted accounting principles enables us to ascertain certain information concerning the magnitude, timing, and riskiness of a firm's cash flows, important determinants of its value.

Because of their importance as a source of information, a basic knowledge of balance sheets and income statements is required throughout the text. Cash flows arising from long-term capital budgeting projects (Chapters 8 through 10) affect the firm's income statement. A large portion of the text (Chapters 18 through 21) discusses the management of working capital and its components: Current assets and liabilities, which are major parts of the balance sheet. Information concerning the firm's capital structure (Chapter 15) can also be determined from the balance sheet. Additionally, knowledge of how financial statements are developed helps us in understanding the differences between earnings, as defined under generally accepted accounting principles, and cash flow (Chapter 4), which leads to better financial management. The du Pont system shows the relationship between profitability, asset utilization, financial leverage, and its return on equity. In general, financial statement analysis is a useful tool in developing an understanding of a firm and its characteristics.

TOPICAL OUTLINE

I. Different statements for different purposes.
   A. Generally accepted accounting principles (GAAP) guide the recording and reporting to the public of the firm's financial status.
   B. Firms employ three different sets of financial records.
      1. GAAP-prepared statements for reporting to stockholders, creditors, and financial publications.
      2. Statements for tax purposes, employed when dealing with the Internal Revenue Service.
      3. Statements for internal management.

II. The basic financial statements.
   A. The income statement records the flow of revenue and related expenses through the firm over a given period of time.
      1. Sales minus cost of goods sold equals gross margin.
      2. Operating profit measures earnings after all expenses except interest and taxes.
      3. Adjustments can include extraordinary income, discontinued operations, and income from unconsolidated subsidiaries.
      4. Earnings before interest and taxes are earnings before taxes or financing costs associated with debt.
      5. Earnings after taxes are the base from which cash dividends on preferred stock are subtracted to achieve earnings available to common stockholders.
      6. GAAP are prepared on an accrual basis; net income is not the same as cash.
      7. Earnings per share provide some information concerning the firm's fortunes.
   B. The balance sheet is a snapshot of the firm's assets, liabilities, and owner's equity at some specific point in time.
      1. Assets are either current or long-term.
      2. Liabilities are either current or long-term.
      3. Stockholders' equity includes both preferred and common stock.
      4. Retained earnings are earnings not paid out as cash dividends; this is not a cash account.
   C. Information contained in the statements helps the financial community value the firm and form expectations about the expected returns and riskiness of the firm's cash flows.
III. Financial statement analysis.
   A. Provides clues concerning the magnitude, timing, and riskiness of the firm's future cash flows.
   B. Analysis guideline.
      1. Look at trends over 3 to 5 years, since they provide a frame of reference.
      2. Compare the firm's performance to that of its industry.

3. All of the financial statement, including the footnotes, is important.
4. Obtain further information to answer questions raised by the financial analysis.

C. Common size statements: Items are calculated in percentage terms to allow for easy comparison of statements from different periods.
   1. Income statement.
      a. Each component is divided by net sales, so that each item is presented as a percentage of sales.
      b. The common-size net income and EBT are the net profit margin and the gross profit margin respectively.
      c. We can compare common-size income statements to industry common-sized data.
   2. Balance sheet.
      a. All statement components are calculated as a percentage of total assets.
      b. Analysis of balance sheet common-size statements for several years shows trends or changes in these accounts.
      c. We can compare common-size balance sheet data to industry data.

D. Ratio analysis.
   1. Liquidity ratios (current ratio or quick ratio) indicate an ability to meet short-run obligations.
   2. Asset management or efficiency ratios (average collection period, inventory turnover, long-term asset turnover, and total asset turnover) help analysts judge management's skill.
   3. Debt management ratios (total debt to total assets, times interest earned and fixed charges) help in analyzing the firm's capital structure and its ability to meet its legal debt obligations.
   4. Profitability ratios (net profit margin, return on total assets, and return on equity) relate net income to sales, assets, or stockholders' equity.
   5. Market ratios (P/E, dividend yield, and dividend payout) help investors evaluate the attractiveness of a common stock,

considering its price, its earnings, and its cash dividends.
6. The du Pont system relates three ratios--net profit margin, total asset turnover, and total debt to total assets.

IV. Limitations of financial analysis.
  A. Financial accounting data may bear little or no relationship to a firm's cash flows, especially in the short run.
  B. There are a variety of legitimate accounting techniques; identical firms may appear to be different due to different accounting methods.
  C. Firms may undertake steps, called "window dressing," to make their financial statements appear better.
  D. International and multidivisional firms present special problems to analysts; it is difficult to find an appropriate industry benchmark for comparison with multidivisional firms.
  E. Inflation and disinflation can have substantial effects on the firm that are not reflected in the financial statements.
  F. Reporting problems exist for firms with substantial international operations.
  G. Successful firms do not want to be average; be careful in comparing the firm with the industry.

V. International aspects.
  A. Reporting of financial results of foreign operations.
    1. FAS No. 52: Companies must use the primary currency in which the foreign subsidiary operates as the basis for computing and translating currency adjustments.
    2. This new requirement may make financial analysis of multinational firms less meaningful, since assets and equity change every year based on prevailing exchange rates.

FORMULAS

Performance Measures from the Income Statement

Gross margin on sales = sales - cost of goods sold
Operating profit = sales - cost of goods sold - operating expenses
Earnings before interest and taxes (EBIT):
  EBIT = Sales - cost of goods sold - operating expenses - adjustments
Earnings before taxes (EBT) = EBIT - interest

Net income = EBT − taxes

Earnings per share (EPS):

$$\text{EPS} = \frac{\text{earnings available to common stockholders}}{\text{number of common stock shares outstanding}} = \frac{\text{net income} - \text{cash dividends on preferred stock}}{\text{number of common stock shares outstanding}}$$

$$\text{Dividends per share} = \frac{\text{total cash dividends paid to common stockholders}}{\text{number of common stock shares outstanding}}$$

Ratio Analysis

Liquidity ratios:

$$\text{Current ratio} = \frac{\text{current assets}}{\text{current liabilities}}$$

$$\text{Quick ratio} = \frac{\text{current assets} - \text{inventory}}{\text{current liabilities}}$$

Asset management ratios:

$$\text{Average collection period} = \frac{\text{accounts receivable}}{\text{sales}/365}$$

$$\text{Long-term asset turnover} = \frac{\text{sales}}{\text{long-term (fixed) assets}}$$

$$\text{Inventory turnover} = \frac{\text{cost of goods sold}}{\text{inventory}}$$

$$\text{Total asset turnover} = \frac{\text{sales}}{\text{total assets}}$$

Debt management ratios:

$$\text{Total debt to total assets} = \frac{\text{total debt}}{\text{total assets}}$$

$$\text{Times interest earned} = \frac{\text{EBIT}}{\text{interest}}$$

$$\text{Fixed charges coverage} = \frac{\text{EBIT} + \text{lease expenses}}{\text{interest} + \text{lease expenses}}$$

Profitability ratios:

$$\text{Net profit margin} = \frac{\text{net income}}{\text{sales}}$$

$$\text{Return on total assets} = \frac{\text{net income}}{\text{total assets}}$$

$$\text{Return on equity} = \frac{\text{net income}}{\text{stockholders' equity}}$$

Market ratios:

$$\text{Price/earnings ratio} = \frac{\text{market price per share}}{\text{earnings per share}}$$

$$\text{Dividend yield} = \frac{\text{dividends per share}}{\text{market price per share}}$$

$$\text{Dividend payout} = \frac{\text{dividends per share}}{\text{earnings per share}}$$

The du Pont system:

Return on total assets (ROA) = (profitability)(asset utilization)

= (net profit margin)(total asset turnover)

$$= \left[\frac{\text{net income}}{\text{sales}}\right]\left[\frac{\text{sales}}{\text{total assets}}\right]$$

$$\text{Return on equity} = \frac{\text{ROA}}{1 - (\text{total debt to total assets})}$$

WHAT TO LOOK FOR

Financial Statements: Limitations and Uses

Limitations

Financial analysts thrive on financial data. Chapter 3 analyzes the financial data firms provide in annual reports. Generally accepted accounting principles (GAAP), which rely on the ideas of accrual, realization, matching, and historical cost, guide the reporting of a firm's operating results in financial statements.

Although the operating data are not necessarily wrong, financial statements do not give the clearest picture of the firm's potential for generating future cash flows. Financial statements, since they adhere to GAAP, ignore the timing of cash flows. Thus, as we see in Chapter 4, a firm may report a healthy net income while experiencing a severe cash shortage. Such a cash shortage can have significant effects on a firm if interest rates are high or if the firm has used up all its readily available credit.

Analysts use GAAP financial statements to try to estimate the magnitude, timing, and riskiness of the firm's future cash flows. It is upon this cash flow and risk estimate that analysts base their valuation of a firm. We will suppose that you are a financial analyst, and we will walk through the use of the J. C. Penney financial statements in the text.

To begin your analysis of J. C. Penney, take financial statements for several years and put them into a common-size form. For the income statement, this means you would put all expenses into a percentage of sales revenue. We have reproduced below the actual income statements (in billions) for J. C.

Penney and the common-size statements alongside. Notice how much easier it is to see trends when you have a statement in common-size form.

	Actual Income			Common-Size		
	1987	1986	1985	1987	1986	1985
Net sales	$15,332	$14,740	$13,747	100.0%	100.0%	100.0%
Cost of goods sold	10,152	9,786	9,240	66.2	66.4	67.2
Gross profit margin	5,180	4,954	4,507	33.8	33.6	32.8
Operating expenses and adjustments	3,196	3,698	3,143	25.6	25.1	25.0
Net operating income (EBIT)	1,264	1,256	1,064	8.2	8.5	7.8
Interest	300	350	370	1.9	2.4	2.7
Earnings before tax (EBT)	964	906	694	6.3	6.1	5.1
Income tax	356	428	297	2.3	2.9	2.2
Net income (net profit margin)	$ 608	$ 478	$ 397	4.0%	3.2%	2.9%

Common-size statements for J. C. Penney's and for the retail industry in Table 3.3 readily tell you that J. C. Penney's cost of goods sold was lower in 1987 than in 1985 and is lower than the industry average. Although operating expenses for J. C. Penney increased in 1986 and 1987, the net result is a higher net profit margin than the industry's. We would need a few more years to get a reasonable trend for J. C. Penney, but you can see that J. C. Penney outperforms the retail industry.

For common-size balance sheets, all accounts are calculated as a percentage of total assets. Table 3.4 in the text gives you J. C. Penney's and the retail industry's asset, liability, and stockholders' equity accounts in percentage terms. We see that J. C. Penney's equity remained constant, placing no more financial risk on creditors. Accounts receivable have also fallen, suggesting a change in J. C. Penney's willingness to carry its own receivables and perhaps that J. C. Penney's credit policy or collection policy has become more strict.

From common-size analysis, we go naturally into ratio analysis. Table 3.5 summarizes the five types of ratios. You will notice that all the information you need to make these calculations is in either the income statement or the balance sheet.

These ratios point out problem areas for managers and financial analysts. Dun & Bradstreet publishes a short pamphlet called "Key Business Ratios," which you can check when you compare your firm's financial ratios to those of its industry. The average liquidity ratios for the apparel retail sales industry are quite different from those of the automobile industry, as are the turnover ratios. In this way, using your particular industry's average ratios as a benchmark, you can judge the performance of your firm.

Let's look at Table 3.5 in the text. It compares J. C. Penney's ratios to those of the retail industry. By taking several ratios--the liquidity ratios, the profitability ratios, and the debt management ratios, for example--we can make some comments about J. C. Penney. Note that J. C. Penney's net profit margin is high relative to the industry, and that more than half its capital structure is debt. We might decide that, as bankers, we will grant J. C. Penney a line of credit at a higher rate of interest, due to its higher debt than the industry. As investors, we might decide that J. C. Penney's growth prospects have not met our expectations, as reflected by the lower P/E ratio. In making any judgements with ratios, however, remember that they are based on GAAP statements, which rely on the accrual concept, realization, matching, and historical cost, so there is no direct link to expected cash flows.

In the analysis above, we referred to several ratios in order to make a judgement about the riskiness of a firm's cash flows. The du Pont system incorporates three of these key ratios--profitability, asset management, and financial leverage--so that we can see their contribution to return on equity (ROE).

$$ROE = \frac{\text{return on total assets}}{\text{financial leverage}} = \frac{(\text{profitability})(\text{asset management})}{\text{financial leverage}}$$

$$= \frac{(\text{net income/sales})(\text{sales/total assets})}{1 - (\text{total debt to total assets})}$$

You might be a little unclear about what financial leverage is. Basically, financial leverage is the amount of debt (or other fixed cost sources of financing) used by a firm, in comparison to total assets. J. C. Penney's financial leverage is 62 percent. When you look at an income statement, you note that interest payments are deducted from before-tax income. In effect, then, interest increases net income when compared to dividends. This effect is called financial leverage. The use of financial leverage increases the return on assets and thus the return on equity. (This increase continues for increases in debt usage until the interest rate on debt exceeds the return on total assets.) Anything that changes the profit margin, asset turnover, or financial leverage will affect the return on equity. Remember that the usefulness of the du Pont system is limited, since the GAAP data upon which it is based are not directly linked to expected cash flows.

Currency Losses and Gains in International Business

Due to the relatively high return from business operations in developing countries, many firms have foreign subsidiaries and conduct sales in other currencies. Since 1972, exchange rates have been floating. With the growth in foreign sales, the impact of foreign exchange gains and losses is significant for both the firm's returns on these sales and financial analysis. The change from Financial Accounting Standard (FAS) No. 8 to FAS No. 52 has made accounting of foreign exchange gains or losses less meaningful. The assets and equity of the parent firm change with exchange rates. Firms with similar operating results may report different results due to the functional currency employed, and firms need not note the functional currency in the annual report. The analyst, then, is left with little meaningful information in order to evaluate the effect of currency transactions on expected cash flows from foreign sales.

COMPLETION QUESTIONS

3.1 Generally accepted accounting principle (GAAP) underlie consistent and objective financial statements. But GAAP do not provide a direct link to _____, which are so crucial in evaluating the performance of the firm.

3.2 The payment of taxes is a direct cash _____ for the firm, so separate statements are prepared for tax purposes. These differ from those required for GAAP purposes.

3.3 The _____ is a "snapshot" of the firm's assets, liabilities, and owners' claims as of a specific date. The _____ records the flow of income and related expenses through the firm over a period of time.

3.4 _____ reflects the firm's earnings before costs of financing and income taxes.

3.5 The figures on the balance sheet are presented in terms of historical costs and do not reflect _____ values or the effects of _____.

3.6 Retained earnings is an account that reflects all prior _____ not paid out as _____, but it does not contain any cash.

3.7 _____ ratios indicate the firm's ability to meet its short-run obligations.

3.8 If we want to know how effective a firm's credit granting and management activities are, we should use the _____ ratio.

3.9 Times interest earned helps measure the ability of a firm to meet its _____. A high ratio is safer, but if too high, it may indicate the firm does not use enough financial leverage.

3.10 The _____ ratio provides an accounting-based indication of the effectiveness of management from the stockholder's perspective. This ratio is directly affected by the return on _____ and by the amount of _____ employed.

3.11 The dividend payout ratio indicates how the firm is splitting earnings between _____ and _____.

3.12 The _____ is the currency under which a firm's foreign subsidiary operates.

3.13 Both common-size statements and financial ratios should be analyzed over time, be compared to those of _____, and be used as a basis for asking further questions about the firm.

PROBLEMS

3.1 Baylor Book Company has the following current portion of its balance sheet:

Baylor Book Company
December 31
(in Thousands)

Cash	$ 30,000	Accounts payable	$ 42,000
Accounts receivable	60,000	Notes payable	78,000
Inventory	156,000		
Total current assets	$246,000	Total current liabilities	$120,000

Sales $912,500

Cost of goods sold $585,000

Calculate the current ratio, quick ratio, average collection period, and inventory turnover ratio.

3.2 Using the following balance sheet and other financial information for International Electronics Company, calculate the long-term asset turnover, total asset turnover, total debt to total assets, and times interest earned.

International Electronics Company
Balance Sheet
As of December 31

Cash	$ 35,000	Accounts payable	$ 36,000
Accounts receivable	45,000	Notes payable	60,000
Inventory	170,000	Total current liabilities	96,000
Total current assets	250,000		
		Long-term debt	1,164,000
Net long-term assets	2,000,000	Total liabilities	1,260,000
		Common stock	100,000
		Retained earnings	890,000
		Total stockholders' equity	990,000
Total assets	$2,250,000	Total liabilities and stockholders' equity	$2,250,000

Sales $4,500,000
EBIT   3,264,000
Interest expense   170,000

3.3 Xtel Corporation's common stock is selling for $42.50 per share, pays a dividend of $6.30, and has a dividend payout ratio of 75 percent. What is the P/E ratio?

3.4 Using the information given below, complete the following balance sheet and the sales amount.

Jepson Enterprises
Balance Sheet
December 31

Cash	_____	Accounts payable	$ 10,000
Accounts receivable	_____	Notes payable	20,000
Inventory	_____	Total current liabilities	_____
Total current assets	_____		
		Long-term debt	50,000
Net long-term assets	_____	Total liabilities	_____
		Common stock	10,000
		Retained earnings	_____
		Total stockholders' equity	_____
Total assets	_____	Total liabilities and stockholders' equity	_____

Sales _____

Current ratio: 1.7

Quick ratio: 1.2

Average collection period: 36.5 days (based on a 365-day year)

Total asset turnover: 2.0

Total debt to total assets: 0.5

3.5 Engletown Manufacturing Company has set a net profit margin of 4.2 percent, a total asset turnover of 2.5, and a return on equity of 16.8 percent. Using the du Pont formula, determine the company's total debt to total assets ratio.

ANSWERS TO COMPLETION QUESTIONS

3.1 cash flows
3.2 outflow
3.3 balance sheet; income statement
3.4 EBIT (earnings before interest and taxes
3.5 historical; current; inflation
3.6 net income (or earnings); cash dividends
3.7 Liquidity
3.8 collection period
3.9 interest payments
3.10 return on equity; total assets; financial leverage
3.11 common stockholders; reinvesting them in the firm
3.12 functional currency
3.13 the industry

SOLUTIONS TO PROBLEMS

3.1

Step 1. Current ratio = $\dfrac{\text{current assets}}{\text{current liabilities}} = \dfrac{\$246{,}000}{\$120{,}000} = 2.05$

Step 2. Quick ratio = $\dfrac{\text{current assets} - \text{inventory}}{\text{current liabilities}}$

$= \dfrac{\$246{,}000 - \$156{,}000}{\$120{,}000} = 0.75$

Step 3. Average collection period = $\dfrac{\text{accounts receivable}}{\text{sales}/365} = \dfrac{\$60{,}000}{\$912{,}500/365} = 24$ days

Step 4. Inventory turnover = $\dfrac{\text{cost of goods sold}}{\text{inventory}} = \dfrac{\$585{,}000}{\$156{,}000} = 3.75$

3.2

Step 1. Long-term asset turnover = $\dfrac{\text{sales}}{\text{long-term assets}} = \dfrac{\$4{,}500{,}000}{\$2{,}000{,}000} = 2.25$

Step 2. Total asset turnover = $\dfrac{\text{sales}}{\text{total assets}} = \dfrac{\$4{,}500{,}000}{\$2{,}250{,}000} = 2.00$

Step 3. Total debt to total assets = $\dfrac{\text{total debt}}{\text{total assets}} = \dfrac{\$1{,}260{,}000}{\$2{,}250{,}000} = 0.56$

Step 4. Times interest earned = $\dfrac{\text{EBIT}}{\text{interest expense}} = \dfrac{\$3{,}264{,}000}{\$170{,}000} = 19.20$

3.3

Step 1. Dividend payout ratio = $\dfrac{\text{DPS}}{\text{EPS}}$, so EPS = $\dfrac{\text{DPS}}{\text{dividend payout ratio}}$

$= \dfrac{6.30}{0.75} = \$8.40$

Step 2. P/E = $\dfrac{\text{market price}}{\text{EPS}} = \dfrac{\$42.50}{\$8.40} = 5.06$ times

3.4

Step 1. Total current liabilities = accounts payable + notes payable
$$= \$10{,}000 + \$20{,}000 = \$30{,}000$$

Step 2. Total liabilities = total current liabilities + long-term debt
$$= \$30{,}000 + \$50{,}000 = \$80{,}000$$

Step 3. Since total assets = total liabilities + stockholders' equity, and $\frac{\text{total debt}}{\text{total assets}} = 0.5$,

$$\text{Total assets} = \text{total liabilities} + \text{stockholders' equity} = \frac{\text{total debt}}{0.5}$$
$$= \frac{\$80{,}000}{0.5}$$
$$= \$160{,}000$$

Step 4. Total stockholders' equity = (total liabilities + stockholders' equity) − total liabilities
$$= \$160{,}000 - \$80{,}000 = \$80{,}000$$

Step 5. Total stockholders' equity = common stock + retained earnings

Retained earnings = total stockholders' equity − common stock
$$= \$80{,}000 - \$10{,}000 = \$70{,}000$$

Step 6. Total asset turnover = $\frac{\text{sales}}{\text{total assets}} = 2.0$

Sales = (2.0)(total assets)
$$= (2.0)(\$160{,}000) = \$320{,}000$$

Step 7. Current ratio = $\frac{\text{current assets}}{\text{current liabilities}} = 1.7$

Current assets = (1.7)(current liabilities)
$$= (1.7)(\$30{,}000) = \$51{,}000$$

Step 8. Total assets = current assets + net long-term assets

Net long-term assets = total assets − current assets
$$= \$160{,}000 - \$51{,}000 = \$109{,}000$$

Step 9. Quick ratio = $\frac{\text{current assets} - \text{inventory}}{\text{current liabilities}} = 1.2$

Current assets − inventory = (1.2)(current liabilities)
$$= (1.2)(\$30{,}000) = \$36{,}000$$

Step 10. Inventory = current assets − (current assets − inventory)
$$= \$51{,}000 - \$36{,}000 = \$15{,}000$$

Step 11. Average collection period = $\dfrac{\text{accounts receivable}}{\text{sales per day}}$ = 36.5

Accounts receivable = (36.5)(sales per day)

= (36.5)($320,000/365) = $32,000

Step 12. Current assets = cash + accounts receivable + inventory

Cash = current assets − accounts receivable − inventory

= $51,000 − $32,000 − $15,000 = $4,000

Jepson Enterprises
Balance Sheet
December 31

Cash	$ 4,000	Accounts payable	$ 10,000
Accounts receivable	32,000	Notes payable	20,000
Inventory	15,000	Total current liabilities	30,000
Total current assets	51,000	Long-term debt	50,000
		Total liabilities	80,000
Net long-term assets	109,000		
		Common stock	10,000
		Retained earnings	70,000
		Total stockholders' equity	80,000
Total assets	$160,000	Total liabilities and stockholders' equity	$160,000

3.5

Step 1. Return on total assets = (net profit margin)(total asset turnover)

= (4.2%)(2.5) = 10.5%

Step 2. Return on equity = $\dfrac{\text{return on total assets}}{(1 - \text{total debt to total assets})}$

16.8% = $\dfrac{10.5\%}{(1 - \text{total debt to total assets})}$

16.8%(1− total debt to total assets) = 10.5%

16.8% − (16.8%)(total debt to total assets) = 10.5%

(16.8)(total debt to total assets) = 16.8 − 10.5 = 6.3

total debt to total assets = 6.3/16.8

= 0.375 or 37.5%

CHAPTER 4

THE EMPHASIS ON CASH FLOWS

HOW THIS CHAPTER RELATES TO THE REST OF THE TEXT

Cash flow is a major component of value. The value of an asset is a function of its cash flow, timing (Chapter 5), and riskiness (Chapter 7). Valuation (Chapter 6) requires the calculation of the cash flow and a recognition of the difference between cash flow and earnings. Cash flow is also an important input in capital budgeting (Chapters 8, 9, 10, and 11), is useful in the management of accounts receivable (Chapter 20), and is an essential tool in financial planning (Chapter 23). A financial manager should understand how depreciation and taxes affect cash flow and how cash flow concepts relate to such decisions as leasing (Chapter 17), and mergers and corporate restructuring (Chapter 22).

TOPICAL OUTLINE

I. Cash flow versus net income.
   A. What is depreciation?
      1. Under generally accepted accounting principles (GAAP), depreciation is an annual charge designed to reflect the wearing out of the firm's assets over its lifetime.
      2. Depreciation is deducted from pretax income, reducing taxes.
      3. Depreciation is a noncash charge; no money changes hands.
      4. The Warner Manufacturing example in the text shows net income versus cash flow, with depreciation as a tax shield. If no depreciation had been charged,
         a. Cash outflow for taxes would have increased.
         b. Net cash flow would have decreased.
   B. Deferred taxes.
      1. GAAP taxes and IRS taxes can differ due to the use of different depreciation methods and/or periods on the financial statements versus the tax statements.
      2. Firms account for differences between GAAP taxes and IRS taxes by creating a deferred tax account.

3. A decrease in the depreciation recovery period or the use of an accelerated method of depreciation will decrease the current cash outflow for taxes and increase the current net cash flow.
4. By "depreciation," we mean depreciation as required for tax purposes.

C. Other factors affecting cash flows.
1. Any accounting treatment affecting taxes will affect cash flows.
2. FAS 96 will change the accounting requirement for deferred taxes; deferred tax accounts will generally be smaller and there will be greater accounting-induced volability in taxes reported.

II. Why cash flow?
A. It is theoretically correct.
B. It removes ambiguities in the accounting process.
C. Cash flow is essential to the well-being of the firm.

III. Cash flow analysis.
A. Statement of cash flows.
1. Operatiing activities: The firm generates cash flow by producing goods or services to be sold.
2. Investing activities: Firms earn cash by investing in bonds which pay interest, stocks which pay dividends, or other marketable securities.
3. Financing activities: Cash flow can arise from issuing stocks or bonds in the capital market or through short-term borrowing.
4. Advantages of the statement of cash flows.
   a. It focuses on the three main functions of the firm; operations, investment, and financing.
   b. It removes the effects of accruals.
   c. It breaks out gross rather than net figures for such items as long-term debt transactions.
5. Disadvantages.
   a. There are two methods, yielding different results, for presenting the statements.

b. The statement does not reconcile reported taxes and taxes paid.
c. Reporting problems exist with discontinued operations and extraordinary expenses, noncash investing and financing, and dividends.

B. The cash budget.
1. Includes all cash inflows and outflows expected by the firm.
2. Alerts the firm to future cash needs and provides a standard of comparison for subsequent performance.

C. Forecasting cash.
1. Create a scenario with an explicit set of assumptions.
   a. Assumptions concerning the state of the economy, competitors' actions, and conditions in the money and capital markets should reflect future possibilities.
   b. Scenario analysis enables the manager to see how sensitive cash flow forecasts are to changes in inputs or assumptions.
2. Estimate Sales.
   a. Internal sales forecasts are based on past sales or information provided by sales personnel and the marketing department. Linear extrapolation is discussed in Appendix 4A.
   b. External forecasts employ factors, such as economic conditions, projected gross national product, etc. outside the firm.
3. Determine cash inflows arising from operations.
4. Determine cash outflows from operations.
5. Calculate other cash inflows and outflows.
6. Determine the short-term financing needs or surplus available.

IV. How to calculate cash flows.
A. Express cash inflows and outflows on an after-tax basis.
B. Ignore all irrelevant costs and benefits, such as overhead.
C. Divide all cash flows into three kinds:
1. Initial investment at time zero--the initial cash outflow.

2. Operating net cash flows for each year in the life of the investment--the periodic cash flow.
3. Terminal cash flows when the project is completed.
D. Opportunity costs, the costs associated with an alternative or foregone opportunity bypassed in choosing another alternative, should be considered.

V. Pro forma financial statements.
A. Pro forma statements project expected revenues, expenses, and financial position at the end of the forecast period.
B. Approaches to developing pro forma statements:
1. Use projections arising from the cash budget and modify to reflect GAAP.
2. The percentage of sales method is based on the historical relationship between balance sheet and income statement entries and sales.
C. Balance sheet and income statement items are assumed to vary directly with sales or must be forecasted.
D. External funds needed equal required increase in assets less spontaneous increase in liabilities less increase in retained earnings.

VI. Forecasting in practice.
A. Inflation and disinflation have a profound impact on cash flows. Firms and their suppliers may be required to change strategies in order to cope with these impacts.
B. Firm growth must be accounted for. High growth rates may put the firm in a cash bind and require external financing. Failure to plan for future needs is one of the primary shortcomings of many growing firms.
C. Electronic spreadsheets allow for rapid scenario analysis and the ability to update forecasts quickly and easily.

VII. Appendix 4A: Linear forecasting (located at the end of the text).
A. Simple linear regression is used to develop sales forecasts.
B. Sales are the dependent variable (Y_i); the time period is the independent variable (X_i). The model is:
$$Y_i = \alpha + \beta X_i$$

C. By using future values for time (X_i), we can forecast future values of sales (Y_i).

D. Although this approach is simple and inexpensive to implement, it may provide misleading results because sales are often affected by factors not captured by the time component.

FORMULAS

<u>Measures of Earnings</u>

Earnings before taxes (EBT):

EBT = Revenue - costs and expenses - depreciation

Net income = EBT(1 - T)

<u>Measures of Cash Flow</u>

Cash flow before taxes (CFBT):

CFBT = Cash inflows - cash outflows

Cash flow after taxes (CF):

CF = (Cash inflows - cash outflows) - taxes

    = CFBT - taxes

    = (CFBT)(1 - T) + (Depreciation)(T)

<u>Appendix 4A: Linear Forecasting</u>

Notation:

Y_t = sales in period t

X_t = time period

Formulas:

$$\bar{Y} = \sum_{t=1}^{n} Y_t/n$$

$$\bar{X_t} = \sum_{t=1}^{n} X_t/n$$

$$Y_t = \alpha + \beta X_t$$

$$\beta = \frac{\sum_{t=1}^{n} X_t Y_t - (n)(\bar{Y})(\bar{X})}{\sum_{t=1}^{n} X_t^2 - n(\bar{X}^2)}$$

$$\alpha = \bar{Y} - \beta \bar{X}$$

WHAT TO LOOK FOR

In this section, we will highlight taxes, depreciation, and cash flows and discuss some aspects that may be confusing.

After-Tax Cash Flow versus Net Income

The difference between cash flow and net income

You noted from this chapter that earnings figures and cash flow figures often do not agree. Why does this difference exist? The purposes of earnings figures and cash flow figures differ. Earnings figures, whose calculation is guided by generally accepted accounting principles, can be calculated in a variety of ways depending upon which generally accepted procedures are employed. Sometimes the choice of a procedure is an attempt to put forth the most attractive financial picture of the firm. In addition, earnings figures also attempt to match costs and revenues in the period in which they occur, based upon historical cost. Earnings are only a clue to the firm's ability to generate cash flows.

Cash flow figures, however, report the inflow and outflow of cash. The value of the firm can be estimated as the present value of the expected future cash flows of the firm. Poor management cannot be masked as easily by cash flow figures as it can be by earnings figures.

Management problems indicated by cash flow figures

In fact, cash flow figures can indicate areas for improvement in management. Let's look at the Zeigler Tire Company, for example. Suppose that Zeigler Tire has annual sales of $700,000, with 75 percent on credit. Credit terms require full payment within 90 days. These sales are relatively seasonal, with about 60 percent in the autumn months. The projected cash flows for the three months ending November 30 are below:

Cash Inflows		Cash Outflows	
Sales in cash	$105,000	Cash expenses	$200,000
Cash on hand	10,000	Taxes	63,000
Credit sales coming in	70,000	Repayment of short-term debt	100,000
Total	$185,000	Total	$363,000

Cash shortfall = $185,000 - $363,000 = -$178,000

As we see, the cash shortfall is $178,000. Now let's compare these cash flow figures with the GAAP balance sheet and income statement. Notice that while the income statement reports a healthy $147,000 income, Zeigler is actually experienceing a cash shortage of $178,000.

Balance Sheet as of November 30

Assets		Liabilities and Stockholders' Equity	
Cash	$ 10,000	Short-term debt	$100,000
Accounts receivable	70,000	Long-term debt	150,000
Inventory	500,000	Equity	330,000
Total	$580,000	Total	$580,000

Income Statement (for Three Months Ending November 30)

Sales (0.25 in cash)	$420,000
Cash expenses	200,000
Depreciation	10,000
EBT	$210,000
Taxes (0.30)	63,000
Net Income	$147,000

Zeigler has excellent earnings figures but very poor cash flow, since its outflows exceed its inflows. With 75 percent of its tires sold on credit, the cash flow is slowed down. The sales are recorded, but the cash will not be coming in for 90 days. Meanwhile, Zeigler must continue to replace inventories. Zeigler's cash flow figures show a cash shortfall of $178,000 and indicate the need to change its credit terms policy to speed up its cash flow, consider selling its receivables, and perhaps cut down the percentage of customers using credit.

Cash Flow Analysis

While understanding the difference between cash flow and earnings is important to financial management, it is also important to know how to estimate future cash flows. Cash inflows and outflows can be categorized as arising from operations, investments, or financing. Firms must be sensitive to the balance between inflows and outflows over both the short run and the long run. Excessive cash outflows can ultimately result in the failure of the firm. In order to prevent this, firms often develop cash budgets to provide an indication of future problems and to use as a standard of comparison for future performance.

The cash budget is a detailed statement of all expected cash inflows and outflows and can be developed for any period of time such as a month or a quarter of a year. The procedure for developing a cash budget includes developing a scenario with explicit assumptions estimating sales, determining cash inflows and outflows from operations, estimating other cash inflows and outflows, and determining the expected cash surplus or funds needed.

To see how a cash budget can be developed, consider the case of Rand Manufacturing. The firm had sales of $460 thousand in January, had sales of $396 thousand for February, and forecasts sales of $530 thousand in March. Fifty percent of sales are for cash, 40 percent are collected in one month, and the remainder are collected in two months.

In order to maintain operations, the company purchases raw materials equivalent to 75 percent of sales. Forty percent of the monthly purchase is paid in cash, the remaining 60 percent is paid for one month later. Wages and other expenses are estimated at $125 thousand for March; interest expenses are estimated to be $12 thousand, and the firm expects to pay $35 thousand in taxes. At the end of February, Rand has $75 thousand in cash on hand and expects to receive $6,000 in dividends on stock owned. The company must maintain a minimum cash balance of $30,000 and has to pay an insurance bill of $50,000 in March. What are Rand Manufacturing's cash needs for March?

First, let us estimate cash inflows from operations. These cash inflows come from either sales or collections on prior sales. Following Table 4.5, we can estimate these cash inflows as follows:

Estimated Cash Inflows from Operations (in Thousands)
Rand Manufacturing

		January	February	March
1.	Total sales	$460.00	$396.00	$530.00
2.	Collections: one-month lag (40% of total sales)			158.40
3.	Collections: two-month lag (10% of total sales)			46.00
4.	Total collections (2+3)			204.40
5.	Cash sales (50% of total sales)			265.00
6.	Total operating cash inflow (4+5)			$469.40

In a similar fashion, we calculate the net cash outflows from operations.

Estimated Cash Outflows from Operations (in Thousands)
Rand Manufacturing

	February	March
1. Total sales	$396.00	$530.00
2. Credit purchases (75% of sales)(0.60)	178.20	238.60
3. Payment of credit purchases (one month-lag)		178.20
4. Cash purchases (75% of sales)(0.40)		159.00
5. Wages and other expenses		125.00
6. Interest		12.00
7. Taxes		35.00
8. Total operating cash outflows (3+4+5+6+7)		$509.20

Other cash inflows are $6,000 from dividends and outflows are $50,000 for insurance expenses, or -$44,000 overall. For March, the net cash inflow is as follows:

	March
1. Total operating cash inflow	$469.40
2. Total operating cash outflow	- 509.20
3. Other cash inflow or outflow	- 44.00
4. Net cash inflow (+) or outflow (-)	-$ 83.80

Rand Manufacturing has some cash on hand, but is it sufficient? Let's determine the short-term financing needed:

	March
1. Cash	$ 75.00
2. Net cash inflow or outflow	- 83.80
3. Cash at end of period	- 8.80
4. Minimum cash balance required	- 30.00
5. Short-term financing needed	-$ 38.80

Rand needs to obtain $38,800 in cash in order to maintain operations. In reality, Rand would forecast its financing needs over a longer period of time in order to make arrangements with a lender to prevent any sort of cash crisis.

Pro Forma Financial Statements

Other useful tools in estimating expected future cash flows are pro forma financial statements. These statements project the firm's expected revenues, expenses, and financial position at the end of the forecast period.

Two basic approaches are used in developing pro forma statements. The first uses projections arising from the cash budget and modifies them to reflect GAAP. The second, or percentage of sales method, starts with the historical relationship between sales and various income statement and balance sheet items. These relationships are then applied to the firm's sales forecast to determine net income and external financing needs.

Consider the following abbreviated financial statement for Voltex Company, a manufacturer of synthetic fabrics. Voltex believes that sales next year will be $39,000,000 and wishes to develop pro forma statements to estimate cash needs. The firm also wishes to increase net long-term assets by $3,000,000 next year.

Income Statement (in Thousands)
Voltex Company
Year Ending December 31

	Actual	% of Sales
Sales	$36,000	
Cost of goods sold	22,320	62.00%
Gross margin	13,680	
Selling, general, and administrative expenses	2,500	6.94
EBIT	11,180	
Interest	1,200	3.33
EBT	9,980	
Taxes (40%)	3,992	-
Net income	5,988	-
Cash dividends	4,491	-
Transferred to retained earnings	$ 1,497	-

Balance Sheet (in Thousands)
Voltex Company
December 31

	Actual	% of Sales
Assets		
Cash	$ 2,000	5.56%
Accounts receivable	3,000	8.33
Inventory	10,000	27.77
Total current	15,000	41.66
Net long-term assets	18,000	-
Total assets	$33,000	-
Liabilities and stockholders' equity		
Accounts payable	$ 1,000	2.78%
Notes payable	3,500	-
Accrued taxes and wages	1,500	4.17
Total current	6,000	-
Long-term debt and leases	16,000	-
Deferred taxes	1,000	2.78
Total long-term debt	17,000	-
Common stock and additional paid in capital	3,000	-
Retained earnings	7,000	-
Total stockholders' equity	10,000	-
Total liabilities and stockholders' equity	$33,000	-

The column marked "percent of sales" is simply the line item divided by sales. The percentage is not listed for many items. These are thought not to vary directly with sales or require managerial action to change. An example is notes payable; any change must be negotiated with a lending officer at the firm's bank.

By multiplying these percentages by our estimated sales of $39,000,000, we can calculate next year's projected net income for Voltex.

Pro Forma Income Statement
Voltex Company
(in Thousands)
Year Ending December 31

Sales	$39,000
Cost of goods sold	24,180
Gross margin	14,820
Selling, general, and administrative expenses	2,707
EBIT	12,113
Interest	1,299
EBT	10,814
Taxes (40%)	4,326
Net income	$ 6,488

If the dividend payout ratio remains constant at 75 percent, $4,866,000 will be paid in dividends and $1,622,000 will be added to retained earnings. Using this figure and applying the same logic as above, we can estimate the pro forma balance sheet, assuming those entries not affected by sales (except net long-term assets) remain constant.

Pro Forma Balance Sheet
Voltex Company
(in Thousands)
December 31

Assets		Liabilities and Stockholders' Equity	
Cash	$ 2,168	Accounts payable	$ 1,084
Accounts receivable	3,249	Notes payable	3,500
Inventory	10,830	Accrued taxes and wages	1,626
Total current assets	16,247	Total current	6,210
Net long-term assets	21,000	Long-term debt and leases	16,000
Total assets	$37,247	Deferred taxes	1,084
		Total long-term debt	17,084
		Common stock and additional paid-in capital	3,000
		Retained earnings	8,622
		Total stockholders' equity	11,622
		Additional funds needed to balance total	2,331
		Total	$37,247

Note that total assets do not equal total liabilities and stockholders' equity. The difference, in this case $2,331,000, is the external funds needed by the firm. The firm could raise these funds through increasing notes payable, issuing long-term debt, or issuing stock. You should see that the method of financing will affect the external funds needed. More notes payable or long-term debt will increase interest expenses; additional stock will require larger dividend payments. Once a method of financing has been decided upon, new pro forma statements should be developed to determine actual financing needs.

Forecasting in Practice

Cash flow analysis is obviously a powerful tool for financial managers. In practice, a good cash flow analysis is consideration of a variety of conditions not discussed to this point. Inflation and disinflation, for instance, have an obvious impact on the firm's cash flows. Also, it may be necessary for a firm to change its strategies to cope with these conditions. The firm may not be able to pass the effects of inflation or disinflation along to its consumers and may cause suppliers of funds to change strategies. A complete cash flow analysis should consider these possibilities.

Growing firms have special problems that need careful attention. As firms grow, so do their sales. This requires additional assets and, hence, additional capital. High growth rates may put the firm in a cash bind. Internally generated funds may not be sufficient and the firm may need to acquire long-term sources of financing. Failure to consider and plan for the effects of growth is one of the primary shortcomings of growing firms.

Appendix 4A: Linear Forecasting (located at the end of the text)

Simple linear regression techniques provide a naive approach to forecasting sales. In this approach, it is assumed that

$$\text{Sales} = \alpha + \beta \times \text{time}$$

By varying time, we can forecast sales for any period in the future. However, this method ignores all factors except time and may yield misleading results.

COMPLETION QUESTIONS

4.1 Three advantages of using cash flow rather than net income are that cash flow is _____, _____, and _____.

4.2 Once we have calculated the after-tax cash flow of an investment project, it is necessary to consider the _____.

4.3 The cost associated with a foregone alternative bypassed to accept another investment is called an _____.

4.4 _____ is a noncash expense which acts as a tax shield to reduce a firm's taxable income, provided the firm is profitable.

4.5 Managers must give special attention to the _____, _____, and _____ of the firm's expected cash flows.

4.6 Smith and Company is investing in a capital project which requires an increase in inventory of $40,000 during the life of the project. At time 0, the investment is an _____ of cash. At the end of the project's life, the inventory (dis)investment is an _____ of cash.

4.7 Global Corporation is considering the introduction of a new line of small electronic switches to its products. In evaluating this investment, Global should look at the _____ cash flows.

4.8 When a firm uses different depreciation periods and methods for GAAP purposes than for reporting to the IRS, it sets up a _____ _____ on the balance sheet for the difference in the IRS versus the GAAP taxes.

4.9 If a firm chooses a shorter rather than longer recovery period for depreciation, its current cash outflow for taxes _____, while its net current cash flow _____.

4.10 The cash budget is a detailed statement of the firm's expected _____ and _____.

4.11 An external sales forecast is based on factors _____ to the firm, such as the state of the economy.

4.12 Scenario analysis enables a manager to determine how _____ cash flows are to changes in inputs or _____.

4.13 To estimate the firm's cash needs, the firm should take into account internally generated _____, increases in the investment in current assets, the timing and magnitude of the firm's projected _____ _____, repayment of principal, and short-term financing costs. The free internally generated funds available for reinvestment depend on the firm's _____ policy.

4.14 In financial planning, GAAP-based accounting statements are not very useful since they are not based upon _____.

PROBLEMS

4.1 Essex Industries has approached Union First Bank about the possibility of obtaining a $600,000 three month loan to purchase new manufacturing equipment. (The equipment has a normal recovery period of 5 years.) Kenneth Lawrence, the corporation's financial officer, has drawn up a projected three-month income statement for the period of the loan. The income statement does not reflect the impact of the loan.

Projected Income Statement

Sales	$2,000,000
Cash expenses	950,000
Depreciation	450,000
EBIT	600,000
Interest	50,000
EBT	550,000
Taxes (36%)	198,000
Net income	$ 352,000

Mr. Lawrence has provided the following information:

1. All sales and expenses are for cash.
2. The depreciation is straight-line and is pro-rated on a quarterly basis
3. Essex Industries has $400,000 cash on hand.
4. A $500,000 construction progress payment is due this quarter.

If the interest rate is 12 percent annually (3 percent this quarter), will Essex Industries have sufficient funds to repay the loan? Prepare a new income statement and go on to consider the cash inflows and outflows.

4.2 Manson Electronics is considering conversion of an existing warehouse into a production facility. For the new facility, Manson must buy manufacturing equipment for $1,500,000. The new facility will allow Manson to increase sales by $3,000,000 per year. The following should be considered in the analysis

1. Expenses associated with the new facility are:
   Fixed cash flows = $100,000
   Variable cash flows = 60 percent of sales
2. The manufacturing equipment will be depreciated over its 5-year normal recovery period using straight-line depreciation for tax purposes.
3. At present, Manson Electronics leases the warehouse to a local moving company for $100,000 (before taxes) per year.
4. The new facility will require a $500,000 increase in raw materials inventory. Manson expects to recover this at the end of the project's life.
5. The value of the equipment at the end of 5 years is estimated to be zero.
6. Manson's marginal tax rate is 30 percent.

What are the cash flows associated with the above project?

4.3 Green's Golf Equipment is a manufacturer of golf balls and is attempting to plan for its future cash flow needs. Historically, 45 percent of sales are for cash, 35 percent are collected with a one month lag, and 20 percent are collected with a two month lag. Purchases are 60 percent of sales and are made one month in advance. Forty percent of the purchases are for cash; the remainder is paid after one month. Estimates of wages, interest, and taxes are listed below. The firm also intends to pay an $185 insurance bill in May. Using the data below, forecast Green's cash flow needs for March, April, and May.

	January	February	March	April	May	June
Estimated sales	$1,200	$1,300	$2,100	$2,300	$1,800	$2,500
Wages	250	250	260	280	280	280
Interest	100	100	100	100	100	100
Taxes	–	–	–	80	–	–

4.4 Laird Transit Company is attempting to forecast its short-term financing needs for the next year. Its cash flow forecasts are as follows:

	Quarter 1	Quarter 2	Quarter 3	Quarter 4
Total operating cash inflow	$300	$400	$250	$180
Total operating cash outflow	-250	-320	-230	-150
Other net inflow (+) or outflow (-)	-70	+50	-160	-20

Laird's starting cash balance is $10, which is the minimum it requires. What are its cumulative short-term financing needs by quarter?

4.5 The following is the income statement for Clearwater Distillery, a distributor of bottled mineral water:

Sales	$1,450.00
Operating expenses	1,044.00
Income from operations	406.00
Other income	55.00
EBIT	461.00
Interest	120.00
EBT	341.00
Taxes	102.30
Net income	$ 238.70

Sales are expected to increase by 12 percent over the next year; other income is expected to remain constant, as is the interest expense. Using the percentage of sales method, estimate the income statement for next year.

4.6 The 1989 balance sheet for Tyrone Enterprises is as follows:

Balance Sheet
(in Thousands)

Cash	$ 70	Accounts payable	$ 100
Accounts receivable	240	Notes payable	220
Inventory	500	Total current liabilities	320
Total current assets	810	Long-term bonds	540
Net long-term assets	1,200	Common stock	600
Total	$2,010	Retained earnings	550
		Total	$2,010

Sales for 1989 were $5,000. The company expects sales to increase by 15 percent for 1990. This increase in sales can be obtained without expanding net long-term assets due to sufficient capacity. The firm's after-tax profit as a percent of sales is typically 2 percent, and the firm pays out 60 percent of net income as cash dividends. The firm will raise additional funds needed through the use of notes payable so long as the current ratio is at least 2.5. Remaining funds needed will be raised by equal amounts of long-term bonds and common stock. Using the percent of sales method and the above limitations, develop a pro forma balance sheet for 1990 for Tyrone Enterprises.

4A.1 Becker's Building Supply is trying to forecast sales for 1990. Using the data below, develop a linear forecast using simple linear regression for Becker.

Year	Sales (in Thousands)
1980	$170
1981	180
1982	195
1983	225
1984	218
1985	260
1986	245
1987	265
1988	270
1989	290

ANSWERS TO COMPLETION QUESTIONS

4.1 theoretically correct; unambiguous; essential to the firm's financial well being

4.2 riskiness (or uncertainty) of the cash flows

4.3 opportunity cost

4.4 Depreciation

4.5 magnitude; timing; riskiness

4.6 outflow; inflow

4.7 incremental after-tax

4.8 deferred tax account

4.9 decreases; increases

4.10 inflows; outflows

4.11 external

4.12 sensitive; assumptions

4.13 funds; capital expenditures; cash dividend

4.14 cash flows

SOLUTIONS TO PROBLEMS

4.1

Step 1. To determine if Essex Industries will have sufficient cash on hand, recalculate the income statement under the assumption that the loan will be granted.

Sales		$2,000,000
Expenses		950,000
Depreciation: Old	$450,000	
New[a]	30,000	480,000
EBIT		570,000
Interest: Old	50,000	
New[b]	18,000	68,000
EBT		502,000
Taxes (36%)		180,720
Net income		$321,280

[a] New depreciation: Depreciation for 1 year = (1/5)(cost), so
Depreciation = ($600,000)(0.20)/4 = $30,000 per quarter

[b] New interest expense: The firm wishes to borrow $600,000 at an interest rate of 12 percent per year. The quarterly interest will be
Interest = ($600,000)(0.12)/4 = $18,000

Step 2. Cash inflows

Sales	$2,000,000
Cash on hand	400,000
Total cash available	$2,400,000

Step 3. Cash outflows

Expenses	$ 950,000
Interest	68,000
Taxes	180,720
Construction progress payment	500,000
Loan repayment	600,000
Total outflows	$2,298,720

The firm will have a cash surplus of $101,280 ($2,400,000 - $2,298,720) if the loan is made.

4.2

Step 1. (in thousands)

Initial investment

Manufacturing equipment	$1,500
Inventory	500
Net initial cash outflow	$2,000

Step 2. For years 1-5:

CFBT = sales - variable cash flows - fixed cash flows
= [$3,000 - (0.60)($3,000) - $100] = $1,100

Step 3. Depreciable base = $1,500

Depreciation = (1/5)($1,500) = $300 per year

Step 4. $CF_{1,2,3,4,5}$ = $1,100(1 - 0.30) + 0.30(300) = $860

	Year				
	1	2	3	4	5
CF	$860	$860	$860	$860	$860
Opportunity loss					
$100(1 - 0.30) = $70	(70)	(70)	(70)	(70)	(70)
Recovery of inventory					500
Net CF	$790	$790	$790	$790	$1,290

Step 5. The total cash flow stream is:

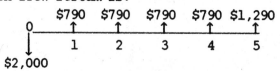

4.3

Step 1. Estimated Cash Inflows from Operations

	January	February	March	April	May
1. Total sales	$1,200	$1,300	$2,100	$2,300	$1,800
2. Collections--one-month lag (35% of sales)		420	455	735	805
3. Collections--two-month lag (20% of sales)			240	260	420
4. Total collections (2 + 3)			695	995	1,225
5. Cash sales (45% of total sales)			945	1,035	810
6. Total operating cash inflows			$1,640	$2,030	$2,035

Step 2. Estimated Cash Outflows from Operations

	February	March	April	May	June
1. Total sales	$1,300	$2,100	$2,300	$1,800	$2,500
2. Total purchases (60% of sales made one month in advance)	1,260	1,380	1,080	1,500	
3. Credit purchases (60% of purchases)	756	828	648	900	
4. Payment of credit purchases (one-month lag)		756	828	648	
5. Cash purchases (40% of purchases)		552	432	600	
6. Wages		260	280	280	
7. Interest		100	100	100	
8. Taxes			80		
9. Total operating cash outflows (4+5+6+7+8)		$1,668	$1,720	$1,628	

Step 3. Net Cash Flow for Green's Golf Equipment

	March	April	May
1. Total operating cash inflow	$1,640	$2,030	$2,035
2. Total operating cash outflow	-1,668	-1,720	-1,628
3. Other net outflows			- 185
4. Net cash inflow (+) or outflow (-)	-$ 28	+$ 310	+$ 222

4.4

Step 1. Determine net inflow or outflow:

	Q1	Q2	Q3	Q4
Total operating cash inflow	$300	$400	$250	$180
Total operating cash outflow	- 250	- 320	- 230	- 150
Other net inflow or outflow	- 70	+ 50	- 160	- 20
Net inflow (+) or outflow (-)	-$ 20	+$130	-$140	+$ 10

Step 2. Short-term financing needs:

	Q1	Q2	Q3	Q4
Cash at start of period	+$ 10	-$ 10	+$120	-$ 20
Net cash inflow or outflow	- 20 ↱	+ 130 ↱	- 140 ↱	+ 10
Cash at end of period	-$ 10	+$120	-$ 20	-$ 10
Minimum balance required	- 10	- 10	- 10	- 10
Cumulative needed(-) or surplus(+)	-$ 20	+$110	-$ 30	-$ 20

4.5

Step 1. Operating expense as a percent of sales = $1,044/$1,450 = 0.72 = 72%

Tax rate = $102.30/$341 = 30%

Step 2.

Sales ($1,450)(1.12)	$1,624.00
Operating expenses ($1,624)(0.72)	1,169.28
Income from operations	454.72
Plus: Other income	55.00
EBIT	509.72
Interest	120.00
EBT	389.72
Taxes (30%)	116.92
Net income	$ 272.80

4.6

Step 1. Assets as a percent of sales   Liabilities as a percent of sales

$$\frac{\text{Cash}}{\text{sales}} = \frac{\$70}{\$5,000} = 1.4\% \qquad \frac{\text{Accounts payable}}{\text{sales}} = \frac{\$100}{\$5,000} = 2\%$$

$$\frac{\text{Accounts receivable}}{\text{sales}} = \frac{\$240}{\$5,000} = 4.8\%$$

$$\frac{\text{Inventory}}{\text{sales}} = \frac{\$500}{\$5,000} = 10\%$$

Sales$_{1989}$ = $5,000(1.15) = $5,750

Cash = ($5,750)(0.014) = $80.5

Accounts payable = ($5,750)(0.02) = $115

Accounts receivable = ($5,750)(0.048) = $276

Inventory = ($5,750)(0.10) = $575

Step 2. Assets

Cash	$ 80.50
Accounts receivable	276.00
Inventory	575.00
Total current assets	931.50
Net long-term assets	1,200.00
Total assets	$2,131.50

Necessary increase in assets = $2,131.50 − $2,010 = $121.50

External funds needs = $121.50 − ($115 − $100)
$$\qquad - [(0.02)(\$5,750)(1 - 0.60)]$$
$$= \$121.50 - \$15 - \$46 = \$60.5$$

Step 3. Retained earnings = $550 + [($5,750)(0.02)(1 - 0.60)] = $596

The firm needs to raise $60.50 externally. Assuming that the firm wishes to maintain a current ratio of 2.5,

$$\text{Current ratio} = \frac{\text{current assets}}{\text{current liabilities}} = 2.5$$

$$= \frac{\$931.50}{\text{current liabilities}} = 2.5$$

Current liabilities = $931.50/2.5 = $372.60

Current liabilities = accounts payable + notes payable

$372.60 = $115 + notes payable

Notes payable = $372.60 - $115 = $257.60

The increase in notes payable is $257.60 - $220 = $37.60

The firm still needs to raise $60.50 - $37.50 = $22.90 by using new long-term bonds and common stock. Since half comes from each source,

Increase in common stock = $22.90/2 = $11.45

Increase in long-term bonds = $22.90/2 = $11.45

Step 4. The pro forma balance sheet is then

Cash	$ 80.50	Accounts payable	$ 115.00
Accounts receivable	276.00	Notes payable	257.60
Inventory	575.00		
		Total current liabilities	372.60
Total current assets	931.50	Long-term debt	551.45
Net long-term assets	1,200.00	Common stock	611.45
Total assets	$2,131.50	Retained earnings	596.00
		Total liabilities and stockholders' equity	$2,131.50

4A.1

Step 1.

Year	Sales(Y_t)	Time(X_t)	$Y_t X_t$	X_t^2
1980	170	1	170	1
1981	180	2	360	4
1982	195	3	585	9
1983	225	4	900	16
1984	218	5	1,090	25
1985	260	6	1,560	36
1986	245	7	1,715	49
1987	265	8	2,120	64
1988	270	9	2,430	81
1989	290	10	2,900	100
	2,318	55	13,830	385

Means:

$$\bar{Y} = \frac{\sum Y_t}{n} = \frac{2,318}{10} = 231.8$$

$$\bar{X} = \frac{\sum X_t}{n} = \frac{55}{10} = 5.5$$

$$\beta = \frac{\sum X_t Y_t - n(\bar{Y})(\bar{X})}{\sum X_t^2 - n(\bar{X})^2} = \frac{13,830 - 10(231.8)(5.5)}{385 - 10(5.5^2)}$$

$$= \frac{13,830 - 12,749}{385 - 302.5} = \frac{1,081}{82.5} = 13.103$$

$$\alpha = \bar{Y} - \beta \bar{X} = 231.8 - 13.103(5.5)$$

$$= 231.8 - 72.066 = 159.734$$

For 1990, $X_t = 11$

$$\text{Sales}_{1990} = 159.734 + 13.103(11)$$

$$= 159.734 + 144.133 = \$303.867$$

CHAPTER 5

TIME VALUE OF MONEY

HOW THIS CHAPTER RELATES TO THE REST OF THE TEXT

The time value of money is the first fundamental concept of finance discussed in this book. All valuation techniques such as bond and stock pricing (Chapter 6) and capital budgeting (Chapters 8-10) rely on present value. Time value concepts enable us to determine implied interest rates such as yield to maturity (Chapter 6) and the internal rate of return (Chapter 8). Other uses include leasing (Chapter 17), working capital management (Chapters 20 and 21), and mergers and corporate restructuring (Chapter 22).

TOPICAL OUTLINE

I. Basic concepts.
   A. Future value or compounding.
      1. Involves taking today's dollar amount and figuring what it will be worth sometime in the future if it earns a return of k percent each year or compounding period.
      2. Use the formula: $FV_n = PV_0(1 + k)^n$ or $FV_n = PV_0(FV_{k,n})$
      3. Table F.1 at the end of the text presents future value factors (FVs) for your use.
   B. Present value or discounting.
      1. Involves taking a future amount and figuring out what it is worth today when it is discounted at k percent each year or compounding period.
      2. Useful for financial or investment planning, answering such questions as: How much would I have to put away at k percent today in order to have $X in 5 years to pay for a college education?
      3. Equation: $PV_0 = FV_n/(1 + k)^n$ or $PV_0 = FV_n(PV_{k,n})$
      4. Table F.3 at the end of the text has present value factors (PVs) for your use.
   C. Comparing future value and present value.
      1. Mathematically and theoretically, present value and future value are inverses of each other.

a. Present value takes a future amount in period n and values it today, given a specific discount rate over time from period n to today.

b. Future value takes a present amount today and calculates its value in the future, given a specific compounding rate over the time from today to period n.

2. FVs are the reciprocals of PVs.

II. Multiple cash flows: Annuities, uneven payments, and perpetuities.

A. Future value of an annuity.

1. Annuity A, is a series of fixed dollar payments for each of a number of periods.

2. Future value of an investment of a fixed dollar amount per period for n periods at k percent; the first payment at the end of the first period.

a. Payments begin one year from now, so the number of compounding periods is n - 1.

b. $FV_n = PMT \sum_{t=0}^{n-1} (1 + k)^t = PMT \left[\frac{(1 + k)^n - 1}{k} \right] = PMT(FVA_{k,n})$

3. Table F.2 at the end of the text has future value factors for annuities ($FVA_{k,n}$) for you to use: $FVA_n = PMT(FVA_{k,n})$.

4. The FVAs are actually the sum of the FVs for the n - 1 number of periods plus 1.000.

5. An annuity due assumes the first payment is made at the beginning rather than the end of a period.

a. $FV_n(\text{annuity due}) = PMT \left[\frac{(1+k)^n - 1}{k} \right](1+k) = PMT(FVA_{k,n})(1+k)$

B. Present value of an annuity.

1. Present value of a series of n annual payments of A dollars invested at k percent; the first receipt to be received in exactly one year.

2. Formula:
$PV_0 = PMT \sum_{t=1}^{n} \frac{1}{(1+k)^t} = PMT \left[\frac{1 - [1/(1 + k)^n]}{k} \right] = PMT(PVA_{k,n})$

3. Table F.A at the end of the textbook has PVAs for you to use: $PV_0 = PMT(PVA_{k,n})$.

C. Present value of an uneven series.
  1. Since the payments or receipts are uneven, PVs must be used instead of PVAs.
  2. Each receipt must be discounted separately, unless some can be treated as an annuity.
     a. Use PVs on cash flows which are unlike the other cash flows in the series.
     b. If an even series of cash flows exists within the total series of cash flows, use a PVA (for the number of years it is received or paid) to discount these flows back to the period when these even flows begin; then discount this amount back to the present with a PV.
D. Perpetuities.
  1. Perpetuities are fixed annuities into infinity, like preferred stock or a perpetual bond.
  2. Formula: $PV_0 = \dfrac{\text{annual receipt}}{\text{discount rate}} = \dfrac{PMT}{k}$

III. Determining interest rates.
  A. Single cash flow.
    1. If you borrowed $1,000 today and paid interest and principal in a $2,012.07 lump sum in five years, what would be the implied rate?
       a. Equation: $PV_0 = FV_n(PV_{k,n})$
       b. $PV_{k,n} = PV_0/FV_n$
       c. When you have solved for PV, look in Table F.3 across the appropriate year row; in this case, the implied interest rate is 15 percent.
  B. Annuities: Do as for a single cash flow, except $PVA_{k,n} = PV_0/PMT$.
  C. Uneven series.
    1. Trial-and-error approach. Choose an interest rate and use present value factors to attempt to exactly equal your present value; see Table 5.5 for an example.
    2. Interpolate the implied interest rate for an uneven cash flow series.
    3. Use a financial calculator.

IV. Applications in financial management.
   A. Growth rates.
      1. Determine the number of time periods involved--one less than the number of years (or periods) with which you are dealing.
      2. Use the following formula:

         Implied growth factor = rate associated with $PV_{k,n} = \dfrac{\text{beginning value}}{\text{ending value}}$

      3. Look in Table F.3 at the number of periods for the PV factor to find the implied growth rate.
   B. Future Sums.
      1. You can determine annual funds necessary to accumulate a certain sum in the future.
      2. $PMT = \dfrac{FV_n}{FVA_{k,n}}$
   C. Loan Amortization.
      1. Determine the periodic payment needed to pay off a loan.
      2. $PMT = \dfrac{PV_0}{PVA_{k,n}}$
      3. An amortization schedule shows how much of each payment is principal and interest.
   D. Effective rate of interest.
      1. $k_{effective} = (1 + \dfrac{k_{adjusted\ nom}}{m})^m - 1$
      2. Some nominal rates are based on a 360-day year. To adjust: $k_{nominal} = k_{360\ nom}(365/360)$
   E. Semiannual and other compounding and discounting periods.
      1. For compounding, use the equation: $FV_n = PV_0 [1 + (k/m)]^{mn}$
      2. m = number of periods per year; n = number of years.
      3. For discounting, use: $PV_0 = \dfrac{FV_n}{(1 + k/m)^{mn}}$
V. Linear interpolation.
   A. If the factor lies between two interest rates, you can easily interpolate.

      Example: n = 8, $PV_{?\%,8yr} = 0.500$
      1. Table F.3 says this factor is between 9 and 10 percent.
      2. Interpolation takes the ratio of the difference between the calculated factor and the 9 percent factor to the difference

between the 9 percent factor and the 10 percent factor:
$$\frac{0.502 - 0.500}{0.502 - 0.467} = 0.002/0.035 = 0.0571.$$
3. The implied interest rate is 9 percent plus 0.0571 or 9.0571 percent.

B. The same procedure can be used for future value factors and future value factors for annuities.

FORMULAS

Notation

PV = Present (or discounted) value of future amount that will be invested

k = compounding or discount rate

FV = future (or compounded) value of the present amount you will invest

n = number of discounting or compounding periods or number of annuity periods

Σ = sigma, or take the sum of

PMT = annuity that starts in time period 1 and extends to time period n

m = number of times per year the interest is compounded

t = number of periods you invest the money

Future Value

$$FV_n = PV_0(1 + k)^n = PV_0(FV_{k,n}) \quad \text{(Use Table F.1)}$$

Present Value

$$PV_0 = \frac{FV_n}{(1 + k)^n} = FV_n(PV_{k,n}) \quad \text{(Use Table F.3)}$$

Present Value versus Future Value

$$PV_{k,n} = \frac{1}{FV_{k,n}}$$

Annuities or Perpetuities

Future value:

$$FV_n = PMT \sum_{t=0}^{n-1}(1+k)^t = PMT\left[\frac{(1+k)^n - 1}{k}\right]$$

$$= PMT(FVA_{k,n}) \quad \text{(Use Table F.2)}$$

Present value:

$$PV_0 = PMT \sum_{t=1}^{n} \frac{1}{(1+k)^t} = PMT \left[\frac{1 - [(1/1+k)^n]}{k} \right]$$

$$= PMT(PVA_{k,n}) \quad \text{(Use Table F.4)}$$

Perpetuity:

$$PV_0 = \frac{PMT}{k}$$

Determining Interest Rates

Rearrange the above equations as below:

$$PV_{k,n} = PV_0/FV_n$$

$$PVA_{k,n} = PVA_0/PMT$$

Semiannual and Other Compounding and Discounting Periods

Compounding:

$$FV_n = PV_0 [1+(k/m)]^{mn}$$

Discounting:

$$PV_0 = \frac{FV_n}{[1 + (k/m)]^{mn}}$$

Effective Rate of Interest:

$$k_{effective} = (1 + \frac{k_{nom}}{m})^m - 1$$

$$k_{nom} = k_{360\ nom}(365/360)$$

Interpolation

$$\text{Implied interest rate} = \text{lower interest rate} + \frac{\text{PV at lower interest rate} - \text{calculated PV}}{\text{PV at lower interest rate} - \text{PV at higher interest rate}}$$

$$\text{Implied growth factor} = \text{rate associated with } PV_{k,n} = \frac{\text{beginning value}}{\text{ending value}}$$

WHAT TO LOOK FOR

Chapter 5 is the first of three critical chapters in this text; here we look at the time value of money. In Chapter 6, we examine value, and in Chapter 7, risk and return. Up to now, we have made only general comments about interest or discount rates. In Chapter 5, we begin using interest rates. If your accounting class has covered the time value of money, you will find these concepts familiar. If you have never studied the time value of money, you will find it is a simple, commonsense approach for dealing with cash flows that occur at different points in time.

Terminology and Examples of Time Value

The study of time value will be easier if we understand a few terms.

Time value of money.

Since money can be invested productively to earn a positive rate of return, a dollar received today is worth more than a dollar to be received sometime in the future. The difference in value depends upon the expected rate of return on that dollar received today.

Future value (FV).

Since the dollar received today can be invested, its future value would be its present value, $1, compounded at the expected rate of return—$1 $(1+k)^n$—where k = the rate of return and n = the number of compounding periods. If k = 15 percent, and n = 10, what is the future value of the $1 received today earning 15 percent annually for 10 years?

```
 0   1   2   3   4   5   6   7   8   9   10    $1 compounded
 |                                                at 15% for
$1 |─────────────────────────────────→ $4.05    10 years
```

$$FV_{10} = PV_0(1+k)^n = \$1(1 + 0.15)^{10} = \$1(4.0455578) = \$4.0455578$$

If you use the FVs in Table F.1 and the following equation, the computation is even simpler:

$$FV_n = PV_0(FV_{k,n}) = PV_0(FV_{15\%,10yr}) = \$1(4.046) = \$4.046$$

Present value (PV_0)

A dollar to be received in 10 years is worth much less than if received today. We should be able to calculate that future dollar's present value by reversing the process we used for future value. Suppose, again, that in delaying this $1 receipt by 10 years, we are foregoing a 15 percent rate of return on it. To find that future dollar's present value, we must discount it back to the present at the 15 percent discount rate:

```
      0   1   3   4   5   6   7   8   9   10
                                            |        $1 discounted back
                                           $1        10 years to t_0 at 15%
  $0.25 ←─────────────────────────────────|
```

$$PV_0 = \$1[1/(1+k)^n] = \$1(1/4.0455578)^{10}$$
$$= \$1(0.2471847) = \$0.2471847$$

So, a dollar to be received in 10 years is worth 25 cents today. Again, this computation could be even simpler if you use the PVs from Table F.3 and the following equation:

$$PV_0 = FV_n(PV_{k,n}) = \$1(PV_{15\%,10yr}) = \$1(0.247) = \$0.247$$

Annuity (PMT)

People who pay car or mortgage payments are often involved in paying an annuity. An annuity is a series of equal payments for a specified number of periods, typically years or months, with each payment occurring at the end of the period.

Suppose you received an annual gift from your grandparents of $1,500 from your 13th birthday to your 18th birthday, with the understanding that the money is to be saved to finance your college education. It would be invested each year at 10 percent annually in a local savings and loan. What would the future value of that annuity be by the time you were eighteen? Let's calculate n first: end of 12th year (13th birthday) to the end of the 17th year (18th birhtday) = 6 = n. We can calculate the future value of this annuity, which will be your college tuition nest egg, as follows:

```
Age      13       14       15       16       17       18
       $1,500   $1,500   $1,500   $1,500   $1,500   $1,500.00    $1,500
                                                    1,650.00     each year
                                          (1.100)                for six
                                                    1,815.00     years, com-
                                       (1.210)                   pounded at
                                                    1,996.50     10%
                                    (1.331)
                                                    2,196.00
                                 (1.464)
                                                    2,416.50
                              (1.611)
                                                    $11,574.00
```

or, using the Equation 5.11, we can solve this as follows:

$$FV_0 = PMT\left[\frac{(1+k)^n - 1}{K}\right] = \$1,500\left[\frac{(1+0.10)^6 - 1}{0.10}\right]$$
$$= \$1,500[(1.771561 - 1)/0.10] = \$11,573.415$$

A simpler method of calculating the future value of this annuity is to use the FVAs from Table F.2 and the following equation:

$$FV_n = PMT(FVA_{k,n}) = \$1,500(FVA_{10\%,6yr}) = \$1,500(7.716) = \$11,574$$

Suppose you are guaranteed that a public college education (for tuition) will cost only $4,000 each year for four years. Will this $11,574 nest egg be large enough to make this series of tuition annuities? Let's remember that the money that you do not pay out in the first year's tuition stays invested until it is used sometime during the annuity series. What is the present value of this annuity of $4,000 for four years?

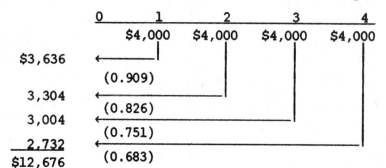

Present value of a $4,000 annuity for four years if k = 10%

or we can calculate the present value of this annuity as follows:

$$PV_0 = PMT\left[\frac{1 - [1/(1 + k)^n]}{k}\right] = \$4,000\left[\frac{1 - (1 + 0.10)^4}{0.10}\right]$$

$$= \$4,000\left[\frac{1 - (1/1.4641)}{0.10}\right] = \$4,000\left[\frac{1 - 0.68301346}{0.10}\right]$$

$$= \$4,000(3.1698654) = \$12,679.462$$

By the time you reach eighteen, you would need a nest egg of $12,679.462 in order to pay your tuition, so you must add about $1,100 to your grandparents' contribution. Again, an even simpler method of calculating the present value of an annuity is to use the PVAs in Table F.4 and the following equation:

$$PV_0 = PMT(PVA_{k,n}) = \$4,000(PVA_{10\%, 4yr}) = \$4,000(3.170) = \$12,680.$$

We can easily find the present value of an uneven series of payments or receipts. We should first look at the payments on a time line to get a better idea of how to solve for the present value. Look at the two time lines below; each represents an uneven series.

```
               0        1         2         3
                      $250      $445      $525
  $227.250   ←────────┘           │         │
                (0.909)           │         │
    367.570   ←───────────────────┘         │
                (0.826)                     │
    394.275   ←─────────────────────────────┘
  $989.095    (0.751)
```

Present value of an uneven series for 3 years, if k=10%

- 76 -

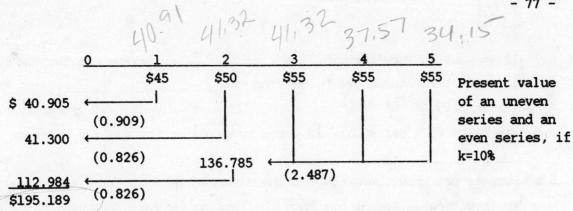

Present value of an uneven series and an even series, if k=10%

Using this approach and drawing time lines makes the calculation of the present value of any uneven time series easy.

Determining interest rates

Just as in any problem using time values, practice is necessary to feel comfortable with determining interest rates. This chapter discusses how to determine interest rates for single cash flows, annuities, uneven series, and growth rates. The key here is to try to solve for the interest factor and then match it to the implied rate. Examples in the text should help you in practicing this type of problem.

COMPLETION QUESTIONS

5.1 If you compare a dollar received today versus a dollar received in one year, the dollar to be received _____ is more valuable, because money has _____.

5.2 You want to find out how much money you will have in 10 years if you leave $1,000 in a savings account earning 10 percent. To solve this problem, you must calculate the _____ of the $1,000.

5.3 You want to know how much money you will need when you are 21 in order to pay graduate school tuition of $5,000 for each of four years, given that the unused balance stays invested at 10 percent until used. For the solution to this problem, you need to find the _____ of the annuity.

5.4 The present value factors are actually the inverse of the _____ _____ factors.

5.5 The _____ is the rate we use in calculating present value. It represents the required rate of return.

5.6 A _____ is an annuity that continues at a constant amount into infinity, like cash dividends on preferred stock.

5.7 If we want to know the cumulative savings after saving $15 per month at 12 percent for three years, we find the _____ of the annuity.

5.8 The value of a perpetuity is found by dividing the annuity by the _____.

5.9 Suppose you know the price and the expected uneven cash flow series for an investment. You do not know the rate of return. You use the trial-and-error method to find the discount rate that makes the present value of the cash inflows exactly equal to the investment's _____ _____.

5.10 If the implied rate of return is between two percentages, you will need to _____ to find the exact rate.

PROBLEMS

FV 61420.57

5.1 Suppose you deposited $3,500 a year for 10 years in a savings account paying 12 percent interest, compounded annually. The first deposit will be made exactly one year from now. How much could you withdraw per year from years 11 through 20 if you wanted to have a balance of $1,000 one year after (i.e., at the end of year 21) the last withdrawal?

5.2 Suppose your parents had decided to plan for your college education at a private college. Their intent was to make equal deposits on each year of your first 17 birthdays to give you $20,000 a year for four years starting on your 18th birthday. If the savings account paid 6 percent interest compounded annually, how much should the yearly deposits have been?

5.3 Mr. Michael Andrews will purchase one of two bonds. Bond A is a zero-coupon bond. (That is, it is issued at a discount and pays no cash interest over its life. But it matures at a value greater than the issuance price.) It will be issued at $295 and will pay a lump sum of $1,000 ten years from now. Bond B promises coupon payments of $100 per year for ten years as well as the $1,000 principal repayment in the tenth year. What price would Andrews be willing to pay for bond B if he thought both should offer the same compound rate of return?

5.4 Using an interest rate of 15 percent, calculate the present value of the following stream of cash flows.

Year	Cash Flows
1	$100
2	300
3	500
4	600
5	300
6	200

Then calculate the future value of this stream of payments in year 6. Use a time line to illustrate your point.

5.5 Arvin Custom Clothiers has just borrowed $150,000. The loan has an annual interest rate of 9 percent and requires five equal payments with the first payment made one year from today. Calculate the annual loan payment and develop a loan amortization schedule for Arvin.

5.6 Suppose you deposited $2,000 in a savings account 15 years ago. For the first five years, the account paid 5 percent interest compounded annually. For the second five years, it paid 6 percent compounded semiannually. For the last 5 years, it paid 8 percent compounded quarterly.

 a. What is the balance in the account today?

 b. What is the average annual compound rate over the entire life of the deposit?

5.7 Many credit cards charge an interest rate of 1.5 percent per month, or a nominal rate of 18 percent per year. What is the effective interest rate on such credit cards?

5.8 Marion Willoughby recently purchased a new automobile for $12,500. She made a $1,000 downpayment and financed the balance over 24 months using a loan with a 12 percent annual nominal rate of interest. What are her monthly payments?

5.9 Russell Gula recently purchased a bond offering a yield (based on 360 days) of 7.65 percent and monthly compounding of interest. What is the effective rate of interest on the bond?

5.10 Many states in the United States now offer lotteries as a method of raising funds. Some lotteries offer prizes as either a lump sum or an annuity. Suppose you are offered your choice between a $50,000 lifetime annuity with the first payment a year from today, or a prize of $1,000,000 today. If your life expectancy is 50 more years, at what interest rate would you be better off with the annuity? (Ignore any tax effects.)

ANSWERS TO COMPLETION QUESTIONS

5.1 today; time value
5.2 future value
5.3 present value
5.4 future value
5.5 discount rate
5.6 perpetuity
5.7 future value
5.8 discount rate (or rate of return)
5.9 present value (or price)
5.10 interpolate

SOLUTIONS TO PROBLEMS

5.1

Step 1. Find the balance in year 10.

$$FV_{10} = \$3,500(FVA_{12\%, 10yr}) = \$3,500(17.549) = \$61,421.50$$

Step 2. Set this balance equal to the 10-year annuity plus the $1,000 balance desired at the end of year 21, and solve for the annuity A.

$$FV_{10} = PMT(PVA_{12\%, 10yr}) + \$1,000(PV_{12\%, 11yr})$$

$$\$61,421.50 = PMT(5.650) + \$1,000(0.287)$$

$$PMT = \frac{\$61,421.50 - \$287.00}{5.650} = \$10,820.27$$

5.2

Step 1. Find out how much money would have to be on deposit in year 17 to allow the withdrawal of $20,000 a year for 4 years if the interest rate is 6 percent.

$$PV_{17} = \$20,000(PVA_{6\%, 4yr}) = \$20,000(3.465) = \$69,300$$

Step 2. Now find the annuity that will give you a value of $69,300 after 17 deposits.

$$FV_{17} = PMT(FVA_{6\%,17yr})$$

$$PMT = \frac{FV_{17}}{FVA_{6\%,17yr}} = \frac{\$69,300}{28.213} = \$2,456.31$$

5.3

Step 1. Calculate the rate of return (or discount rate) on bond A, the zero-coupon bond.

$$PV_A = FV_n(PV_{k\%,10yr}), \text{ so } \$295 = \$1,000(PV_{k\%,10yr})$$

$$PV_{k\%,10yr} = \$295/\$1,000 = 0.295$$

From Table F.3, k = 13%

Step 2. Bond B is a 10-year annuity of $100 per year plus a lump sum of $1,000 in year 10. At a discount rate of 13 percent:

$$PV_B = \$100(PVA_{13\%,10yr}) + \$1,000(PV_{13\%,10yr})$$

$$= \$100(5.426) + \$1,000(0.295) = \$837.60$$

Andrews would pay $837.60.

5.4

Step 1.

```
0       1       2       3       4       5       6
       $100    $300    $500    $600    $300    $200
```

$$PV_0 = \$100(PV_{15\%,1yr}) + \$300(PV_{15\%,2yr}) + \$500(PV_{15\%,3yr})$$

$$+ \$600(PV_{15\%,4yr}) + \$300(PV_{15\%,5yr}) + \$200(PV_{15\%,6yr})$$

$$= \$100(0.870) + \$300(0.756) + \$500(0.658) + \$600(0.572)$$

$$+ \$300(0.497) + \$200(0.432)$$

$$= \$87.00 + \$226.80 + \$329.00 + \$343.20 + \$149.10 + \$86.40$$

$$= \$1,221.50$$

Step 2.

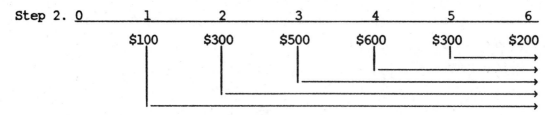

$$FV_6 = \$100(FV_{15\%,5yr}) + \$300(FV_{15\%,4yr}) + \$500(FV_{15\%,3yr})$$
$$+ \$600(FV_{15\%,2yr}) + \$300(FV_{15\%,1yr}) + \$200$$

$$= \$100(2.011) + \$300(1.749) + \$500(1.521) + \$600(1.323)$$
$$+ \$300(1.150) + \$200$$

$$= \$201.10 + \$524.70 + \$760.50 + \$793.80 + \$345.00 + \$200.00$$

$$= \$2,825.10$$

However, a far easier way is to start from the answer to step 1. Thus,

```
 0    1    2    3    4    5    6
 |
$1,221.50
 |————————————————————————————>
```

$$FV_6 = PV_0(FV_{15\%,6yr}) = \$1,221.50(2.313) = \$2,825.33$$

5.5

Step 1. $$PMT = \frac{\$150,000}{PVA_{9\%,5yr}} = \frac{\$150,000}{3.890} = \$38,560.41$$

Step 2. Amortization Schedule

Year	Beginning Balance	+ Interest[a]	− Payment[b]	= Remaining Balance	Principal[c] Repayment
1	$150,000.00	$13,500.00	$38,560.41	$124,939.59	$ 25,060.41
2	124,939.59	11,244.56	38,560.41	97,623.74	27,315.85
3	97,623.74	8,786.14	38,560.41	67,849.47	29,774.27
4	67,849.47	6,106.45	38,560.41	35,395.51	32,453.96
5	35,395.51	3,185.60	38,581.11[d]	-0-	35,395.51
					$150,000.00

a Interest = (0.09)(balance)

b Payment is calculated above

c Principal repayment = payment − interest
           = beginning balance − remaining balance

d Due to rounding, the last payment must be different in order to completely pay off the loan: Last payment = beginning balance for year 5 + interest for year 5.

5.6a

Step 1.

Years (n)	Annual Rate (k)	Periodic Rate (k/m)	Number of Periods (mn)
1-5	5%	5%	5
6-10	6%	6%/2 = 3%	2 × 5 = 10
11-15	8%	8%/4 = 2%	4 × 5 = 20

Step 2. $FV_{15} = \$2,000(FV_{5\%,5\ periods})(FV_{3\%,10\ periods})(FV_{2\%,20\ periods})$

$= \$2,000(1.276)(1.344)(1.486) = \$5,096.81$

or

$FV_{15} = \$2,000(1.05)^5(1 + \frac{0.06}{2})^{2\times5}(1 + \frac{0.08}{4})^{4\times5}$

$= \$2,000(1.05)^5(1.03)^{10}(1.02)^{20} = \$5,097.44$

5.6b

Step 3. $FV_{15} = PV_0(FV_{k\%,15yr})$

$\$5,096.81 = \$2,000(FV_{k\%,15yr})$

$FV_{k\%,15yr} = \frac{\$5,096.81}{\$2,000} = 2.5484$

Step 4. Using Table F.1, the factor is between 6 and 7 percent.

Using linear interpolation:

$k = 6\% + \frac{2.5484 - 2.397}{2.759 - 2.397} = 6\% + \frac{0.1514}{0.3620} = 6.42\%$

(Via financial calculator, the rate is 6.435%.)

5.7

$k_{effective} = (1 + \frac{k_{nom}}{m})^m - 1$

$= (1 + \frac{0.18}{12})^{12} - 1$

$= (1.015)^{12} - 1 = 0.1956\ or\ 19.56\%$

5.8

Step 1. $A = \$12,500 - 1,000 = \$11,500$

$k = \frac{12\%}{12mo} = 1\%/month$

Step 2. $A = \frac{PV_0}{PVA_{k,n}} = \frac{\$11,500}{PVA_{1\%,24}} = \frac{\$11,500}{21.243} = \$541.35/month$

5.9

Step 1. $k_{nom} = k_{360\ nom}(365/360)$

$= 0.0765(365/360) = 0.0775625$

Step 2. $k_{effective} = (1 + \frac{k_{nom}}{m})^m - 1$

$= (1 + \frac{0.0775625}{12})^{12} - 1$

$= (1.0064635)^{12} - 1 = 0.08038$ or 8.038%

5.10

Step 1. If the present value of the annuity equals $1,000,000, you should be indifferent between the two payment plans. Find the rate where

$\$1,000,000 = \$50,000(PVA_{k\%,50yr})$

$PVA_{k\%,50yr} = \frac{\$1,000,000}{\$50,000} = 20.000$

Step 2. From the PVA table, 20.000 lies between the factors for 4 percent and 5 percent. Using linear interpolation,

$k = 4\% + \frac{21.482 - 20.000}{21.482 - 18.256} = 4.46\%$

(Via financial calculator, the rate is 4.427%.)

If you could reinvest at a rate greater than 4.46 percent, you would be better off with the $1,000,000. For rates greater than 4.46 percent, the present value of the annuity is less than $1,000,000.

CHAPTER 6

BOND AND STOCK VALUATION

HOW THIS CHAPTER RELATES TO THE REST OF THE TEXT

Common stocks and bonds are the two main sources of external capital for a firm (Chapter 11). The value of these assets is a function of their cash flows (Chapter 4), timing (Chapter 5), and riskiness (Chapter 7). The firm's required rate of return (Chapter 14) is a function of the returns on stocks and bonds. Many managerial decisions such as capital budgeting (Chapters 8-10) and capital structure (Chapter 15) have an impact on the value of the firm's securities.

TOPICAL OUTLINE

I. Determining bond values and yields.
   A. Bond characteristics.
      1. Promissory notes are issued by a firm or government.
      2. Issued for the short term (less than one year), intermediate term (1 to 10 years), or long term (10 to 30 years).
      3. Par value or stated face value of a bond is generally $1,000; this is how much the firm promises to pay the bondholder at maturity.
      4. Coupon interest rate is the stated interest rate that will be paid every year.
      5. Maturity is the length of time in years until repayment of the bond is legally due.
      6. New issues are bonds that have not been in the market before and are sold in the primary market to generate funds for the issuer.
      7. Outstanding issues are bonds traded in the secondary market, providing no new money to the issuer.
      8. The market price of coupon bonds will typically be at or close to par when newly issued; an outstanding bond's market price may be far from par value.

B. The bond valuation model.
1. The value of a bond is the present value of its expected cash flows in terms of interest and maturity repayment.
2. Value = $I(PVA_{k_b,n}) + M(PV_{k_b,n})$
3. Some bonds sell at a premium (discount) because the current market interest rate for bonds of that risk level is less (greater) than the bond's coupon interest rate. Prices of shorter maturity bonds fluctuate less than those of longer maturity bonds as market interest rates change.

C. Interest rates and bond prices.
1. Most bonds do not sell at par because of current economic conditions.
    a. If the required return on a bond is greater than the coupon rate, the bond will sell at a discount; that is, for less than its face value.
    b. If the required rate of return is less than the coupon rate, the bond will sell at a premium; that is, for more than its face value.
    c. There is an inverse relationship between market rates of interest and bond prices.
2. Risk premiums on bonds.
    a. Expected inflation increases required returns and decreases bond prices.
    b. Interest rate risk is the tendency of short-term bond prices to fluctuate less than long-term bond prices when interest rates change.
    c. Default risk reflects the possibility of bankruptcy.
    d. Liquidity risk results if there is a "thin" market for the bonds.
    e. Issue specific risk occurs because of differing features of a bond.
    f. Reinvestment risk is the risk that an investor's income may fall if there is a need to reinvest in another bond issue.

g. Event risk occurs if there is a drastic change in circumstances and the bond changes from "safe" to "risky."
D. Yield to maturity.
1. Use the bond valuation formula above.
a. Set up a relationship among missing present value factors, cash flow sums, and the market price.
b. Use the tables to find the correct discount rate to balance the equation.
2. In searching for the correct discount rate, remember that as the discount rate increases, the present value decreases.
E. Bonds with semiannual interest.
1. Most bonds pay interest semiannually.
2. For semiannual interest payments:

$$B_0 = \sum_{t=1}^{2n} \frac{I}{2} \left\{ \frac{1}{1 + (k_b/2)} \right\}^t + M \left\{ \frac{1}{1 + (k_b/2)} \right\}^{2n}$$

$$= \frac{I}{2} (PVA_{k_b/2, 2n}) + M(PV_{k_b/2, 2n})$$

F. A consol is a perpetual coupon rate bond.
1. Value of a perpetual bond: $B_0 = \dfrac{I_1}{k_b}$
2. Preferred stock is priced similarly.
G. Bond valuation and financial management.
1. Bonds are one of the main sources of capital for firms; understanding the valuation process is important for financial managers.
2. Determining the firm's required rate of return (Chapter 14), and capital structure (Chapter 15) requires knowledge of bond pricing.
3. Managers must understand bond valuation in order to determine the appropriate form of financing for the firm.
II. Valuing common stock.
A. The value of common stock is the present value of the expected cash flows; it is adjusted for expected growth in the stock price and cash dividends.

B. The dividend valuation model.
   1. Value of common stock is equal to the present value of the expected cash dividends and future market price.
   2. Value = $P_0 = \sum_{t=1}^{n} \frac{D_t}{(1+k_s)^t} + \frac{P_n}{(1+k_s)^n}$
      a. Each year's cash dividend is discounted separately with its own PV.
      b. When you assume infinite dividends, the future market price component, P_n drops out.
      $$P_0 = \sum_{t=0}^{\infty} \frac{D_t}{(1+k_s)^t}$$
C. No growth in cash dividends.
   1. An unrealistic, but useful simplification for calculating common stock value is to suppose no growth in cash dividends.
   2. Value = $P_0 = D_1/k_s$
   3. Use cash dividends for one year hence.
D. Constant growth in cash dividends.
   1. $P_0 = \frac{D_1}{k_s - g}$
   2. Use cash dividends for one year hence.
E. Nonconstant growth in cash dividends.
   1. Figure 6.4 suggests a 10 percent dividend growth for three years followed by a constant dividend growth of 3 percent.
   2. The text gives step-by-step directions to calculate the present value of these dividends; Figure 6.5 may be helpful.
F. Pricing non-dividend paying stocks.
   1. Estimate when dividends will be paid, then discount them to time 0.
   2. Estimate a future price and discount.
   3. Use an earnings multiple approach.
G. Stock valuation and financial management.
   1. While ex ante returns are always positive, ex post or realized returns may be negative. Managers may be able to take actions that increase the chance that the firm is a winner rather than a loser.

2. The realized return on a stock is defined as:

$$k = \frac{D_1 + P_1 - P_0}{P_0}$$

3. Because it is impossible to predict the future with certainty, realized (actual) returns will likely differ from expected returns.

4. Value has three components; the magnitude, timing, and riskiness of cash flows. Most managerial actions have an impact on at least one of these components and hence, stock values.

FORMULAS

Notation

B_0 = current market price of the bond

I = dollar amount of interest expected to be received each year (or par value x coupon interest)

n = number of years to maturity of the bond

k_b = required rate of return for the bond

M = par or maturity value of the bond (typically $1,000)

D_t = annual amount of cash dividends expected to be received on common stock in the tth year

D_0 = cash dividend just paid on the common stock

D_1 = cash dividend on common stock expected in one year

k_s = required rate of return on a common stock, based on the risk-free rate and a risk premium appropriate to the particular stock

P_t = market price of the stock at time t

P_0 = market price of common stock today (t=0) right after receipt of the cash dividend D_0

P_1 = market price of common stock one year from now after receiving the cash dividend D_1

g = expected (compound) growth rate for a common stock's cash dividend

k_M = expected return on the market

k_{RF} = the risk-free rate (the yield on U.S. Treasury bills)

k_j = required rate of return on asset j (Note: The subscript s refers specifically to stocks, while the subscript j refers to any asset)

Bond Valuation Model

$$\text{Value} = B_0 = \sum_{t=1}^{n} \frac{I}{(1+k_b)^t} + \frac{M}{(1+k_b)^n}$$

$$= I(PVA_{k_b,n}) + M(PV_{k_b,n})$$

Yield to Maturity

Use formula above. In trial-and-error form, use PVAs and PVs for year n, one interest rate at a time. <u>Hint</u>: If B_0 is below par, the yield is below the coupon rate. When you achieve B_0, you have found the yield to maturity. Interpolate if necessary.

Interpolation

$$\text{Yield to maturity} = \text{lower interest rate} + \frac{\text{lower interest rate price} - B_0}{\text{lower interest rate price} - \text{higher interest rate price}}$$

Common Stock Valuation

Dividend valuation model for valuing common stock:

$$P_0 = \sum_{t=1}^{n} \frac{D_t}{(1+k)^t} + \frac{P_n}{(1+k_s)^n}$$

Fundamental common stock valuation model if we assume that cash dividends go on forever:

$$P_0 = \sum_{t=1}^{\infty} \frac{D_t}{(1+k_s)^t}$$

No-growth dividend valuation model:

$$P_0 = \frac{D_1}{k_s}$$

Constant growth dividend valuation model:

$$P_0 = \frac{D_1}{k_s - g} = \frac{D_0(1+g)}{k_s - g}$$

Non-constant growth in cash dividends: See four-step procedure in the text.

Returns:

$$k = \frac{D_1 + P_1 - P_0}{P_0}$$

WHAT TO LOOK FOR

Valuation: How We Use It

The value of any investment results from the present value of its expected cash flows. You already have nearly all of the raw materials for valuation: You first measure the cash flows (Chapter 4), measure their riskiness (Chapter 7), determine the appropriate rate of return given the risk (Chapter 7), and use the appropriate rate to discount these expected cash flows back to the present (Chapter 5). We will use this procedure for many types of valuation problems in this course.

Bond Valuation

Bond value is merely the present value of the expected cash flows from a bond. Bond cash flows come from two sources, coupon interest and repayment of the principal. Since bond cash flows occur through time, present value factors help us discount these cash flows back to the present. The time line below illustrates a 10 percent coupon bond's cash flows. The bond has five years until maturity, and the going market rate of interest is 10 percent. The interest for this year has just been paid.

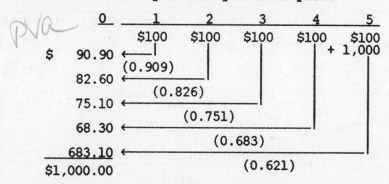

A simpler method of calculating the bond value is to use the following equation:

$$B_0 = I(PVA_{k_b,n}) + M(PV_{k_b,n})$$

$$= \$100(PVA_{10\%,5yr}) + \$1,000(PV_{10\%,5yr})$$

$$= \$100(3.791) + \$1,000(0.621) = \$379.10 + \$621 = \$1,000.10 = \$1,000$$

The present value of this particular bond is its par value, since the coupon interest rate equals the current market-determined required rate of return (or yield to maturity). Once a bond is issued, its stated coupon rate does not change, although the market-determined required rate of return may rise or fall. If the required rate of return rises above the coupon rate, investors buying the bond on the secondary market can achieve their required rate of return only if they pay less than par for the bond. So, as the required rate rises above the coupon rate, the bond's market value falls below par. The required rate on a bond, k_b, will rise as the structure of interest rates rises or as the risk of the bond itself increases. This process works in reverse as the required rate of return falls below the coupon rate. The two examples below, where k_b = 15% and where k_b = 8%, illustrate this process for a five-year 10 percent coupon bond:

15%: $B_0 = \$100(PVA_{15\%,5yr}) + \$1,000(PV_{15\%,5yr})$

          $= \$100(3.352) + \$1,000(0.497) = \$335.20 + \$497 = \$832.20$

8%: $B_0 = \$100(PVA_{8\%,5yr}) + \$1,000(PV_{8\%,5yr})$

          $= \$100(3.993) + \$1,000(0.681) = \$399.30 + \$681 = \$1,080.30$

It is possible to know a bond's value or current market price and not its yield to maturity, k_b. However, by trial-and-error, you can plug PVAs and PVs into the equation above until you come close to the bond's price. If your trial-and-error places the rate between two percentages, you can interpolate. Remember, if your price is below par, the yield to maturity is above the coupon rate and vice versa. Suppose you have a four-year 6 percent coupon bond selling for $830. What is the yield to maturity? It must be above 6 percent, but how much? We will use trial-and-error.

Try 12%: $B = \$60(PVA_{12\%,4yr}) + \$1,000(PV_{12\%,4yr})$

             $= \$60(3.037) + \$1,000(0.636) = \$182.22 + \$636.00 = \$818.22$

Try 11%: $B = \$60(PVA_{11\%,4yr}) + \$1,000(PV_{11\%,4yr})$

             $= \$60(3.102) + \$1,000(0.659) = \$186.12 + \$659.00 = \$845.12$

The yield is between 11 and 12 percent. Next we interpolate to find the yield:

$$\text{Yield to maturity} = \text{lower interest rate} + \frac{\text{lower interest rate price} - \text{market price}}{\text{lower interest rate price} - \text{higher interest rate price}}$$

$$= 11\% + \frac{(\$845.12 - \$830)}{(\$845.12 - \$818.22)} = 11\% + \frac{\$15.12}{\$26.90}$$

$$= 11\% + 0.5621 = 11.56\%$$

Common Stock Valuation Techniques

In common stock valuation, you again are looking at cash flows. The cash flow on common stock is in the form of cash dividends and the ending market price. The dividends may be nonexistent, stable, growing evenly, or growing unevenly. The valuation technique used depends upon the assumptions you make concerning the dividend cash flows. Let's review the basic common stock valuation techniques, based upon the various dividend assumptions above. Here we will assume that cash dividends do occur for all common stocks.

Suppose we want to use a basic equation that will work no matter what the dividend assumptions. If we follow the same format as for bond valuation, we will discount each cash dividend to be received until the next year we expect to sell the stock, and then discount the stock's expected market price. This is Equation 6.3; we must use this formula if cash dividends are uneven or if some selling price is expected.

Suppose, however, that we expect cash dividends to be $2 next year and to grow at 5 percent each year thereafter. It would be a waste of your time to discount each year's dividends separately. Instead, we can use the constant growth formula, Equation 6.6. Assume k_s = 13 percent.

$$P_0 = D_1/(k_s - g) = \$2.00/(0.13 - 0.05) = \$25$$

Sometimes dividends do not actually grow at a constant rate, but the assumption of constant growth makes the valuation calculations simple.

A perpetuity results if we assume that a firm's dividend will continue at the same amount forever--i.e., $g = 0$. Here, we divide the cash dividends by the required rate of return: $P_0 = D_1/k_s$. This same formula is also useful for valuing preferred stock, which is a perpetuity.

Finally, if we expect a firm's cash dividends to grow unevenly, we must discount all unlike dividends separately. If we have a series of equal dollar dividends, these can be discounted as an annuity. Suppose you are valuing the shares of Vic Chemical Corporation, and you have the following expectations for cash dividends:

Year 1 = $2.00
Year 2 = $2.15
Year 3 = $2.15(1+0.08) = $2.322
Year 4 = $2.15(1+0.08)^2 = $2.50776 = $2.508
Year n = $2.15(1+0.08)$^{n-2}$

The constant dividend growth of 8 percent begins in year 3.

How would we value this dividend cash flow if our required return on Vic Chemical were 16 percent? First, we discount back to time zero the cash dividends for years 1 and 2 separately, since they are uneven. Then, we discount the constant growth dividend series back to year 2 (the year before the constant growth series begins). Once we have a value for the constant growth dividend series, we discount that value back two years to time zero. The value of Vic Chemical is then the sum of the first two present values, plus the series' present value: $1.724 + $1.597 + $21.887. The calculations and the timeline below will clarify the process:

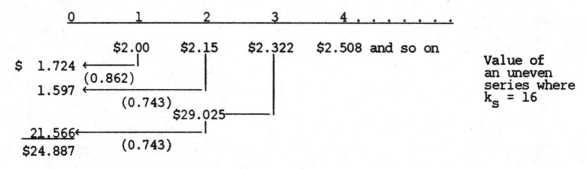

The calculation for years 3 through infinity is

$$P_2 = \frac{D_3}{k_s - g} = \frac{\$2.322}{0.16 - 0.08} = \$29.025$$

Changes That Affect Required Return and Valuation

The risk premium depends upon investors' current attitudes toward bearing risk. For example, during a recession, investors become more reluctant to bear risk, since their uncertainty about the economy and their own livelihood has increased. As a result, they raise their risk premiums. The risk premium of relatively more risky investments will rise more than that of relatively less risky investments, while the riskless rate may be unaffected.

As the required rate of return on a security increases, the value or market price of the security decreases. To see this, compare the constant growth valuation based on a k_s of 12 percent to one based on a k_s of 14 percent. Assume that D_1 is $2.50 and g is 6 percent:

$P_0 = D_1/(k_s - g) = \$2.50/(0.12 - 0.06) = \$41.67$

versus $P_0 = \$2.50/(0.14 - 0.06) = \$31.25$

You can see that the dividend growth assumptions and the required rate of return can have a marked effect upon the stock's market price. Since the managers' objective is to maximize shareholder wealth, they must pay attention to how their decisions affect the magnitude, timing, and riskiness of their firm's expected cash flows.

For example, consider the case of Edge Razor Company. The firm expects to pay a dividend next year of $5.00 per share. Presently, k_s is 16% and dividends are growing at a constant rate of 3%. Edge is considering the addition of shaving products (shaving cream, aftershave, ect.) to its line. It is expected that the new line will allow the firm to pay a dividend of $6.00 per share next year and growth will increase to 5%. Since this is a new venture to Edge, risk will also increase and its k_s will rise to 20%. Should Edge do it?

To determine if the new product line is in the best interest of stockholders, look at what happens to the stock prices. Currently, Edge is selling for:

$$P_0 = \frac{D_1}{k_s - g} = \frac{\$5.00}{0.16 - 0.03} = \$38.46$$

If Edge adds the shaving products line, the price will be:

$$P_0 = \frac{\$6.00}{0.20 - 0.05} = \$40.00$$

Share price will increase by $40.00 - $38.46 = $1.54 per share if Edge adds the new line; stockholders will be better off.

Valuation is important for financial managers for two reasons. First, value is determined in the financial market and provides an assessment of managerial decisions. Second, by understanding value, managers can learn what is important to bond- and stockholders, and hence make appropriate decisions.

COMPLETION QUESTIONS

6.1 As the risk of a financial asset increases, its required rate of return _____. So, the financial asset's market value must _____.

6.2 In bond valuation, the coupon payment can be thought of as an _____, while the par value can be thought of as a _____ payment.

6.3 Coupon interest is the stated amount of interest. To calculate the amount of the annuity in dollars, multiply the stated coupon rate times the _____.

6.4 If a 10 percent coupon bond is currently selling at par, its yield to maturity must be _____.

6.5 If an 8 percent coupon rate bond is yielding 12 percent, its current market price must be _____ its par value.

6.6 In comparing the price variability of bonds of various maturities, market prices of bonds with longer maturities vary _____ than prices of bonds with shorter maturities in response to general market interest rate changes.

6.7 The yield to maturity is that discount rate which makes the present value of the bond's expected cash flows equal to _____ _____.

6.8 When the risk aversion of investors rises, the risk-free rate _____ _____ while other required rates of return _____.

6.9 When the rate of expected inflation increases, the risk-free rate _____, and all other required rates of return _____.

6.10 When a firm's beta or nondiversifiable risk increases and the risk-free rate stays the same, the required rate of return on that stock _____. The required rate of return on the stock market as a whole _____.

6.11 Suppose a firm has been expecting constant growth in its cash dividends. The marketing department announces that a newly tested product should increase net income substantially for the next five years and that cash dividends too will increase substantially. Experts believe this prediction. The market price for this firm will _____ _____ in response to this news.

6.12 In the dividend valuation model, the present market value of a share of common stock is equal to the present value of _____ _____.

6.13 When we value a share of common stock which is expected to provide constant growth in its cash dividends, we divide the expected cash dividend for the _____ year by the difference between the required rate of return and the _____.

6.14 When looking at the relationship between the growth rate in expected cash dividends and the current market value of the stock, we expect the value of a no-dividend-growth stock to be _____ than that of a growing dividend stock, all other things being equal.

PROBLEMS

6.1 Butte Copper Mining Company has outstanding a bond with 17 years to maturity. The coupon rate on the bond is 11 percent, the face value is $1,000, and the current market price is $809.03. What is its yield to maturity?

6.2 The bonds of Scott Chemical Company promise annual interest payments of $120, have a $1,000 face value, mature in 15 years, and are priced to yield 8 percent. If interest payments are made semiannually, what is the price of the bond?

6.3 McElroy Aviation is expected to pay a cash dividend of $2.31 per share next year. The company is quite risky; its required return is 22%, and P_0 = $19.25. What is this year's (at t = 0) cash dividend, assuming a constant growth rate in cash dividends until infinity?

6.4 Solar Energy Research Company is a new enterprise and is not expected to pay any cash dividends for the next five years. Its first dividend (D_6) is expected to be $2, and dividends are expected to grow for the next four years (through t=10) at 25 percent. After that, dividends are expected to grow at a more normal 5 percent. If k_s = 18 percent over the entire time period, what is P_0?

6.5 Processed Food Company is a well-established firm that pays a cash dividend of $5 per share and has for several years experienced no growth. Its current required rate of return (without the new investment described below) is 14 percent. The firm has asked shareholders to forego the cash dividend payment for the next five years to free funds for investment in a new process that will ultimately allow the firm to increase the $5 dividend by 10 percent per year. If the firm intends to resume the dividend in year 6 (at $5.50, or $5.00 × 1.10) and the new k_s = 18 percent, will the present shareholders be better or worse off?

6.6 Dana Neal has observed the following prices and dividends for her 100 shares of Tennessee Power Company. Calculate the rate of return on this stock for each month listed below.

Month	Ending Price	Dividend
January	$60	-
February	$62	$3
March	$65	-
April	$58	$3
May	$64	-

ANSWERS TO COMPLETION QUESTIONS

6.1 increases; decrease
6.2 annuity; lump sum
6.3 par (or face) value
6.4 10 percent
6.5 below
6.6 more widely
6.7 current market price

6.8 stays the same; increase
6.9 increases; increase also
6.10 increase; stays the same
6.11 increase immediately
6.12 all future cash dividends
6.13 next; compound growth rate
6.14 less

SOLUTIONS TO PROBLEMS

6.1
Step 1. Since the bond is selling at a discount, the yield to maturity must be greater than the coupon rate.

Step 2. at 12%: $B_0 = \$110(PVA_{12\%,17yr}) + \$1,000(PV_{12\%,17yr})$

$= \$110(7.120) + \$1,000(0.146) = \$929.20$, which is too high

at 13%: $B_0 = \$110(PVA_{13\%,17yr}) + \$1,000(PV_{13\%,17yr})$

$= \$110(6.729) + \$1,000(0.125) = \$865.19$, which is still too high

at 14%: $B_0 = \$100(PVA_{14\%,17yr}) + \$1,000(PV_{14\%,17yr})$

$= \$110(6.373) + \$1,000(0.108) = \$809.03$

The yield to maturity is 14 percent.

6.2 For semiannual interest payments:

$$B_0 = \frac{I}{2}(PVA_{k/2,2n}) + M(PV_{k/2,2n})$$

$$= \frac{\$120}{2}(PVA_{8\%/2,2\times15}) + \$1,000(PV_{8\%/2,2\times15})$$

$$= \$60(PVA_{4\%,30}) + \$1,000(PV_{4\%,30})$$

$$= \$60(17.292) + \$1,000(0.308)$$

$$= \$1,037.52 + \$308.00 = \$1,345.52$$

6.3

Step 1. Assuming constant growth:

$$P_0 = \frac{D_1}{k_s - g}$$

$$\$19.25 = \frac{\$2.31}{0.22 - g}$$

$$0.22 - g = \frac{\$2.31}{\$19.25}$$

$$g = 0.22 - \frac{\$2.31}{\$19.25} = 0.22 - 0.12 = 0.10$$

Step 2. Since $D_1 = D_0(1 + g)$

$$D_0 = \frac{D_1}{(1 + g)} = \frac{\$2.31}{1.10} = \$2.10$$

6.4

Step 1. $D_6 = \$2.00$

$D_7 = \$2.00(1.25) = \$2.50$

$D_8 = \$2.50(1.25) = \$3.125$

$D_9 = \$3.125(1.25) = \$3.906$

$D_{10} = \$3.906(1.25) = \$4.883$

$D_{11} = \$4.883(1.05) = \$5.127$

Step 2. $P_{10} = \dfrac{D_{11}}{k_s - g} = \dfrac{\$5.127}{0.18 - 0.05} = \$39.438$

Step 3. $P_0 = \$2.00(PV_{18\%,6yr}) + \$2.50(PV_{18\%,7yr}) + \$3.125(PV_{18\%,8yr})$

$\qquad + \$3.906(PV_{18\%,9yr}) + \$4.883(PV_{18\%,10yr}) + \$39.438(PV_{18\%,10yr})$

$\qquad = \$2.00(0.370) + \$2.50(0.314) + \$3.125(0.266) + \$3.906(0.225)$

$\qquad + \$4.883(0.191) + \$39.438(0.191)$

$\qquad = \$0.7400 + \$0.7850 + \$0.8312 + \$0.8788 + \$0.9327 + \$7.5327$

$\qquad = \$11.70$

6.5

Step 1. With no investment:
$$P_0 = \frac{D_1}{k_s} = \frac{\$5.00}{0.14} = \$35.71$$

Step 2. With the investment:
$$P_5 = \frac{D_6}{k_s - g} = \frac{\$5.50}{0.18 - 0.10} = \$68.75$$

Step 3. $P_0 = (P_5)(PV_{18\%, 5yr}) = \$68.75(0.437) = \$30.04$

The current shareholders will be worse off. The shareholders will lose $5.67 ($35.71 - $30.04) per share.

6.6

$$k_{Feb} = \frac{D_{Feb} + P_{Feb} - P_{Jan}}{P_{Jan}} = \frac{\$3 + \$62 - \$60}{\$60} = 0.0833 \text{ or } 8.33\%$$

$$k_{Mar} = \frac{D_{Mar} + P_{Mar} - P_{Feb}}{P_{Feb}} = \frac{\$0 + \$65 - \$62}{\$62} = 0.0484 \text{ or } 4.84\%$$

$$k_{Apr} = \frac{D_{Apr} + P_{Apr} - P_{Mar}}{P_{Mar}} = \frac{\$3 + \$58 - \$65}{\$65} = -0.0615 \text{ or } -6.15\%$$

$$k_{May} = \frac{D_{May} + P_{May} - P_{Apr}}{P_{Apr}} = \frac{\$0 + \$64 - \$58}{\$58} = 0.1034 \text{ or } 10.34\%$$

CHAPTER 7

RISK AND RETURN

HOW THIS CHAPTER RELATES TO THE REST OF THE TEXT

The relationship between risk and return is another fundamental concept of finance. Risk and return influence the value of financial assets (Chapter 6) and the required rate of return (Chapter 14) and is an important consideration in capital budgeting (Chapters 8-11). The capital asset pricing model, which shows the relationship between risk and return, enables a financial manager to identify profitable (or undervalued) investments. In fact, this tradeoff between risk and return underlies all financial decisions--both corporate and personal.

TOPICAL OUTLINE

I. The meaning of risk.
   A. Uncertainty about future developments results in risk.
   B. General economic forces increase the uncertainty of future outcomes for businesses, individuals, and consumers.
   C. Inflation decreases the purchasing power of the dollar and increases the risk that the desired result will not be achieved.
   D. Firm- and issue-specific risk.
      1. Business risk is the inherent uncertainty or variability in a firm's EBIT.
      2. Financial risk arises from the use of fixed-cost financing, since the financing costs must be paid before the common stockholders receive anything.
      3. Issue-specific risk.
         a. Common stock is riskier than preferred stock, which is riskier than debt.
         b. The riskiness of debt issues depends upon such things as sinking fund agreements, covenants, and liens.
   E. International risk results when a firm exposes itself to international forces, which add to increased uncertainty or variability in its EBIT.

II. Measuring risk.
   A. Probability distributions show the chances of various outcomes occurring.
   B. Expected value or mean is the probability weighted average of possible outcomes.
   C. Standard deviation is the risk measure which measures dispersion around the mean; this total risk measure contains both diversifiable and nondiversifiable risk.
III. Portfolio risk and diversification.
   A. A portfolio's return is the average return of the securities in the portfolio weighted by the proportion of the portfolio invested in each security.
   B. Portfolio risk.
      1. When you combine securities in a portfolio, the total riskiness is generally less than an average of the individual risks.
      2. Correlation measures the degree with which two variables, such as the return on two securities, move together.
         a. Perfect positive correlation: No risk reduction; portfolio standard deviation is a weighted average of the individual standard deviations.
         b. Perfect negative correlation: Maximum risk reduction.
         c. Negative correlation or positive correlation which is less than perfect: Benefits from diversification in terms of risk reduction.
         d. The returns on most assets are positively correlated, since they tend to move with the general movements of the economy.
   C. Two-security portfolios.
      1. Expected return for a portfolio is the average of the returns for the two securities, weighted by the proportion devoted to each security.

2. The standard deviation, or risk, of the portfolio is affected by the correlation of the rates of returns on the two securities.
   a. If perfect positive correlation exists, the portfolio's standard deviation is the weighted average of the individual security's standard deviations, and no risk-reducing benefits result.
   b. As the correlation becomes less positive, the diversifiable risk becomes less.

D. The efficient frontier.
   1. The feasible set is a graph of all possible portfolios that can be developed from a group of securities.
   2. An efficient portfolio is one that offers the lowest risk at a given return or the highest return at a given level of risk.
   3. The efficient frontier is a graph of all efficient portfolios; rational investors will choose the portfolio on the efficient frontier that best suits his or her risk preferences.
   4. For N securities, the feasible set is given in Figure 7.4. All investors will prefer a portfolio on the curve EF, since they dominate all other portfolios at the same level of risk.

E. Diversifiable and nondiversifiable risk.
   1. If securities are perfectly positively correlated, no reduction in risk is possible.
   2. For correlations less than +1.0, there are some benefits to diversification. Possible risk reduction increases as the correlation decreases.
   3. If the correlation is -1.0, all risk can be eliminated.
   4. Returns on most securities are positively correlated and tend to be from +0.40 to 0.75.
   5. Since some risk can be diversified away,
      total risk = diversifiable risk + nondiversifiable risk
      a. Diversifiable (company-specific, unsystematic) risk relates to events affecting individual companies.

b. Nondiversifiable (market, systematic) risk includes general economic conditions, monetary and fiscal policy, inflation and other events affecting all firms.

c. Since a well diversified portfolio has no diversifiable risk, only nondiversifiable risk is relevant to investors.

IV. The capital asset pricing model (CAPM).
   A. The capital market line.
      1. Investors who can lend and borrow at the risk-free rate of return will combine risk-free investments with a risky portfolio on the efficient frontier.
      2. The risky portfolio that maximizes the risk-return tradeoff, when combined with the risk-free asset, is the tangent portfolio (portfolio M).
         a. M is the market portfolio; a value-weighted portfolio of all risky assets.
         b. All investors will choose portfolio M, then satisfy their risk preferences by lending or borrowing at the risk-free rate.
            i. Investors on the segment $k_{RF}M$ (see Figure 7.9) invest in both portfolio M and the risk-free asset (lending portfolios).
            ii. Investors on the segment ML borrow at k_{RF} and invest the proceeds in portfolio M (borrowing portfolios).
      3. The capital market line (CML) shows the relationship between total risk (σ_P) and expected return (K_P) for efficient portfolios only. Equation for the CML:
      $$K_P = k_{RF} + \left[\frac{k_M - k_{RF}}{\sigma_M}\right]\sigma_P$$
      4. Efficient portfolios are made up of the market portfolio (M) in linear combination with the risk-free security.
   B. Beta is a measure of risk.
      1. Beta is the measure of the stock's price volatility relative to the volatility of the market as a whole as measured by some market index, such as the Standard & Poor's 500.

2. Beta is the measure of nondiversifiable risk for stocks in a diversified portfolio.
3. The market has a beta of 1.0; it is our frame of reference.
4. Stable firms with stable cash flows have betas of less than 1.0, since their market prices fluctuate less than the market as a whole.
5. Risky firms, whose cash flows are more volatile, have more volatile market prices than the market index; thus, they have betas greater than 1.0.

C. A portfolio beta is a weighted average of the betas of the individual stocks within the portfolio.

D. The security market line (SML) shows the relationship between systematic risk (β) and the expected return for all assets.
   1. Equation of the SML: $k_j = k_{RF} + \beta_j(k_M - k_{RF})$

E. Using the capital asset pricing model (CAPM).
   1. Components: Risk-free rate (k_{RF}), expected return on the market (k_M), and the stock's beta (β_j). The value of each component changes as conditions change.
      a. Risk-free rate depends upon expected inflation, economic conditions, and monetary policy.
      b. Expected return on the market can be estimated based on expected inflation, expected real growth in the economy, and the risk premium commanded for owning common stocks rather than bonds.
      c. Betas for stocks change over time but can be found in <u>Value Line</u>, reports from stockbrokers, or by using the techniques outlined in Appendix 7B.
   2. Beta measures nondiversifiable risk.

F. The equilibrium nature of the CAPM.
   1. In equilibrium, the expected rate of return equals the required rate of return.
   2. In disequilibrium, the stock is either overpriced or underpriced, providing an actual rate of return less or greater than the return required.

> > a. In an efficient market, investors will see the possibilities of excess return from an underpriced stock, and will bid up the price.
> > b. Investors will do just the opposite to overpriced stocks.
> G. Words of caution when using the CAPM.
> > 1. The CAPM is an ex ante model; using historical data without adjustment for future expectations invites trouble.
> > 2. Both the SML and beta can shift over time.
> > 3. Persistent evidence on the risk-return tradeoffs for small-capitalization stocks and low P/E stocks as well as seasonal effects casts some doubt as to the total efficiency of the markets and/or the validity of the CAPM.

V. The efficient market hypothesis.
> A. The efficient market hypothesis states that prices react unambiguously and quickly to new information.
> > 1. Weak-form efficiency: Current stock prices reflect all historical information about stock prices.
> > 2. Semistrong-form efficiency: Current stock prices reflect all publicly available information about earnings, dividends, mergers, etc.
> > 3. Strong-form efficiency: Current stock prices reflect all information, both public and private.
> B. Tests of the efficient market hypothesis suggest that the market is highly weak-form efficient, generally semi-strong efficient, but not strong-form efficient.
> C. Implications of the efficient market hypothesis.
> > 1. On average, expected and realized returns are equal.
> > 2. Prices react quickly to new information.
> > 3. Abnormal (risk-adjusted) returns require private information.
> > 4. Without private information, increased returns require increased risk.
> > 5. The best estimate of firm value is what the market will pay for its stock (S) plus its bonds (B).

VI. Arbitrage pricing theory (APT).
   A. The arbitrage pricing theory is based on fewer assumptions than the CAPM.
   B. In the APT, stock returns are assumed to be a linear function of a number of factors common to all securities.
      1. Equation: $k_j = k_{RF} + \sum_{n=1}^{N} b_{jn}(k_n - k_{RF})$
      2. k_n is the required return on the Nth factor.
   C. A problem with APT is that the factors are unknown ex ante.
   D. The CAPM is a single factor APT.
VII. Appendix 7A: Calculating covariances and correlations (located at the back of the text).
   A. Covariance measures the degree of linear relationship between any two random variables.
      1. Formula for calculating covariance from expected returns:
         $$Cov_{AB} = \sum_{i=1}^{n} (k_{Ai} - \bar{k}_A)(k_{Bi} - \bar{k}_B)P_i$$
      2. Formula for calculating covariance from historical returns:
         $$Cov_{FG} = \frac{\sum_{t=1}^{n} (k_{Ft} - \bar{k}_F)(k_{Gt} - \bar{k}_G)}{n - 1}$$
   B. The correlation coefficient ranges from -1 to +1 and measures the degree of linearity between two random variables.
      1. Formula: $Corr_{AB} = \frac{Cov_{AB}}{\sigma_A \sigma_B}$
VIII. Appendix 7B: Calculating security betas (located at the back of the text).
   A. Use linear regression to fit a least-squares regression line in the form $Y = \alpha + \beta X$.
      1. The "α" is the return on the stock when the market is returning nothing at all--the Y-intercept.
      2. The "β" is the sensitivity of the returns of the security to the returns of the market index (beta).
      3. The "Y" is the required return on stock; "X" is the expected return on the market.
   B. Beta equals the covariance between the stock's return and the market's returns divided by the variance of the market's returns.

1. Covariance of the returns of the security and the market is equal to the standard deviation of the security times the standard deviation of the market times the correlation between the security and the market:

$$Cov_{jM} = \sigma_j \sigma_M Corr_{jM}.$$

2. Use the standard deviation of the stock's return, the standard deviation of the market's returns, and the correlation between the two returns:

$$\beta_j = \sigma_j Corr_{jM}/\sigma_M.$$

FORMULAS

<u>Notation</u>

k	= return
P_0	= price in period 0
D_1	= dividend in period 1
$\bar{k}$	= the expected value or expected return
k_i	= rate of return or outcome associated with the ith possible state
n	= number of possible states of the economy
P_i	= probability of the ith state or outcome occurring
σ	= standard deviation--how tightly the probability distribution is centered around the rate of return or expected value. Also, the square root of the variance
σ^2	= variance, the square of the standard deviation
W_i	= proportion of portfolio invested in stock i
β_j	= beta coefficient for asset j
k_M	= expected return on the market in general
k_{RF}	= risk-free rate of return, generally measured by the return on U.S. Treasury bills
$(k_M - k_{RF})$	= market risk premium required to encourage investment in the market rather than in riskless securities
$\beta_j(k_M - k_{RF})$	= risk premium required for the security in question
Cov_{AB}	= covariance between A and B
$Corr_{AB}$	= correlation between A and B

Expected Value or Mean Rate of Return

$$\text{Expected value} = \bar{k} = \sum_{i=1}^{n} k_i P_i$$

Standard Deviation

$$\sigma = \sqrt{\sum_{i=1}^{n} (k_i - \bar{k})^2 P_i}$$

Portfolio Return

$$\bar{K}_p = W_A \bar{k}_A + W_B \bar{k}_B + \ldots + W_Z \bar{k}_Z$$

Standard deviation of a two-security portfolio:

$$\sigma_p = \sqrt{W_A^2 \sigma_A^2 + W_B^2 \sigma_B^2 + 2 W_A W_B \sigma_A \sigma_B \text{Corr}_{AB}}$$

Portfolio Beta

$$\beta_p = \sum_{j=1}^{n} W_j \beta_j$$

Capital Asset Pricing Model

Capital market line:

$$k_p = k_{RF} + \left[\frac{k_M - k_{RF}}{\sigma_M}\right] \sigma_p = \text{the required return on an efficient portfolio}$$

Security market line:

$$k_j = k_{RF} + \beta_j (k_M - k_{RF}) = \text{required rate of return on any security}$$

Appendix 7A Equations

Covariance

From expected returns:

$$\text{Cov}_{AB} = \sum_{i=1}^{n} (k_{Ai} - \bar{k}_A)(k_{Bi} - \bar{k}_B) P_i$$

From historical returns:

$$\text{Cov}_{AB} = \frac{\sum_{t=1}^{n} (k_{At} - \bar{k}_A)(k_{Bt} - \bar{k}_B)}{n - 1}$$

Correlation

$$\text{Corr}_{AB} = \frac{\text{Cov}_{AB}}{\sigma_A \sigma_B}$$

Appendix 7B Equations

Notation:

- α = Y-intercept of the characteristic line, the return on the stock when risk or beta is zero
- Cov_{jM} = covariance between returns on security j and returns on the market

Fitted regression or least squares line:

$$k_j = \alpha + \beta k_M$$

Calculation of beta:

$$\beta_j = \frac{\text{Cov}_{jM}}{\sigma_M^2} = \frac{\sigma_j \sigma_M \text{Corr}_{jM}}{\sigma_M^2} = \frac{\sigma_j \text{Corr}_{jM}}{\sigma_M}$$

Calculation of covariance:

$$\text{Cov}_{jM} = \sigma_j \sigma_M \text{Corr}_{jM}$$

WHAT TO LOOK FOR

We will discuss risk, economic forces resulting in risk, measures of risk, and required rates of return in order to develop the concepts of risk and return. Although we want to understand risk from a business standpoint, we begin by seeing it from an investor's viewpoint. The investor's viewpoint is essential for the manager; the firm's required return is determined by the perceived riskiness (variability) of the firm's cash flows.

Where Does Risk Come From?

As noted in Chapter 2, monetary policy set by the Federal Reserve controls the money supply, helps stabilize the economy, and affects interest rates. For example, when the Federal Reserve wants to cool down a hot economy, it conducts open market operations to sell U.S. government securities to federal banks and the money supply contracts. Money becomes more expensive, and interest rates rise. Since the cost of borrowing has risen, managers postpone capital spending projects, and the economy cools. The risk comes from not being able to predict Federal Reserve policy and its full effect on the economy. In some cases, the market may believe that a Federal Reserve decision will have serious effects on business, so investors push up their required returns.

Monetary policy may be reinforced or counteracted by a second force, fiscal policy. Fiscal policy may mean raising taxes or borrowing money to fund the budget. Sometimes the goals of fiscal and monetary policy conflict, so the decisions counteract one another. Again, the risk results from not knowing what the effect of the actions may be.

Inflation is a third force active in the market environment. Inflation results from too many dollars chasing too few goods in the marketplace. As you can probably guess, inflation can result in a heated economy in which the money supply has increased too fast. Inflation expectations increase investors' required rate of return, since they want to achieve a certain rate of return, net of inflation.

Measurement of Risk: A Practical Example

Risk measurement is difficult to describe in the abstract. We know we expect higher risk, but how do we measure this risk? In Chapter 7, we use probability, standard deviation, and variance to measure the risk of a firm's return. We associate a probability with each of a spectrum of states of the economy. For example, the probability of an expansion might be 40 percent. With each of these states of nature, we associate a potential rate of return for each stock. Below, for example, we predict that in an expansion, Dr. Pepper will return 20 percent, while Eastman Kodak will return 14 percent. Remember, these are just predictions, not actual returns. Given this probability distribution and these return estimates, we can find the probability-weighted expected return for these two stocks, and discover the predicted variability around these expected returns.

Let's measure the variability of two stocks' returns to see how risk is measured and how it affects the expected rate of return. Suppose you had access to information through an investment advisory service such as Value Line. Suppose those experts made some informed guesses about next year's economy and the probable return on the common stock of Dr. Pepper and Eastman Kodak.

Step 1: Calculate expected return:

State of the Economy	Associated Probability P_i	Associated Dr. Pepper Total Return k_i	=	Dr. Pepper Expected Return $\bar{k}$
Recession	0.20	8.0%		1.6%
Normal	0.40	14.0%		5.6%
Expansion	0.40	20.0%		8.0%

Dr. Pepper's mean or expected return = $\bar{k}$ = 15.2%

State of the Economy	Associated Probability P_i	Associated Eastman Kodak Total Return k_i	=	Eastman Kodak Expected Return $\bar{k}$
Recession	0.20	8.0%		1.6%
Normal	0.40	11.0%		4.4%
Expansion	0.40	14.0%		5.6%

Eastman Kodak's mean or expected return = $\bar{k}$ = 11.6%

Now you have calculated the expected return on these two stocks. You know that in the next period you might expect, on average, a 15.2 percent return on Dr. Pepper and an 11.6 percent return on Eastman Kodak. Take time to note a few things about the total return distributions of these two firms. Over the course of the business cycle, the returns on Eastman Kodak are expected to vary less widely (6 percent) than those of Dr. Pepper (12 percent).

Step 2: Calculate variance and standard deviation:

The wider return variability of the Dr. Pepper stock is a sign of the greater total risk in holding such stock as one's sole investment. We can measure this variability with the use of the variance or standard deviation. We will use the return values from the previous table.

Dr. Pepper:

Outcome − Expected Value (deviation from mean) $(k_i - \bar{k})$	Deviation Squared $(k_i - \bar{k})^2$	×	Probability of ith Outcome P_i	=	$(k_i - \bar{k})^2 P_i$
8.0 − 15.2 = −7.2	51.84		0.20		10.368
14.0 − 15.2 = −1.2	1.44		0.40		0.576
20.0 − 15.2 = 4.8	23.04		0.40		9.216

$$\text{Dr. Pepper variance} = \sigma^2 = 20.160$$

$$\text{Dr. Pepper standard deviation} = \sigma = \sqrt{\sigma^2} = 4.490$$

Eastman Kodak:

Outcome − Expected Value (deviation from mean) $(k_i - \bar{k})$	Deviation Squared $(k_i - \bar{k})^2$	×	Probability of ith Outcome P_i	=	$(k_i - \bar{k})^2 P_i$
8.0 − 11.6 = −3.6	12.96		0.20		2.592
11.0 − 11.6 = −0.6	0.36		0.40		0.144
14.0 − 11.6 = 2.4	5.76		0.40		2.304

$$\text{Eastman Kodak variance} = \sigma^2 = 5.040$$

$$\text{Eastman Kodak standard deviation} = \sigma = \sqrt{\sigma^2} = 2.245$$

As you can see, the standard deviation of Dr. Pepper is twice that of Eastman Kodak. Over the course of the business cycle, Eastman Kodak's return seems to be the less variable or risky. It is a less cyclical stock. Logically, Dr. Pepper requires a higher return--15.2 percent versus 11.6 percent.

Risk and Diversification

By now, a question should arise in your mind: Does total risk matter? After all, few investors own single securities; most own portfolios. Does owning more than one security eliminate risk? The answer is generally yes, risk reduction can be achieved by diversifying our holdings. For example, suppose you own some Ford stock. You estimate that if gasoline prices rise, car sales (and hence Ford's profitability) will fall. Holding Ford stock alone exposes you to risk.

Now, suppose that you sold half of your Ford stock and purchased shares of Shell Oil with the proceeds. If gasoline prices rise, Ford profitability falls, but Shell's profits should rise. By diversifying your holdings, you have eliminated some of the risk to which you were exposed.

The key to diversification is the correlation between the returns to the securities in your portfolio. In the above example, suppose:

	Ford	Shell
Expected return	15%	21%
σ	20%	40%

and that $Corr_{Ford, Shell} = -0.50$. What is the expected return and risk of a portfolio of 50% Ford stock and 50% Shell stock?

$$\bar{k}_P = W_F k_S + W_S k_S = 0.50(15\%) + 0.50(21\%) = 18\%$$

$$P \quad \sqrt{W_F \sigma_F + W_S \sigma_F + 2W_F W_S \sigma_F \sigma_S \, corr_{F,S}}$$

$$= \sqrt{(0.5)^2 (20)^2 + (0.5)^2 (40) + 2(0.5)(0.5)(40)(-0.5)}$$

$$= \sqrt{100 + 400 - 200} = \sqrt{300} = 17.32\%$$

Note that because the correlation is negative, the risk of the portfolio is less than the risk of either stock.

Most individuals hold portfolios of securities rather than individual stocks. While the return to a portfolio is simply the weighted average of the returns of the stocks in the portfolio, a portfolio's risk is not. A portfolio's risk is a function of the risk of the stocks and their correlations. If stocks are less than perfectly positively correlated, the portfolio's risk will be less than the weighted average of the stocks' risk.

Risk reduction through diversification is an important concept. Portfolio risk declines to a minimum level as more and more randomly selected stocks (up to 25) are added. Since investors can eliminate part of the portfolio's risk through diversification, they do not expect to be compensated for it. Only nondiversifiable risk, associated with general economic conditions, is priced in the market.

Risk and Portfolio Returns

All rational investors will strive to hold efficient portfolios, those portfolios that offer the highest return for a given level of risk. Investors also have the ability to invest in a risk-free security such as U.S. Treasury bills. As Chapter 7 shows us, investors can get the best trade-off between risk and return by combining the market portfolio with the risk-free security. The equation for the relationship between return and total risk for efficient portfolios is called the capital market line (CML). The equation for the CML is:

$$k_P = k_{RF} + \left[\frac{k_M - k_{RF}}{\sigma_M}\right]\sigma_P$$

Investors can expect to earn the risk-free return plus a premium based on how much risk they are willing to bear. For instance, suppose k_M = 18%, k_{RF} = 7%, and σ_M = 12. What is the required return on a portfolio with σ_P = 20? From the CML,

$$k_P = 7\% + \left[\frac{18\% - 7\%}{12}\right] = 25.33\%$$

The portfolio is expected to earn 25.33%; no portfolio with σ_P = 20 will offer a higher return.

Risk and Security Returns

An implication of the CML is that all rational investors will hold the market portfolio in combination with the risk-free security (this is sometimes known as two-fund separation). A benefit of this implication is that it is possible to show that for individual securities, the risk that is important is the contribution that security makes to the riskiness of the market portfolio. This leads to the security market line (SML), which shows the relationship between systematic risk and required return for individual assets. The equation for the SML is:

$$k_j = k_{RF} + \beta_j(k_M - k_{RF})$$

The market portfolio is the reference point for beta calculation. Let's assume k_M equals 13 percent. If a firm has a beta above (below) 1.0, its required return is above (below) k_M. Let us suppose that we have calculated the betas for Dr. Pepper and Eastman Kodak, as explained in Appendix 7B.

Since Dr. Pepper's 15.2 percent expected return is above k_M, we would expect its beta to exceed 1.0. Likewise, since Eastman Kodak's 11.6 percent expected return is below k_M, we would expect its beta to be below 1.0. Let's assume the calculated betas would be 1.55 for Dr. Pepper and 0.65 for Eastman Kodak.

Security Market Line and the Capital Asset Pricing Model

We can take these betas and plug them into the security market line equation, introduced in Chapter 7. If the risk-free rate, k_{RF}, equals 9.0 percent, these are the required returns for both stocks:

Security market line = $k_j = k_{RF} + \beta_j(k_M - k_{RF})$

For Dr. Pepper: $k_{DP} = 9.0\% + 1.55(13.0\% - 9.0\%) = 15.2\%$

For Eastman Kodak: $k_{EK} = 9.0\% + 0.65(13.0\% - 9.0\%) = 11.6\%$

We can graph the security market line below, using the directions in Chapter 7:

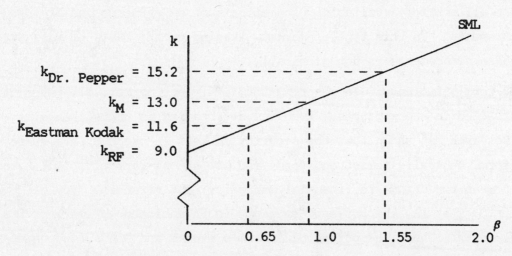

The capital asset pricing model states that in a competitive market the expected risk premium varies proportionately with beta, as we see above. The model goes on to suggest that everyone could buy the same portfolio of assets, the market portfolio, and they could vary the risk of the portfolio by borrowing or lending at the risk-free rate. If the market is not at equilibrium--that is, if some asset is returning more than is required, investors will bid up the price of that asset and push its return down to the required level.

The Efficient Market Hypothesis

You have no doubt heard someone say "you get what you pay for" or "there's no such thing as a free lunch." While most individuals are willing to accept both statements, most have problems with the notion of an efficient market.

In an efficient market, security prices rapidly accurately reflect all relevant information about that security. The efficient market hypothesis is ususlly broken into three components. They are:

Weak-form efficiency: In a weak-form efficient market, prices reflect all histoical information concerning a security. In a weak-form efficient market, trading on the basis of patterns in prices won't generate excess returns.

Semistrong-form efficiency: In a semistrong-form efficient market, prices reflect all publicly available information such as earnings and dividend announcements. In this type of market, trading on the basis of <u>Wall Street Journal</u> announcements is not profitable.

Strong-form efficiency: In a strong-form efficient market, all information is reflected in stock prices. Even insider trading is unprofitable.

Research has shown that the security markets in the U.S. are quite weak-form, generally semistrong-form, and not strong-form efficient. This should mean two things to financial managers. The first is, "you get what you pay for." That is, the price of an asset is an unbiased estimate of its actual worth. Thus, the prices of a firm's stocks and bonds (and changes in those prices upon the announcement of new information) accurately reflect what investors think a firm is worth; maximizing these values is the appropriate goal for financial managers.

Second, "there is no such thing as a free lunch." In an efficient market, the only way to earn increased returns is to bear additional risk. For both investors and managers this is extremely important and should be considered in making an informed investment decision.

COMPLETION QUESTIONS

7.1 Uncertainty about a firm's future earnings before interest and taxes is called _____ risk.

7.2 _____ measures the sensitivity of a security's returns to movements in the market.

7.3 The _____ of a security measures how tightly the probability distribution of possible return outcomes is centered around the expected return.

7.4 _____ is the process of combining assets in a portfolio in order to reduce the variability in the total investment's return.

7.5 When the returns of stock A and stock B tend to move together, we can say their returns are positively _____.

7.6 If a stock's beta is 0.95, then its required return would be _____ than the expected return on the market portfolio.

7.7 The proxy for the risk-free rate is the rate on _____.

7.8 According to the capital asset pricing model, the required rate of return on an asset is the sum of the risk-free rate and a _____ _____.

7.9 _____ measures nondiversifiable risk in a diversified portfolio.

7.10 Maximum risk reduction occurs in a two-security portfolio when the returns of the two securities move _____.

7.11 In a diversified portfolio, the riskiness of the stocks is _____ than the simple average of their individual risks.

7.12 If a stock is providing expected returns over its required return, it is underpriced. A stock cannot remain underpriced, since investors will _____.

7.13 If two stocks' returns move exactly opposite to each other, their correlation is _____. The returns on most assets, however, are _____.

7.14 The _____ shows the relationship between both risk and returns for efficient portfolios.

7.15 The market portfolio is a _____ portfolio of all risky assets.

7.16 In a _____ market, prices reflect all publicly available information.

PROBLEMS

7.1 The following is a probability distribution of possible security returns for Dixon Medical Supply:

State	Probability	Return
Boom	0.15	16.0%
High growth	0.20	14.0
Normal growth	0.30	9.0
Recession	0.25	7.0
Deep recession	0.10	3.5

What is the expected security return and standard deviation?

7.2 Vidmar Industries and Mansfield Manufacturing Company have the following distributions of rates of return:

		Distribution of Security Returns	
State	Probability	Vidmar Industries	Mansfield Manufacturing
1	0.10	40%	-10%
2	0.20	20	- 5
3	0.30	16	6
4	0.25	9	18
5	0.15	3	30

a. Calculate the expected return and standard deviation for both companies.

b. Construct a portfolio composed of 60 percent Vidmar Industries and 40 percent Mansfield. What is the expected return and standard deviation of the portfolio?

7.3 Bob Wilkens owns an efficient portfolio. He estimates that k_M = 20 percent, k_{RF} = 12 percent, and σ_M = 10. If the standard deviation of his portfolio is 16, what is his expected return?

7.4 Bachman Corporation, a manufacturer of home building products, has an expected return of 18 percent. If the expected market return is 16 percent and the risk-free rate is 8 percent, what is the stock's beta if the market is in equilibrium?

7.5 First Investment Trust is a mutual fund investing in the common stock of six firms. The firms, market value of shares held, and the beta of each stock are as follows:

Firm	Market Value of Shares Held (In millions)	Beta
Anderson Industries	$ 90	0.6
Evans International	110	1.2
Fargo Power Company	60	0.7
Omicron Corporation	130	1.8
Pennsylvania Trucking Company	70	0.9
Space Satellite Corporation	40	2.5
	$500	

a. Calculate the beta of the mutual fund.

b. Suppose k_M = 16 percent and k_{RF} = 6 percent; what is the expected portfolio return?

c. Using the individual security betas, calculate the expected return for each security. Show that the weighted average of the individual security returns equals the expected return of the portfolio calculated above.

7.6 Walter Abercrombie has invested $10,000 in the stock of St. Louis Brewing Company and $15,000 in the stock of Amalgamated Aluminum. The expected return on the St. Louis Brewing is 18.6 percent and its standard deviation is 19 percent. The expected return on Amalgamated is 25.8 percent and its standard deviation is 31 percent. If the correlation between the two securities' returns is 0.45, what is the expected return and standard deviation of his portfolio?

7A.1 Consider the following probability distributions for Applegate Industries and the market portfolio.

State(i)	P_i	$k_{Applegate}$	k_{market}
Depression	0.1	-20%	-10%
Recession	0.3	50%	10%
Normal economy	0.4	30%	25%
Boom	0.2	10%	35%

Calculate the correlation between the returns on Applegate and the market.

7B.1 Consider the following information.

Stock	Expected Return	Standard Deviation	Corr$_{jM}$
Michaelson Company	16.70%	10%	0.88
Williams Corp.	13.00	14	0.40
Woods Computers	24.00	22	0.64
Miller Grain Co.	19.08	16	0.72
Market portfolio	16.00	8	1.00

a. Calculate the beta for each stock.

b. Suppose k_{RF} = 9 percent. Calculate the required security returns implied by the CAPM and compare these to the expected returns to determine if the securities are correctly priced.

ANSWERS TO COMPLETION QUESTIONS

7.1 business

7.2 Beta

7.3 standard deviation

7.4 Diversification

7.5 correlated

7.6 less

7.7 U.S. Treasury bills

7.8 risk premium

7.9 Beta

7.10 exactly opposite one another

7.11 less

7.12 buy the stock and bid the price up

7.13 -1.0; positively correlated

7.14 capital market line

7.15 value weighted

7.16 semistrong-form efficient

SOLUTIONS TO PROBLEMS

7.1

Step 1. Expected Return:

Probability	×	Security Return	=	Expected Return
0.15		16.0%		2.40%
0.20		14.0		2.80
0.30		9.0		2.70
0.25		7.0		1.75
0.10		3.5		0.35

Expected return = $\bar{k}$ = 10.00%

Step 2. Standard Deviation:

$(k_i - \bar{k})$	$(k_i - \bar{k})^2$	× Probability =	$(k_i - \bar{k})^2 P_i$
6.0%	36	0.15	5.400
4.0	16	0.20	3.200
-1.0	1	0.30	0.300
-3.0	9	0.25	2.250
-6.5	42.25	0.10	4.225

$$\text{Variance} = \sigma^2 = 15.375\%$$
$$\sigma = \sqrt{15.375\%} = 3.920\%$$

7.2a

Step 1. Vidmar Industries:

$$\bar{k} = 0.10(40\%) + 0.20(20\%) + 0.30(16\%) + 0.25(9\%) + 0.15(3\%)$$
$$= 4\% + 4\% + 4.8\% + 2.25\% + 0.45\% = 15.5\%$$

Step 2. $\sigma^2 = 0.10(40 - 15.5)^2 + 0.20(20 - 15.5)^2 + 0.30(16 - 15.5)^2$
$\qquad + 0.25(9 - 15.5)^2 + 0.15(3 - 15.5)^2$

$\qquad = 0.10(24.5)^2 + 0.20(4.5)^2 + 0.30(0.5)^2 + 0.25(-6.5)^2$
$\qquad + 0.15(-12.5)^2$

$\qquad = 60.025 + 4.05 + 0.075 + 10.5625 + 23.4375 = 98.15\%$

$\sigma = \sqrt{98.15\%} = 9.91\%$

Step 3. Mansfield Manufcturing:

$$\bar{k} = 0.10(-10\%) + 0.20(-5\%) + 0.30(6\%) + 0.25(18\%) + 0.15(30\%)$$
$$= -1\% - 1\% + 1.8\% + 4.5\% + 4.5\% = 8.8\%$$

Step 4. $\sigma^2 = 0.10(-10 - 8.8)^2 + 0.20(-5 - 8.8)^2 + 0.30(6 - 8.8)^2$
$\qquad + 0.25(18 - 8.8\%)^2 + 0.15(30 - 8.8)^2$

$\qquad = 0.10(353.44) + 0.20(190.44) + 0.30(7.84) + 0.25(84.64)$
$\qquad + 0.15(449.44)$

$\qquad = 164.36$

$\sigma = \sqrt{164.36} = 12.82\%$

7.2b

Step 1. Calculate portfolio returns:

State	$\begin{bmatrix}\text{Vidmar}\\ \text{Return}\end{bmatrix} \times$ Weight	+	$\begin{bmatrix}\text{Mansfield}\\ \text{Return}\end{bmatrix} \times$ Weight	= Return
1	40% 0.6		−10% 0.4	20.0%
2	20 0.6		− 5 0.4	10.0
3	16 0.6		6 0.4	12.0
4	9 0.6		18 0.4	12.6
5	3 0.6		30 0.4	13.8

Step 2. Expected portfolio return:

State	Probability ×	Portfolio =	Expected Return
1	0.10	20.0%	2.00%
2	0.20	10.0	2.00
3	0.30	12.0	3.60
4	0.25	12.6	3.15
5	0.15	13.8	2.07

Expected Return = 12.82%

Step 3. Standard Deviation:

$$\sigma^2 = 0.10(20 - 12.82)^2 + 0.20(10 - 12.82)^2 + 0.30(12 - 12.82)^2$$
$$+ 0.25(12.6 - 12.82)^2 + 0.15(13.8 - 12.82)^2$$
$$= 0.10(51.55) + 0.20(7.95) + 0.30(0.67) + 0.25(0.05) + 0.15(0.96)$$
$$= 7.10\%$$
$$\sigma = \sqrt{7.10\%} = 2.67\%$$

7.3

Step 1. CML: $k_P = k_{RF} + \left[\dfrac{k_M - k_{RF}}{\sigma_M}\right]\sigma_P$

$$= 12\% + \left[\dfrac{20\% - 12\%}{10}\right][16]$$

$$= 12\% + (0.8)(16) = 24.8\%$$

7.4

Since $k_j = k_{RF} + \beta_j(k_M - k_{RF})$

$k_j - k_{RF} = \beta_j(k_M - k_{RF})$

$\beta_j = \dfrac{k_j - k_{RF}}{k_M - k_{RF}} = \dfrac{18\% - 8\%}{16\% - 8\%} = \dfrac{10\%}{8\%} = 1.25$

7.5a

Step 1. Calculate the beta of the mutual fund.

$$\beta_P = \frac{\$90}{\$500}(0.6) + \frac{\$110}{\$500}(1.2) + \frac{\$60}{\$500}(0.7) + \frac{\$130}{\$500}(1.8) + \frac{\$70}{\$500}(0.9)$$

$$+ \frac{\$40}{\$500}(2.5)$$

$$= 0.18(0.6) + 0.22(1.2) + 0.12(0.7) + 0.26(1.8) + 0.14(0.9)$$

$$+ 0.08(2.5)$$

$$= 0.108 + 0.264 + 0.084 + 0.468 + 0.126 + 0.200 = 1.25$$

7.5b

Step 2. $k_P = k_{RF} + \beta_P(k_M - k_{RF}) = 6\% + 1.25(16\% - 6\%) = 18.5\%$

7.5c

Step 3. $k_j = k_{RF} + \beta_j(k_M - k_{RF})$

Anderson Industries: $k_j = 6\% + 0.6(16\% - 6\%) = 12\%$

Evans International: $k_j = 6\% + 1.2(16\% - 6\%) = 18\%$

Fargo Power Company: $k_j = 6\% + 0.7(16\% - 6\%) = 13\%$

Omicron Corporation: $k_j = 6\% + 1.8(16\% - 6\%) = 24\%$

Pennsylvania Trucking: $k_j = 6\% + 0.9(16\% - 6\%) = 15\%$

Space Satellite Corp.: $k_j = 6\% + 2.5(16\% - 6\%) = 31\%$

Step 4.

Firm	Expected Return to Security	×	Market Value Weight	=	Expected Portfolio Return
Anderson Industries	12%		$90/$500		2.16%
Evans International	18		$110/$500		3.96
Fargo Power Co.	13		$60/$500		1.56
Omicron Corp.	24		$130/$500		6.24
Penn. Trucking	15		$70/$500		2.10
Space Satellite Corp.	31		$40/$500		2.48 |//					Total portfolio return =	18.50%

Total portfolio return = 18.50%

7.6

Step 1. Total Investment = $10,000 + $15,000 = $25,000

$$W_A = \frac{\text{Investment in A}}{\text{Total Investment}} = \frac{\$10,000}{\$25,000} = 0.4$$

$$W_B = \frac{\text{Investment in B}}{\text{Total Investment}} = \frac{\$15,000}{\$25,000} = 0.6$$

Step 2. $\bar{k}_P = W_A \bar{k}_A + W_B \bar{k}_B$

$$= 0.4(18.6\%) + 0.6(25.8\%) = 7.44\% + 15.48\% = 22.92\%$$

Step 3. $\sigma_P = \sqrt{W_A^2 \sigma_A^2 + W_B^2 \sigma_B^2 + 2W_A W_B \sigma_A \sigma_B \text{Corr}_{AB}}$

$= \sqrt{(0.4)^2(19)^2 + (0.6)^2(31)^2 + 2(0.4)(0.6)(19)(31)(0.45)}$

$= \sqrt{(0.16)(361) + (0.36)(961) + 127.224}$

$= \sqrt{57.76 + 345.96 + 127.224} = \sqrt{530.944} = 23.04\%$

7A.1

Step 1. Calculate expected returns: $\bar{k} = \sum_{i=1}^{n} k_i P_i$

$\bar{k}_{\text{Applegate}(A)} = 0.1(-20\%) + 0.3(50\%) + 0.4(30\%) + 0.2(10\%)$
$= 27\%$

$\bar{k}_{\text{market}(M)} = 0.1(-10\%) + 0.3(10\%) + 0.4(25\%) + 0.2(35\%)$
$= 19\%$

Step 2. Calculate standard deviations: $\sigma_i = \sqrt{\sum_{i=1}^{n}(k_i - \bar{k})^2 P_i}$

$\sigma_A = \sqrt{0.1(-20 - 27)^2 + 0.3(50 - 27)^2 + 0.4(30 - 27)^2 + 0.2(10 - 27)^2}$

$= \sqrt{220.9 + 158.7 + 3.6 + 57.8} = \sqrt{441} = 21$

$\sigma_M = \sqrt{0.1(-10 - 19)^2 + 0.3(10 - 19)^2 + 0.4(25 - 19)^2 + 0.2(35 - 19)^2}$

$= \sqrt{84.1 + 24.3 + 14.4 + 51.2} = \sqrt{174} = 13.19$

Step 3. Calculate the covariance: $\text{Cov}_{A,M} = (k_{A,i} - \bar{k}_A)(k_{M,i} - \bar{k}_M)P_i$

State	P_i	$\times (k_{A,i} - \bar{k}_A)$	$\times (k_{M,i} - \bar{k}_M)$	$= (k_{A,i} - \bar{k}_A)(k_{M,i} - \bar{k}_M)P_i$
Depression	0.1	(-20 - 27)	(-10 - 19)	136.3
Recession	0.3	(50 - 27)	(10 - 19)	- 62.1
Normal	0.4	(30 - 27)	(25 - 19)	7.2
Boom	0.2	(10 - 27)	(35 - 19)	- 54.4
			$\text{Cov}_{A,M} =$	27.0

Step 4. Calculate the correlation: $\text{Corr}_{A,M} = \dfrac{\text{Cov}_{A,M}}{\sigma_A \sigma_M}$

$\text{Corr}_{A,M} = \dfrac{27}{(21)(13.19)} = \dfrac{27}{276.99} = 0.0975$

7.B1a

Step 1. Calculate the betas for each stock.

From Equation 7B.4: $\beta_j = \dfrac{\sigma_j \text{Corr}_{jM}}{\sigma_M}$

Michaelson Company: $\beta_j = \dfrac{10\%(0.88)}{8\%} = 1.1$

Williams Corp.: $\beta_j = \dfrac{14\%(0.40)}{8\%} = 0.7$

Woods Computers: $\beta_j = \dfrac{22\%(0.64)}{8\%} = 1.76$

Miller Grain Co.: $\beta_j = \dfrac{16\%(0.72)}{8\%} = 1.44$

7B.1b

Step 2. Michaelson Company: k_j = 9% + 1.1(16% - 9%) = 16.7%. The security is correctly priced, since the required rate of return is equal to the expected return.

Williams Corp.: k_j = 9% + 0.7(16% - 9%) = 13.9%. The security is overpriced; the expected return of 13.0 percent is below the required return of 13.9 percent.

Woods Computers: k_j = 9% + 1.76(16% - 9%) = 21.32%. The security is underpriced; its expected return of 24 percent is higher than the required return of 21.32 percent.

Miller Grain Company: k_j = 9% + 1.44(16% - 9%) = 19.08%. The security is correctly priced, since its expected and required rates of return are equal.

CHAPTER 8

CAPITAL BUDGETING TECHNIQUES

HOW THIS CHAPTER RELATES TO THE REST OF THE TEXT

Capital budgeting techniques are used to evaluate proposed investment in long-term assets and build on the concepts of cash flow (Chapter 4), timing (Chapter 5), and risk (Chapter 7). The net present value of an asset is simply the present value of its cash flows less its cost. It is through accepting only positive NPV projects that a manager increases the firm's stock price (Chapter 6). Another decision criterion, the IRR, is mathematically the same as the project's interest rate or implied rate of return (Chapter 5), or the yield to maturity on a bond (Chapter 6). Managers should accept projects with IRRs greater than the project's required return or hurdle rate (Chapter 10). Chapters 9, 10, and 11 further examine the process of capital budgeting.

TOPICAL OUTLINE

I. Introduction.
   A. Capital budgeting techniques are used to evaluate proposed investment in long-term assets whose return is expected to extend beyond one year.
   B. Annually, firms complete an economic forecast, a sales budget, and a production budget in order to estimate internal cash flows and external financing.
II. Capital budgeting and the value of the firm.
   A. Project classification.
      1. One scheme is to classify projects as expansion, replacement, or regulatory.
      2. Another scheme is to classify projects as mutually exclusive or independent.
         a. Mutually exclusive projects must be considered as a group of alternative projects whose individual paybacks, internal rates of return, or net present values can be compared.
         b. Independent projects can be evaluated in isolation.
         c. The cash flow of interdependent projects may interact negatively or positively.

B. Value maximization.
1. There are similarities between the valuation process discussed in Chapter 6 and capital budgeting.
2. A project's net present value is the present value of the cash flows, discounted at the required rate of return, less the project's cost.
3. Only by accepting positive NPV projects can a firm increase its value.

III. Overview of the capital budgeting process.
A. Search and identify project ideas from all areas of the firm.
B. Develop forecasts of magnitude, timing, and riskiness of cash flows.
1. In this chapter, we will assume all projects have identical risk; in Chapter 10, we will consider how to handle risk.
2. Cash flows can be broken into the three parts noted in Chapter 4: Initial, operating, and terminal.
C. Select from among proposed projects using methods consistent with the goal of value maximization.
D. Post-completion audit compares the projections with the project's actual cash flows, suggesting changes in the capital budgeting process.
E. When working through steps B and C above, given equal risk, all projects use the same hurdle or discount rate.
1. The discount rate, k, is the required rate of return on the project.
2. The minimum required rate of return which we will discuss more fully Chapter 14.

IV. How to estimate cash flows.
A. Express cash inflows and outflows on an after-tax basis.
B. Ignore all irrelevant costs and benefits, such as overhead.
C. Divide cash flows into three kinds:
1. Initial investment at time zero--the initial cash outflow.
2. Operating net cash flows for each year in the economic life of the investment--the periodic cash flows.
3. Terminal cash flows when the project is completed.

D. Opportunity cost is the cost associated with an alternative or foregone opportunity bypassed in choosing another alternative.

V. Selecting capital budgeting projects.

A. Payback period.
1. Payback period is the number of years it takes for the firm to recover its initial investment.
2. Payback period is the time (T) such that

$$\left(\sum_{t=1}^{T} CF_t - CF_0\right) = 0$$

3. When the cash inflows are unequal, interpolation is necessary. Example: $500 project with cash inflows of $80, $100, and $400.
   a. Determine the number of whole years of payback: $500 - $80 - $100 = $320, so the payback is 2 years plus some fraction.
   b. Determine the fraction of the last year before full recovery: $320/$400 = 0.80 years.
   c. Payback is 2.80 years.
4. The firm establishes a stated or benchmark payback period; projects whose payback exceed this benchmark are not accepted.
5. Advantages of payback include its simplicity and its rough indication of the riskiness of the project; projects with faster payback may have less risk.
6. Disadvantages of payback are that it does not consider the timing of the cash flows (time value of money), nor cash flows that occur after the payback period.

B. Net present value is the discounted expected cash inflows less the initial investment.
1. The equation for net present value is

$$NPV = \sum_{t=1}^{n} \frac{CF_t}{(1+k)^t} - CF_0$$

2. Projects with positive NPV are candidates for selection. If projects are independent, select all that have positive NPVs.
3. Net present value will lead to a correct capital budgeting decision; payback can lead to erroneous decisions.

4. A present value profile, based upon varying discount rates, can show how sensitive the net present value is to increases or decreases in the discount rate.
5. Projects with the same cash flows can have different net present values if their discount rates differ; the more risky the cash flows, the higher the discount rate, and the lower the NPV.

C. Internal rate of return (IRR).
1. The IRR is the discount rate that equates the present value of the cash inflows with the initial investment.
2. The formula is:

$$\sum_{t=1}^{n} \frac{CF_t}{(1 + IRR)^t} = CF_0, \text{ or } \sum_{t=1}^{n} \frac{CF_t}{(1 + IRR)^t} - CF_0 = 0$$

3. If the IRR exceeds the firm's required rate of return, the project is a candidate for acceptance.
4. Review the steps for determining interest rates in Chapter 5.
5. For the present value profile in Figure 8.2, the internal rate of return occurs where the profile passes through the X (or horizontal) axis, and the net present value equals zero.

D. Which is best: NPV or IRR?
1. Both the IRR and NPV are consistent with the objective of value maximization, but complications can occur.
2. The IRR calculations can produce multiple internal rates of return when the cash flow series involves more than one change in sign.
3. When ranking mutually exclusive projects, IRR and NPV sometimes do not provide consistent rankings; the firm wants to choose the project that will maximize its value.
   a. The initial outlays for mutually exclusive projects may differ significantly, causing the ranking problems.
   b. The timing of the mutually exclusive projects' cash inflows may differ significantly, causing rankings problems.
   c. The ultimate culprit is the implied reinvestment rate assumption.
      i. IRR assumes that all intermediate cash flows can be

reinvested at the same rate of return as the IRR on the project; this assumption can be faulty, especially for longer-term projects.

ii. NPV assumes that the intermediate cash flows are reinvested at the firm's required rate of return; this assumption leads toward value maximization.

4. Reconciliation of NPV and IRR.
   a. Calculate the IRR of both projects.
   b. Select the project with the highest IRR and designate it as the "defender."
   c. Calculate the incremental cash flows of the "challenger" over the "defender."
   d. Calculate the IRR of the incremental cash flows.
   e. If the IRR for the incremental cash flows is greater than the required return, the challenger is preferred.

VI. Capital budgeting decisions.
   A. Expansion project.
      1. Calculate the depreciation schedule, using the normal recovery period ACRS factors.
      2. Calculate the initial, operating, and terminal cash flows, as in Table 8.6.

VII. What leads to positive NPVs?
   A. The net present value from investing in financial assets is equal to zero.
      1. The market for stocks and bonds is reasonably efficient.
      2. In an efficient market, securities are fairly priced based on risk and return.
      3. Any mispricing is quickly exploited by investors and eliminated.
   B. Positive NPVs for capital budgeting projects must come from imperfections in the product and labor markets or bad data.
      1. Evidence suggests that labor and product markets are less than perfectly competitive and hence inefficient. An effective capital budgeting process includes analysis of these imperfections.

2. Some studies suggest that managers are overoptimistic in formulating cash flow and risk estimates. Incorrect specification of these items leads to incorrect NPVs--"garbage in, garbage out."
3. For terminal flows, recall the tax effects of asset disposal.
4. Calculate the net present value of these cash flows, using the appropriate discount rate, which is the required rate of return for the project.

VIII. Appendix 8A: Important depreciation and tax ideas (located at the end of the text).
   A. Depreciation is a means of charging the original cost of long-term assets against revenues.
      1. Two major results of the Economic Recovery Tax Act of 1981 as modified by the Tax Reform Act of 1986: Simplified depreciation for tax purposes and shortened the normal recovery period. Many assets are fully depreciated before the end of their useful lives.
      2. The modified Accelerated Cost Recovery System (ACRS) is relevant for tax purposes.
         a. Estimated salvage values for accounting purposes are irrelevant.
         b. The six normal recovery periods cover all new and used equipment.
         c. Depreciation factors depend upon the recovery period.
         d. Have the option of using modified ACRS or straight-line depreciation over the normal recovery period.
   B. Corporate taxes.
      1. Ordinary income.
         a. Recaptured depreciation is taxed as ordinary income.
         b. We will use tax rates between 30 and 40 percent in the text.
      2. Sale of an asset above its remaining book value results in a tax liability; the gain is treated as ordinary income.
      3. Losses result in a tax credit; tax losses are carried back and then, if necessary, carried forward.

4. Interest received by the firm is fully taxable, but 70 or 80 percent of cash dividend income received by the firm is tax exempt.
5. Firms pay taxes quarterly on tax payment dates, although we will simplify our calculations by assuming they pay taxes once a year.

C. Other tax considerations.
1. Consolidated tax returns combine the income of the parent firm and the income of firms of which it owns 80 percent or more.
2. International considerations: The U.S. Government taxes U.S. based multinationals on their worldwide income.

D. Summary of depreciation and tax considerations: See Table 8.1.

FORMULAS

Tax Rates in This Text

Ordinary tax rate = 30% to 40% = 0.30 to 0.40

Measures of Earnings

Earnings before taxes (EBT):

EBT = Revenue − costs and expenses − depreciation

Net income = $EBT(1 - T)$

Measures of Cash Flow

Cash flow before taxes (CFBT):

$CBFT$ = Revenues − costs and expenses − interest

Cash flow after taxes (CF):

CF = (Cash inflows − cash outflows) − taxes

  = $CFBT$ − taxes

  = $(CFBT)(1 - T) + (depreciation)(T)$

Depreciation for Tax Purposes

Cost of asset × modified ACRS depreciation factor

Tax Effects of Disposal of an Asset

Tax on recapture of depreciation:

(Selling price − remaining book value)(T)

Tax credit on sale if asset sold at a loss, below book value:

(Remaining book value − selling price)(T)

After tax cash flow from sale of asset:

    Selling price + tax credit (if loss)

    Selling price - tax on sale (if gain)

Terminal Cash Flow

Terminal cash flows = funds realized from sale of asset + tax benefit if sold at a loss (or - tax liability if sold at a gain) + release of net working capital

Payback Period

$$\text{Payback, } T, = \left(\sum_{t=1}^{T} CF_t - CF_0\right) = 0$$

Net Present Value (NPV)

$$NPV = \sum_{t=1}^{n} \frac{CF_t}{(1+k)^t} - CF_0$$

Internal Rate of Return (IRR)

$$\text{Rate so that } \sum_{t=1}^{n} \frac{CF_t}{(1+IRR)^t} - CF_0 = 0$$

WHAT TO LOOK FOR

In this chapter, we begin to look at investment in capital assets, assets whose life is expected to extend beyond one year. Capital budgeting decisions are important, since they shape the future of the firm for years to come. In addition, they may represent a relatively large commitment of the firm's resources.

In Chapter 8, we discuss the basics of capital budgeting for expansion projects and assume that all capital budgeting projects have equally risky cash flow streams. In Chapter 9 we consider more complications. In Chapter 10 we relax that assumption and consider variations in risk. In capital budgeting, as in all financial management, the firm's goal is to maximize the value of the firm.

The Capital Budgeting Process

Measuring the cash flows

In making capital budgeting choices, we take into account the timing, magnitude, and riskiness of each project's cash flows. It is easier to estimate a project's expected cash flows if we break down the flows into intial, operating, and terminal. Initial flows are all those necessary to get the project off the ground. These might include (1) purchase of land, building, and equipment; (2) installation and freight-in; (3) special training for using new equipment; (4) increases in net working capital such as an increase in accounts receivable and inventory, less increases in accounts payable and accruals; and (5) tax effects of selling a replaced asset. For simplicity, we assume these flows all occur at time zero, so their net outflow is immediate. In order for a project to be acceptable, the present value of the operating flows plus terminal flows must exceed the initial cash outflow.

Intermediate cash flows are also on an after-tax basis, so we must adjust the operating cash flows (inflows - outflows) for taxes. Since depreciation is a noncash expense that decreases taxable income, we must consider its effect on operating cash flows. The modified ACRS depreciation system has shortened the normal recovery period for most assets, so now it is often shorter than the project's useful life. Thus, for later years of many projects, depreciation does not affect the CF stream.

Terminal flows are those flows which result at the end of the project. These include (1) funds realized from sale of an asset; (2) the tax benefit if the asset is sold at a loss; (3) the release of net working capital; (4) the tax liability if the asset is sold at a gain.

Taxes and Tax Effects of Selling an Asset

The tax effects of selling an asset are important. We will review the three standard situations: (1) sale of an asset above the original purchase price; (2) sale of an asset below original purchase price, but above remaining book value; and (3) sale of an asset below remaining book value. Suppose the original purchase price of a four-passenger commuter plane was $500,000 and its remaining book value is $300,000. Its selling price in the three situations above is $750,000, $450,000, and $100,000, respectively. The marginal corporate tax rate is 35 percent.

	Sold at a gain price above original cost	Sold at a gain price below original cost	Sold at a loss
Selling price	$750,000	$450,000	$100,000
Remaining book value	300,000	300,000	300,000
Gain (loss) on sale	450,000	150,000	(200,000)
Tax at 35%	-157,500	-52,500	+70,000
Net proceeds	$750,000 - $157,500 = $542,500	$150,000 - $52,500 = $97,500	$100,000 + $70,000 = $170,000

Rationale for Taxes on Recapture of Depreciation

You may still be wondering what recapture of depreciation is, and why it is taxed. As you will remember, when a firm buys an asset, the firm is allowed to write off (or "expense") the cost of an asset over the normal recovery period of that asset. This expensing is called depreciation. Depreciation, as a noncash expense on the income statement, reduces the firm's taxable income each year over the normal recovery period of the asset. From an accounting perspective, depreciation is designed to match revenues and associated expenses (in this case wear and tear on the equipment) in the same time period. For tax purposes, depreciation is used to stimulate investment. For our purposes, accounting depreciation is irrelevant; what we care about is depreciation for tax purposes, since that is what affects cash flow.

In the example above, the firm's airplane had an original price of $500,000 and a remaining book value of $300,000. These figures indicate that $200,000 of the value of the plane had already been expensed for tax purposes when the firm was ready to sell it. The book value of the airplane declined each year as the firm depreciated it.

In the second situation above, the firm sells the plane for more than its remaining book value, but less than the original purchase price. The firm has to, in effect, recapture depreciation already deducted from book value. The tax code specifies that recapture of depreciation results when the firm depreciates the asset too rapidly and pays too few taxes in the earlier years of the asset's life. So the tax code treats recaptured depreciation as ordinary income.

In the final case, the plane is sold for less than its remaining book value, resulting in a loss to the firm. Losses generate tax rebates; in this case, the firm can reduce taxes otherwise paid by $70,000 in order to recoup part of the loss. This effectively increases the net proceeds from the sale of the plane.

While we are considering tax incentives in this chapter, let's consider another important one. The new depreciation schedule under the modified Accelerated Cost Recovery System (ACRS) provides simplified depreciation for tax purposes and shortens the depreciation (or normal recovery) period for most assets. These changes increase firms' cash flows and serve to spur more capital investment. ACRS was originally a tax code response to the twofold problem of high inflation and high financing costs borne by corporations in recent years. Although the modified ACRS factors depreciate assets more slowly, they still are an important determinant of a project's cash flows. The simplified ACRS factors can be forund in Table F.5 in the back of your text.

Cash Flow: A Comprehensive Example

The following example will demonstrate more fully depreciation, taxes, and cash flow. We will look at the after-tax cash flows throughout the life of an investment, after calculating the component cash inflows and outflows.

Initial outflow

Suppose you purchase an IBM computer system for $15,000, and you expect to use it for two years. Installation expenses are $1,500 and the corporate tax rate is 34 percent. The installation expenses will be tax deductible and will result in a tax savings of $1,500(0.34) = $525. The initial outlay will be $15,000 + $1,500 - $510 = $15,990.

Operating cash flows

Out-of-pocket costs each year are $1,500 in materials and maintenance, while out-of-pocket savings per year in time and personnel costs are $3,000. To calculate the depreciation for years one and two, we will use ACRS. The computer has a five year recovery period, so the depreciation for the two years is: ($15,000)(0.20) = $3,000; ($15,000)(0.32) = $4,800. At the end of year two, the remaining book value is: $15,000 - $3,000 - $4,800 = $7,200.

Terminal cash flow

Suppose that at the end of year two you plan to sell the computer, and you estimate its selling price to be $13,000. We need to calculate the after-tax cash flows. Since the sale price is above the remaining book value, you have recaptured depreciation: $13,000 - $7,200 = $5,800. The tax on this recapture would be ($5,800)(0.34) = $1,972. So the after-tax terminal cash flow on the sale is $13,000 - $1,972 = $11,028.

Net cash flows

The chart and figure below will help us find the net after-tax cash flows for each period.

Time	Type	Cash Flow Calculations	Net Cash Flows
Yr 0	Initial	-$15,000 - $1,500 + $510	-$15,990
Yr 1	Operating	($3,000-$1,500)(1-0.34) + ($3,000)(0.34)	2,010
Yr 2	Operating	($3,000-$1,500)(1-0.34) + ($4,800)(0.34)	2,622
Yr 2	Terminal	$13,000 - $1,972	11,028

```
                                              $11,028
                                            +   2,622
                  Cash Inflows $2,010       = $13,650
                         ↑                     ↑
         0_____1_____2
         ↓
      $15,990 Cash Outflows
```

Measuring the Timing of the Cash Flows

Two selection techniques that consider the timing as well as the magnitude and riskiness of the cash flows are net present value (NPV) and the internal rate of return (IRR). The payback period does not consider the timing or riskiness of the cash flows, but it implies that a shorter payback makes a project less risky.

The net present value calculation allows the manager to discount the proposed project's expected cash flows using the required rate of return (or for projects of average risk, the weighted average cost of capital). In calculating net present value, the manager is not only considering the riskiness of the project, but assuming that its cash flows are reinvested at the required rate of return.

When choosing among independent projects, the manager chooses all projects with a positive net present value. If two projects are mutually exclusive, the manager chooses the project that will increase the value of the firm more--the project with the higher net present value. By doing so, the manager maximizes the value of the firm.

The internal rate of return (IRR) is the rate of return the project's inflows must earn in order to exactly offset the initial investment. The project is accepted if the IRR exceeds the required rate of return. The IRR method assumes that the intermediate cash flows are reinvested at the IRR of that specific project. This assumption can be unrealistic if the IRR is relatively high and if the project's life is long.

In ranking mutually exclusive capital projects, NPV and IRR do not always give consistent results. NPV, however, always gives a value maximizing decision. We'll demonstrate both the calculation of NPV and IRR and their ranking differences. Breckenridge Manufacturing is considering two capital projects, project A and project B. Both were due to the marketing department's suggestions to expand production.

Project A is a completely automated bottling system while project B uses the company's current technology. The two projects are mutually exclusive. Both machines will be depreciated over five years using the modified ACRS factors.

Project A:

    Cost = $180,000

    Installation costs = $500 (this will be treated as an expense)

    Resale value (in year five) = $40,000

    Increase in working capital = $5,000

    Increase in sales per year (cash inflows) = $105,000

    Increase in costs per year (cash outflows) = $50,000

    Tax rate = 30 percent

    k = 12 percent

Project A: Cash flows

    Initial investment = cost + installation + increase in working capital − tax effect of installation expense

        = $180,000 + $500 + $5,000 − $500(0.30)

        = $185,350

Operating flows = (cash inflows − cash outflows)(1 − T)
                  + depreciation(T)

Year 1 = ($105,000 − $50,000)(1 − 0.30) + $180,000(0.20)(0.30)
       = $49,300

Year 2 = ($105,000 − $50,000)(1 − 0.30) + $180,000(0.32)(0.30)
       = $55,780

Year 3 = ($105,000 − $50,000)(1 − 0.30) + $180,000(0.19)(0.30)
       = $48,760

Year 4 = ($105,000 − $50,000)(1 − 0.30) + $180,000(0.15)(0.30)
       = $46,600

Year 5 = ($105,000 − $50,000)(1 − 0.30) + $180,000(0.14)(0.30)
       = $46,060

Terminal flow = cash from sale + release of working capital + tax effect of asset sale

       = $40,000 + $5,000 − $40,000(0.30)

       = $33,000

With these data, we can calculate the NPV and IRR of Project A. Since k = 12 percent,

Time	Type	Cash Flow	$PV_{12\%,n}$	Present Value of Cash Flows
1	Operating	$49,300	0.893	$ 44,024.90
2	Operating	55,780	0.797	44,456.66
3	Operating	48,760	0.712	34,717.12
4	Operating	46,600	0.636	29,637.60
5	Operating	46,060	0.567	26,116.02
5	Terminal	33,000	0.567	18,711.00

Present value of cash flows = $197,663.30

Net Present Value = $197,663.30 − $185,350 = $ 12,313.30

Using a financial calculator, the IRR = 14.50%

Project B:

    Cost = $100,000

    Installation costs = $500 (this will be treated as an expense)

    Resale value (in year five) = $20,000

    Increase in working capital = $5,000

    Increase in sales per year (cash inflows) = $105,000

    Increase in costs per year (cash outflows) = $72,000

    Tax rate = 30 percent

    k = 12 percent

Using the same formula as before,

Project B: Cash flows

    Initial investment = $100,000 + $500 + $5,000 - $500(0.30)

                  = $105,350

    Operating flows:

        Year 1 = ($105,000 - $72,000)(1 - 0.30) + $100,000(0.20)(0.30)

              = $29,100

        Year 2 = ($105,000 - $72,000)(1 - 0.30) + $100,000(0.32)(0.30)

              = $32,700

        Year 3 = ($105,000 - $72,000)(1 - 0.30) + $100,000(0.19)(0.30)

              = $28,800

        Year 4 = ($105,000 - $72,000)(1 - 0.30) + $100,000(0.15)(0.30)

              = $27,600

        Year 5 = ($105,000 - $72,000)(1 - 0.30) + $100,000(0.14)(0.30)

              = $27,300

    Terminal flow = $20,000 + $5,000 - $20,000(0.30)

                = $19,000

Time	Type	Cash Flow	$PV_{12\%,n}$	Present Value of Cash Flows
1	Operating	$29,100	0.893	$ 25,986.30
2	Operating	32,700	0.797	26,061.90
3	Operating	28,800	0.712	20,505.60
4	Operating	27,600	0.636	17,553.60
5	Operating	27,300	0.567	15,479.10
5	Terminal	19,000	0.567	10,773.00

Present value of cash flows = $116,359.50

Net Present Value = $116,359.50 - $105,350 = $ 11,009.50

Using a financial calculator, the IRR = 15.91%

Net present value ranks project A above project B, but IRR ranks project B above project A. The NPV ranking is the one to use. Its reinvestment assumption leads to value maximization.

We can show that the above statement is true by examining the incremental cash flows. Since project B has the higher IRR, let's define it as the "defender" and let project A be the "challenger." The incremental cash flows are calculated as:

Time	Challenger (A)	−	Defender (B)	=	Incremental CF
0	-$185,350		-$105,350		-$80,000
1	49,300		29,100		20,200
2	55,780		32,700		23,080
3	48,760		28,800		19,960
4	46,600		27,600		19,000
5	46,060		27,300		18,760
5	33,000		19,000		14,000

Using a financial calculator, the IRR of the incremental cash flows is 12.62%, which is greater than the required return. Thus, the incremental investment needed to move from B to A is justified and project A should be chosen.

When using single value estimates of initial investment, inflows, outflows, terminal values, project life, and so forth, managers should consider how sensitive the project rankings are to variations from these expected values. In Chapter 10, we will adjust NPV calculations for this variability, and look at other methods of dealing with project risk.

COMPLETION QUESTIONS

8.1 Long-term investments have a major impact on the magnitude, timing, and riskiness of the firm's _____.

8.2 In searching for and indentifying capital project ideas, managers must be certain that the projects are in line with the firm's _____ _____.

8.3 The _____ contains estimates of the cash flows for long-term projects.

8.4 _____ projects are those designed to improve the firm's ability to produce and market its products. _____ projects are those designed to take the place of existing assets which have become obsolete.

8.5 When two capital projects are _____ the acceptance of one precludes the acceptance of the other. The firm would choose that project whose NPV was _____.

8.6 The tax benefits arising from the sale of replaced assets and costs related to purchases are all part of the _____.

8.7 Sale of an asset above book value but below the original purchase price would result in the _____

8.8 Under the Accelerated Cost Recovery System (ACRS) of depreciation, salvage value is _____.

8.9 The _____ is the cost of a foregone opportunity, such as the loss of rental income when a firm decides to use its own warehouse space.

8.10 The release of net working capital occurs in the _____.

8.11 The _____ is a nondiscounted cash flow technique measuring the number of years it takes for the firm to recover its initial investment. It does not, however, consider the cash flows that _____ _____.

8.12 The net present value is determined by discounting the _____ _____ back to the present and then _____.

8.13 Among the three selection techniques, the _____ technique provides the correct ranking decisions.

8.14 On the present value profile, the internal rate of return is where the net present value would be _____.

PROBLEMS

8.1 Kiser Kitchenware is considering the construction of a new assembly line requiring an initial outlay of $1,500,000. The assembly line is expected to last for ten years, and the firm expects constant yearly after-tax cash flows (CF) over the life of the project. The payback period on the assembly line is 4.92 years. Assuming a required return of 12 percent, what is the project's NPV? What is its IRR?

8.2 Baker Publishing Company is considering converting a warehouse to enable the firm to increase production. The renovation will require the purchase of $3,000,000 worth of printing and binding equipment and will be depreciated over five years according to the modified ACRS tables. The warehouse is presently being rented out for $75,000 per year.

    The new facility has an expected lifetime of 10 years and zero salvage value. Because of the increased productive capability, Baker expects additional sales of $2,000,000 in year 1, and sales are expected to increase (primarily due to inflation) by 5 percent per year. The fixed costs associated with this facility are $100,000 per year, and variable costs are 60 percent of sales. If the corporate tax rate is 35 percent, and the discount rate is 16 percent, should the warehouse be renovated?

8.3 Miles Office Supply is considering two mutually exclusive inventory management systems each with five-year lives. Project A is an office computing system to facilitate record-keeping costing $20,000 and yielding a CF of $6,540.22 per year. Project B is a fully automated system costing $100,000 with a CF of $29,832.94 per year.

    a. Calculate the IRR of each project and select the preferred project.
    b. Assuming that the required rate of return is 10 percent, which project is preferable?
    c. At what discount rate would the firm be indifferent between the two projects?

8.4 Okeefe Printing is considering the purchase of one of two mutually exclusive printing presses. The cash flows with each are listed below.

Year	Project A CF	Project B CF
0	-4,000.00	-2,000.00
1	1,401.05	743.49
2	1,401.05	743.49
3	1,401.05	743.49
4	1,401.05	743.49

The required rate of return on each project is 10%. Calculate the NPV and IRR of each project. Which project should be chosen? Use the incremental approach to show that your answer is correct.

ANSWERS TO COMPLETION QUESTIONS

8.1 cash flows

8.2 strategic goals and objectives

8.3 capital budget

8.4 Expansion; Replacement

8.5 mutually exclusive; greater (assuming both NPVs are positive)

8.6 initial investment

8.7 recapture of depreciation

8.8 ignored

8.9 opportunity cost

8.10 terminal cash flow

8.11 payback period; occur after the payback period

8.12 expected cash inflows; subtracting the initial investment

8.13 net present value

8.14 zero

SOLUTIONS TO PROBLEMS

8.1

Step 1. When cash flows are constant, payback period = $\frac{\text{Initial outlay}}{\text{CF}}$

so, CF = $\frac{\text{Initial outlay}}{\text{Payback period}} = \frac{\$1,500,000}{4.92}$ = \$304,878.05 per year

Step 2. NPV = $\sum_{t=1}^{n} \frac{CF_t}{(1+k_t)} - CF_0$

= $304,878.05(PVA_{12\%,10yr})$ - $1,500,000

= $304,878.05(5.650)$ - $1,500,000

= $1,722,560.99 - $1,500,000

NPV = $222,560.99

Step 3. IRR: At the IRR, $\sum_{t=1}^{n} \frac{CF_t}{(1+IRR)^t} - CF_0 = 0$

so, $304,878.05(PVA_{IRR\%,10yr}) - \$1,500,000 = 0$

$PVA_{IRR\%,10yr} = \frac{\$1,500,000}{\$304,878.05} = 4.920$

Step 4. Using Table F.3, we can see that the $PVA_{IRR\%,10yr}$ lies between the factors for 15% and 16%. Interpolating,

$IRR = 15\% + \frac{PVA_{15\%,10yr} - PVA_{IRR\%,10yr}}{PVA_{15\%,10yr} - PVA_{16\%,10yr}}$

$= 15\% + \frac{5.019 - 4.920}{5.019 - 4.833} = 15\% + \frac{0.099}{0.186} = 15.53\%$

8.2

Step 1. Cash Flows Year 0: Cost of equipment, $CF_0 = \$3,000,000$

Step 2. CFBT

Year	Sales	- Variable Cost	- Fixed Cost	- Opportunity Cost of Rent	= CFBT
1	$2,000,000	$1,200,000	$100,000	$75,000	$ 625,000
2	2,100,000	1,260,000	100,000	75,000	665,000
3	2,205,000	1,323,000	100,000	75,000	707,000
4	2,315,250	1,389,150	100,000	75,000	751,100
5	2,431,012	1,458,607	100,000	75,000	797,405
6	2,552,563	1,531,538	100,000	75,000	846,025
7	2,680,191	1,608,115	100,000	75,000	897,076
8	2,814,201	1,688,521	100,000	75,000	950,680
9	2,954,911	1,772,947	100,000	75,000	1,006,964
10	3,102,656	1,861,594	100,000	75,000	1,066,062

Step 3. Depreciation

Year	Original Cost	× ACRS Factors	= Depreciation
1	$3,000,000	0.20	$600,000
2	3,000,000	0.32	960,000
3	3,000,000	0.19	570,000
4	3,000,000	0.15	450,000
5	3,000,000	0.14	420,000

Step 4. Operating Cash Flows

Year	CFBT	CFBT(1 - T)	+	Dep(T)	=	CF
1	$ 625,000	$406,250		$210,000		$616,250
2	665,000	432,250		336,000		768,250
3	707,000	459,550		199,500		659,050
4	751,100	488,215		157,500		645,715
5	797,405	518,313		147,000		665,313
6	846,025	549,916		0		549,916
7	897,076	583,099		0		583,099
8	950,680	617,942		0		617,942
9	1,006,964	654,527		0		654,527
10	1,066,062	692,940		0		692,940

Step 5. Present Value of Cash Inflows

Year	CF	×	PV at 16%	=	PV of CF
1	$616,250		0.862		$ 531,207.50
2	768,250		0.743		570,809.75
3	659,050		0.641		422,451.05
4	645,715		0.552		356,434.68
5	665,313		0.476		316,688.99
6	549,916		0.410		225,465.56
7	583,099		0.354		206,417.05
8	617,942		0.305		188,472.31
9	654,527		0.263		172,140.60
10	692,940		0.227		157,297.38

Present Value of CFs = $3,147,384.87

Step 6. NPV = Present value of cash inflows - CF_0

= $3,147,384.87 - $3,000,000 = $147,384.87

Accept the project; the net present value is positive.

8.3a

Step 1. Project A

$20,000 = $6,540.22(PVA$_{?\%, 5yr}$)

PVA$_{?\%, 5yr}$ = ($20,000/$6,540.22) = 3.058

From Table F.4, this PVA is associated with 19 percent.

Thus, the IRR for project A is 19 percent.

Project B

$$PVA_{?\%,5yr} = (\$100,000/\$29,832.94) = 3.352 \qquad IRR = 15\%$$

Select project A since it has the higher IRR.

8.3b

Step 2. Calculate the NPV for each project

$$NPV_A = \$6,540.22(PVA_{10\%,5yr}) - \$20,000$$

$$= \$6,540.22(3.791) - \$20,000$$

$$= \$24,793.97 - \$20,000 = \$4,793.97$$

$$NPV_B = \$29,832.94(3.791) - \$100,000 = \$113,096.68 - \$100,000$$

$$= \$13,096.68$$

Since our goal is to maximize the value of firm, select project B, which has the larger NPV.

8.3c

Step 3. Set the two projects equal to each other and solve for the discount rate.

$$\$6,540.22(PVA_{?\%,5yr}) - \$20,000$$

$$= \$29,832.94(PVA_{?\%,5yr}) - \$100,000$$

$$\$23,292.72(PVA_{?\%,5yr}) = \$80,000$$

$$PVA_{?\%,5yr} = (\$80,000/\$23,292.72) = 3.435$$

The rate associated with a PVA of 3.517 is 13 percent, while that associated with 3.433 is 14 percent. By interpolation, the rate is:

$$13\% + \frac{3.517 - 3.435}{3.517 - 3.433} = 13\% + \frac{0.082}{0.084} = 13\% + 0.98\% = 13.98\%$$

8.4

Step 1. Project A: $NPV = \$1,401.05(PVA_{10\%,4yr}) - \$4,000$

$$= \$1,401.05(3.170) - \$4,000$$

$$= \$4,441.33 - \$4,000$$

$$= \$441.33$$

$$IRR = \$1,401.05(PVA_{?\%,4yr}) - \$4,000 = 0$$

$$PVA_{?\%,4yr} = \frac{\$4,000}{\$1,401.05} = 2.855$$

From Table F.4, $IRR_A = 15\%$

Step 2. Project B: NPV = $743.49(PVA$_{10\%, 4yr}$) − $2,000

$\qquad\qquad\qquad\quad$ = $743.49(3.170) − $2,000

$\qquad\qquad\qquad\quad$ = $2,356.86 − $2,000

$\qquad\qquad\qquad\quad$ = $356.86

$\qquad\qquad\quad$ IRR = $743.49(PVA$_{?\%, 4yr}$) − $2,000 = 0

$\qquad\qquad\quad$ PVA$_{?\%, 4yr}$ = $\dfrac{\$2,000}{\$743.49}$ = 2.690

From Table F.4, IRR$_B$ = 18%

Step 3. You should choose Project A since it has a higher NPV, even though it has a lower IRR.

Step 4.
Time	Challenger (A)	−	Defender (B)	=	Incremental CF
0	−4,000.00		−2,000.00		−2,000.00
1	1,401.05		743.49		657.56
2	1,401.05		743.49		657.56
3	1,401.05		743.49		657.56
4	1,401.05		743.49		657.56

Step 5. IRR$_{Incremental}$: $657.56(PVA$_{?\%, 4yr}$ − $2,000 = 0

$\qquad\qquad\quad$ PV$_{?\%, 4yr}$ = $\dfrac{\$2,000}{\$657.56}$ = 3.042

From Table F.4, the IRR is between 11% and 12%. Interpolating,

IRR = 11% + $\dfrac{3.102 - 3.042}{3.102 - 3.037}$

$\quad$ = 11.92%

Since the IRR of the incremental cash flows is greater than the required return, choose the challenger, project A.

CHAPTER 9

REPLACEMENT DECISIONS, CASH FLOWS, AND CAPITAL RATIONING

HOW THIS CHAPTER RELATES TO THE REST OF THE TEXT

In Chapter 8, we discussed the basics of capital budgeting. The net present value of a project is a function of the cash flows (Chapter 4), their timing (Chapter 5), and their riskiness (Chapter 7). In this chapter, we examine problems such as the replacement decision, how to compare mutually exclusive projects with unequal lives, how to cope with inflation and disinflation, and decision making in a world of capital rationing. The third chapter in this section (Chapter 10) discusses risk and capital budgeting, while the fourth chapter (Chapter 11) discusses options and capital budgeting.

TOPICAL OUTLINE

I. Replacement decisions--focus on incremental cash flows; cash flows related to the new equipment less cash flows related to the old.
   A. For initial flows, consider the increase in net working capital, the tax effects of the sale or disposal of the replaced asset, and the purchase price and installation costs.
   B. In calculating the terminal flows, consider the tax effects of the sale or disposal of the asset and the release of net working capital.
   C. For operating flows, consider the changes in cash inflows, cash outflows, and depreciation.

$$\Delta CF_t = \Delta CFBT_t(1 - T) + \Delta DEP_t(T)$$

   D. If the net present value of the incremental cash flows is positive, the existing asset should be replaced.
II. Interrelated projects--the acceptance of one project can partially affect (either positively or negatively) the cash flows of other possible projects.
   A. Joint cash flows for two or more interrelated projects must be analyzed together.
   B. Identify all possible combinations of interrelated projects.

C. Determine the initial investment and after-tax cash flow stream for each combination, in addition to the total NPV for each project.
D. Choose the combination with the greatest NPV.
III. Mutually exclusive projects with unequal lives.
A. In order to make a valid comparison, the lives of mutually exclusive projects must be equalized.
B. Solving the unequal life problem.
1. Equivalent annual NPV method.
a. Converts the net present value to a yearly net present value figure.
b. Formula:
Equivalent annual NPV = $NPV_n/PVA_{k,n}$
c. Choose the project with the highest equivalent annual NPV.
C. Remember, unequal lives are a problem only in deciding among mutually exclusive alternatives.
IV. More on cash flow estimation.
A. Inflation and disinflation.
1. Inflation and disinflation affect both cash flows and the required rate of return. Only in the case where both CFs and the required return properly anticipate and adjust for the same percentage rate of inflation will the effects cancel each other out.
2. If inflation is accounted for in the required rate of return, but not CF, NPVs will be downward biased.
3. In adjusting for inflation, managers should remember the following:
a. Be consistent; make sure inflation or disinflation consequences are built into both CFs and the required rates of return.
b. Even if inflows and outflows change in line with inflation, CF will not due to the U.S. tax structure.
c. Inflation is not constant across sections of the economy.

        d. Differential price changes may occur due to supply and
            demand. These changes are due to factors other than
            inflation and should be considered.
B. Financing costs should, under most cases, be excluded from the
    calculation of CFs. Capital budgeting and financing decisions are
    separate.
C. Abandonment.
    1. In order to insure that all options have been examined,
        consider abandonment.
    2. The selling price of an asset is an opportunity cost that must
        be considered.
    3. An additional option is to consider modernization. The
        relevant set of cash flows for this decision is the combination
        of existing and new cash flows.
D. Capital rationing occurs when the firm sets a dollar limit to the
    capital budget, generally due to the amount of external funds the
    firm can raise.
    1. The goal in capital rationing is to maximize the value of the
        firm over all projects accepted.
    2. For small numbers of projects, one can list all feasible
        combinations of projects within the budget constraint and
        choose the combination with the largest NPV.
    3. For large numbers of projects, linear programming can produce an
        optimal combination of projects.

FORMULAS

Depreciation

Depreciation per year for tax purposes = (original cost)(ACRS factor)

Total depreciation taken for tax purposes = $\sum_{t=1}^{n}$ (original cost)(ACRS factor)

Initial Investment

Initial investment = cost of equipment and land + costs related to purchase + additional net working capital required + tax liability of replaced assets sold − funds realized from the sale of replaced assets − tax benefits from sale of replaced assets.

Operating Cash Flows

$\text{CFBT} = \text{cash inflows} - \text{cash outflows}$

$\text{CF} = \text{CFBT}(1 - T) + \text{Dep}(T)$

Terminal Cash Flows

Terminal cash flows = funds realized from sale of asset + tax benefit if sold at a loss + release of net working capital − tax liability if sold at a gain

Incremental Operating Cash Flows

$\Delta \text{CF}_t = \Delta \text{CFBT}_t (1 - T) + \Delta \text{Dep}_t (T)$

Equivalent Annual NPV

Equivalent annual NPV = $\text{NPV}_n / \text{PVA}_{k,n}$

WHAT TO LOOK FOR

In Chapter 8, we examined the basics of capital budgeting and applied a variety of techniques to the expansion decision. Managers must also be able to apply these techniques to a variety of other types of decisions such as replacement and abandonment of existing assets.

This chapter examines those issues as well as discusses a variety of problems facing financial managers. These problems include how to evaluate interrelated projects, how to deal with mutually exclusive projects with unequal lives, how inflation and disinflation affect capital budgeting, and how to decide which projects to invest in when faced with a limited investment budget. In all cases, we base our decision on the goal of maximizing the value of the firm by accepting positive NPV projects.

Replacement Decisions

The firm is often faced with the alternative of keeping or replacing an existing asset due to normal wear or technological innovation. The replacement decision is especially complex because the manager must concentrate on incremental cash flows, that is, the cash flows related to the new equipment less that associated with the old.

In calculating incremental cash flows, a variety of factors need to be considered. The initial investment includes cost of equipment, all other costs related to the investment, additional working capital required, and any tax effects and opportunity costs. The change in operating CF contains the change in CFBT as well as the change in depreciation due to the new equipment.

It is also important to consider any terminal cash flows associated with the new project such as recovery of working capital. If the NPV of the incremental cash flows is positive, replacement should take place.

For example, suppose that Northwest Lumber Company is considering the replacement of a plywood glueing machine. Their present machine was purchased three years ago for $500,000 and is being depreciated according to the modified ACRS-five year factors. It can be sold for $250,000. The new machine can be bought for $700,000, has a lifetime of five years, and a zero resale value. The machine will result in labor savings of $150,000 per year over the old machine. The tax rate is 35 percent. If the required rate of return is 12 percent, should the existing machine be replaced?

First, let's calculate the initial outlay, CF_0.

CF_0 = Cost of new - selling price of old + tax effects of sale of old

Since the depreciated value of the old machine is $500,000 - (0.20 + 0.32 + 0.19)($500,000) = $145,000, the tax effect of the sale of the old equipment is 0.35($250,000 - $145,000) = $36,750, so CF_0 = $700,000 - $250,000 + $36,750 = $450,000 + $36,750 = $486,750.

According to the modified ACRS tables, the old machine would be depreciated at a rate of ($500,000)(0.15) = $75,000 in year 4, and ($500,000)(0.14) = $70,000 in year 5, so we can calculate ΔDep_t.

Year	Cost of New Machine	× ACRS Factor	= New Depreciation	− Old Depreciation	= ΔDep_t
1	$700,000	0.20	$140,000	$75,000	$ 65,000
2	700,000	0.32	224,000	70,000	154,000
3	700,000	0.19	133,000	0	133,000
4	700,000	0.15	105,000	0	105,000
5	700,000	0.14	98,000	0	98,000

Using this result, we can calculate ΔCF_t.

$$\Delta CF_t = \Delta CFBT_t(1 - T) + \Delta Dep_t$$

Year
1. $150,000(1 - 0.35) + \$ 65,000(0.35) = \$120,250$
2. $150,000(1 - 0.35) + 154,000(0.35) = 151,400$
3. $150,000(1 - 0.35) + 133,000(0.35) = 144,050$
4. $150,000(1 - 0.35) + 105,000(0.35) = 134,250$
5. $150,000(1 - 0.35) + 98,000(0.35) = 131,800$

The net present value of the incremental CF is

$$\begin{aligned}
NPV &= \$120,250(PV_{12\%,1yr}) + \$151,400(PV_{12\%,2yr}) + \$144,050(PV_{12\%,3yr}) \\
&\quad + 134,250(PV_{12\%,4yr}) + \$131,800(PV_{12\%,5yr}) - \$486,750 \\
&= \$120,250(0.893) + \$151,500(0.797) + \$44,0500(0.712) \\
&\quad + \$134,250(0.636) + \$131,800(0.567) - \$486,750 \\
&= \$107,383.25 + \$120,665.80 + \$102,563.60 + \$85,383.00 + \$74,730.60 \\
&\quad - \$486,750 = \$3,976.25
\end{aligned}$$

Since the NPV is positive, Northwest should replace its existing machine.

Interrelated Projects

Many projects cannot be analyzed independently as one project complements another. For example, suppose a developer owns a large tract of land and is considering three projects; a restaurant, a shopping center, and an apartment building. Unless the developer intends to accept only one project, he must consider the interrelationship between projects in order to decide how the land should be developed. The restaurant will do more business if the apartment building or the shopping center is nearby. Likewise, the proximity to shopping may be an important consideration for those moving into the apartment building and so on. The developer would need to evaluate the joint cash flows from seven possible combinations of projects in order to reach the optimal decision. These combinations are:

1. Restaurant alone.
2. Shopping center alone.
3. Apartment building alone.
4. Restaurant and shopping center.
5. Restaurant and apartment building.
6. Shopping center and apartment building.
7. Shopping center, apartment building, and restaurant.

After identifying all the possible combinations, the developer must determine the initial investment and cash flow stream for each project and calculate the NPV. The appropriate decision is to choose the combination with the highest NPV.

Mutually Exclusive Projects with Unequal Lives

Firms must often make decisions between mutually exclusive projects with unequal lives. Simply choosing the project with the highest NPV can be suboptimal; longer-lived projects have more time to build up positive NPVs. In order to make a valid comparison, it is necessary to equalize the lives of the projects.

One method of equalizing project lives is the equivalent annual NPV approach. This technique converts the project's original NPV to a yearly NPV and assumes that the projects are replicated over time in perpetuity so that NPVs can be stated as yearly figures. To see how the method is used, consider Fairchild Fasteners Company. Fairchild is contemplating the purchase of one of two mutually exclusive staple-making machines. Machine A costs $6,000 and promises CFs of $2,750 per year for its four year life. Machine B is more expensive; it costs $10,000, but the machine promises CFs of $3,000, and is expected to last seven years. Both machines have a required return of 16%. Which should be purchased?

First, let's calculate the NPV of each machine.

For machine A: $NPV_A = \$2,750(PVA_{16\%, 4yr}) - \$6,000$
$= \$2,750(2.798) - \$6,000$
$= \$7,694.50 - \$6,000 = \$1,694.50$

For machine B: $NPV_B = \$3,000(PVA_{16\%, 7yr}) - \$10,000$
$= \$3,000(4.039) - \$10,000$
$= \$12,117.00 - \$10,000 = \$2,117.00$

Machine B has a higher NPV, but it also has a longer life. Since the two NPVs are calculated over different lengths of time, you cannot directly compare them; you'll generally end up accepting the machine with the longer life since it has a longer time to build up its NPV.

To choose between the machines, you must convert the original NPVs to an equivalent annual NPV. To do so,

Equivalent annual $NPV_A = NPV_A/PVA_{16\%, 4yr} = \$1,694.50/2,798 = \$605.61$

Equivalent annual $NPV_B = NPV_B/PVA_{16\%, 7yr} = \$2,117.00/4.039 = \$524.14$

Machine A has the highest equivalent annual NPV and should be chosen over machine B. You should choose the project with the highest equivalent annual NPV since you have equalized the project lives and the approach is consistent with the goal of stockholder wealth maximization.

Remember that only in the case of mutually exclusive projects do we worry about unequal lives. For independent projects, you should choose the ones with positive NPVs.

More on Cash Flow Estimation

To this point, we've ignored some issues in cash flow estimation that are important. First, how do we adjust for inflation and disinflation? If inflation and disinflation affect both cash flows after taxes and required rate of return proportionally, we can ignore the effects. In other cases, we must incorporate our estimates into both. It is not an easy task, but it must be done in order to reach appropriate decisions.

Another issue is financing costs. Since interest on debt is tax deductible, you would think that we should account for its effect in calculating cash flows. This is generally not the case. For most projects, the capital budgeting decision is separate from the decision on how to finance the project.

Financial managers must make sure that they have examined all of the options available to the firm. One option often ignored is the option to abandon a present asset. If the firm can sell an asset for more than the present value of its CF, stockholders will be better off if the asset is sold. If modernization is an option, the relevant set of cash flows for decision making is the combination of existing cash flows and new cash flows due to modernization.

Capital Rationing

Capital rationing occurs when the firm places a limit on the money available for investment in long-term projects. In this case, not all positive NPV projects can be accepted. If this happens, you should choose the set of projects that fits the capital budget and has the highest total NPV. If the number of projects is small, this can be done by listing all possible combinations and calculating the NPV of each combination. If there are a large number of projects, linear programming should be used.

COMPLETION QUESTIONS

9.1 In replacement decisions, the relevant cash flows for analysis are _____.

9.2 Incremental operating CF includes the after-tax change in CFBT and _____.

9.3 If one of several _____ projects is undertaken, the cash flows to all related projects also increase.

9.4 The joint cash flows for two or more interrelated projects must be _____.

9.5 In deciding among _____ projects, you must insure that the lifetimes are equal.

9.6 The method for equalizing lifetimes is _____.

9.7 If both CFs and _____ are proportionally affected by inflation, inflation will not affect the capital budgeting decision.

9.8 The capital budgeting decision is separate from the _____ decision.

9.9 In cases in which inflation might be a factor, the projected _____ _____ should be adjusted to reflect inflation.

9.10 When the firm sets a limit on the size of the capital budget, it is faced with _____. In order to select from among the alternative projects, the firm will consider all possible combinations of positive net present value projects within the budget limit. The set of projects with the _____ will be selected.

PROBLEMS

9.1 Hebert Manufacturing is considering the replacement of a lathe used to turn table legs. The machine, which was purchased three years ago for $50,000 still has a useful life of five years. A more efficient lathe with a cost of $75,000 is being considered because the new machine will result in a reduction of expenses of $20,000 year over its five-year life. Both machines are being depreciated to zero using the modified ACRS factors for five years. The old machine could be sold now for $25,000 but, like the new machine, will be worthless at the end of five years. If the required rate of return is 10 percent, should the machine be replaced? The corporate tax rate is 40 percent.

9.2 Suppose a firm has available to it the following projects:

Project	Initial Investment	After-Tax Cash Flow per Year	Life
A	$100,000	$ 50,000	3
B	250,000	75,000	8
C	350,000	100,000	5
D	60,000	10,000	10
E	85,000	30,000	4
F	150,000	60,000	5
G	500,000	150,000	6
H	275,000	65,000	8

If the required rate of return is 18 percent, and the firm has available for investment only $600,000, which projects should be chosen?

9.3 Imported Auto Repair Center has recently purchased a plot of land to allow for expansion. Three possible projects are under consideration: a parts store, a gas station, and an automobile dealership. Each project has an expected life of 15 years. The parts store will cost $2 million and is expected to produce after-tax cash flows of $375,000 per year. The gas station would cost $500,000 and will produce after-tax cash flows of $85,000 per year. The dealership would cost $4 million and produce after-tax cash flows of $718,000 per year. Because of certain scale economies, the parts store could be combined with the dealership for a total cost of $5 million and would produce after-tax cash flows of $900,000. The gas station could be combined with any of the projects, but it is not expected that such a combination will result in any investment savings or changes in the cash flows. If Imported's required rate of return is 16 percent, what should it do?

9.4 Milliken Manufacturing Company, a producer of airplane parts, is considering two different plans for moving raw materials into its work area. Plan A is to invest $10 million in a fully automated assembly line that will result in labor savings of $3.0 million (before-tax) per year. Plan B is for a system of conveyor belts to bring raw materials into the work area where they will be moved manually into the appropriate work station. The conveyor belts are less costly, requiring an investment of $2 million; however, because of the labor intensity, the reduction in labor expense will be only $600,000 per year (before-tax). Both investments will be depreciated over five years according to the modified ACRS tables and have no resale value. If the fully automated assembly line has a useful lifetime of six years and the conveyors have a lifetime of ten years, which plan should the firm undertake if its required rate of return is 12 percent and the tax rate is 30 percent? Use the equivalent annual NPV approach to show your answer is correct.

ANSWERS TO COMPLETION QUESTIONS

9.1 incremental cash flows
9.2 the tax rate times the change in depreciation
9.3 complementary
9.4 analyzed together
9.5 mutually exclusive
9.6 the equivalent annual NPV approach
9.7 required rate of return
9.8 financing
9.9 cash flows
9.10 capital rationing; maximum total NPV

SOLUTIONS TO PROBLEMS

9.1

Step 1. Calculate the depreciated value of the old lathe.

Year	Original Cost	× ACRS Factors	= Depreciation
1	$50,000	0.20	$10,000
2	50,000	0.32	16,000
3	50,000	0.19	9,500
4	50,000	0.15	7,500
5	50,000	0.14	7,000

Undepreciated book value = $50,000 − ($10,000 + $16,000 + $9,500)
= $14,500

Step 2. Calculate incremental initial investment.

Cost of new lathe	$75,000
Less: Sale of old lathe	− 25,000
Plus: Tax on sale of old lathe ($25,000 − $14,500)(0.40)	4,200
Incremental initial investment	$54,200

Step 3. Calculate incremental depreciation.

Depreciation on new lathe

Year	Original Cost	× ACRS Factors	= Depreciation
1	$75,000	0.20	$15,000
2	75,000	0.32	24,000
3	75,000	0.19	14,250
4	75,000	0.15	11,250
5	75,000	0.14	10,500

Year	Depreciation on New Lathe	− Depreciation on Old Lathe	= Incremental Depreciation
1	$15,000	$7,500	$ 7,500
2	24,000	7,000	17,000
3	14,250	0	14,250
4	11,250	0	11,250
5	10,500	0	10.500

Step 4. There are no terminal cash flows.

Step 5. Calculate operating CFs.

Year	Δ CFBT	× (1 − T)	+ Δ Dep	× T =	Δ CF
1	$20,000	0.60	$ 7,500	0.40	$12,000 + $3,000 = $15,000
2	20,000	0.60	17,000	0.40	12,000 + 6,800 = 18,800
3	20,000	0.60	14,250	0.40	12,000 + 5,700 = 17,700
4	20,000	0.60	11,250	0.40	12,000 + 4,500 = 16,500
5	20,000	0.60	10,500	0.40	12,000 + 4,200 = 16,200

Step 6. NPV = $15,000(PV$_{10\%,1yr}$) + $18,800(PV$_{10\%,2yr}$) + $17,700(PV$_{10\%,3yr}$)

+ $16,500(PV$_{10\%,4yr}$) + $16,200(PV$_{10\%,5yr}$) − $54,200

= $15,000(0.909) + $18,800(0.826) + $17,700(0.751)

+ $16,500(0.683) + $16,200(0.621) − $54,200

= $13,635.00 + $15,528.80 + $13,292.70 + $11,269.50 + $10,060.20

− $54,200 = $9,586.20

Since the NPV is positive, replace the old lathe.

9.2

Step 1. Calculate the NPV of each project.

NPV$_A$ = $50,000(PVA$_{18\%,3yr}$) − $100,000 = $50,000(2.174) − $100,000
= $8,700

NPV$_B$ = $75,000(PVA$_{18\%,8yr}$) − $250,000 = $75,000(4.078) − $250,000
= $55,850

NPV$_C$ = $100,000(PVA$_{18\%,5yr}$) − $350,000 = $100,000(3.127) − $350,000
= −$37,300

NPV$_D$ = $10,000(PVA$_{18\%,10yr}$) − $60,000 = $10,000(4.494) − $60,000
= −$15,060

NPV$_E$ = $30,000(PVA$_{18\%,4yr}$) − $85,000 = $30,000(2.690) − $85,000
= −$4,300

NPV$_F$ = $60,000(PVA$_{18\%,5yr}$) − $150,000 = $60,000(3.127) − $150,000
= $37,620

NPV$_G$ = $150,000(PVA$_{18\%,6yr}$) − $500,000 = $150,000(3.498) − $500,000
= $24,700

NPV$_H$ = $65,000(PVA$_{18\%,8yr}$) − $275,000 = $65,000(4.078) − $275,000
= −$9,930

Step 2. Since projects C, D, E, and H have negative NPVs, the firm would never accept them. Consider only the remaining projects.

Project	Cost	NPV
A	$100,000	$ 8,700
B	250,000	55,850
F	150,000	37,620
G	500,000	24,700

Step 3. The firm can invest in combination A, B, F or combination A and G and remain within the capital budget.

$NPV_{ABF} = NPV_A + NPV_B + NPV_F$
$= \$8,700 + \$55,850 + \$37,620 = \$102,170$

$NPV_{AG} = NPV_A + NPV_G = \$8,700 + \$24,700 = \$33,400$

The appropriate combination is projects A, B, and F. Note that the firm does not exhaust its capital budget with this combination.

9.3

Step 1. Calculate the NPVs of the following projects:

   The parts store
   The gas station
   The automobile dealership
   The dealership and the parts store

If the NPV of the parts store is positive, we can add it to the alternative with the highest NPV.

Step 2. Parts store

$$NPV = \$375,000(PVA_{16\%,15yr}) - \$2,000,000$$
$$= \$375,000(5.575) - \$2,000,000 = \$90,625$$

Gas station

$$NPV = \$85,000(PVA_{16\%,15yr}) - \$500,000$$
$$= \$85,000(5.575) - \$500,000 = -\$26,125$$

Dealership

$$NPV = \$718,000(PVA_{16\%,15yr}) - \$4,000,000$$
$$= \$718,000(5.575) - \$4,000,000 = \$2,850$$

Dealership and parts store

$$NPV = \$900,000(PVA_{16\%,15yr}) - \$5,000,000$$
$$= \$900,000(5.575) - \$5,000,000 = \$17,500$$

Imported should build just the parts store. (Note: If the gas station had a positive NPV, the combinations to consider would increase since the gas station would have to be evaluated with each of the projects above.)

9.4

Step 1. Plan A

Calculate initial investment

Cost of equipment, $CF_0 = \$10,000,000$

Step 2. Calculate depreciation

Year	Cost of Equipment (in units of $1,000)	Modified ACRS Factors	Depreciation
1	$10,000	0.20	$2,000
2	10,000	0.32	3,200
3	10,000	0.19	1,900
4	10,000	0.15	1,500
5	10,000	0.14	1,400

Step 3. Operating cash flows (units of $1,000)

Year	CFBT	CFBT(1 − T)	+ Dep(T)	= CF
1	$3,000	$2,100	$600	$2,700
2	3,000	2,100	960	3,060
3	3,000	2,100	570	2,670
4	3,000	2,100	450	2,550
5	3,000	2,100	420	2,520
6	3,000	2,100	0	2,100

Step 4. $\text{NPV} = CF_1(PV_{12\%,1yr}) + CF_2(PV_{12\%,2yr}) + CF_3(PV_{12\%,3yr})$
$\qquad + CF_4(PV_{12\%,4yr}) + CF_5(PV_{12\%,5yr}) + CF_6(PV_{12\%,6yr}) - CF_0$

$\qquad = \$2{,}700(0.893) + \$3{,}060(0.797) + \$2{,}670(0.712) + \$2{,}550(0.636)$
$\qquad + \$2{,}520(0.567) + \$2{,}100(0.507) - \$10{,}000$

$\qquad = \$2{,}411.10 + \$2{,}438.82 + \$1{,}901.04 + \$1{,}621.80 + \$1{,}428.84$
$\qquad + \$1{,}064.70 - \$10{,}000 = \$866.30 \text{ or } \$866{,}300$

Step 5. Equivalent annual NPV

$$= \frac{\text{NPV}_n}{\text{PVA}_{12\%,6yr}} = \frac{\$866{,}300}{4.111} = \$210{,}727.32$$

Step 6. Plan B

Calculate initial investment

Cost of equipment, $CF_0 = \$2{,}000{,}000$

Step 7. Calculate depreciation

Year	Cost of Equipment (in units of $1,000)	Modified ACRS Factors	Depreciation
1	$2,000	0.20	$400
2	2,000	0.32	640
3	2,000	0.19	380
4	2,000	0.15	300
5	2,000	0.14	280

Step 8. Operating cash flows (units of $1,000)

Year	CFBT	CFBT(1 − T)	+ Dep(T)	= CF
1	$600	$420	$120	$540
2	600	420	192	612
3	600	420	114	534
4	600	420	90	510
5	600	420	84	504
6	600	420	0	420
7	600	420	0	420
8	600	420	0	420
9	600	420	0	420
10	600	420	0	420

Step 9. NPV = $CF_1(PV_{12\%,1yr}) + CF_2(PV_{12\%,2yr}) + CF_3(PV_{12\%,3yr})$

$+ CF_4(PV_{12\%,4yr}) + CF_5(PV_{12\%,5yr}) + CF_{6-10}(PVA_{12\%,5yr})$

$(PV_{12\%,5yr}) - CF_0$

= $540(0.893) + $612(0.797) + $534(0.712)+ $510(0.636)

+ $504(0.567) + $420(3.605)(0.567) - $2,000

= $482.22 + $487.76 + $380.21 + $324.36 + $285.77 + $858.49

- $2,000 = $818.81 or $818,100

Step 10. Equivalent annual NPV

$= \dfrac{NPV_n}{PVA_{12\%,10yr}} = \dfrac{\$818,100}{5.650} = \$144,796.46$

Choose plan A; it has the slightly higher equivalent annual NPV.

CHAPTER 10

RISK AND CAPITAL BUDGETING

HOW THIS CHAPTER RELATES TO THE REST OF THE TEXT

As we have seen in Chapters 8 and 9, capital budgeting decisions are based on cash flows (Chapter 4), their timing (Chapter 5), and the valuation process (Chapter 6). An important factor in determining value is the required rate of return, which is a function of risk (Chapter 7). This chapter discusses various methods of adjusting the required return to reflect the riskiness of the project. If the project is similar in risk to the firm, the firm's weighted average cost of capital (Chapter 14) can be employed. The riskiness of a project affects the business risk (Chapter 15) of the firm. Risk in international capital budgeting is discussed in Chapter 24.

TOPICAL OUTLINE

I. Risk and strategic decisions.
   A. Sources of risk.
      1. General economic conditions, such as a recession, can decrease the firm's cash flows below the expected level.
      2. Inflation can cause losses in capital budgeting projects if the projected inflation is below the actual inflation and if the firm is unable to pass the cost increases on to the customers.
      3. Projects themselves have unique risks due to the technological considerations of the individual project.
      4. Investments outside the United States are subject to the risk of currency fluctuations, unstable host governments, and expropriation.
      5. Risks can result in cash flows varying dramatically from their expected levels.
   B. Strategic decisions.
      1. All sources of risk are important in the capital budgeting process.
      2. Taking into account risk is one of the most difficult aspects in capital budgeting, but it cannot be ignored.

3. Risk may be beneficial; firms must expose themselves to risk in order to earn positive NPVs.
4. It is a mistake to think that discount rates must be increased in order to account for the greater riskiness of distant cash flows; the use of any rate above k_{RF} recognizes that more distant cash flows are proportionately more risky.

II. Required returns for capital budgeting decisions.
   A. Firm, divisional and project required returns.
      1. Some corporations use a single, firm-wide required rate of return, reflecting the cost of funds to the firm. That is, some firms use the weighted average cost of capital approach (Chapter 14).
      2. The divisional cost of capital approach assigns different required returns to projects in different divisions, based on the perceived risk of that division.
      3. Project-specific discount rates are based on the riskiness of the individual project.
         a. One such approach is the CAPM.
         b. The stand-alone principle states that a proposed project should be evaluated on its own merits; consider the opportunity costs of investing in another project of the same risk.
         c. Project-specific required returns are hard to estimate; part science and part judgement.
   B. What about portfolio effects?
      1. Investors diversify their own portfolios, so diversification should not be the goal of the firm.
      2. However, cash flow interactions among projects should be considered, since these interactions can affect the actual cash flows and their estimates.
   C. When a single discount rate cannot be used; sequential analysis.
      1. Probability distributions can produce the sequential outcomes of cash flows related to a capital budgeting project.
      2. The sum of the joint probabilities times the respective NPVs result in the project's NPV.

III. Information about project riskiness.
  A. Sensitivity analysis determines how sensitive NPV or IRR is to changes in input variables (cash flows, costs, discount rates, etc.).
  B. Break-even analysis: The break-even point occurs when the present value of inflows equals the present value of outflows.
    1. Use present values of cash inflows and outflows.
    2. Use equivalent annual cash flows.
        a. Equivalent annual cost = $\dfrac{\text{Initial investment}}{PVA_{k,n}}$
        b. Net equivalent annual cash flow =
           Gross cash inflow − (Variable cost + Fixed costs + Taxes + Equivalent annual cost)
    3. Break-even points calculated using GAAP ignore the opportunity cost of investment and are incorrect.
  C. Simulation is a technique that allows for changing all of the relevant variables in an analysis.
    1. Specify the relevant variables and interdependencies.
    2. Specify a probability distribution of possible values for each relevant variable.
    3. Randomly select values for each relevant variable.
    4. Calculate NPVs and IRRs using the values selected.
    5. Repeat the simulation, using new randomly selected variables, and graph NPVs and IRRs.
    6. Problems with simulation.
        a. Simulations are costly, time-consuming, and usually require computers.
        b. It is difficult to correctly specify interdependencies.
        c. Results are often difficult to interpret.
IV. Appendix 10A: Certainty equivalents (located at the end of the text).
  A. The certainty equivalent method adjusts the cash flows for risk and then discounts these cash flows using the risk-free rate.
  B. Certainty equivalent cash flows are what the firm would be willing to receive for certain in lieu of the possible distribution of cash flows for each year.

C. Steps for certainty equivalent method.
1. Determine the most likely cash flows for each year.
2. Calculate the certainty equivalent factors for each year.
3. Calculate the net present value using the following formula

$$NPV = \sum_{t=1}^{n} \frac{\alpha_t \overline{CF_t}}{(1 + k_{RF})^t} - \alpha_0 \overline{CF_0}$$

D. The major drawback is deriving the certainty equivalents; this process tends to be subjective.
E. To equate certainty equivalents with required return solutions, the implied certainty equivalent is equal to the risky PV divided by the risk-free PV.

FORMULAS

Required Return

Required return = risk-free rate + risk premium based on project risk

Capital Asset Pricing Model

Risk-adjusted discount rate = $k_{project} = k_{RF} + \beta_{project}(k_M - k_{RF})$

Appendix 10A

Certainty equivalent NPV = $\sum_{t=1}^{n} \frac{\alpha_t \overline{(CF)_t}}{(1 + k_{RF})^t} - \alpha_0 \overline{CF_0}$

$\alpha_t \, PV_{risk-free_t} = PV_{risky_t}$

$\alpha_t = \dfrac{PV_{risky_t}}{PV_{risk-free_t}}$

WHAT TO LOOK FOR

If we could predict the future accurately, we would not need to adjust our required returns for risk. We could have our fortunes made. Chapters 8 and 9 assumed that we could predict cash flows accurately. The discounting process we conducted merely adjusted the capital project cash flows for the time value of money and the firm's cost of funds, since we could invest in something else if we did not invest in the project.

In Chapter 10, we recognize that actual cash flows will probably vary from the expected cash flows. Managers must assign probabilities to the possible levels of cash flow and assign a discount rate appropriate to the cash flow riskiness. This discount rate increases as the cash flows' variability or risk increases. We will look at several methods of considering project risk, including firm-wide, divisional, and project-specific required rates of return, break-even analysis, sequential analysis, and sensitivity analysis.

Risk-Adjusted Discount Rates

Essentially, the required return should be the risk-free rate plus some risk premium appropriate to the project. We use this just as we used the required rate of return in Chapters 8 and 9 when we calculated net present value. Alternatively, the required return can be the hurdle rate when the internal rate of return method is employed. The required rate of return approach implicitly compensates for risk by assuming it increases as a function of time. If you suspect that a project's risk will vary for other reasons, you might assign a different rate for each year's cash flows. Although it is difficult to decide how and when the risk of a project will change, this adjustment is necessary and appropriate.

Measuring Project Risk

In Chapter 7, we considered risk as variability from the expected value. This variability is due to economic factors, inflation and disinflation, international factors, and project-specific factors. These factors can significantly affect the required rate of return and the variability of the project's expected cash flows. For example, a recession can reduce expected sales revenue, or a Federal Reserve tightening of money can push inflation down and increase the whole structure of interest rates.

Firms use a variety of approaches to analyze risk in capital budgeting. The technique used depends on your assumptions about risk. For instance, some approaches assume that risk is constant throughout the project's life. They are:

Weighted average cost of capital

The weighted average cost of capital (WACC) approach, suggests that the return from an acceptable project will exceed the firm's cost of the last dollar of new funds. This rate is appropriate for projects such as replacement projects that are similar to the firm.

Divisional required returns

The divisional required rate of return approach requires that the risk involved in each division's projects be evaluated. Each division is then assigned an appropriate required return, assuming risk is the same for all projects within the division. For example, consider Xerox Corporation. They have a division that produces office equipment, such as copiers, and a division that retails office products, such as paper. Each division has associated with it certain risk characteristics and it is likely that each should use its own discount rate.

Project-specific reuired rates of return

Each project is unique, and as such, has its own risk characteristics. Appropriate capital budgeting requires that this risk be reflected in discount rates. One method of doing so is to employ the CAPM using the project's beta. However, in practice, this procedure can be difficult to implement since project betas are hard to calculate.

Other Techniques for Analyzing Project Risk

Sequential analysis

Sequential analysis uses the probability distribution information to consider sequential cash flow outcomes and NPVs for a capital budgeting project. The sum of the joint probabilities times the net present values gives the project's expected NPV. Use of sequential analysis is limited since it cannot easily consider all possible outcomes in many realistic situations.

Sensitivity analysis

Sensitivity analysis focuses on how sensitive the NPV or IRR is to change in any of the input variables, such as initial investment or the discount rate. Managers can ask "what if" questions and look at how much variability can occur in each variable before the project's NPV becomes negative. They can then focus on these critical variables. Recent advances in computer technology have made this kind of analysis much more available.

Break-even analysis

Break-even analysis enables you to determine the point at which the present value of the cash inflows equals the present values of the outflows; the point at which NPV equals zero. From this point, you can calculate the minimum level of sales needed to justify the project.

For example, Moonbeam Herbal Tea is considering the addition of a new tea bag packaging machine. The machine costs $10,000 and is expected to last ten years. It will be depreciated using straight-line depreciation. Costs of goods sold amount to 80% of sales and fixed costs are $2,000. If the tax rate is 30%, and the required rate of return is 16%, what kind of sales are necessary?

To solve this problem, first calculate the equivalent annual cost:

$$\text{Equivalent annual cost} = \frac{\text{Initial investment}}{PVA_{16\%,10yr}} = \frac{\$10,000}{4.833} = \$2,069.10$$

The machine needs to generate cash inflows of $2,069.10 per year to be justifiable.

Yearly cash inflow is equal to:

CF_t = sales - variable and fixed costs - taxes

Variable costs equal (0.80)(sales), and taxes equal

(sales - variable + fixed costs - depreciation)(T)

= [sales - (0.80 sales + $2,000) - $\frac{\$10,000}{10 \text{ yrs}}$](0.30)

= 0.06sales - $900

so, CF_t = sales - (0.80 sales + $2,000) - (0.06sales - $900)

= 0.14sales - $1,100

Setting CF_t equal to the equivalent annual cost,

CF_t = 0.14sales - $1,100 = $2,069.10

sales = $3,169.10/0.14 = $22,636.43

If the company can increase sales by $22,636.43 per year, the new machine will have a positive NPV.

Simulation

The advent of modern computers has allowed more firms to use simulation to evaluate capital budgeting projects. In a simulation, all relevant variables can be changed and a profile of possible values of NPVs and IRRs can be generated. Although difficult, simulation is useful in determining the liklihood that a project will have a positive NPV. With this additional information, managers can make more informed decisions about project acceptability.

COMPLETION QUESTIONS

10.1 Since the actual returns from a project are not known until after the firm invests in the project, _____ exists.

10.2 Firms unable to pass on the impact of inflation to their customers have _____ inflation or disinflation risk than those which can readily increase their prices.

10.3 A project employing advanced state-of-the-art technology would have more _____ than a replacement project.

10.4 The CAPM is a _____ model which is not entirely appropriate for making long-term capital budgeting decisions.

10.5 The risk premium approach assumes that risk changes purely as _____. The required return is equal to the risk-free rate and _____. To take into account risk changes that are not time related, _____ may be employed.

10.6 _____ is the risk apparent in the cash flows associated with a project resulting from sensitivity to the economy, inflation, and other risk sources.

10.7 A project less risky than the firm as a whole would have a required return that is _____ the firm's weighted average cost of capital.

10.8 _____ uses probability distribution information to consider cash flow outcomes and NPVs for a capital budgeting project.

10.9 _____ does not formally quantify risk, but focuses on determining which factors have the greatest effect on net present value.

10.10 The _____ is the point where the present value of cash inflows equals the present value of the outflows and the NPV equals zero.

10.11 In an efficient market, firms should ignore _____ effects since investors can diversify themselves.

10.12 A _____ is the risk-free cash flow that has the same present value as a risky cash flow occuring in the same time period.

PROBLEMS

10.1 J. M. Richardson Company has under consideration a project with a cost of $50,000 and the following cash flows:

Year	CF
1	$10,000
2	14,000
3	18,000
4	15,000
5	14,000
6	21,849

If k_{RF} = 8 percent and k_M = 16 percent, what is the maximum beta the project could have and still be acceptable?

10.2 Snap-Tight Tool Company is considering a project with a cost of $100,000 and CFs of $22,500 per year for the eight year life of the project.

a. If the k_{RF} is 10 percent and the risk premium is 3 percent, should the project be accepted?

b. Suppose the firm used a WACC approach. If the WACC for Snap-Tight is 17 percent and the risk premium is the same, should the project be accepted?

10.3 Miller Snack Stand is considering the installation of ice cream making equipment with a cost of $150,000 and an expected life of nine years. The machine has expected CFs of $40,000 for each year of its life. Since Miller does not currently make ice cream, the manager regards this as a risky venture, at least initially. He has determined the appropriate discount rates are as follows:

Years	Required Return
1-3	20%
4-6	16
7-9	10

Calculate the NPV and determine if the equipment should be bought.

10.4 Morely Vacuum Cleaners is considering an expansion project that will enable them to make vacuum cleaner bags. The necessary equipment will require an initial cash outflow today of $100,000 and an increase in working capital of $20,000 <u>next</u> year. The equipment will be depreciated over five years using straight-line depreciation and the working capital investment will be recovered in year 5. Costs of goods sold amount to 60% of sales and fixed costs are $10,000 per year. If the required return on investment is 14%, and the tax rate is 35%, what is the break-even level of sales?

10.5 CK Enterprises is considering a two-phase project to enable them to produce bottled soft drinks. Phase 1 requires a cash outflow of $1 million in year 0 and is expected to generate CFs in year 1 of $1.2 million with probability 0.6 or $0.5 million with probability 0.4. If, in fact, the year 1 cash flow is $1.2 million, the firm will invest (also in year 1) another $5 million in Phase 2, which is expected to yield CFs of $1.5 million per year for five years (in years 2-6). Since Phase 1 is more risky, its required return is 15%; Phase 2's required return is 10%. Using sequential analysis, determine if this project is acceptable.

10A.1 Mountaintop Preserves, a manufacturer of homemade jams and jellies, is considering the purchase of a new canning machine and wishes to use a certainty equivalent approach. Cash flows and certainty equivalents are listed below:

Year	$\overline{CF}_t$	α_t
Initial Investment	$7,000	1.00
1	1,200	0.94
2	1,500	0.88
3	1,800	0.82
4	1,900	0.76
5	2,000	0.71
6	2,200	0.67

If k_{RF} = 6 percent, should the machine be purchased?

ANSWERS TO COMPLETION QUESTIONS

10.1 uncertainty (or risk)
10.2 more
10.3 project-specific risk
10.4 single-period
10.5 a function of time; a risk premium; a different required return for each year

10.6 Project-specific risk
10.7 less thanl analysis
10.8 Sequential analysis
10.9 Sensitivity analysis
10.10 break-even point
10.11 portfolio
10.12 certainty equivalent

SOLUTIONS TO PROBLEMS

10.1

Step 1. Find the IRR of the project using the technique presented in Chapter 8. To find the average cash flow:

$$\overline{CF} = \frac{\$10,000 + \$14,000 + \$18,000 + \$15,000 + \$14,000 + \$21,849}{6}$$

$$= \$15,474.83$$

The simulated annuity IRR is found where

$$\$15,474.83(PVA_{IRR,6yr}) - \$50,000 = 0$$

$$PVA_{IRR,6yr} = 50,000/\$15,474.83 = 3.231$$

The factor lies between 21 percent and 22 percent in the PVA tables. Thus, the simulated annuity based IRR is between 21 and 22 percent. This provides a starting point for determining the actual IRR on the project.

Step 2. Starting at 21 percent

$$NPV = \$10,000(PV_{21\%,1yr}) + \$14,000(PV_{21\%,2yr}) + \$18,000(PV_{21\%,3yr})$$
$$+ \$15,000(PV_{21\%,4yr}) + \$14,000(PV_{21\%,5yr}) + \$21,849(PV_{21\%,6yr})$$
$$- \$50,000$$

$$= \$10,000(0.826) + \$14,000(0.683) + \$18,000(0.564)$$
$$+ \$15,000(0.467) + \$14,000(0.386) + \$21,849(0.319) - \$50,000$$

$$= \$8,260 + \$9,562 + \$10,152 + \$7,005 + \$5,404 + \$6,970 - \$50,000$$

$$= -\$2,647$$

Since the NPV is negative, the IRR is lower than 21 percent.

Step 3. Try 19 percent

$$NPV = \$10,000(0.840) + \$14,000(0.706) + \$18,000(0.593)$$
$$+ \$15,000(0.499) + \$14,000(0.419) + \$21,849(0.352) - \$50,000$$
$$= \$8,400 + \$9,884 + \$10,674 + \$7,485 + \$5,866 + \$7,691 - \$50,000$$
$$= 0$$

The IRR is 19 percent.

Step 4. From the CAPM, $k_{project\ j} = k_{RF} + \beta_j(k_M - k_{RF})$

$$19\% = 8\% + \beta_j(16\% - 8\%)$$

$$\beta_j = \frac{19\% - 8\%}{16\% - 8\%} = \frac{11\%}{8\%} = 1.375$$

If the project's beta is greater than 1.375, its required rate of return (or discount rate) will be greater than its IRR, and its NPV will be negative.

10.2a

Step 1. $k = k_{RF} + \text{risk premium} = 10\% + 3\% = 13\%$

Step 2. $NPV = CF_{1-8}(PVA_{13\%,8yr}) - CF_0 = \$22,500(4.799) - \$100,000$

$$= \$7,977.50$$

Since the NPV is positive, the project is acceptable.

10.2b

Step 3. $NPV = CF_{1-8}(PVA_{17\%,8yr}) - CF_0 = \$22,500(4.207) - \$100,000$

$$= -\$5,342.50$$

Since the NPV is negative, the project should not be accepted.

10.3 $NPV = CF_{1-3}(PVA_{20\%,3yr}) + CF_{4-6}(PVA_{16\%,3yr})(PV_{20\%,3yr})$

$$+ CF_{7-9}(PVA_{10\%,3yr})(PV_{16\%,3yr})(PV_{20\%,3yr}) - CF_0$$

$$= \$40,000(2.106) + \$40,000(2.246)(0.579) + \$40,000(2.487)(0.641)$$
$$(0.579) - \$150,000$$

$$= \$84,240 + \$52,017.36 + \$36,920.91 - \$150,000 = \$23,178.27$$

Since the NPV is positive, the project should be accepted.

10.4

Step 1. Calculate the present value of the cash outflows less the present value of the inflow from the recovery of working capital. (This accounts for all cash flows that do not occur _each_ year). The answer is the present value of the investment we need to recoup.

PV_0 = $100,000 + $20,000($PV_{14\%, 1yr}$) - $20,000($PV_{14\%, 5yr}$)

= $100,000 + $20,000(0.877) - $20,000(0.519)

= $100,000 + $17,540 - $10,380

= $107,160

Step 2. Calculate the equivalent annual cost.

equivalent annual cost = $107,160/$PVA_{14\%, 5yr}$ = $107,160/3.433

= $31,214.68

Step 3. Calculate depreciation.

$depreciation_{1-5}$ = $100,000/5 = $20,000

Step 4. Express CF in terms of sales.

CF_t = sales - (variable + fixed costs) - taxes

= sales - (0.60sales + $10,000) - (sales - 0.60sales - $10,000 - $20,000)(0.35)

= 0.40sales - $10,000 - (0.14sales - $10,500)

= 0.26sales + $500

Step 5. Set CF_t equal to the equivalent annual cost and solve for sales.

0.26sales + $500 = $31,214.68

0.26sales = $31,214.68 - $500

sales = $30,714.69/0.26 = $118,133.39

10.5

Step 1. We can represent the cash flows in the following fashion:
(using units of $1,000)

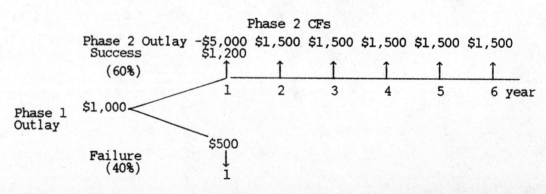

Step 2. Phase 2 NPV (in year 1) = $1,500(PVA$_{10\%,5yr}$) - $5,000
(if successful)

$$= \$1,500(3.791) - \$5,000$$

$$= \$5,686.50 - \$5,000 = \$686.50$$

Step 3. Phase 2 Expected Present Value in year 1 = 0.6(686.50) = $411.90

Step 4. Phase 2 Expected NPV in year 0 = $411.90(PV$_{15\%,1yr}$)

$$= \$411.90(0.870) = \$358.35$$

Step 5. Phase 1 Expected CF in year 1 = 0.6($1,200) + 0.4($500)

$$= \$720 + \$200 = \$920$$

Step 6. Phase 1 NPV in year 0 = $920(PV$_{15\%,1yr}$) - $1,000

$$= \$920(0.870) - \$1,000$$

$$= \$800.40 - \$1,000 = -\$199.60$$

So NPV = $358.35 - $199.60 = $158.75 and the project is acceptable.

10A.1 NPV = $1,200(0.94)(PV$_{6\%,1yr}$) + $1,500(0.88)(PV$_{6\%,2yr}$)

$\quad$ + $1,800(0.82)(PV$_{6\%,3yr}$) + $1,900(0.76)(PV$_{6\%,4yr}$)

$\quad$ + $2,000(0.71)(PV$_{6\%,5yr}$) + $2,200(0.67)(PV$_{6\%,6yr}$) - $7,000

$\quad$ = $1,128(0.943) + $1,320(0.890) + $1,476(0.840) + $1,444(0.792)

$\quad$ + $1,420(0.747) + $1,474(0.705) - $7,000

$\quad$ = $1,063.70 + $1,174.80 + $1,239.84 + $1,143.65 + $1,060.74

$\quad$ + $1,039.17 - $7,000

$\quad$ = -$278.10

Since the NPV is negative, the machine should not be purchased.

CHAPTER 11

OPTIONS AND INVESTMENT DECISIONS

HOW THIS CHAPTER RELATES TO THE REST OF THE TEXT

Options are contracts that give the owner the right to buy or sell assets at a fixed price over a specified period of time. Many aspects of financial management, such as warrants attached to bonds (Chapter 12), rights offerings (Chapter 12), options to buy other firms and merge (Chapter 22), and capital budgeting (Chapters 8 - 10) have options imbedded in them. Good financial management requires that the firm understand options and their requirements.

TOPICAL OUTLINE

I. Some definitions of option terms.
   A. A call option provides the owner the right to buy the underlying asset at a specified price (the exercise or strike price) over some time period.
   B. A put option provides the owner the right to sell the underlying asset at a specified price over some time period.
   C. The act of purchasing or selling the underlying asset is called exercising the option.
   D. The maturity (exercise) date is when the option expires. After expiration, the option is worthless.
   E. An American option can be exercised anytime up to and including the expiration date; an European option can be exercised only on the expiration date.
   F. An option contract is written on 100 shares, but option prices are quoted on a per share basis.
   G. The option contract specifies the underlying security, the exercise price, and the expiration date.
II. Valuing European call options.
   A. Basic determinants of call option value.
      1. Everything else being equal, the higher the exercise price (X), the lower the value of the call option.

2. The longer the time to expiration (t), the higher the call option value, other things being equal.
3. The value of the call option is positively related to the risk-free rate of interest (k_{RF}).
4. Other things being equal, the higher the stock price (P_0), the higher the value of a call option.
5. The greater the variability (standard deviation) of the underlying asset (σ), the higher the value of a call option.

B. The Black-Scholes option pricing model.
   1. Terms:
      a. V_c = the value of the call option.
      b. P_0 = the current stock price.
      c. X = the exercise price.
      d. t = time to expiration.
      e. k_{RF} = the risk-free rate of interest in decimal form.
      f. σ = the stock's standard deviation.
      g. e = 2.71828
      h. ln() = the natural logarithm.
      i. N(d) = the probability from a standard normal distribution that a variable will be less than or equal to d.
   2. The model: $V_c = P_0 N(d_1) - \dfrac{X}{e^{k_{RF}t}} N(d_2)$

      where $d_1 = \dfrac{\ln(P_0/X) + (k_{RF} + 0.5\sigma^2)t}{\sigma\sqrt{t}}$

      $d_2 = d_1 - \sigma\sqrt{t}$

      a. Calculate d_1 and d_2.
      b. Look up the values for $N(d_1)$ and $N(d_2)$ in Table F.6
      c. Using $N(d_1)$ and $N(d_2)$, compute the value of the call option, V_c.
   3. Assumptions in the Black-Scholes option pricing model.
      a. No taxes or transactions costs.
      b. k_{RF} is constant over the option's life.
      c. The stock market operates continually.
      d. The stock price is continuous; there are no sudden jumps in price.

e. The stock pays no cash dividends.

f. The option can only be exercised at expiration.

g. Short selling is allowed.

h. The distribution of returns is log-normal.

4. In spite of the restrictive assumptions, the Black-Scholes model is a good predictor of actual option prices.

C. A short-cut approach to valuing call options.

1. Calculate the standard deviation times the square root of time.

2. Calculate the market price divided by the present value of the exercise price.

3. Using the two values, determine the factor using Table F.7.

4. Multiply the tabled factor by the share price to determine the value of a call.

III. Valuing put options.

A. A put option is an option to sell the underlying asset at a specified price.

B. Put call parity: The value of a call plus the present value of the exercise price equals the value of a put plus the value of the stock.

1. Formula for calculating the value of a put option:

$$V_p = V_c + X/e^{k_{RF}t} - P_0$$

C. Use Table F.8 to calculate put values using the short-cut method.

IV. Options in financial management.

A. A warrant is a long-term call option; the owner has the right to buy shares of stock at a fixed price over a period of time.

1. Warrants are often attached to privately placed debt.

B. Options in capital investment.

1. An example of a call option is an option to purchase another firm.

2. The acceptance of a capital budgeting project often carries with it an option for future investment.

3. The option to abandon a capital investment is a put option.

4. Guarantees are also put options.

5. If a capital expenditure contains an option, the option value must be considered in calculating the true net present value of the expenditure.

V. Appendix 11A: Valuing the firm using the option pricing model (located at the end of the text).
   A. Common stock in a levered firm is similar to a call option.
      1. The face value of debt is the exercise price.
      2. Stockholders can exercise the option by paying off the bondholders.
   B. Stockholders also own a put option (or option to default).
   C. The value of the stock plus the value of riskless bonds equals the value of the right to default plus the market value of the firm's assets.
   D. Use the option pricing model to calculate the value of the stock (a call option) using the value of the firm's assets as the stock price.
   E. Use the put call parity relationship to calculate the value of the option to default.

FORMULAS

Notation

P_0 = the price of the underlying asset

X = the exercise price of the option

t = time to expiration

σ = the standard deviation of the underlying asset

k_{RF} = the continuously compounded risk-free rate

e = 2.71828

$\ln()$ = the natural logarithm of the number in the brackets

$N(d)$ = the probability from a cumulative standard normal distribution that a random number will be less than or equal to d.

Black-Scholes Option Pricing Model

$$V_c = P_0 N(d_1) - \frac{X}{e^{k_{RF}t}} N(d_2)$$

$$d_1 = \frac{\ln(P_0/X) + (k_{RF} + 0.5\sigma^2)t}{\sigma\sqrt{t}}$$

$$d_2 = d_1 - \sigma\sqrt{t}$$

Value of a Put Option

$$V_p = V_c + X/e^{k_{RF}t} - P_0$$

Valuing the Firm Using the Option Pricing Model

Notation

default option = value of the option to default
V = market value of the firm
S = market value of stock
V_B = value of riskless bonds
M = face value of bonds
B = value of risky debt

Formulas

$$V_B = M/e^{k_{RF}t}$$

$$S = VN(d_1) - \frac{M}{e^{k_{RF}t}} N(d_2)$$

$$d_1 = \frac{\ln(V/M) + [k_{RF} + 0.5\sigma^2]t}{\sigma\sqrt{t}}$$

$$d_2 = d_1 - \sigma\sqrt{t}$$

default option = $S + V_B - V$

$B = V - S = V_B$ - default option

WHAT TO LOOK FOR

Many decisions made by financial managers contain options. An option is simply a contract that gives the owner the right to buy or sell an asset at a specific price over some specified time period. For instance, a firm may purchase a piece of manufacturing equipment from a supplier and the supplier may agree to sell additional pieces at the same price for the next year. This option has value; correct decisionmaking requires that managers understand what affects option values and how they are calculated.

Call Options

A call option gives the option owner the right to purchase the underlying asset at a fixed price over some time period. The owner of a May $55 call option on Hewlett Packard stock has the right to purchase 100 shares of Hewlett Packard stock at $55 per share ($5,500 total) up until the end of May, irrespective of the market price of the stock. If HP is trading for $58 per share when the option expires, the owner of the call will exercise the option and buy the stock for $55 per share, $3 less than the market price. Buying a call option is a bet that the market price of the stock will rise above the exercise price before expiration.

Put Options

The owner of a put option has the right to sell an asset at a specified price over some period of time. For example, suppose your firm buys a fleet of trucks. The truck dealer agrees to buy the trucks back at the end of three years for $10,000 each. Your firm owns a put option. If, three years from now, the value of a truck falls below $10,000, your firm still has the right to sell the trucks for that price. The owner of a put option is wagering that the market price of an asset will fall below the exercise price.

Factors Affecting Call Option Values

In an important paper, Fischer Black and Myron Scholes developed a model for calculating call options. The model shows that a call option's value is related to five factors. Let's examine how each factor affects value while holding the others constant.

Exercise price

The higher the exercise price, the lower the value of a call option. Imagine two options, one with an exercise price of $10, and one with an exercise price of $100. If the stock is trading today for $25, and the option expires in one week, it is quite likely that, at expiration, the stock will be worth more than $10, but less than $100 per share. Thus, the option with the lower exercise price will be worth more since its owner will make a profit.

Time to expiration

Imagine two call options on the same stock, both with exercise prices of $25 per share. The first option expires in one month, the second in six months. If the stock is trading for $20 per share, it would need to increase in value by at least $5 per share (25%) for the option to be exercised. It is more likely that the stock price will increase by that amount over six months than over one month. The longer the term to expiration, the higher the value of the call option.

The risk-free rate of interest

The value of a call option must be at least today's stock price less the present value of the exercise price. As the risk-free rate rises, the present value of the exercise price falls and the value of the call option increases.

Stock price

The profit from investing in call options is the difference between the stock price and the exercise price. The higher the stock price, the larger the profit. Thus, call option values are positively related to the stock price.

Standard deviation of the stock

The more variable the stock price is, the higher the value of the call option. The higher the variability in stock prices, the more likely it is that the stock price will be above the exercise price at maturity.

Using the Black-Scholes Option Pricing Model

The Black-Scholes option pricing model looks (and is) very complex, but with the help of a good calculator and Table F.6 in your text, we can use the model to value call options. The Black-Scholes model is:

$$V_c = P_0 N(d_1) - \frac{X}{e^{k_{RF} t}} N(d_2)$$

where

$$d_1 = \frac{\ln(P_0/X) + (k_{RF} + 0.5\sigma^2)t}{\sigma\sqrt{t}}$$

and

$$d_2 = d_1 - \sigma\sqrt{t}$$

Suppose we wish to calculate the value of a call option on Westland, Inc.'s common stock. The exercise price is $75 per share and the stock price is $71 per share. The option expires in three months (25% of one year), the risk-free rate is 10% per year, and $\sigma = 36\%$. What is the value of the call option?

First, calculate d_1 and d_2.

$$d_1 = \frac{\ln(P_0/X) + (k_{RF} + 0.5\sigma^2)t}{\sigma\sqrt{t}}$$

$$= \frac{\ln(71/75) + [0.10 + 0.5(0.36)^2](0.25)}{0.36\sqrt{0.25}}$$

$$= \frac{-0.0548 + (0.1648)(0.25)}{(0.36)(0.50)}$$

$$= -0.0756$$

$$d_2 = d_1 - \sigma\sqrt{t}$$

$$= -0.0756 - 0.36\sqrt{0.25}$$

$$= -0.2256$$

Now, look up $N(d_1)$ and $N(d_2)$ in Table F.6 in the text. If you interpolate correctly, $N(d_1) = 0.4699$, and $N(d_2) = 0.3991$.

Next, use the Black-Scholes formula to solve for the value of a call.

$$V_c = P_0 N(d_1) - \frac{X}{e^{k_{RF}t}} N(d_2)$$

$$= 71(0.4699) + \frac{75}{e^{0.10(0.25)}} (0.3991)$$

$$= 33.3629 + \frac{75}{e^{0.025}} (0.3991)$$

$$= 33.3629 - 29.1935$$

$$= \$4.17$$

An individual purchasing this call option would pay $4.17 per share or $417.00 ($4.17 × 100 shares) for it.

Calculating option values using the Black-Scholes model can be quite complex. The text discusses a short-cut approach using Table F.7 to estimate call option values. Although the answers using this approach are not precise, they are easier to compute.

Valuing Put Options

Puts are options to sell. Put values can be calculated by taking advantage of put call parity. The value of a put is:

$$V_p = V_c + \frac{X}{e^{k_{RF}t}} - P_0$$

A put option on the above stock with the same exercise price and expiration date can be valued as:

$$V_p = \$4.17 + \frac{75}{e^{0.10(0.25)}} - 71$$

$$= 4.17 + 73.15 - 71$$

$$= \$6.32$$

An investor will be willing to pay $6.32 per share for the right to sell this stock at $75 per share in three months. Again, there is a short-cut method using Table F.8 to estimate put values.

Options in Financial Management

Most people think of options traded on major exchanges when the topic is mentioned. However, options are present in many of the firm's activities. An obvious example of a call option is a warrant. When firms privately place new debt, they often attach warrants as a "sweetener" to make the issue more attractive. A warrant is simply a long-term call option; its owner has a right to buy shares of a company at a fixed price over some time period.

For example, suppose Morrison Communications plans to issue ten year $1,000 bonds. The current market rate of interest on bonds of equivalent risk is 12%, but the company will issue the debt with a 10% coupon rate. The bond owner will also receive warrants allowing the purchase of 10 shares of common stock at $50 per share. The stock is presently trading for $30 per share, the risk-free rate is 8%, and $\sigma = 36\%$. If the warrants expire in five years, what should be the issue price of the bond package?

We can calculate the value of the bond by computing the value of each component (the straight bond and the warrant) and adding them together. From Chapter 6, the value of a straight bond is:

$$B_0 = I(PVA_{k\%, n \text{ yr}}) + M(PV_{k\%, n \text{ yr}})$$

$$= \$100(PVA_{12\%, 10yr}) + \$1,000(PV_{12\%, 10yr})$$

$$= \$100(5.650) + \$1,000(0.322)$$

$$= \$887.00$$

To value each warrant, first calculate $\sigma\sqrt{t} = 0.36\sqrt{5} = 0.80$. Next, calculate the share price divided by the present value of the exercise price.

$$\frac{30}{50/e^{0.08(5)}} = \frac{30}{33.516} = 0.90$$

From Table F.7, the factor is 0.2752, so the value of each warrant = $30(0.2752) = $8.26. Since there are ten warrants per bond, the issue should sell for:

$$P_0 = \$887.00 + 10(\$8.26) = \$969.60$$

Other options exist as well. For example, a firm may engage in a contract to purchase shares in another firm for a fixed price, or a supplier may agree to sell goods at a contracted price. Capital budgeting projects often contain implied options since they may lead to future projects. The value of each of these call options must be considered in order to make appropriate decisions.

Put options also exist for the firm. The option to sell an existing asset at a specified price and abandon a project is a put option. Suppose a firm is considering a project with a cost of $1,000,000 and a PV of cash flows of $940,000. The NPV of the project is $940,000 - $1,000,000 = -$60,000, which is negative. But, suppose the firm has the option to abandon the project at the end of one year and sell the assets for $800,000. The risk-free rate is 10%, and $\sigma = 0.60$. The put option's value must be considered before the decision can be made. Using the three-step short-cut:

$$\sigma\sqrt{t} = 0.60\sqrt{1} = 0.60$$

$$\frac{P_0}{X/e^{k_{RF}t}} = \frac{\$940,000}{\$800,000/e^{0.10(1)}} = 1.30$$

From Table F.8, the factor is 0.1121, so the value of the put option is 0.1121(940,000) = $105,374. The "true" NPV of the project, including the option value, is -$60,000 + $105,374 = $45,374, which is positive. Failure to include the option value would have led to an incorrect decision.

<u>Valuing the Firm Using Option Pricing</u> (Appendix 11A located at the end of the text)

Option pricing is useful in determining where stock values come from. Consider a typical firm. The firm owns assets which generate cash flows. The firm is financed in part, by common stock and in part, by debt. The presence of debt in a firm's capital structure leads to two options.

First, common stock can be viewed as a call option. If the firm does well, stockholders have the right to buy the firm's assets from the bondholders for a fixed price (the face value of debt). From the put call parity relationship,

$$V_c = P_0 - \frac{X}{e^{k_{RF}t}} + V_p$$

We can see that the owners of the stock also own a put option. In this case, the put option is the right to default on debt if the firm does poorly. Because of limited liability, stockholders can lose only their investment, they cannot be held liable for the firm's debt. This default option is valuable to stockholders. In other words,

$$\text{Value of stock} = \text{value of the firm's assets} - \text{value of riskless bonds} + \text{default options}$$

If we know the various factors necessary to use the option pricing model, we can use it to calculate the value of the firm's stocks and bonds. The model can also provide insights into the sources of conflict between stock and bondholders.

COMPLETION QUESTIONS

11.1 A _____ option is the right to buy an asset at a specific price over some time period.

11.2 A put option is the right to _____ an asset at a specific price over some period of time.

11.3 Call option values are inversely related to the _____.

11.4 The _____ price of an option is the stated purchase or sale price.

11.5 _____ are often attached to privately placed debt issues and can be valued as call options.

11.6 _____ options can only be exercised on the expiration date, while _____ options can be exercised up to and including the expiration date.

11.7 A call option is a bet that the asset will _____ in price while a put option is a bet that the asset will _____ in price.

11.8 A guarantee is an example of a _____ option.

11.9 Common stock in a firm can be considered a _____ option since the stockholders can buy the firm's assets from the bondholders by paying the _____.

11.10 Stockholders own a put option since they can _____ on the firm's debt.

11.11 Capital budgeting projects often contain _____ since they can lead to future investments.

11.12 The decision to _____ a project and sell the assets is really a put option.

PROBLEMS

11.1 Nordik Sports' common stock is selling for $16 per share. Using the Black-Scholes option pricing model, calculate the value of a call option and a put option with six months to maturity and an exercise price of $20 per share assuming $\sigma = 0.40$, and $k_{RF} = 0.12$.

For the problems 11.2 to 11.6, approximate the option values using the factors in Tables F.7 and F.8.

11.2 The common stock of Edwards Electrical Supply is presently selling for $69 per share. Approximate the value of a three-month call option and a three-month put option with an exercise price of $75 assuming $k_{RF} = 0.08$ and $\sigma = 0.30$.

11.3 Bulldog Lock Company is issuing debt with warrants attached. Each warrant enables the owner to purchase a share of common stock at $35 per share in eight years. The stock is presently trading for $20 per share, the risk-free rate is 7%, and $\sigma = 0.30$. What is the value of a warrant?

11.4 Mideast Semiconductor is considering a merger with one of its major competitors, Computer Components Corporation. CCC has offered to sell a 90 day option with an exercise price of $120 per share. If $k_{RF} = 11\%$, $\sigma = 0.40$, and CCC's stock price is currently $94 per share, how much should Mideast be willing to pay for options on the 2 million shares of CCC outstanding?

11.5 Minnesota Adhesives is considering the purchase of American Glue's contact cement division. Forecasted cash flows after tax are:

Year	CF
1	$200,000
2	400,000
3	500,000
4	600,000
5	600,000

American Glue is trying to get rid of the division and has offered to guarantee CFs of $450,000 per year. Minnesota Adhesives believes the CFs should be discounted at 20%, k_{RF} = 7%, and σ = 0.80. What is the maximum price Minnesota Adhesives should be willing to pay for this division? (Assume continuous compounding in calculating the PV of the CFs).

11.6 Exact Precision Tools is considering the purchase of a computerized manufacturing machine. The present value in year 0 of the cash flows after year 1 is $775,000, and the company has the option of abandoning the machine after 1 year and selling the equipment for $500,000. If k_{RF} = 12%, and σ = 0.55, what is the value of the option to abandon?

11A.1 LaBarge Garden Products has a total market value of $10 million and 10 year zero coupon bonds with a face value of $3 million. If k_{RF} = 9%, and the annual standard deviation of the firm's value is 0.80, what is the value of the default option on the bonds using the Black-Scholes option pricing model?

ANSWERS TO COMPLETION QUESTIONS

11.1 call
11.2 sell
11.3 exercise price
11.4 exercise
11.5 Warrants
11.6 European; American
11.7 increase; decrease
11.8 put
11.9 call; face value of debt
11.10 default
11.11 call options
11.12 abandon

SOLUTIONS TO PROBLEMS

11.1

Step 1. $d_1 = \dfrac{\ln(P_0/X) + (k_{RF} + 0.5\sigma^2)t}{\sigma\sqrt{t}}$

$= \dfrac{\ln(16/20) + [0.12 + 0.5(0.40)^2]6/12}{0.40\sqrt{6/12}}$

$= \dfrac{-0.2231 + 0.10}{0.2828}$

$= -0.44$

Step 2. $d_2 = -0.44 - 0.40\sqrt{6/12}$

$= -0.44 - 0.28$

$= -0.72$

Step 3. Calculate $N(d_1)$ and $N(d_2)$

$N(-0.44) = 0.3264 + \dfrac{-0.44 - (-0.45)}{-0.40 - (-0.45)}(0.3446 - 0.3264)$

$N(d_1) = 0.3300$

$N(d_2) = N(-0.72) = 0.2266 + \dfrac{-0.72 - (-0.75)}{-0.70 - (-0.75)}(0.2420 - 0.2266)$

$= 0.2382$

Step 4. $V_c = P_0 N(d_1) - \dfrac{X}{e^{k_{RF}t}} N(d_2)$

$= \$16(0.3300) - \dfrac{\$20}{e^{0.12(6/12)}}(0.2382)$

$= \$5.28 - \$18.8353(0.2382)$

$= \$5.28 - \$4.4866$

$= \$0.79$

Step 5. $V_p = V_c + \dfrac{X}{e^{k_{RF}t}} - P_0$

$= \$0.79 + \dfrac{\$20}{e^{0.12(6/12)}} - \$16$

$= \$0.79 + \$18.8353 - \$16$

$= \$3.63$

11.2

Step 1. Calculate the standard deviation times the square root of time.

$\sigma\sqrt{t} = 0.3\sqrt{3/12} = 0.3\sqrt{0.25} = 0.15$

Step 2. Calculate the market price divided by the present value of the exercise price.

$$\frac{P_0}{X/e^{k_{RF}t}} = \frac{\$69}{\$75/e^{0.08 \times 3/12}} = \frac{\$69}{\$73.5149} = 0.9386$$

Step 3. Using Table F.7 and the two values calculated above, find the tabled factor for a call option and multiply it by the share price:

tabled factor = 0.0349

$$V_c = 0.0349(\$69)$$
$$= \$2.4081$$
$$= \$2.41$$

Step 4. Using Table F.8 and the two values calculated above, find the tabled factor for a put option and multiply it by the share price:

tabled factor = 0.0988

$$V_p = 0.0988(\$69)$$
$$= \$6.8172$$
$$= \$6.82$$

11.3

Step 1. Calculate $\sigma\sqrt{t} = 0.30\sqrt{8}$

$$= 0.30(2.8284)$$
$$= 0.85$$

Step 2. Calculate the $\dfrac{P_0}{X/e^{k_{RF}t}} = \dfrac{\$20}{\$35/e^{0.07(8)}}$

$$= \frac{\$20}{\$35/1.7507}$$
$$= \frac{\$20}{\$19.9923}$$
$$= 1.00$$

Step 3. Using Table F.7 and the two values above, look up the tabled factor and multiply it by the share price.

tabled factor = 0.3292

value of a warrant = 0.3292($20)
$$= \$6.584$$
$$= \$6.58$$

11.4

Step 1. $\sigma\sqrt{t} = 0.40\sqrt{90/365} = 0.20$

Step 2. $\dfrac{P_0}{X/e^{k_{RF}t}} = \dfrac{\$94}{\$120/e^{0.11(90/365)}} = \dfrac{\$94}{\$116.7889} = \$0.80$

Step 3. From Table F.7, the tabled factor = 0.0148, so

$V_c = 0.0148(\$94)$

$= \$1.3912$

Step 4. For options on 2 million shares, Mideast should pay:

2,000,000($1.3912) = $2,782,400

11.5
Step 1.

Year	CF	Present Value of CFs at 20%	
1	$200,000	$200,000/e^{0.07(1)}$ =	$ 186,478.76
2	400,000	$400,000/e^{0.07(2)}$ =	347,743.29
3	500,000	$500,000/e^{0.07(3)}$ =	405,292.12
4	600,000	$600,000/e^{0.07(4)}$ =	453,470.24
5	600,000	$600,000/e^{0.07(5)}$ =	422,812.85
		Total PV of CFs	$1,815,797.26

Step 2. Calculate the factors needed to use Table F.8 to value the put options, rounding the factors to the closest tabled values.

Year	$\sigma\sqrt{t}$	$\dfrac{P_0}{X/e^{k_{RF}t}}$
1	$0.80\sqrt{1} = 0.80$	$\dfrac{186,478.76}{450,000/e^{0.07(1)}} = 0.44 \approx 0.50$
2	$0.80\sqrt{2} = 1.13 \approx 1.15$	$\dfrac{347,743.29}{450,000/e^{0.07(2)}} = 0.89 \approx 0.90$
3	$0.80\sqrt{3} = 1.39 \approx 1.40$	$\dfrac{405,292.12}{450,000/e^{0.07(3)}} = 1.11 \approx 1.12$
4	$0.80\sqrt{4} = 1.60 \approx 1.50$	$\dfrac{453,470.24}{450,000/e^{0.07(4)}} = 1.33 \approx 1.35$
5	$0.80\sqrt{5} = 1.79 \approx 1.75$	$\dfrac{422,812.85}{450,000/e^{0.07(5)}} = 1.33 \approx 1.35$

Step 3.

Year	Tabled factor	×	P_0	=	Value of the put
1	1.1151		$186,478.76		$207,942.47
2	0.5161		$347,743.29		$179,470.31
3	0.4362		$405,292.12		$176,788.42
4	0.3540		$453,470.24		$160,528.47
5	0.4147		$422,812.85		$175,340.49

Total value of the puts = $900,070.16

Step 4. Maximum price = PV of CF + value of put option

$$= \$1,815,797.26 + \$900,070.16$$
$$= \$2,715,867.42$$

11.6

Step 1. $\sigma\sqrt{t} = 0.55\sqrt{1} = 0.55$

Step 2. $\dfrac{P_0}{X/e^{k_{RF}t}} = \dfrac{\$775,000}{\$500,000/e^{0.12(1)}} = 1.75$

Step 3. From Table F.8, the factor = 0.0327, so

Value of option to abandon = 0.0327($775,000)

$$= \$25,342.50$$

11A.1

Step 1. $S + V_B$ = default option + V

The value of the bonds if risk free (V_B) is:

$$V_B = \text{(face value)}/e^{k_{RF}t}$$

$$= \dfrac{\$3,000,000}{e^{0.09 \times 10}} = \$1,219,708.98$$

Step 2. Use the Black-Scholes model to calculate the value of the stock (S).

$$d_1 = \dfrac{\ln(V/\text{face value of bonds}) + [k_{RF} + 0.5(\sigma)^2]t}{\sigma\sqrt{t}}$$

$$= \dfrac{\ln(\$10\text{ m}/\$3\text{ m}) + [0.09 + 0.5(0.8)^2] \times 10}{0.8\sqrt{10}}$$

$$= \dfrac{1.2040 + 4.10}{2.5298}$$

$$= 2.0966$$

$d_1 \approx 2.10$

$$d_2 = d_1 - \sigma\sqrt{t}$$
$$= 2.0966 - 0.8\sqrt{10}$$
$$= -0.4332$$
$$d_2 \approx -0.45$$

From Table F.6, $N(d_1) = 0.9821$
$$N(d_2) = 0.3264$$

Step 3. $S = V \times N(d_1) - \dfrac{\text{face value of bond}}{e^{k_{RF}t}} N(d_2)$

$$= \$10,000,000(0.9821) - \dfrac{\$3,000,000}{e^{0.09 \times 10}}(0.3264)$$

$$= \$9,821,000 - (\$1,219,708.98)(0.3264)$$

$$= \$9,422,886.99$$

Step 4. $S + V_B$ = default option + V

$\$9,422,886.99 + \$1,219,708.98$ = default option + $\$10,000,000$

default option = $\$9,422,886.99 + \$1,219,708.98 - \$10,000,000$

$$= \$642,595.97$$

CHAPTER 12

OBTAINING LONG-TERM FINANCING AND COMMON STOCK

HOW THIS CHAPTER RELATES TO THE REST OF THE TEXT

Chapters 8-11 provided us with the tools needed to evaluate long-term capital projects. In order to take advantage of positive NPV projects, firms often must raise funds in the capital markets. In Chapter 2, we saw how these markets operate; in this chapter, we see how they relate to long-term financing and common stock. Other long-term sources of funds--bonds and preferred stock--are covered in Chapter 13. Short-term sources of funds are discussed in Chapter 21. The cost of capital (Chapter 14), capital structure (Chapter 15), and dividend policy (Chapter 16) are closely related to the firm's ability and need to secure external financing.

TOPICAL OUTLINE

I. Public offerings versus private placement.
   A. Public offerings.
      1. Offered for sale to the general public (general cash offer) or through privilged subscription (rights offering).
      2. Typically uses an investment banker.
   B. Private placements provide funds from financial institutions such as insurance companies.
   C. The vast majority of externally raised funds have been long-term debt, since firms can generate equity internally.
   D. When raising external capital, firms must plan in order to provide flexibility and to be able to minimize financing costs.
II. General cash offerings.
   A. Types of placement.
      1. Underwriting by an investment banker.
         a. An investment banker purchases the issue from the firm at a fixed price and then resells it.
         b. The risk of the issue not selling is borne by the investment banker.
         c. The firm is guaranteed a fixed dollar amount from the issue.

2. Best effort basis.
   a. The investment banker agrees to sell as much of the issue as he or she can for a fixed commission.
   b. Large, well-known firms that feel the issue will sell easily may use best efforts investment banking.
   c. Very small firms use best efforts investment banking when the risks and costs are too great for underwriting.
3. Direct placement is generally through a rights offering to stockholders. It may or may not require an investment banker.

B. Selection of an investment banker.
1. The negotiated underwriting process involves simply selecting or negotiating with one investment banker.
2. Competitive bidding involves announcing an intention to sell the securities, and inviting bids to select the investment banker.

C. The underwriting process.
1. At the pre-underwriting conferences, the issuing firm and the investment banker discuss the general details of the issue.
   a. They discuss the amount of capital needed, the type(s) of security to issue, and the terms of the agreement.
   b. The investment banker, a specialist in selling new securities, offers advice.
   c. The investment banker begins the underwriting investigation, which will be followed up by an auditor and lawyers.
   d. The firm and the underwriter draw up an underwriting agreement after the investigation.
2. The registration statement filed with the SEC presents all the facts of the issue and the issuing firm.
   a. The SEC will judge the factual accuracy of the registration statement.
   b. During the registration period, a red herring statement can be distributed.
   c. During this period, the underwriters can make oral offers and discover the interest of potential buyers, but the price is decided after the registration period.

i. When a new issue of existing stock is sold, the investment banker might buy the security at a price a few points below the closing price of the security on the last day of its registration.
ii. If the new stock issue is for a firm just going public, the investment banker and the issuer must negotiate on a price.
iii. For bonds and preferred stock, the ratings services rate the issue, and the issue is priced according to the current rate of return on that rating of security.
d. After the registration period, the underwriting firm will often run a tombstone advertisement in the financial newspapers, telling from whom the prospectus may be obtained.
3. An underwriting syndicate (wholesalers) and a selling group (retailers) are formed in order to spread the risk and ensure national marketability.

III. Costs of flotation to the issuing firm.
A. Costs include the underwriting fee and all other expenses related to the offering.
B. Total selling costs are the difference between what the securities are sold for and what the firm actually receives.
C. The cost of selling common stock is substantially greater than for selling preferred stock and debt.
1. Common stock is sold to a large number of investors, whereas preferred stock and debt are issued in large blocks and are sold to fewer investors.
2. The price of common stock is more erratic, and entails greater risk for the investment banker.

IV. Private placements.
A. Advantages of private placements.
1. The issuing firm saves the time, expense, and trouble of having to register the issue with the SEC.

2. The firm can maintain a lower profile, since it need not go through the registration process.

3. The firm can discuss the financing problem directly with the lender and often make modifications in the offering.

B. Disadvantages of private issues.

1. The lender may monitor the firm's activities more closely, either directly or through loan provisions.

2. If common stock financing is used, the investor is likely to gain substantial influence on or even control of the firm.

3. The cost of privately placed debt is generally higher than on public issues.

4. It is more difficult to raise large amounts of capital through private placements.

C. Shelf registration: Adopted by the SEC in 1982 (Rule 415).

1. A firm must file a short form describing the securities and financing needed over the next two years.

2. The rule streamlines the registration procedure for debt and equity issues; firms can take issues "off the shelf" in a matter of minutes when they think market conditions are favorable.

3. Shelf registration is welcomed by financial officers but results in bypassing some investment banking firms.

4. More volatile interest rates and market conditions as well as Rule 415 have led to a decline in syndicating.

V. Rights and privileges of common stockholders.

A. Common stockholders have a residual right to the income of the firm.

1. Creditors, lessors, the government, and preferred stockholders receive their claims before common stockholders receive cash dividends.

2. Firms are not obligated to pay cash dividends.

3. Since risk is greater for common stock, so is the expected return; cash dividends may increase, and the value of the firm may also increase as funds are reinvested in the firm.

B. In theory, stockholders control the firm through election of the board of directors, but this control is limited.

1. Individual stockholders generally hold only a small fraction of the total shares.
2. Management often nominates only enough directors to fill the board positions, requesting stockholders to vote for this slate.
3. Outside or dissident groups may challenge management and propose a different slate of directors.
4. The board is selected either by majority voting or cumulative voting, with the total number of per share votes equal to the number of directors being elected.
    a. Majority voting requires that the stockholders place only one vote per share per director; the candidates with the most votes win.
    b. Cumulative voting allows investors to distribute their total votes among the candidates in any manner they wish, allowing minority groups to elect representatives on the board.
- C. Stockholders have the right to obtain information from management about the firm' operations.
- D. Common stockholders can (in most circumstances) lose no more than their initial investment, since they have no liability for the debts incurred by the firm.
- E. Stockholders may have the preemptive right to buy new shares of common stock in the same percentage as their current ownership.
    1. Some charters have eliminated this right in order to make mergers and acquisitions easier.
    2. If the preemptive right does not exist, the stockholder may experience dilution of ownership.
- F. Common stockholders may transfer ownership of shares to another investor.

VI. Features of common stock.
- A. Authorized, outstanding, and treasury shares.
    1. The firm's charter states the maximum number of shares the firm is authorized to issue without amending the charter.
    2. Outstanding shares are those held by the public.

3. Treasury stock is issued shares bought back by the firm.
B. Par value and book value.
1. Common stock can be issued with or without par value.
    a. The common stockholder is responsible to creditors for the difference between par value and the issuance price if that price is below par value, so par value is generally low.
    b. If the firm does not state a par value, it uses some stated value for accounting purposes.
    c. The difference between the issuance price and the par (or stated) value is recorded on the firm's balance sheet as additional paid-in capital.
2. The book value per share reflects the stockholder's equity divided by the number of shares outstanding.
    a. Due to the effects of inflation, this figure has little economic meaning.
    b. Some analysts prefer to use net working capital to estimate the value of the firm in potential liquidations.
C. Forms of common stock.
1. Sometimes the firm issues a nonvoting class and reserves the voting class for the founder's group.
2. The founders' class of stock may have more votes per share than the class of stock for other stockholders, in order for founders to maintain their voting power.

VII. Common stock financing.
A. Recent studies have indicated that issuing new common stock causes a stock price decline of approximately 3%. Debt issues leave stock prices unaffected.
1. The decline may be due to information asymmetries. Managers should be inclined to issue (sell) new shares if they feel that the firm's stock is overpriced. A new issue signals this belief to investors and stock prices fall.

2. Investors may interpret the issue as a signal about the firm's investment prospects. If the prospects are good, investors would prefer debt financing since the gains from the prospect would not have to be shared with new stockholders.

B. Initial public offerings (IPOs) are often underpriced by 15-20% due to difficulties in selling the issue or lack of information about the firm.

C. Pricing new issues.
   1. For firms having outstanding shares, the new shares typically are priced a few dollars below the closing price on the day the stock clears SEC registration.
   2. For firms going public, no market exists for the stock, so the investment banker must determine the issue price.
      a. Estimate what the total market value of the firm would be after the issue.
         i. Use a valuation approach appropriate to the firm, such as the constant dividend growth approach: $S_0 = D_1/(k_s - g)$.
            (a) The D_1 estimate depends upon the firm's projected net income and dividend payout.
            (b) The g estimate depends upon the firm's expectations for earnings and dividends.
            (c) Estimating k_s is difficult; the investment banker might use some approach such as adding a risk premium to the expected interest rate on long-term bonds.
            (d) This approach is not very helpful, since both k_s and D_1 are difficult to determine for a new issue.
         ii. Use the comparative P/E approach for valuation.
            (a) Examine the P/E ratios for publicly traded firms in the same industry and of firms which have recently gone public.

(b) Compare other pertinent information.
  (1) Financial condition growth prospects, quality and stability of management, and size.
  (2) Some of these comparisons are qualitative rather than quantitative.
(c) Establish an appropriate P/E ratio, and determine the value of the firm: S_0 = (expected net income)(expected P/E per share).
   b. Divide this total market value by the number of shares that will be outstanding, including privately held or founders' shares.
D. Recording a stock issue on the firm's balance sheet.
   1. Increase the common stock account by the number of shares times the par value per share.
   2. Increase the capital surplus account by the number of shares times the difference between the issuance price and the par value per share.
   3. Increase cash by the amount of the new capital net of issuance and flotation costs.
E. Rights offering.
   1. The rights offering is the issuance of new shares of common stock, with the firm's current stockholders having first option to buy the issue.
   2. The importance of right's offerings has diminished.
      a. Some firms have eliminated the preemptive right.
      b. Investors have increased participation in dividend reinvestment plans.
      c. Shelf registration has been introduced.
   3. The number of rights needed to purchase an additional share can be calculated using the formula presented in the appendix.
   4. Value of stock and rights.
      a. Rights-on is the period of time when the right is attached and purchasable with the share of common stock.

b. Ex rights day is the day the stock and the right begin trading separately; the price of the stock drops by the value of the right.
5. Effect on the position of the stockholders.
   a. As long as stockholders take positive action, they do not suffer any loss from a rights offering.
   b. If they let the rights expire, they incur a loss equal to the value of the rights.
6. Pricing the offering.
   a. If the firm wants to lower its per share price substantially, it would set a low subscription price.
   b. If the firm does not want to lower its price much, the subscription price will be set just low enough to ensure the market price remains above it during the rights offering.

VIII. Listing the stock.
   A. Small firms generally do not list their stock but trade on the over-the-counter market.
   B. In order to apply for listing, a firm must meet certain conditions, file a listing application, pay a listing fee, and agree to meet the additional financial reporting requirements.

IX. Regulation of public issues.
   A. Primary market issues are regulated by the Securities Act of 1933.
   B. Secondary issues are regulated by the Securities Exchange Act of 1934.

FORMULAS

Notation

S_0 = value of the firm at time = 0
D_1 = expected cash dividend to be paid to stockholders next year
k_s = common stock investors' required rate of return
g = constant growth rate in cash dividends
P/E = price/earnings ratio
EPS = earnings per share

Estimated Selling Price for Common Stock of a Firm Going Public

Value of firm after the issue/number of shares of common stock

Constant Growth Formula for Valuing the Firm

$S_0 = D_1/(k_s - g)$

Comparative P/E Approach to Valuing the Firm

S_0 = (expected net total income)(expected P/E per share of stock)

Effect of a Stock Repurchase

Current EPS = total earnings/number of shares outstanding

Current P/E = market price per share/EPS

EPS after repurchase = total earnings/decreased number of shares

Expected market price after repurchase = (current P/E)(new EPS)

Rights Offerings

Notation

v_r = value of one right

P_0 = rights on market price per share

P_s = subscription price

N = number of rights needed to purchase an additional share of stock

P_x = ex rights stock price per share

Number of rights needed to purchase an additional share

Number of additional shares, N = funds to be raised/subscription price, P_s

Number of rights to buy one additional share = existing shares/additional shares

Cost to shareholders for one additional share of stock = P_s + required rights per share

Value of stock and rights

Rights-on:

Value of one right = $\dfrac{\text{market value of stock, rights-on} - \text{subscription price}}{\text{number of rights needed to purchase one share} + 1}$

$= (P_0 - P_x)/(N + 1)$

Ex rights:

Value of one right = $\dfrac{\text{market value of stock, ex rights} - \text{subscription price}}{\text{number of rights needed to purchase one share}}$

$= (P_x - P_s)/N$

WHAT TO LOOK FOR

We have spent four chapters preparing to make long-term financing decisions by evaluating the capital budget (Chapters 8-11). Now, we are ready to look for long-term funding sources. In Chapter 12, we see that firms can generate equity internally by retaining cash flows. In order to maintain their operation, however, firms may also need to find sources of external long-term financing. In Chapter 12, we focus on the process of obtaining these long-term external funds.

Obtaining External Long-Term Funds

Public offerings

Firms which offer new securities publicly have several alternatives. They can place the issue directly with current stockholders through a rights offering. They can hire an investment banker to underwrite the issue, shifting the risk of the sale to the investment banker. Finally, they can hire an investment banker to sell the issue on a best efforts basis. To select an investment banker, the firm could simply negotiate with a single investment banker or accept competitive bids. The text discusses the underwriting process.

The 1982 SEC shelf registration rule may have a significant impact on both the firm's long-term funding procedures and the investment banking industry. Shelf registration allows larger firms, with market capitalization of over $100 million, to register their planned debt and equity issues with a short form far in advance of the actual offerings. Astute managers can then pull the registered securities "off the shelf" when they decide market conditions are favorable. This increased flexibility may decrease the need for investment banking firms, intensifying the competition in that industry.

Private placements

Private placements are securities the firm issues directly to a financial institution, such as insurance companies, banks, or pension funds. Firms can privately place either debt or equity. Firms that place equity privately transfer a substantial amount of control to the investor, so firms are often reluctant to place equity privately. A potential buyer of privately placed equity is a venture capitalist. Firms choosing to place equity privately with a venture capitalist should choose the investor carefully, looking for one that will not only provide the funds, but also nurture and wisely advise the firm.

The interest rate paid on privately placed debt is often 10 to 40 basis points (or 0.10 to 0.40 percent) higher than on a public offering. Most privately placed debt is in the form of term loans, sometimes at a variable interest rate, repayable on an amortized basis. Term loans may be carried by a bank for the first few years and an insurance company in the later years, since the lenders match their loan maturities with the maturities of their liabilities. Lending institutions protect themselves by attaching restrictive covenants to privately placed debt.

Long-Term Funding and Managers

A broad array of decisions face managers in the process of obtaining long-term external funds. First, they must decide which type of funding they want to use: common stock, preferred stock, debt, warrants, or convertibles. They must then decide whether to place the issue privately or to offer it publicly.

If they choose a public offering, they must decide whether to use an investment banker. If an investment banker is used, managers must decide whether the issue should be underwritten (insured) or sold on a best efforts basis. They must also decide whether to choose an investment banker or to have competitive bidding. In all these choices, the goal is to maximize the value of the firm, so managers should weigh the costs and benefits of each of these decisions.

Managers must have greater sophistication today than in the recent past when raising long-term capital. Inflation has risen and then fallen, as have interest rates. To protect themselves, lenders have shifted much of the interest rate risk to their customers through the use of variable-rate loans. In addition, larger firms are increasingly using shelf registration procedures to time the issuance of new securities. The use of shelf registration may result in bypassing the investment banker in the registration procedure.

Rights of Common Stockholders

Stockholders, in theory, control the firm through the election of the firm's board of directors. As the text notes, the control of the individual stockholder is limited. Two voting systems exist, majority voting and cumulative voting. In the majority voting system, stockholders may cast one vote per share for a candidate for each director's position. For example, if a stockholder held 200 shares of stock, and the firm was electing 8 directors, the stockholder could vote a total of 1,600 votes--with 200 per director candidate. In the cumulative voting system, the same stockholder could vote 1,600 votes any way desired. The stockholder could cast 1,600 votes for a single director candidate. Through this concentration of votes, the cumulative voting system allows minority groups to place representatives on the board of directors.

Stockholders have the right to receive information about the operations of the firm. Management screens this information in order to protect the firm's competitive position in its industry.

All About Common Stock

What do the balance sheet figures mean?

The details in the stockholders' equity section of the balance sheet may be confusing. Authorized shares are shares the firm's charter allows the firm to issue. Outstanding shares are the shares held by the public. Par value of common stock is the value stated in the firm's charter. It helps determine the liability of stockholders. If the par value is above the issuance price, the stockholders are liable to creditors for the difference between the par value and the issuance price. For this reason, firms generally set a low par value. If the firm has no par value, it assumes (states) some value for accounting purposes. The difference between the issuance price and the par (or stated) value is the capital surplus or additional paid-in capital.

Treasury stock are shares held by or repurchased by the firm. Capital stock is outstanding stock held by the public. Under this heading, you will find the computation of the par value of the outstanding stock. As noted above, the capital surplus account is the capital stock in excess of par value. Finally, as you already know, the retained earnings account is equal to the sum of all income (over the years) from the firm's income statements less all cash dividends paid. Remember, there is no cash in the retained earnings account.

How does a firm price a new issue of common stock?

Firms with outstanding stock tend to price new issues a few dollars below its price on the day the stock cleared SEC registration. Firms going public with an initial stock offering, however, have more trouble pricing their issues. The firm should use several methods to value the firm. These methods are subjective, but if several are employed, they should produce a usable value.

The firm divides this calculated market value by the number of shares to be issued in order to obtain an issuance price. The setting of the issuance price is important. If the price is set too high, it will be difficult to sell the issue; a price that is too low will not bring in enough capital for the firm. Remember, the firm's capital proceeds from selling common stock are based on the issuance price, not the subsequent market price after the stock is outstanding.

COMPLETION QUESTIONS

12.1 Firms have two primary sources of funds. They can generate funds internally from continuing operations or _____ _____.

12.2 When firms publicly offer new issues of long-term capital, they frequently use the services of an _____, who helps register the new issue and assist in its distribution and sale.

12.3 Investment bankers can be hired either to _____ the issue or to sell the issue on a _____ basis.

12.4 To select an investment banker and the issue price, some firms (especially those the in public utility industry) use _____ _____.

12.5 A _____ is the first part of the SEC registration statement, which can be distributed prior to the issue's SEC approval.

12.6 When the issuing firm has outstanding stock, the investment banking firm typically buys the new issue at _____ _____.

12.7 _____ is a streamlined procedure that qualifying firms can use for issuing both debt and equity issues.

12.8 Among new issue securities, _____ involves higher flotation costs, since it involves more risk and is distributed to more investors.

12.9 Common stockholders play two roles. They both own the firm and provide _____ for the firm.

12.10 Common stockholders have a _____ to the income of the firm. This claim comes _____ the claims of creditors, lessors, the government, and preferred stockholders.

12.11 Under the majority voting system, each stockholder has _____ vote per director per share. Under _____ voting, the stockholder has the same number of votes as the majority voting system, but can distribute these votes to any director(s) as deemed appropriate.

12.12 The _____ is a provision granting stockholders the right to purchase new shares of common stock in the same proportion as their current ownership. When stockholders have this option, the stock issuance is called a _____ offering.

12.13 _____ shares are the shares a firm is allowed to issue without amending its charter. _____ shares are the shares currently issued. _____ stock are shares the firm has repurchased for such needs as the firm's stock option plan or for mergers or acquisitions.

12.14 If a firm is making an initial stock offering, the pricing of the issue is difficult since there is no _____ for the stock. In this case, the firm or investment banker may use a _____ approach like those in Chapter 6 or the _____ _____ approach.

12.15 When the firm records a new stock issue, the common stock account is increased by the amount of the _____ times the number of shares. The _____ account is increased by the amount of the number of shares times the difference between the issuance price and the par value. On the asset side, the _____ account has an offsetting entry.

PROBLEMS

12.1 Deighton Bank intends to issue 2 million shares of common stock. The bank's investment banker has offered two alternatives:

Plan A: A best efforts offering at $16 per share subject to an underwriting commission of 2 percent of the expected gross proceeds plus $300,000. The investment banking firm expects 93 percent of the issue will be sold.

Plan B: An underwritten offer at $15.50 per share plus an underwriting fee of 7 percent of the gross proceeds.

Which plan offers the highest net proceeds to Deighton Bank?

12.2 Gray Enterprises is considering the issuance of 1 million shares of common stock. The stock is expected to pay a $2.50 cash dividend next year and cash dividends and earnings are expected to grow at a rate of 8 percent per year. If k_s is 20 percent and the cost of issuing the stock is 7 percent of the gross proceeds from the sale, how much should Gray expect to receive if 100 percent of the issue is sold?

12.3 Stevenson Industries is planning its first issue of common stock. The company expects to pay a cash dividend of $2.28 per share next year-- a dividend payout ratio of 60 percent. Firms in the same industry typically have a P/E ratio of 22 times and earnings growth of 6 percent.

a. What price should Stevenson expect per share of stock?

b. Assuming that the price in (a) is correct, what is the required rate of return (k_s) for Stevenson?

12.4 Converse Industries, in order to protect existing stockholders, has decided to attach a rights offering to its latest equity issue. The firm presently has 2 million shares of common stock and is attempting to raise $8.5 million by issuing an additional 400,000 shares. At present, the company's EPS is $2.50 per share and its P/E ratio is 10 times. Determine the value of the right and the ex rights price of the stock.

ANSWERS TO COMPLETION QUESTIONS

12.1 secure them externally from creditors or investors
12.2 investment banker
12.3 underwrite; best efforts
12.4 competitive bidding
12.5 red herring
12.6 a few points below the securities' closing price on the last day of the registration period
12.7 Shelf registration
12.8 common stock
12.9 long-term capital
12.10 residual right; after
12.11 one; cumulative
12.12 preemptive right; rights
12.13 Authorized; Outstanding; Treasury
12.14 existing market; valuation; comparative P/E
12.15 par value; additional paid in capital; cash

SOLUTIONS TO PROBLEMS

12.1

Step 1. Plan A: Expected gross proceeds = (2,000,000)($16)(0.93)
= $29,760,000

Commissions

Underwriting = ($29,760,000)(0.02) = $595,200
Fee   300,000
Total commissions $895,200

Net proceeds = $29,760,000 − $895,200 = $28,864,800

Step 2. Plan B: Expected gross proceeds = (2,000,000)($15.50) = $31,000,000

Underwriting = ($31,000,000)(0.07) = $2,170,000

Net proceeds = $31,000,000 − $2,170,000 = $28,830,000

The net proceeds from Plan A are greater by $34,800.

12.2

Step 1. Total dividends paid next year = (1,000,000 shares)($2.50 per share)
= $2,500,000

Step 2. $S_0 = D_1/(k_s - g)$

$$= \frac{\$2,500,000}{0.20 - 0.08} = \frac{\$2,500,000}{0.12} = \$20,833,333$$

The net proceeds = $20,833,333 (1 − 0.07) = $19,375,000

12.3a

Step 1. Dividends per share = (earnings per share)(dividend payout)

So EPS = DPS/dividend payout = $2.28/0.60 = $3.80 per share

Step 2. P_0 = (EPS)(P/E) = ($3.80)(22) = $83.60 per share

12.3b

Step 3. $k_s = (D_1/P_0) + g$

$= (\$2.28/\$83.69) + 0.06 = 0.0272 + 0.06 = 0.0872 = 8.72\%$

12.4

Step 1. The present market price = (EPS)(P/E) = ($2.50)(10) = $25 per share

Step 2. Subscription price = $\dfrac{\text{funds to be raised}}{\text{number of additional shares}}$

= $8,500,000/400,000 = $21.25 per share

Step 3. Number of rights to buy one additional share = $\dfrac{\text{existing shares}}{\text{additional shares}}$

$= \dfrac{2,000,000}{400,000} = 5$ rights

Step 4. The value of the right = $v_r = \dfrac{P_0 - P_s}{N + 1} = \dfrac{\$25.000 - \$21.25}{5 + 1} = \dfrac{\$3.75}{6}$

= $0.625

Step 5. The ex rights price can be found by solving for P_x in the following equation:

$v_r = \dfrac{P_x - P_s}{N}$, or $P_x = N(v_r) + P_s = 5(\$0.625) + \$21.25 = \$24.375$

An alternative approach not presented in the text is:

$P_x = P_0 - v_r = \$25.00 - \$0.625 = \$24.375$

CHAPTER 13

LIABILITY MANAGEMENT

HOW THIS CHAPTER RELATES TO THE REST OF THE TEXT

Chapter 12 discussed obtaining external funds and common stock. In Chapter 13, we examine the two other sources of long-term financing--bonds and preferred stock. Bonds trade based on their yield to maturity (Chapter 6) and are priced according to present values (Chapter 5). For both bonds and preferred stock, risk (Chapter 7) is an important determinant of price. Required returns on bonds and preferred stocks are important components of the cost of capital (Chapter 14) and the amount of debt a firm carries affects its capital structure (Chapter 15).

TOPICAL OUTLINE

I. Features of bonds.
    A. Reasons for issuing debt.
        1. Firms may deduct bond interest payments from pretax income; cash dividends on preferred stock and common stock are not tax deductible.
        2. If unexpected inflation occurs, purchasing power is eroded; thus firms that borrow repay the debt in cheaper dollars.
        3. Firms might employ debt if they have a low level of debt usage compared to their industry.
        4. Firms might use debt if the sale of additional common stock would weaken the majority owner's control.
    B. The bond terms.
        1. All debt holders are guaranteed a prior claim to the firm's income over the common and preferred stockholders.
        2. The contract between the borrowing firm and the lender is called the bond indenture, which specifies the provisions of the bond.
        3. The prospectus, which is available through brokers and other sources, summarizes the bond indenture position.

C. The role of the trustee.
1. Since bonds are issued to many investors, a trustee is appointed to ease communication between the firm and the investors.
2. The trustee sees that all the legal requirements for the bond indenture are met before issuance.
3. The trustee monitors the issuing firm's performance to see that it meets the conditions of the indenture.
4. The trustee takes action on the bondholder's behalf if the firm defaults on interest or principal payments.

D. Security and seniority.
1. Forms of secured debt, and their respective seniority.
   a. Mortgage bonds can be open- or closed-end; open-end provisions do not limit the amount of debt secured by the firm's assets, while closed-end provisions prohibit issuing further debt.
      i. First mortgage bonds have prior claim on assets.
      ii. Second mortgage bonds are subordinate to first mortgage bonds.
   b. Collateral trust bonds are claims against securities rather than against physical assets.
      i. An example of collateral is a holding company's or railway's stock of its subsidiaries.
      ii. Stock takes a junior position to other claims on the subsidiary, so collateral trust bonds usually have detailed restrictions on the subsidiary's issuing senior debt or preferred stock.
   c. Equipment trust certificates frequently finance railroad cars, trucks, buses, and airplanes, giving formal ownership to the trustee.
      i. The issuing firm provides a downpayment of 10 to 25 percent; when the loan is paid off, the title transfers to the firm.
      ii. Equipment trust certificates provide good security to the investor.

2. Forms of unsecured debt, and their respective seniority.
    a. Debentures are unsecured debt and are backed by the full faith and credit of the issuing corporation.
        i. Large firms with excellent credit ratings can issue debentures.
        ii. Debentures have a general claim on assets in the event of default; the claim is subordinate to those of bank loans, short-term debt, the government, and any mortgage bonds.
        iii. Debenture restrictions frequently prohibit issuance of new debt with a senior claim to assets.
E. Provisions of the bond indenture.
    1. The call provision allows the issuing firm to call the bond for redemption before its maturity date.
        a. If interest rates fall sufficiently after a bond is issued, it is to the firm's benefit to call back the bond and eventually reissue it at a lower coupon rate.
        b. Firms calling a bond must pay back the par value plus a call premium, which declines over time.
        c. For many new issues, the call period begins after five to ten years.
        d. In recent years, callable bonds sometimes contain a nonrefundable provision so that the firm must wait a stated period of time before reissuing the debt at a lower coupon rate, thus reducing the investors' call risk.
    2. Sinking fund provisions require the firm to retire a given number of bonds at par value over a specified period of time.
        a. If interest rates are high and bond prices are low, the firm buys the bonds in the open market.
        b. If interest rates are low and bond prices are high, the firm calls the bond by lottery.
        c. Investors face call risk when they invest in bonds with sinking funds, but the sinking fund also decreases the risk that remaining bondholders will not be repaid.

d. Equipment trust certificates and other serial bonds are packages of bonds maturing in different years; the bonds are refunded at par when they mature.
3. Some bonds and preferred stock are convertible into shares of common stock.
    a. The conversion price per share is stated on the bond or share of preferred stock.
    b. Virtually all convertible bonds are convertible subordinated debentures.
    c. The coupon rate on convertibles is typically less than for nonconvertibles.
    d. The conversion price is set above the current market price of the stock when the bond is issued.
    e. The firm has the ability to call the bonds at its discretion.
4. Other restrictive covenants.
    a. Limited open-end and closed-end provisions stipulate the amount of additional mortgage debt that can be issued using the firm's existing assets as collateral.
    b. Provisions also limit the payment of cash dividends, require the firm to maintain its property, limit the sale of assets, and limit sale and leaseback arrangements.
    c. For private placements, and for bonds with a speculating grade rating (Ba or B and below), the lender often requires the firm to maintain minimum levels of net working capital and net worth.

II. Considerations involved if financing with long-term debt.
  A. Pricing and selling the issue.
    1. The price of a bond is expressed as a percentage of its face value; 99.5 percent of $1,000 is $995, for example.
    2. The market interest rate at the time the bond is issued determines its issuance price; if the market rate is above the coupon rate, the bonds are issued below par and vice versa.

3. Bonds pay interest semiannually, and most often are fully registered so that interest and principal are sent directly to the registered owner.
4. Bearer bonds, which are becoming rare, have coupons which the owner clips to obtain the interest payments; the certificate is evidence of ownership.
5. Bonds are quoted net of accrued interest; the bond purchaser pays the purchase price plus interest that has accrued since the last payment date.
6. The firm's net receipt from bond sales is reduced by the underwriting costs.
7. The firm often applies to list its bond issue on the New York Exchange to improve its secondary marketability and its initial attractiveness to investors.

B. Bond ratings.
1. Bond ratings signify the probability of payment of both interest and principal.
2. Moody's Investor Service and Standard & Poor's Corporation are two rating agencies; their ratings are described in Table 13.1.
   a. Aaa and Aa rated bonds are of high quality, while A and Baa bonds are also investment grade; banks and institutions hold these top four grades of bonds.
   b. Ba and B rated bonds are more speculative in respect to interest and principal payment, while bonds rated below B are either in default or have highly speculative characteristics.
3. Factors influencing the bond rating include the debt/equity ratio, the firm's competitive position, the firm's regulatory status, and special provisions of the bond itself.
4. Most bonds are rated B or above.
5. The higher the bond rating, the lower the risk of default, and the lower the required return (the lower the coupon rate).
6. Even the highest-rated corporate bonds involve risk and thus require a premium over the risk-free rate.

7. Yield spreads or risk premiums among bond risk groups change over time depending upon the risk aversion of the investors.
8. Bond ratings are assigned before bonds are issued and are revised as necessary if changes occur in the perceived ability of the firm to pay interest and principal.

C. Debt financing and firm value.
1. Public debt issues may adversely affect the price of common stock, but the magnitude of the effect is much smaller than for the issuance of new common stock.
2. Bank borrowing may be regarded as good news because of the bank's ability to evaluate and monitor the borrowing firm.

III. Recent debt financing developments.
A. Deep discount and zero-coupon bonds.
1. Deep discount bond's coupons offer both coupon return and price appreciation.
2. Zero-coupon bonds are non-coupon-bearing bonds whose entire yield is realized over time in the form of price appreciation.
a. The value of these bonds increases gradually over the bond's life; taxpaying investors pay taxes annually on this gradual price appreciation.
b. Pension funds and other tax-exempt or lightly taxed institutions are the main investors in deep discount or zero-coupon bonds, since they avoid the taxation on the implied interest income resulting from value appreciation.
c. Deep discounted zero-coupon bonds are much more sensitive to changes in interest rates than are normal interest bearing bonds.

B. Junk bonds are those rated Ba and below. Most are issued by growing firms who would rather borrow from the public than from banks.
C. Variable rate bonds are bonds whose interest rate is tied to some short-term rate, such as the rate on 90-day U.S. Treasury bills.
D. The international bond market involves Eurobonds and foreign bonds.

1. The Eurobond is underwritten by an international syndicate and sold primarily in countries other than that in which the issue is denominated.
   a. Most Eurobonds pay interest once a year, reducing Eurobond yields in comparison to bonds issued in the United States, which pay interest semiannually.
   b. Most Eurobonds are issued in bearer form, rather than being fully registered as are most bonds issued in the United States.
   c. Almost all Eurodollar bonds are listed on one or more recognized financial exchange.
2. A foreign bond is one issued by a foreign borrower, but underwritten, sold, and denominated in one country.
3. Many firms are turning to the international bond market for long-term debt capital.

IV. Managing long-term debt.
   A. In bond refunding, a firm calls all of its old bonds at a fixed price and reissues new lower-coupon bonds to take advantage of lower interest rates. (Appendix 13A located at the end of the text).
   B. Alternatives to bond refunding.
      1. The firm issues a public tender offer in an attempt to buy back outstanding bonds.
      2. The firm arranges a private market purchase from one or several institutional investors.
      3. Defeasance--the firm enters into an arrangement with a trustee. The obligation for the bond as well as a portfolio of securities sufficient to cover the bonds are passed to the trustee.
   C. Interest rate swaps: Separate interest payments and principal payments. Convert fixed-rate payments to floating rate payments (and vice versa) by swapping interest payments with another party.

V. Preferred stock.
   A. Characteristics of preferred stock.
      1. Preferred stock is generally used by public utility firms that want to reduce their debt-equity ratio; it is rarely used by other firms.
      2. Preferred stock generally has a par value, typically $25, $50, or $100, and is issued at a price close to this value.
      3. The market price on preferred stock fluctuates with market yields; as the market yields go up, its price goes down.
      4. If the firm does not have the money to pay cash dividends on preferred stock, it can skip the payment.
         a. Unpaid dividends on preferred stock are called arrearages.
         b. Most preferred stock have cumulative cash dividends; all dividends in arrears must be paid before the common stockholders can receive cash dividends.
      5. Preferred stock has no fixed maturity date, but many recent issues make a provision for periodic repayment via a sinking fund.
      6. Virtually all preferred stock is callable at the option of the issuing firm.
      7. The claims of the preferred stockholder are junior to the claim of creditors, but senior to those of common stockholders.
      8. The use of preferred stock may result in restrictions on the firm's issuance of more senior securities, payment of cash dividends to common stockholders, and maintenance of a minimum level of common equity.
      9. Some preferred stock provides voting rights, especially if there are cash dividends in arrearage.
   B. Advantages to the firm using preferred stock.
      1. Preferred stock dividends are generally fixed, so preferred stock provides financial leverage.
      2. Nonpayment of cash dividends to preferred stockholders does not throw the firm into default.
      3. Control of the firm generally remains in the hands of the common stockholders.

C. Adjustable rate preferred stock is a new security tying the dividend rate on the preferred stock to a treasury index, with upper and lower limits on the rates.

VI. Long-term financing and financial distress.
   A. Because of limited liability, stockholders are more inclined to bear risk than bondholders; if the firm is profitible, stockholders pay off bondholders and claim the rest. If the firm fails, stockholders walk away and bondholders may receive something.
   B. Financial distress occurs when the firm has insufficient cash to meet current financial obligations.
      1. Out-of-court options.
         a. In an extension, creditors agree to accept delayed payments from the firm.
         b. In a composition, creditors receive a pro rata settlement on their claims.
         c. In an assignment, the firm voluntarily liquidates and pays off its creditors with the proceeds.
      2. In-court options are covered in the Bankruptcy Reform Act of 1978.
         a. In a liquidation, the firm's assets are sold under the direction of the courts and the creditors are paid off with the proceeds on the basis of priority.
         b. In a reorganization, the firm is restructured in terms of its businesses, creditors, and ownership, and is put back on its feet.

VII. Appendix 13A: Refunding a bond or preferred stock issue (located at the end of the text).
   A. Refunding is the issuance of new securities to replace an existing bond or preferred stock issue.
      1. A firm occasionally calls and refunds an issue to get rid of overly restrictive provisions.
      2. More often, a firm calls and refunds an issue because interest rates have fallen and the firm wants to issue securities at a lower yield.

B. Approach a refunding decision like a capital budgeting decision by calculating the net present value of the proposed refunding.
 1. Find the after-tax initial outlay (ΔCF_0) associated with the refunding.
    a. The call price on old bonds plus additional interest during the overlap period is an outflow.
    b. The net proceeds from a new issue are an inflow, as are tax savings from tax-deductible expenses.
 2. Find the incremental after-tax cash flows (ΔCF_t) resulting from the refunding.
    a. The interest on the old bonds less the tax savings on the old bond's tax-deductible expenses is the cash outflow on the old bonds.
    b. The interest on the new bonds less the tax savings on the new bond's tax-deductible expenses is the cash outflow on the new bonds.
    c. The annual cash savings from the refunding (ΔCF_0) equals the cash outflow on the old bond less the cash outflow on the new bond.
 3. Find the after-tax cost, k_i, of the new bond issue; multiply the coupon rate by 1 - T.
 4. Use the following formula to calculate the NPV:
$$NPV = \sum_{t=1}^{n} \frac{\Delta CF_t}{(1 + k_i)^t} - \Delta CF_0$$
 5. Refund if the NPV is positive.
C. Preferred stock refinancing follows these same general steps; however, some differences, as noted in the text, exist.

FORMULAS

Accrued Interest on a Bond

  Accrued interest payments = (coupon percent)($1,000)(number of days/365)

Zero Coupon

  B_0(zero coupon) = par($PV_{k,n}$)

Appendix 13A: Refunding a Bond or Preferred Stock Issue

Notation

ΔCF_t = incremental after-tax cash flows from refunding

k_i = after-tax cost of the new bond issue

ΔCF_0 = after-tax initial outlay for the refunding

NPV of proposed refunding

$$NPV = \sum_{t=1}^{n} \frac{\Delta CF_t}{(1 + k_i)^t} - \Delta CF_0$$

WHAT TO LOOK FOR

With Chapter 13, we continue our examination of the firm's sources of long-term capital. In this chapter, you learn about long-term debt and preferred stocks, which are fixed-income securities. As you will notice, long-term debt or bonds are the main feature of the chapter, since bonds are more widely issued and occur in more varied forms than preferred stock.

The Various Forms of Corporate Bonds

Corporate bonds vary in their collateral, their seniority, their various restrictions, their riskiness, and their return.

Seniority of debt

If a college grants tuition aid on a seniority basis, the students who have been with the college the longest or who are at the higher levels receive college tuition grants first. If the tuition grant money runs out before all applicants receive aid, so be it. Similarly, a seniority system is established setting out which claims are paid first in the case the firm liquidates its assets. A firm that does not make its interest payments is in default. It must pay the interest on debt, restructure its debt to allow for repayment, or go into liquidation proceedings. If the firm must liquidate its holdings, the provisions of each security's claims show its seniority. According to the new bankruptcy code that went into effect in 1979, creditors, bondholders, and preferred stockholders have a prior claim (on a relative basis) on assets before common stockholders. As we discuss the collateral status of various bond issues, we will discuss their respective seniority.

Collateral of bonds and their respective seniority

Secured bonds backed by mortgages to specific assets of the firm are called first mortgage bonds and second mortgage bonds. First mortgage bonds have prior claim to assets in the event of a default, while second mortgage bonds have a subordinate claim. Open-end provisions allow the firm to pledge the same asset for additional debt. Closed-end provisions prohibit this additional pledging.

Collateral trust bonds are securities of the issuing firm, typically a railroad or holding company, and use common stock as collateral. Claims of these assets are junior to other mortgage bonds of the firm. Equipment trust certificates give the trustee formal ownership to the specific assets being financed. Since the trustee holds the title, these securities provide excellent collateral for their purchasers.

Unsecured bonds are debentures, subordinated debentures, or income bonds. These are backed by the full faith and credit of the issuing corporation. Debentures are often issued by firms with excellent credit ratings. The claims of debentures come after those of bank loans, short-term debt, the government, and any mortgage bonds. Subordinated debentures have even more junior claims to assets. Income bonds require interest to be paid only if it is earned. For the firm, this arrangement is somewhat similar to preferred stock, except that the interest is a tax-deductible expense, whereas cash dividend payments are not tax-deductible.

Bonds can also be callable or convertible. Callable bonds can be repurchased at any time (usually after some grace period) by the firm for specified prices. Convertible bonds can be exchanged for shares of common stock at a fixed conversion price. Convertibles usually carry a lower coupon rate than nonconvertible bonds.

Restrictions on issuing debt

Restrictions on issuing debt help reduce the riskiness of the debt issue for the investor. Therefore, the more risky the firm or the characteristics of the debt issue, the more restrictive will be the covenants. For example, privately placed issues may be more risky than public issues. The lender often requires the borrowing firm to maintain a minimum level of net working capital and a minimum net worth. These restrictions help insure that the lender will receive interest payments and the firm will survive to repay the principal.

Bond restrictive covenants also include a restriction on the payment of cash dividends, a prohibition against issuing additional senior debt, and limitations on the sale of the firm's assets. Again, these restrictions help reduce the investor's risk of not receiving payment of interest and principal. These restrictions can and sometimes do impede the borrowing firm's ability to operate. In such cases, the borrowing firm attempts to modify the indenture or call the issue.

Bond risk and bond ratings

We discussed issue-specific and firm-specific risk in Chapter 7. Issue-specific risk concerns the type of bond and the indenture. A bond with good collateral, a sinking fund, and reasonably good covenants has less issue-specific risk than a subordinated debenture with no sinking fund or restrictive covenants. Call provisions introduce call risk into the debt issue; the nonrefundable provision included in a bond's indenture will help to minimize the call risk. Sinking funds introduce call risk into the debt issue, but also increase the probability that the issue will eventually be retired.

Firms that have stable or growing positive cash flow and a history of meeting their obligations in a timely fashion have low firm-specific risk. Firms that often have cash flow deficits and pay creditors late or default on their obligations have relatively high firm-specific risk.

Investors require a lower return from less risky firms and bond issues. It is in the firm's best interest, then, to maintain a good credit rating in order to minimize its financing costs. Typically, debt issues acquire a bond rating prior to their issuance. Two major rating agencies are Standard & Poor's Corporation and Moody's Investor Service. The text discusses their ratings.

The return on bonds

The bond's rating goes hand in hand with its required rate of return. The riskier the bond, the higher its required yield. Although the coupon on a bond stays fixed over the bond's life (except for variable-rate bonds), the required yield changes over time as the level of inflation, risk, and investors' attitudes change. With increases in expected inflation, the required rate of return on bonds of all quality ratings increases. In addition, the yield difference or risk premium between bonds of different qualities narrows or widens over time. We call this difference the yield spread. The more risk averse investors become, the wider the yield spread, since investors require a greater reward for taking on additional risk. Conversly, as investors become less risk averse, the yield spread narrows.

Deep discount bonds and zero-coupon bonds have a yield that relies on a low purchase or issuance price. These bonds provide some or all of their return in the form of bond value appreciation. Deep discount bonds have a low coupon rate but provide a higher yield through a deep discount issuance price. Zero-coupon bonds carry no coupon rate and are deeply discounted to provide a large value appreciation yield over the life of the bond. Tax-exempt institutions such as pension funds are the chief purchasers of these securities.

Financial Distress

On occasion, firms overextend themselves and have difficulty meeting their current obligations. Financial distress can be caused by a variety of conditions such as economic conditions, increased competition, or bad management. Firms have available to them several mechanisms for dealing with financial distress, the most drastic of which is liquidation. Long-range financial planning (Chapter 23) can help prevent the difficulties caused by financial distress.

Preferred Stock

Preferred stock is most frequently employed by public utilities that must temper their debt/equity ratios. Preferred stock, except for variable-rate issues, provides a fixed return to investors. Like debt, the required return on preferred stock varies as the structure of interest rates changes. As the required yield falls, the market price of outstanding preferred stock rises. Firms need not pay cash dividends on preferred stock unless they have sufficient cash flows. Dividends in arrears must be paid before cash dividends on common stock can be paid. Finally, in the case of default, the preferred stockholder has a claim junior to creditors but senior to common stockholders.

COMPLETION QUESTIONS

13.1 _____ securities obligate the firm to pay a fixed annual return for financing.

13.2 In contrast to the tax treatment of cash dividends on common stock and preferred stock, the interest on debt is a _____ expense for the firm.

13.3 The _____ is the contract between the firm and the lender. It spells out the interest payment schedule, the term of the bond, and the maturity value. In addition, it may include _____ to help protect the bond investors.

13.4 _____ are bonds which have primary claim on specific assets in the event of a default by the firm. The _____ bond has a claim against securities rather than physical assets.

13.5 _____ are backed by the full faith and credit of the issuing corporation, and have no specific assets pledged as collateral.

13.6 The right to redeem a bond before it matures is called a _____ _____. In redeeming the bond early, the firm must pay an amount _____ the par value of the bond. This extra amount, the _____, declines over time.

13.7 A firm's indenture might contain a _____ provision requiring the firm to retire a given number of bonds over a specified time period.

13.8 If a firm is retiring debt for its sinking fund, it will buy the debt _____ if the interest rates are high and the bond price is low. Otherwise, the firm will retire the same issue at par value using a _____.

13.9 The restrictive covenants for private placements may be _____ than those for public issues, since the lending institution is the sole purchaser of the issue and wants to maximize the value of its claim.

13.10 The greatest percentage of large bond issues are underwritten and are _____, recording the ownership of the bond.

13.11 Purchasers of bonds pay the price of the bond plus any _____ _____. The issuer of a bond receives less than $1,000 per bond due to the _____ involved.

13.12 _____ reflect the probability of payment of both interest and principal. The higher the rating, the _____ the required return on the bond.

13.13 A difference in required yield exists between bonds of different quality ratings, Aaa and Aa, for example. This difference is called the _____. As investors become more risk averse, this difference _____, since investors want to be rewarded for taking on additional risk.

13.14 _____-specific conditions can result in the lowering of a bond's rating. If a firm's executives do not improve the quality rating of the firm's debt, the next long-term financing may be _____ costly. In addition, the increased riskiness of the firm's debt may increase the firm's stock _____, resulting in a reduced market value of the stock.

13.15 Bonds which are issued at a low price and which carry no coupon are called _____ bonds. Since the value appreciation of these bonds is taxable, the main investors in them are _____.

13.16 Unpaid cash dividends on preferred stocks are called _____. With _____ preferred stock, these unpaid dividends must be paid before common stockholders can receive _____.

PROBLEMS

13.1 California Public Power Company has an abbreviated balance sheet as follows (in millions):

Current assets	$15	Current liabilities	$ 6
Net long-term assets	70	Long-term debt (12% coupon)	24
Total assets	$85	Stockholders' equity	55
		Total liabilities and stockholders' equity	$85

The firm has earnings after taxes (EAT) of $7 million and is subject to a marginal corporate tax rate of 30 percent. The company wishes to issue new long-term debt at 8 percent to increase its base of net fixed assets. The present debt, however, carries several restrictive covenants as follows:

a. Interest coverage (EBIT/I) must be at least 4.
b. The ratio of net long-term assets to long-term debt must be at least 2.
c. The total debt to equity ratio must remain below 0.80.

How much additional debt can the firm issue? (Assume there are no interest costs associated with current liabilities.)

13.2 Halburton Home Construction has outstanding a 15 percent bond issue with 8 years left until maturity. The bonds have a face value of $1,000, pay interest annually, and have a provision that will allow them to be called with a premium of $100 per bond. The company is considering two options.

Option A: Call the bonds and replace them with new 10 percent coupon bonds also with 8 years to maturity. The firm will incur no transactions costs. These bonds will sell at par.

Option B: Repurchase present bonds in the open market and replace them with the above new issue. The purchase in the open market results in a transaction cost of 1 percent of the market price.

Should the firm repurchase or call the bonds?

13.3 Abecrombie Limited, a wholesale importer, is in the process of issuing $6,000,000 of 12 percent coupon debt with a maturity of 5 years. A sinking fund must be established to retire 60 percent of the issue prior to maturity. Assuming the bonds are retired at par and the tax rate is 35 percent, how large must the annual sinking fund payments be if the firm wishes to retire the bonds in four equal installments starting one year from now, with the balance paid in year 5? What will be the annual after-tax cash outflow for each of the 5 years?

13.4 Blackstone Enterprises wishes to raise $12.4 million through the issuance of new preferred stock. The stock will have a par value of $50 per share and a 9.3 percent cash dividend. The existing preferred stock, which has a dividend of $3.00 per share, sells for $20 per share. Assuming that the required return on the new preferred stock is the same as that on the old, how many shares of preferred stock will have to be issued? (Ignore flotation costs.)

13A.1 Lacey Carpet Manufacturers is considering the refunding of its present $50,000,000 issue of outstanding bonds. The bonds, which were issued 5 years ago with a coupon rate of 15 percent, have a remaining term to maturity of 15 years but can be called at face value with a premium of 1 year's interest. The flotation costs of the original issue were $600,000. The bonds will be replaced with $50,000,000 of 13.5 percent coupon rate bonds, which will be issued at par. The flotation costs of these new bonds, which will mature in 15 years, are expected to be $960,000. To insure that funds will be available when needed, there will be a one month overlap, and net proceeds from the new issue will be invested at 8 percent. Lacey's tax rate is 30 percent. Should the firm refund its existing debt? (Round k_i to the nearest whole percent.)

ANSWERS TO COMPLETION QUESTIONS

13.1 Fixed income

13.2 tax deductible

13.3 indenture; restrictive provisions

13.4 First mortgage bonds; collateral trust

13.5 Debentures

13.6 call provision; greater than; call premium

13.7 sinking fund

13.8 on the open market; lottery

13.9 more onerous (or burdensome)

13.10 fully registered

13.11 accrued interest; underwriting costs

13.12 Bond ratings; lower

13.13 yield spread; widens

13.14 Firm; more; beta

13.15 zero-coupon; pension fund (or other tax-exempt institutions)

13.16 arrearages; cumulative; cash dividends

SOLUTIONS TO PROBLEMS

13.1

Step 1. Starting with covenant A, find the maximum amount of debt the firm can issue and have an interest coverage ratio of at least 4.

Since EAT = EBT(1 - T)

$$EBT = \frac{EAT}{1 - T} = \frac{\$7,000,000}{1 - 0.30} = \$10,000,000$$

Step 2. EBIT = EBT + I

= $10,000,000 + $24,000,000(0.12) = $12,880,000

Step 3. If times interest earned must be greater than or equal to 4, $\frac{EBIT}{I} \geq 4$, so I must be less than or equal to $\frac{EBIT}{4}$

$$I \leq \frac{EBIT}{4} \leq \frac{12.88}{4} \leq \$3.22 \text{ million}$$

The firm can increase its interest expense by $0.34 million ($3.22 million - $2.88 million) which means it can issue $4.25 million = (0.35/0.08) of additional debt without violating covenant A.

Step 4. Covenant B: $\frac{\text{net long-term assets}}{\text{long-term debt}} = \frac{\$70M}{\$24M} = 2.91667$

since any new debt (W) will be used to purchase net long-term assets, according to covenant B.

$$\frac{70M + W}{24M + W} \leq 2 \qquad \begin{aligned} 70 + W &= 2(24 + W) \\ 70 + W &= 48 + 2W \\ W &= \$22 \text{ million} \end{aligned}$$

The firm could issue $22 million in debt and not violate covenant B.

Step 5. Covenant C: $\frac{\text{Total Debt}}{\text{Total Equity}} = \frac{\$30M}{\$55M} = 0.54545$

Since $\frac{\text{Total Debt}}{\text{Total Equity}} \leq 0.80$, $\frac{\text{Total Debt}}{55} \leq 0.80$

Total debt ≤ $44M

The firm could issue up to $44M - $30M = $14 million in new devt without violating covenant C.

The binding covenant is A; the firm can issue only $4.25 million in new debt.

13.2

Step 1. Option A

The cost per bond of recalling = face value + premium

= $1,000 + $100 = $1,100 per bond

Step 2. Option B

To figure out the cost of repurchasing the bonds, we need to know the market price. Since the 10 percent coupon bonds will sell at par, the market rate of interest is 10 percent.

$B_0 = \$150(PVA_{10\%, 8yr}) + \$1,000(PV_{10\%, 8yr})$

$B_0 = \$150(5.335) + \$1,000(0.467) = \$800.25 + \$467.00$

$\quad = \$1,267.25$

Step 3. The transactions cost would be ($1,267.25)(0.01) = $12.67. The total cost of repurchasing the bond = $1,267.25 + $12.67 = $1,279.92. It is more expensive to repurchase than to call the bonds.

13.3

Step 1. The firm needs to retire (0.60)($6,000,000) = $3,600,000 prior to maturity. Since the bonds mature in 5 years, the retirement must take place in only 4 years. So, Abecrombie should retire $3,600,000/4 = $900,000 per year.

Step 2. The after-tax cash outflows:

Year	Bonds Outstanding	Interest(12%)	After-Tax Interest Expense [Interest(1-0.35)]	Sinking Fund Payment =	Total
1	$6,000,000	$720,000	$468,000	$ 900,000	$1,368,000
2	5,100,000	612,000	397,800	900,000	1,297,800
3	4,200,000	504,000	327,600	900,000	1,227,600
4	3,300,000	396,000	257,400	900,000	1,157,400
5	2,400,000	288,000	187,200	2,400,000	2,587,200

13.4

Step 1. The yield on existing preferred is $3.00/$20 = 0.15 or 15%

Step 2. The price of the new preferred = D_{ps}/k_p

$\quad$ Dividend = $50(0.093) = $4.65

$\quad$ Price = $4.65/0.15 = $31 per share

Step 3. Number of shares = $\dfrac{\text{total proceeds}}{\text{price per share}} = \dfrac{\$12,400,000}{\$31} = 400,000$ shares

13A.1

Step 1. Calculate the initial outlay:

    Before taxes

Face value of existing debt	$50,000,000
Call premium (15% of $50,000,000)	7,500,000
Additional interest ($50,000,000)(0.15)(1/12)	625,000
Less: Net proceeds of new issue ($50,000,000 − $960,000)	−49,040,000
Less: Interest earned on net proceeds ($49,040,000)(0.08)(1/12)	− 326,933
	$ 8,758,067

    Tax-deductible expenses

Call premium on old bond	$ 7,500,000
Unamortized flotation cost on old bond ($600,000)(15/20yr)	450,000
Additional interest during overlap period	625,000
Total tax-deductible expenses	$ 8,575,000
Tax savings ($8,575,000)(0.30)	$ 2,572,500

Step 2.

    Initial outlay:

Before-tax outlay	$ 8,758,067
Less: Tax savings	2,572,500
Initial outlay, ΔCF_0	$ 6,185,567

Step 3.

    Incremental savings:

Interest on old bonds (0.15)($50,000,000)		$ 7,500,000

    Tax deductions

Interest	$7,500,000	
Amortization of flotation costs ($600,000/20 yr)	30,000	
Total	$7,530,000	
Tax savings ($7,530,000)(0.30)		$ 2,259,000
After-tax cash outflow on old bond per year		$ 5,241,000
Interest on new bonds (0.135)($50,000,000)		$ 6,750,000

    Tax deductions:

Interest	$6,750,000	
Amortization of flotation cost ($960,000/15 yr)	64,000	
Total	$6,814,000	
Tax savings ($6,814,000)(0.30)		$ 2,044,200
After-tax cash outflow on new bond per year		$ 4,705,800

Step 4.

    ΔCF_t = $5,241,000 − $4,705,800 = $535,200

Step 5.

    Discount rate = 13.5%(1 − 0.30) = 9.45%

    Recall from equation 5.9 that:

$$PVA_{k\%,nyr} = \frac{1 - 1/(1+k)^n}{k}$$

$$PVA_{15\%,15yr} = \frac{1 - 1/(1.0945)^{15}}{0.0945}$$

$$= \frac{1 - 1/3.8747}{0.0945}$$

$$= 7.851$$

    NPV = $\Delta CF_t(PVA_{9.45\%,15yr}) - \Delta CF_0$

         = $535,200(7.851) − $6,185,567

         = $4,201,855.20 − $6,185,567 = −$1,983,711.80

Since the NPV is negative, the firm should not refund the bonds.

CHAPTER 14

REQUIRED RETURNS FOR COMPANIES AND PROJECTS

HOW THIS CHAPTER RELATES TO THE REST OF THE TEXT

A major component of a project's NPV (Chapters 8-11) is the firm's required return. Calculation of the cost of capital requires knowledge of common stocks (Chapter 12), bonds and preferred stock (Chapter 13), and the valuation process (Chapter 6). A firm's cost of capital is dependent on its capital structure (Chapter 15). It is useful also in accounts receivable and inventory decisions (Chapter 19), lease evaluation (Chapter 17), and mergers and corporate restructuring (Chapter 22).

TOPICAL OUTLINE

I. The concept of required returns.
   A. Financial decision making requires an understanding of capital budgeting. An important component of NPV is the required return on the project.
   B. If project risk is the same as risk to the firm as a whole, the proper rate of return can be viewed in two fashions.
      1. The opportunity cost of capital is the rate of return that the firm, or its investors, could earn if it invested its funds in alternative uses.
      2. The weighted average cost of capital is the average after-tax cost of funds to the firm.
   C. Definitions and calculations of the weighted average cost of capital.
      1. WACC = $k_i W_{debt} + k_{ps} W_{preferred\ stock} + k_s W_{common\ equity}$
      2. The W's are the proportions of funding to be raised by debt, preferred stock, and common equity.
      3. k_i is the after-tax cost of issuing new debt: $k_i = k_b(1 - T)$.
      4. k_{ps} is the after-tax cost of issuing new preferred stock.
      5. k_s is the after-tax cost of common equity.
   D. Basic assumptions in order to use the WACC for decision making.
      1. The project's risk must be typical of the firm's risk.
      2. The firm will not materially change its financing policies to undertake the investments.

II. Calculating specific costs and financing proportions.
   A. Cost of debt.
      1. Interest is a tax-deductible expense, so the cost of debt is reduced by that tax deduction (assuming the firm is profitable).
         a. $k_i = k_b (1 - T)$
         b. $B_0 = I(PVA_{k_b},n) + M(PV_{k_b},n)$
      2. Debt is the least costly of the three sources, since bondholders have a fixed legal claim, and since interest is tax deductible for profitable firms.
   B. Cost of preferred stock.
      1. Cash dividends paid on preferred stock are not a tax deductible expense.
      2. $k_{ps} = D_{ps}/P_0$.
   C. Cost of common equity.
      1. The cost of internally generated funds.
         a. Actually, this is an opportunity cost, because stockholders forgo cash dividends in lieu of the retention of cash flows.
            i. Management can distribute the cash flows or reinvest them in the firm.
            ii. Stockholders could have invested the dividend payments for some rate of return if the cash flows had been paid out as cash dividends rather than retained.
            iii. If a firm cannot earn a return of at least k_s on reinvested internally generated funds, it should distribute the funds to investors so they can invest them in other assets to provide a return equal to k_s.
            iv. Estimating the cost of equity capital requires both judgment and an understanding of what the firm's stockholders expect of the firm.

b. Three approaches to calculating k_s.
   i. Dividend valuation approach: $k_s = (D_1/P_0) + g$.
   ii. CAPM approach: $k_s = k_{RF} + \beta_j(k_M - k_{RF})$.
   iii. Bond yield plus risk premium approach:
   k_s = bond yield + risk premium.
   (a) Useful for firm that does not pay cash dividends.
   (b) Useful when stock is not traded.
2. Cost of new common stock, k_s (external common equity).
   a. The cost of newly issued common stock is the same as the cost of internally generated equity, except for the adjustment in flotation costs and the underpricing that occurs when new common stock is sold.
   b. Because flotation costs are relatively small, we generally ignore them.
D. The financing proportions.
1. The weights should be determined by the current proportions of the market values of the firm's outstanding securities.
2. We assume that in investing in assets, the firm will not significantly change its financing mix.

III. The weighted average cost of capital in practice.
A. Steps in calculating the weighted average cost of capital.
1. Calculate the cost of long-term debt, preferred stock, internally generated funds using the formulas above.
   a. The before-tax cost of debt is what the firm would have to pay to raise additional debt.
   b. In calculating the WACC, the manager is interested in the after-tax cost of debt.
   c. In estimating the cost of internally generated common equity via the dividend valuation approach, the manager should begin by estimating the expected growth in cash dividends.

2. Calculate the market value proportions of financing to be employed.
   a. Multiply the market price per bond by the number of bonds outstanding; if no current market price is available, use the term structure of interest rates to estimate the required yield and price.
   b. Multiply the common stock market price by the number of shares outstanding.
   c. Multiply the preferred stock market price by the number of shares outstanding.
   d. Add all these market values, and divide each by this base to get the proportions of each.
3. Use the formula, given before, to calculate the WACC.
4. The WACC can be used to discount cash flows of projects that are as risky as the firm; projects with a positive NPV are candidates for selection.
5. The WACC can be used as a hurdle rate for IRR calculations on projects as risky as the firm.
6. Accepting projects with less return than the WACC is not consistent with the goal of value maximization.

B. How often should the WACC be calculated?
   1. When the financing proportions have or are expected to change.
   2. When economic conditions have changed.
   3. At least every two years.

IV. Divisional and project specific required rates of return.
   A. Reasons for calculating divisional costs of capital.
      1. Riskiness varies among divisional cash flows.
      2. If a firm uses a firm-wide WACC, it may be too low for high-risk projects and too high for low-risk projects.
      3. A firm-wide WACC will under-allocate funds to low-risk divisions and over-allocate funds to high-risk divisions.
   B. Steps in calculating divisional costs of capital.
      1. Determine the firm's cost of debt, k_i, and use as the cost of debt for the division.

2. Identify one or more publicly traded firms that are similar in terms of product line and capital structure. (If the capital structure differs, an adjustment to the beta used will be necessary.)

   a. $\beta_{asset} = \dfrac{\beta_{levered\ firm}}{1 + (1 - T)B/S}$

3. Calculate the division's cost of equity capital, using the beta of the publicly traded firm.
4. Estimate the division's target or appropriate capital structure as if it were a free-standing firm.
5. Calculate the division's cost of capital as though you were calculating the firm-wide WACC.

C. Divisional costs in practice.
   1. Estimating each division's cost of capital requires a thorough understanding of the firm's divisions and appropriate publicly traded firms similar to the divisions.
   2. Since some bonds might not be publicly traded, you might estimate the rating and yield to maturity of newly issued bonds for the firm.

D. Project specific required rates of return can be calculated using the same basic steps used in calculating divisional required rates of return.

FORMULAS

Notation

- WACC = weighted average cost of new capital
- k_b = before-tax cost of new debt issued by the firm
- k_i = after-tax cost of new debt issued by the firm, $k_b(1 - T)$
- k_{ps} = after-tax cost of new preferred stock issued by the firm
- k_s = after-tax cost of new equity capital
- W_i = weights indicate the future financing proportions to be employed by the firm for debt, preferred stock, and common equity
- I = annual dollar interest on a bond
- M = maturity value (typically $1,000) of a bond
- B_0 = net proceeds from the sale of a bond after considering any premium or discount in price, and the flotation costs involved

n = number of years to bond's maturity
D_{ps} = cash dividend expected on the preferred stock
k_{RF} = risk-free rate; often use U.S. Treasury bill rate as proxy
k_M = expected return on the market portfolio
β_j = market risk measure for security j
g = expected compound percentage growth in cash dividends
D_1 = expected cash dividend for next year
P_0 = current value or price

Weighted Average Cost of Capital

$$WACC = k_i W_{debt} + k_{ps} W_{preferred\ stock} + k_s W_{common\ equity}$$

Before-Tax Cost of Debt, k_b

$$B_0 = I(PVA_{k_b},n) + M(PV_{k_b},n)$$

After-Tax Cost of Debt, k_i

$$k_i = k_b(1 - T)$$

Cost of Preferred Stock, k_{ps}

$$k_{ps} = (D_{ps}/P_0)$$

Cost of Internally Generated Funds, k_s (Opportunity Cost)

Dividend valuation approach: $k_s = (D_1/P_0) + g$

CAPM approach: $k_s = k_{RF} + \beta_j(k_M - k_{RF})$

Bond yield plus risk premium approach: k_s = bond yield + risk premium

Divisional Cost of Capital

Divisional cost of equity = $k_{RF} + \beta_{similar\ firm}(k_M - k_{RF})$

Unlevered Beta

$$\beta_{asset} = \frac{\beta_{levered\ firm}}{1 + (T - 1)B/S}$$

WHAT TO LOOK FOR

Any craftsman will tell you that you must have the right tool for the job at hand in order to complete the task well. Financial management is an art and a science. Managers use techniques such as the time value of money (Chapter 5) and cash flow (Chapter 4) to make valuation estimates for short-term and long-term asset investments. The discount rate they use in these calculations is determined by a combination of theory and guess work. If the discount rate is wrong, the valuation results will be wrong, no matter how accurate the cash flow estimates. Chapter 14 addresses the craft of estimating the discount rate. While we want to be as precise as possible, errors of 1 to 2 percent in a firm's discount rate rarely make any important difference in practice.

We know the discount rate by several names--the required rate of return, the weighted average cost of capital, and the hurdle rate. We use these terms interchangably in this chapter.

The Theory Underlying Weighted Average Cost of Capital

During the life of a firm, managers invest the firm's borrowed and equity funds in short- and long-term assets. If every opportunity presented is accepted, the firm will not remain a going concern. Managers must decide among investment alternatives, as we saw in Chapters 8-11. The key criterion for selecting investments is that the investment should increase or maximize the value of the firm.

Net present value (NPV) and internal rate of return (IRR) are two discounting procedures managers can use to value investment alternatives. If the proposed project's NPV is negative, or if the IRR does not exceed the required rate of return for that project, acceptance of the project will reduce the value of the firm.

What is this required rate of return, however? In Chapter 14, we calculate the financing costs of generating new capital. This weighted average cost of capital is the cost of the last dollar of additional funds and is used as a hurdle rate or as the discount rate for making investment decisions for projects with risk similar to the firm.

As you know, investors require a higher return from common stock than from preferred stock or debt, since there is no stated cash dividend rate and they share in both the good and bad times of the firm. So, in calculating the component costs of financing, the cost of equity will be higher than that of preferred stock or debt. Changes in economic risk, inflation risk, firm- and issue-specific risk, and international risk will also increase the firm's cost of some or all of the capital components and thus increase the weighted average cost of capital.

The Art of Estimating the Weighted Average Cost of Capital

Many of the values used in calculating the component costs of capital are rough estimates. The more skillful the manager, the closer the estimates will be to the actual values. In calculating any of the component costs, the proceeds, net of flotation costs and any discount (or underpricing), must be estimated. Discounts and flotation costs increase the effective cost of new capital. In addition, the manager must estimate the expected interest, I, or cash dividend, D_{ps} or D_1, on the new debt or stock, and the expected compound growth in common stock cash dividends, g. If the economy and the financial markets are especially unstable, this estimate may need frequent revision to reflect changes in the supply and demand for money and possible internally generated cash flows available for distribution as common stock cash dividends.

Managers must also estimate the future required return on the stock market, k_M, the future risk-free rate, k_{RF}, and the firm's future beta, β_j. Chapter 7 discusses how to approximate k_M; we will go through the process in the next section. A careful study of the term structure of interest rates can help in approximating k_{RF}. Value Line and other financial services can give a reasonable estimate of the firm's beta, but remember that betas for individual firms are not stable and may change over time.

Calculating the Weighted Average Cost of Capital

Now, let's run through a WACC calculation for a hypothetical company, the Webb Bicycle Corporation. The firm's bonds are rated AA, as is its preferred stock. Its beta is 1.2. Suppose we look at the financial section of the Wall Street Journal and find that AA industrial bonds are yielding 12 percent, while AA preferred stock is yielding 13.25 percent. We look at the trends in the U.S. Treasury bill rate, and deduce that the risk-free rate is 9 percent. Finally, we project the expected rate of inflation (8 percent), and the real rate of return in the economy (2 percent). Then, we add the historical risk premium of stocks over bonds (about 4 percent) and we get an expected k_M of 14 percent.

In selling new bonds, we estimate that the proceeds, B_0, will be $980. We predict that the proceeds from each new $100 par preferred share, P_0, will be $96. Finally, the current market price, P_0, of Webb Bicycle common stock is $30 per share. First, calculate the bond price:

$$P_0 = I(PVA_{k_b,n}) + M(PV_{k_b,n})$$

$$= \$85(PVA_{12\%, 9yr}) + \$1,000(PV_{12\%, 9yr})$$

$$= \$85(5.328) + \$1,000(0.361) = \$452.88 + \$361.00 = \$813.88$$

Now, calculate the price of preferred stock:

$$D = \$200(0.1875) = \$37.50$$

$$P_0 = D/k_{ps} = \$37.50/01325 = \$283.02$$

Below is the capital structure of Webb Bicycle Corporation and the calculation of its market value weights:

Liabilities and Stockholders' Equity for Webb Corporation

	Book Value	Market Price	×	Number Outstanding	=	Market Value
Debt:						
8.5 percent coupon rate due in 9 years $1,000 par, 5,000 bonds	$5,000,000	$813.88		5,000		$ 4,069,400
Preferred stock:						
18 3/4 percent dividend, 10,000 shares, $200 par	1,000,000	283.02		10,000		2,830,200
Stockholders' equity:						
Common stock, 1,000,000 shares outstanding, $10 par	10,000,000	30.00		1,000,000		30,000,000
Total						$36,899,600

The market value weights are: Debt = $4,069,400/$36,899,600 = 11.03%; preferred stock = $2,830,200/$36,899,600 = 7.67%; and common stock = $30,000,000/$36,899,600 = 81.30%.

We can calculate the required rate of return on Webb Bicycle by using the equations in Chapter 14. Let's list again the estimates we made above: M = \$1,000; B_0 = \$980; P_0 = \$96; k_{RF} = 9%; k_M = 14%; β_j = 1.2; and let's suppose D_1 = \$1.50 and g = 10.5%. We will assume that the new bonds are 15-year bonds and the firm's marginal corporate tax rate is 35 percent. Finally, the firm can finance its common equity needs with internally generated funds.

Now, let's calculate the component costs of capital:

Cost of debt: 12 percent coupon, 15 years to maturity

$$P_0 = I(PVA_{k_b,15yr}) + M(PV_{k_b,15yr})$$

at $k_b = 12\%$

$P_0 = \$120(6.811) + \$1,000(0.183) = \$1,000.32$

at $k_b = 13\%$

$P_0 = \$120(6.462) + \$1,000(0.160) = \$775.44 + \$160.00 = \$935.44$

Interpolating, $k = 12\% + \$1,000.32 - \$980/\$1,000.32 - \$935.44$

$= 12\% + \$20.32/\$64.88 = 12.31\%$

(Via financial calculator, $k_b = 12.30\%$.)

$k_i = k_b(1 - T) = 12.31\%(1 - 0.35) = 8.00\%$

Cost of preferred stock: 13.25 percent dividend rate

$k_{ps} = D_{ps}/P_0 = \$13.25/\$96 = 13.80\%$

Cost of internally generated funds:

CAPM approach: $k_s = k_{RF} + \beta_j(k_M - k_{RF}) = 9\% + 1.2(14\% - 9\%) = 15\%$

Dividend valuation approach: $k_s = (D_1/P_0) + g = (\$1.50/\$30) + 10.5\%$

$= 15.5\%$

Bond yield plus risk premium approach: k_s = bond yield + risk premium

$= 12.28\% + 4\% = 16.28\%$

We will use the average of the three approaches (15.59%). Now, using the market value weights, we can weight these costs to find the weighted average cost of capital.

$WACC = k_iW_{debt} + k_{ps}W_{preferred\ stock} + k_sW_{common\ equity}$

$= 0.1103(8.00\%) + 0.0767(13.80\%) + 0.8130(15.59\%) = 14.62\%$

Webb Bicycle Corporation can use the discount rate of 14.62 percent for NPV and IRR calculations if the projects have the same level of risk as the firm.

Divisional Costs of Capital

It is possible to calculate costs of capital or hurdle rates for each division. If, for example, Webb Bicycle had three divisions of varying risk, the most risky division would have more opportunity to invest in risky projects than the least risky division. If the firm used an overall weighted average cost of capital, the most risky division would get more capital budgeting money than the moderately risky and the least risky divisions, simply because of this risk-return difference. To estimate divisional costs of capital, the firm could find other companies which produce the same product line as the most risky division, some which produce the same product as the moderately risky division, and so on. Using the capital structure and beta of the comparable firms, the original firm could calculate divisional costs of equity and then divisional weighted average costs of capital for use in capital budgeting, just as we did above. Each division would have an appropriate discount rate to use when evaluating possible capital investment projects. Managers should take care when using this method, however, since one or more firms similar to the firm's divisions must be found.

COMPLETION QUESTIONS

14.1 The _____ is the minimum acceptable rate of return on new investments of average risk.

14.2 The WACC is the weighted average of the firm's _____ _____.

14.3 In making investment decisions, projects should be chosen which _____. Any projects whose return is _____ the WACC should be rejected, since they will impair the firm's value.

14.4 As inflation and other sources of risk increase, the firm's WACC will _____. In response, the market value of the firm's debt and equity outstanding will _____.

14.5 During the calculation of WACC, the relevant cost of debt is the _____, since it is the cost to the firm.

14.6 In order to calculate the cost of _____, the returns demanded by existing equity investors must be estimated. This cost is an _____, since the cash flows are reinvested in the firm's projects at some rate of return rather than paid out as cash dividends.

14.7 _____ increase the cost of new common equity, making it a more costly source of financing than internally generated funds.

14.8 The cost of common equity is _____ the cost of preferred stock or the cost of debt. From the investor's standpoint, there is _____ risk, since the common stockholders participate in both the good and bad times of the firm.

14.9 The weights used in calculating the weighted average cost of capital are based on the current proportions of the _____ of the firm's outstanding securities.

14.10 The firm's WACC should be recalculated at least _____ or _____.

14.11 Since the riskiness of divisions may vary, the firm might calculate _____ to evaluate possible capital projects. This procedure can help prevent more risky divisions from receiving _____ than their share of capital investment funding.

14.12 When the internal rate of return method is used for screening capital projects, the _____ or some appropriate _____ is the hurdle rate that must be met.

14.13 In calculating the firm's cost of equity with CAPM, the future return on the market can be approximated by adding the _____ _____, _____, and _____. The rate on _____ _____ is used as a proxy for the risk-free rate.

PROBLEMS

14.1 Winchester Industries has outstanding only one bond issue, which will mature in 10 years. The bond is presently selling for $764.23 even though its face value is $1,000. Winchester has estimated its after-tax cost of debt at 7.7 percent. What are the yearly interest payments on the outstanding bonds if the tax rate is 30 percent?

14.2 Washington Petroleum is planning to issue new preferred stock. The present preferred is selling for $58.50 and pays dividends of $7 per year. The new preferred will carry the same dividend, but the net proceeds of the sale are expected to be $3.50 lower than the current market price. What is the percentage cost of new preferred stock?

14.3 Howard Software Company's common stock is presently selling for $45 a share. In 1990, the cash dividend on common stock is expected to be $5.85 per share, an increase over the 1989 dividend of $5.09 per share. What is the cost of internally generated funds using the dividend valuation approach? (Round to the nearest whole percent.)

14.4 Hanson Piano Company wishes to estimate its weighted average cost of capital. The following financial data has been provided.

Balance Sheet (in thousands)

Total assets	$3,710	Accounts payable	$ 200
		Notes payable	300
		Bonds ($1,000 par)	800
		Preferred stock (10,000 shares)	100
		Common stock (1 million shares)	1,000
		Retained earnings	1,310
			$3,710

Common stock
    1983 cash dividend = $0.20
    1990 cash dividend = $0.30
    Current price = $2.375
    Beta = 1.05

Preferred stock
    Dividend = $2.00
    Current price = $14.00

Debt
    Term to maturity = 8 years
    Yearly interest rate = 10%
    Market price = $900 ($1,000 par)

Market data
    k_{RF} = 8%
    k_M = 19%

Because of Hanson's good credit rating, both the accounts payable and notes payable have costs (before tax) of approximately 2 percent over the risk-free rate. The tax rate is 30 percent.

a. Determine the after-tax cost of long-term debt.

b. Determine the cost of preferred stock.

c. Determine the after-tax cost of short-term debt.

d. Using both the dividend valuation approach and the CAPM approach, estimate the cost of common equity. Take as your estimate the average of the two approaches.

e. Assuming that short-term debt is valued at its face value, what are the market value proportions of each component of Hanson's capital structure?

f. Determine the weighted average cost of capital.

ANSWERS TO COMPLETION QUESTIONS

14.1 weighted average cost of capital
14.2 after-tax cost of new financing
14.3 maximize the value of the firm; below
14.4 increase; decrease
14.5 after-tax cost
14.6 internally generated funds; opportunity cost
14.7 Flotation costs and underpricing
14.8 more than; more
14.9 market value
14.10 every two years; when economic conditions change
14.11 divisional costs of capital; more
14.12 weighted average cost of capital; required rate of return
14.13 expected real growth in the economy; next year's expected inflation; a risk premium for riskiness of common stock over bonds; U.S. Treasury bills

SOLUTIONS TO PROBLEMS

14.1

Step 1. From Equation 14.2, $k_i = k_b(1 - T)$ or $k_b = \dfrac{k_i}{(1 - T)} = \dfrac{7.7\%}{1 - 0.30} = 11.0\%$

Step 2. $B_0 = I(PVA_{11\%, 10yr}) + \$1,000(PV_{11\%, 10yr})$

$\$764.23 = I(5.889) + \$1,000(0.352)$

$I(5.889) = \$764.23 - \$352.00$

$I = \$412.23/5.889 = \$70.00$

14.2

Step 1. The proceeds from the sale will be $\$58.50 - \$3.50 = \$55.00 = P_0$

Step 2. $k_{ps} = D_{ps}/P_0 = \$7.00/\$55.00 = 12.73\%$

14.3

Step 1. To estimate g, recall that $D_1 = D_0(1 + g)$ or $1 + g = (D_1/D_0)$

$g = \dfrac{D_{1990}}{D_{1989}} - 1 = (\$5.85/\$5.09) - 1 = 1.1493 - 1 = 0.1493 = 14.93\%$

Step 2. $k_s = (D_1/P_0) + g = (\$5.85/\$45.00) + 14.93\% = 13\% + 14.93\% = 27.93\%$

14.4a

Step 1. To estimate k_b,

$$\$900 = \$100(PVA_{k_b\%,8yr}) + \$1,000(PV_{k_b\%,8yr})$$

at 12%,

$$P_0 = \$100(PVA_{12\%,8yr}) + \$1,000(PV_{12\%,8yr})$$

$$= \$100(4.968) + \$1,000(0.404) = \$900.80$$

at 13%,

$$P_0 = \$100(PVA_{13\%,8yr}) + \$1,000(PV_{13\%,8yr})$$

$$= \$100(4.799) + \$1,000(0.376) = \$855.90$$

Interpolating,

$$k_b = 12\% + \frac{\$900.80 - \$900}{\$900.80 - \$855.90} = 12.0178\%$$

Step 2. $k_i = k_b(1 - T) = 12.0178\%(1 - 0.30) = 8.41\%$

14.4b

Step 3. $k_{ps} = D_{ps}/P_0 = \$2/\$14 = 14.29\%$

14.4c

Step 4. The after-tax cost of short-term debt from the last paragraph of the problem is equal to 8% + 2% = 10% before tax or 10(1 - 0.3) = 7.0% after tax.

14.4d

Step 5. Dividend valuation approach:

Estimate g: $D_{1990}(PV_{?\%,7yr}) = D_{1983}$

$$PV_{?\%,7yr} = \frac{D_{1983}}{D_{1990}} = \frac{\$0.20}{\$0.30} = 0.667$$

From the PV tables, g is approximately 6%.

Step 6. $D_1 = D_0(1 + g) = \$0.30(1.06) = \$0.318$

Step 7. $k_s = (D_1/P_0) + g = (\$0.318/\$2.375) + 6\% = 19.39\%$

Step 8. From the CAPM, $k_j = k_{RF} + \beta(k_M - k_{RF}) = 8\% + 1.05(19\% - 8\%) = 19.55\%$

The estimate of $k_s = (19.39\% + 19.55\%)/2 = 19.47\%$

14.4e

Step 9. (In thousands)

Market value of short-term debt:

Accounts payable + notes payable = $200 + $300 = $ 500

Market value of long-term debt:

(Number of bonds)(B_0/M) = (800)($900/$1,000) = 720

Market value of preferred:

(Number of shares)(P_0) = (10)($14) = 140

Market value of common:

(Number of shares)(P_0) = (1,000)($2.375)   2,375

Total market value = $3,735

Step 10.

Component	Market Value of Component	÷ Total Market Value	= Market Value Proportions
Short-term debt	$ 500	$3,735	0.1339
Long-term debt	720	3,735	0.1928
Preferred stock	140	3,735	0.0375
Common stock	2,375	3,735	0.6358

14.4f

Step 11. The weighted average cost is just the after-tax cost of each component weighted by the market value proportions.

WACC = 0.1339(7.0%) + 0.1928(8.41%) + 0.0375(14.29%) + 0.6358(19.47%)

= 0.9373% + 1.6214% + 0.5359% + 12.3790% = 15.47%

CHAPTER 15

CAPITAL STRUCTURE

HOW THIS CHAPTER RELATES TO THE REST OF THE TEXT

Chapters 12 and 13 examined the procedures for issuing bonds and common stock and Chapter 14 discussed how the cost of each long-term source of funds affects the firm's cost of capital. In this chapter, we discuss the firm's capital structure and how debt affects the firm's value. The risk (Chapter 7) of a firm's common stock is related to how much debt financing is used. The business risk of the firm is primarily a function of the firm's past capital budgeting decisions (Chapters 8-11).

TOPICAL OUTLINE

I. Introduction.
   A. Prior to this chapter, we assumed the firm's capital structure was given.
   B. The issue in capital structure is: Does how we slice the pie affect its size? That is, does the value of the firm change as we change its financing proportions? The answers are complex and controversial.
   C. Once the capital structure is determined, the required rate of return can be estimated, and capital budgeting decisions can be made.
II. Risk and capital structure.
   A. Long-term sources of funds make up the firm's capital structure.
      1. Long-term sources include common stock, preferred stock, debt, leases, and internally generated funds.
      2. The chapter looks at what proportion of each of these sources the firm should use.
   B. Business risk.
      1. Business risk is the relative dispersion or variability in the firm's expected EBIT.
      2. The coefficient of variation measures the relative variability of the firm's EBIT.
      3. Business risk is primarily caused by the nature of the firm's operations.

a. The more sensitive the firm's sales are to general economic fluctuations, the higher the business risk.
b. The smaller the firm and its share of the market, the more the business risk.
c. The higher the proportion of fixed versus variable operating costs, the higher the operating leverage, and the greater the business risk.
d. The more uncertain the input prices for the firm's products, the greater the business risk.
e. The greater the firm's ability to adjust output prices, the less the business risk.
4. Business risk is a direct function of the firm's accumulated investment (capital budgeting) decisions.
a. Capital budgeting decisions affect the nature of the firm's business as well as the composition of its assets.
b. Cyclical industries such as steel, have greater business risk than less cyclical industries, such as the grocery industry.
5. Business risk has a major impact on how much financial risk a firm is able to undertake.

C. Financial risk.
1. Financial risk is a result of the firm's long-term financing decisions.
2. Financial risk refers to:
a. The increased variability of earnings available to the firm's common stockholders due to the presence of debt.
b. The increased probability of financial distress borne by the firm's stockholders if financial leverage is employed.
3. The primary sources of financial leverage are debt, leases, and preferred stock. Chapter 15 focuses only on debt.
4. The coefficient of variation of earnings per share (EPS) is higher when more debt is employed, signifying an increase in relative variability and an increase in financial risk.

D. Impact on the value of the firm is more important than impact on EPS.

III. Capital structure theory.
   A. Assumptions.
      1. Only two types of securities are used--long-term debt and common stock.
      2. The firm is not expected to grow, so we can value common stock with the no-growth dividend model.
      3. All earnings are assumed to be paid out in cash dividends, so the market price can be written $P_0 = EPS/k$, while the total market value of the firm, S, can be calculated by $S = E/k_s$.
      4. There are no costs or penalties if the firm does not pay interest on its debt, although bondholders may take over the firm.
   B. The no-tax case: If the firm pays no corporate taxes, what effect does debt financing have on the value of the firm?
      1. For example, an all-equity firm chooses between issuing more common stock or new debt to pay for a capital investment.
         a. If common stock is used, the firm will still be all equity financed, so its total market value will be the present value of the future perpetual dividend stream: $V = S = D/k_s$.
         b. If the firm uses debt rather than common stock, the apparent value of the firm seems higher than if the firm uses all equity, but that is because the change in risk has not been taken into account. The cost of equity, k_s, increases.
      2. Modigliani and Miller (MM) suggest that the value of the firm actually does not change when using debt under a no-tax assumption.
         a. MM assumptions.
            i. Perfect capital markets.
            ii. All debt is risk-free.
            iii. All firms can be grouped into risk classes based on variance in EBIT.
            iv. Homogeneous expectations.

b. Proposition I: The market value of any firm is independent of its capital structure and is found by capitalizing EBIT at the appropriate discount rate for an all equity firm, k_s^U.

c. Proposition II: The cost of equity for a levered firm, k_s^L, is equal to k_s^U plus a risk premium:
$k_s^L = k_s^U + (k_s^U - k_b)\frac{B}{S}$.

d. Propositions I and II hold because individuals can replicate (or undo) anything the firm does; there is no advantage in having the corporation issue debt.

e. See Figure 15.3 for Modigliani and Miller's position; as financial leverage increases, the value of the firm and the marginal cost of capital remain constant.

C. The MM model with corporate taxes. Assume T = 30%.

1. Since the common stock price results from capitalizing the expected income by the required rate of return, the value of the all-equity firm would be lower since the earnings would decline by 30 percent due to taxes.

2. If the firm funds a capital project with debt, any additional earnings are split among the original number of shares. The interest payments on debt are tax deductible.

   a. The firm's common stock market price will increase due to the addition of debt.

   b. In spite of the increase in risk due to debt usage, the presence of corporate taxes subsidizes the use of debt, increasing the value of the firm (S + B) by the amount B × T, and decreasing the firm's marginal cost of capital.

3. Proposition I (adjusted for taxes): $V_L = V_U + T(B)$.

4. Proposition II (adjusted for taxes):
$k_s^L = k_s^U + (k_s^U - k_b)(1 - T)\frac{B}{S}$.

D. Financial distress costs and other factors that affect the level of debt usage.

1. Financial distress may cause additional expenses and serious disruption of the ongoing activities of the firm.

   a. Worried customers may cancel orders.

b. Key employees may leave.
c. The firm may bypass positive NPV projects if they don't produce immediate cash flows.
d. The firm loses financial flexibility.

2. Agency costs.
   a. Unless a firm's equity is completely owned by managers, the managers have an incentive to consume perquisites. This agency cost increases as external equity increases.
   b. Since the claims of bondholders are fixed, equityholders have an incentive to invest in more risky projects. Bondholders demand restrictive covenants and monitoring to guard these agency costs.
   c. Since some forms of agency costs increase with equity and some with debt, there must be an optimal capital structure.
   d. Given financial distress costs (FD) and agency costs (AC), $V_L = V_U + TB - PV(FD) - PV(AC)$.

3. Corporate and personal taxes
   a. While corporations have the benefits of deducting interest payments for tax purposes, investors pay taxes on interest earned.
      i. With personal taxes,
      $$V_L = V_U + \left[1 - \frac{(1-T)(1-T_{ps})}{(1-T_{pb})}\right] B$$
      ii. There is no optimal capital structure for individual firms.
      iii. There may be an equilibrium optimal amount of aggregate debt for the entire economy.
   b. Modigliani and Miller's and Miller's theories ignore non-cash tax shields such as depreciation. DeAngelo and Masulis show that the tradeoff between interest tax shields and other tax shields leads to an optimal capital structure that is less than 100% debt.

4. Managers may use capital structure changes to signal their expectations about the firm's future prospects.
   a. Debt signals higher expected futire cash flows.

b. Under signaling theory, capital structure is an ongoing, dynamic process.

5. A target capital structure is one which maximizes the value of the firm (V) or minimizes the WACC. Under the pecking order theory, managers try to maintain a target capital structure.

   a. Internal financing is preferred because of lack of flotation costs or lack of submission to market disciplinary forces.

   b. Managers develop a target dividend payout ratio and avoid sudden changes in dividends.

   c. When firms have excess cash, they build up cash balances or buy back stock. If cash is less than needed, the firm draws down its cash balances.

   d. External financing is a last resort; if external financing is needed, debt is preferred to new equity.

IV. Some tools for capital structure management.

   A. EPS-EBIT analysis.

      1. Different financing decisions will have differing impacts on EPS; the effects of several alternatives can be found by EPS-EBIT analysis.

         a. By finding $EBIT^*$, one finds the EBIT at which one would be indifferent between the two financing alternatives.

         b. This known crossover (or indifferent) EBIT is found by solving the following equation for $EBIT^*$:

         $$\frac{(EBIT^* - I_1)(1 - T) - D_{ps1}}{N_1} = \frac{(EBIT^* - I_2)(1 - T) - D_{ps2}}{N_2}$$

         c. One should also consider the effects of debt usage on the capitalization rate; as risk increases, will the required rate of return increase and the common stock market price decrease?

   B. Other tools to help select the target capital structure.

      1. Coverage ratios help ascertain whether the firm can cover additional interest payments that result from the use of debt.

2. Lender requirements may impose certain performance standards that must be met before assets can be sold, cash dividends can be paid, and so on.
3. Some firms tie their capital structure decision to the bond rating they want to maintain.
4. Some firms follow the capital structure typical of the industry.
5. A cash flow analysis of how the firm might fare in a severe recession will indicate the firm's ability to take on debt.

V. Guidelines for setting debt/equity ratios.
   A. Firms with high amounts of business risk use less debt.
      1. Business risk is related to the types of assets employed.
   B. Although interest expenses from debt reduce taxes, firms need to consider their future expected tax liabilities as well. If it is unlikely that the firm can take advantage of tax shields in the future, use less debt.
   C. Firms need to maintain some financial slack in order to take advantage of new positive NPV projects.

VI. Appendix 15A: Operating, financial, and total leverage (located at the end of the text).
   A. Operating leverage.
      1. Operating leverage arises if the firm experiences fixed operating costs for such things as labor, rent, and the like; variable operating expenses do not provide operating leverage.
      2. Operating leverage is the responsiveness of the firm's earnings before interest and taxes (EBIT) to fluctuations in sales.
      3. The greater the leverage, the greater the responsiveness of EBIT to a given change in sales:

$$\text{Degree of operating leverage (DOL) from base sales level} = \text{DOL} = \frac{\text{percent change in EBIT}}{\text{percent change in sales}}$$

$$= \frac{\Delta \text{EBIT}/\text{EBIT}}{\Delta \text{sales}/\text{sales}} \quad \text{or DOL} = \frac{\text{sales} - \text{variable costs}}{\text{EBIT}}$$

      4. As the firm's sales increase, if all else stays the same, the degree of operating leverage declines (see Table 15A.1).

B. Financial leverage.
1. Financial leverage is the responsiveness of the firm's earnings per share to fluctuation in EBIT.
2. The greater the financial leverage, the greater the responsiveness of EPS to changes in EBIT.

Degree of financial leverage (DFL) from base level EBIT $= \text{DFL} = \dfrac{\text{percentage change in EPS}}{\text{percentage change in EBIT}}$

$= \dfrac{\Delta \text{EPS}/\text{EPS}}{\Delta \text{EBIT}/\text{EBIT}}$ or $\text{DFL} = \dfrac{\text{EBIT}}{\text{EBIT} - \text{Interest}}$

C. Combining operating and financial leverage.
1. With combined leverage, even small changes in sales can have a large impact on EPS.

Degree of combined leverage (DCL) from base level sales $= \text{DCL} = \dfrac{\text{percentage change in EPS}}{\text{percentage change in sales}}$

$= \dfrac{\Delta \text{EPS}/\text{EPS}}{\Delta \text{sales}/\text{sales}}$

or $\text{DCL} = \dfrac{\text{sales} - \text{variable costs}}{\text{EBIT} - \text{Interest}}$

or $\text{DCL} = (\text{DOL})(\text{DFL})$

2. With both operating and financial leverage, the change in sales affects the change in EBIT, which magnifies the change in EPS.

FORMULAS

Notation

- D_1 = next year's common stock cash dividend
- P_0 = today's common stock price
- k_s = required return on equity
- k_s^U = required return on equity in the unlevered firm
- k_s^L = required return on equity in the levered firm
- EPS = earnings per share
- EBIT = total earnings before interest and taxes
- $\overline{\text{EBIT}}$ = expected earnings before interest and taxes
- EBIT^* = the unknown crossover point in EBIT
- I_1, I_2 = the annual total interest charges under two financing plans
- N_1, N_2 = number of shares of common stock outstanding under two financing plans

D_{ps1}, D_{ps2} = preferred stock cash dividends under two financing plans
P/E = firm's price/earnings ratio
k_i = after-tax cost of debt
k_b = before-tax cost of debt
V_U = total value of the unlevered firm
V_L = total value of the levered firm
S = market value of common stock
B = market value of debt
T = firm's marginal tax rate
T_{ps} = personal tax rate on stock income
T_{pb} = personal tax rate on bond income
G_L = gain from leverage
PV = present value
AC = agency costs
FD = financial distress costs
WACC = weighted average cost of capital
DOL = degree of operating leverage
DFL = degree of financial leverage
DCL = degree of combined leverage

Expected EBIT

$$\overline{EBIT} = \sum_{i=1}^{n} P_i(EBIT_i)$$

Standard Deviation of Expected EBIT

$$= \sqrt{\sum_{i=1}^{n} P_i(EBIT_i - \overline{EBIT})^2}$$

Coefficient of Variation of Expected EBIT

$$CV = \frac{\text{standard deviation}}{\overline{EBIT}}$$

Valuation Approach Where All Earnings Are Paid in Dividends and No Growth is Expected

$P_0 = EPS/k_s$, or S(total firm value) = earnings in perpetuity/k_s

Crossover EBIT. EBIT*

$$\frac{(EBIT^* - I_1)(1 - T) - D_{ps1}}{N_1} = \frac{(EBIT^* - I_2)(1 - T) - D_{ps2}}{N_2}$$

Expected Market Price

$$P_0 = (P/E)(EPS)$$

Earnings per Share

$$EPS = \frac{\text{EBIT - interest - taxes - cash dividends on preferred stock}}{\text{number of shares of common stock outstanding}}$$

After-Tax Cost of Debt (k_i)

$$k_i = k_b(1 - T)$$

Valuation Approach When Dividends Are Constant

$$P_0 = D_1/k_s$$

Valuation Approach Where All Earnings Are Paid in Dividends and No Growth is Expected

$$P_0 = EPS/k_s, \text{ or } S = E/k_s$$

The Modigliani and Miller Model Without Taxes

The Value of an Unlevered Firm:

$$V_U = EBIT/k_s^U$$

The Value of a Levered Firm (Proposition I):

$$V_L = S_L + B = EBIT/k_s^U = V_U$$

The Required Return on Equity (Proposition II):

$$k_s^L = k_s^U + (k_s^U - k_b)\frac{B}{S_L}$$

$$k_s^L = EBIT - k_b B/S_L$$

The Weighted Average Cost of Capital:

$$WACC = k_s^L[S_L/(S_L + B)] + k_i[B/(S_L + B)]$$

The Modigliani-Miller Model With Corporate Taxes

The Value of an Unlevered Firm:

$$V_U = EBIT(1 - T)/k_s^U$$

The Value of a Levered Firm:

$$V_L = V_U + TB$$

The Value of Stock in a Levered Firm (Proposition I Adjusted for Taxes):

$$S_L = V_L - B$$

The Required Return on Equity (Proposition II Adjusted for Taxes):

$$k_s^L = K_s^U + (k_s^U - K_b)(1 - T)\frac{B}{S_L}$$

The Gain From Leverage:

$$G_L = TB$$

The Value of a Levered Firm With Agency and Financial Distress Costs:

$$V_L = V_U + TB - PV(AC) - PV(FD)$$

The Value of a Firm With Corporate and Personal Taxes

$$V_L = V_U + \left[1 - \frac{(1-T)(1-T_{ps})}{(1-T_{pb})}\right]B$$

The Gain From Leverage:

$$G_L = \left[1 - \frac{(1-T)(1-T_{ps})}{(1-T_{pb})}\right]B$$

Appendix 15A (located at the end of the text)

Degree of operating leverage (DOL) from the base level sales:

$$DOL = \frac{\text{percentage change in EBIT}}{\text{percentage change in sales}} = \frac{\Delta EBIT/EBIT}{\Delta sales/sales}$$

$$= \frac{\text{sales - variable costs}}{EBIT}$$

Degree of financial leverage (DFL) from the base level EBIT:

$$DFL = \frac{\text{percentage change in EPS}}{\text{percentage change in EBIT}} = \frac{\Delta EPS/EPS}{\Delta EBIT/EBIT} = \frac{EBIT}{EBIT - \text{interest}}$$

Degree of combined leverage (DCL) from the base level sales:

$$DCL = \frac{\text{percentage change in EPS}}{\text{percentage change in sales}} = \frac{\Delta EPS/EPS}{\Delta sales/sales}$$

$$= \frac{\text{sales - variable costs}}{EBIT - \text{interest}} = (DOL)(DFL)$$

WHAT TO LOOK FOR

Again in Chapter 15, we see that financial management is both an art and a science. There is no single obvious optimum combination of debt, equity, and preferred stock, but skillful managers using the proper tools can determine the appropriate capital structure for their firm. Chapter 15 discusses the theory of capital structure and the tools for selecting a capital structure.

Capital Structures

The use of debt introduces financial leverage. The interest payments on debt are tax deductible, and act as a tax shield to decrease taxable earnings.

In comparison to the payment of an equal dollar amount of cash dividends, interest payments increase the earnings available for distribution to common stockholders. Thus, debt used in place of common stock in prudent amounts can increase earnings per share.

Financial leverage

Interest payments on debt represent a fixed cost which must be paid no matter what the revenues of the firm are. This fixed-cost nature of interest payments increases the variability of EPS with changes in EBIT, and increases the firm's likelihood of financial distress. We call this variability financial leverage. As long as the return on total assets exceeds the interest rate of debt (and risk has not increased too much), financial leverage is beneficial. That is, up to a point, debt usage increases the value of the firm.

Operating leverage

Fixed operating costs introduce operating leverage to the firm. The higher the level of fixed operating costs, the more variable the firm's EBIT is to changes in sales. Appendix 15A at the end of the text lists equations for calculation of the degrees of operating, financial, and combined leverage. When both operating and financial leverage are combined, even small changes in sales will have a major impact on EPS. Figure 15.A1 depicts this magnified effect on EPS due to combined leverage.

Business and financial risk

Although business and financial risk are not synonomous with operating and financial leverage, they are interrelated. Firms which have the following characteristics tend to have more variable EBIT and higher business risk: (1) higher operating leverage due to higher fixed operating costs versus variable operating costs; (2) small market share; (3) greater sensitivity to changes in economic conditions; (4) little control of input prices for its products; and (5) an inability to pass on the effects of inflation to customers. The level of business risk will have a major impact on the amount of financial risk the firm can undertake.

Financial risk, on the other hand, is a result of the firm's long-term financing decisions. It refers to the increased variability in earnings available to the firm's common stockholders and the increased probability of financial distress as the firm employs financial leverage. Financial risk is a result of employing financial leverage, and business risk is partially the result of employing operating leverage.

The Effect of Taxes on Optimal Capital Structure

In the absence of taxes, capital structure does not affect the value of the firm, assuming there is no probability of costly bankruptcy. If we use the dividend valuation model and suppose that dividends will be perpetual, then the value of a share of common stock is the discounted value of this perpetual stream of cash dividends. If we add stock to this all-equity firm in order to fund capital projects, the value of common shares is unaffected. However, when we add taxes to our valuation model, the earnings available to common stockholders (our perpetual dividend stream) will be reduced by that amount of taxes. Thus, the value of each share of common stock is lower than the nontaxed shares.

The use of debt

Now consider the same previously all-equity firm if it chooses to use debt rather than equity to fund its capital projects. Remember, if the firm uses debt rather than increase the number of common shares outstanding, the perpetual dividend stream is divided by the original number of common shares rather than a larger number. If the perpetual dividend stream from the new project is higher than the previous dividend stream, the original common stockholders enjoy higher dividends.

Let's first consider the no-tax case. Debt usage increases the riskiness of the firm's cash flows. Modigliani and Miller suggest that if no taxes existed, the required rate of return on the common stock would increase with an increase in debt usage, so any benefit of debt financing would be directly offset by an increase in the cost of equity. As such, adding debt to a firm's capital structure does not affect value at all.

Taxes and other factors

We will now add taxes to our analysis. We noted above that interest payments are tax deductible and shield some income from taxes. So the earnings available for distribution are higher when the firm pays interest rather than cash dividends on common stock for new financing. Thus, the value of the firm will increase by the present value of the tax shield provided by this debt. If the debt is perpetual,

$$\text{Present value of the debt tax shield} = \frac{\text{(expected interest payment)(corporate tax rate)}}{\text{expected rate of return on debt}}$$

$$= \frac{k_b B(T)}{k_b} = B(T)$$

If the manager's goal is to maximize the value of the firm, he would choose the largest amount of debt possible and the firm's optimal capital structure would be 100% debt!

This surprising result clearly does not hold in the "real world." The Modigliani-Miller world is highly simplified and based on a number of assumptions. In practice, many factors ignored by MM affect the amount of debt a firm can carry. These factors include bankruptcy costs, agency costs, and personal taxes.

As the firm adds more debt, it becomes riskier. With more debt comes larger interest payments and the likelihood that the firm cannot make its interest payments increases. Since bankruptcy is costly, investors will demand higher returns in compensation for possible losses due to financial distress. These financial distress costs can effectively limit the amount of debt a firm is willing to issue.

Agency problems also serve to limit the amount of debt a firm issues. For instance, stockholders (principals) hire managers (agents) to operate the company. While managers supposedly act to maximize the value of the firm, they may choose to maximize their own benefits. If a firm has many outside stockholders, managers may try to maximize their own wealth by demanding high wages or consuming excessive perquisites. This agency cost makes debt the preferred method of financing.

Debt leads to other agency problems as well. Since the amount of money owed to bondholders is fixed, stockholders prefer more risky projects because they have a greater likelihood of being profitable for the stockholders. Because of this, bondholders typically demand restrictive covenants and monitoring devices when they buy debt.

A final factor that limits the use of debt is personal taxation. Corporations gain a tax benefit when they issue bonds; interest payments are tax deductible. But, bondholders pay a penalty since interest income is taxable, and at a rate higher than stock income. According to Miller, bondholders will require higher returns on bonds to compensate for the additonal tax and in equilibrium, the gain to corporations is exactly offset by the loss to bondholders. Consequently, there are no additional gains to be made from issuing more debt.

But, factors other than taxes may affect the choice of debt or equity, and hence capital structure. The issuance of new debt may signal to investors that managers expect future earnings to increase and may be perceived as "good news". Managers may have an order of preference (a "pecking order") in which they raise new funds. Finally, issuing equity may indicate that manager's think that the firm's stock is overpriced. All these explanations are plausible, but as of now, we have not determined which of the various theories of capital structure, if any, is correct.

The optimal capital structure is the one that maximizes the value of the firm or minimizes the WACC. Since risk increases with more debt usage, the increase in the firm's value does not continue to all levels of debt. One way of looking at this maximum debt point is shown in Figure 15.6. When the firm first begins employing debt, the weighted average cost of capital decreases. The cost of equity increases gradually up to some point; then it increases more steeply as the cost of financial distress increases. Gradually WACC levels off and then begins to increase with debt usage as the benefits of cheap debt financing are offset by the increases in the required return on equity. To maximize the value of the firm, the manager should try to find this minimum WACC point (or range) and achieve the corresponding capital structure range.

EPS-EBIT Analysis

EPS-EBIT analysis is a tool to help managers analyze the effects of various financing packages on EPS. Since financial risk increases with debt usage, we want to look at the EBIT at which the alternative financing methods produce the same dollar EPS. At this $EBIT^*$, the firm would be indifferent between the two methods. Once the financial manager has calculated $EBIT^*$, the probability distribution of the firm's EBIT can help assess the risk-return tradeoff. While EPS is important, increased use of debt may raise the required return on equity, and thus, this debt usage could decrease the value of the firm. The analysis must always focus on maximizing the value of the firm--not simply on maximizing EPS.

COMPLETION QUESTIONS

15.1 The firm's _____ affects how much financial risk it can undertake.

15.2 Firms whose sales fluctuate more with changes in economic conditions have _____ business risk than those whose sales fluctuate less.

15.3 The _____ measures the relative variability of the firm's expected EBIT or EPS.

15.4 The higher the proportion of fixed costs to variable costs, the greater the _____.

15.5 Financial risk refers to _____ in earnings available to common stockholders, and the increased probability of _____ as the firm employs more financial leverage.

15.6 The coefficient of variation of the firm's EPS will _____ as a firm employs more debt in its capital structure.

15.7 If there were no taxes, and if an all equity firm financed new projects identical to the firm with more equity, according to Modigliani and Miller, the market price per share of the stock would _____.

15.8 If there were no taxes, Modigliani and Miller argue that the required return on a firm's common stock would _____ as the firm begins to use debt.

15.9 If taxes exist in the MM world, the market price of a firm's common stock _____ when more debt financing is employed. As the firm increases its usage of debt, the total value of the firm will _____ as a result of the tax deductibility of interest.

15.10 _____, including legal fees and disruption of the firm's operations, can decrease the value of the firm.

15.11 For an optimal capital structure to exist, the weighted average cost of capital must first _____ and then _____ as debt usage increases.

15.12 Firms more concerned about maintaining ownership control may tend to issue _____ debt than those who are not so concerned.

15.13 Under the _____, managers use the choice of new debt or equity to indicate to investors their changes in expectations about future cash flows.

15.14 Under the pecking order theory, managers prefer internally generated funds because of lack of _____ and lack of submission to the forces of _____.

PROBLEMS

15.1 North Bay Resorts, an all-equity firm, is planning a $20 million dollar expansion of its hotel complex. The expansion will be financed by the issuance of 400,000 shares of common stock at $50 per share or a bond issue carrying an interest rate of 12 percent. The firm presently has 600,000 shares of common stock outstanding. The firm has a 30 percent marginal tax rate.

North Bay has spent considerable time determining the effects of the expansion. According to its financial analysts, the following scenarios seem likely.

EBIT if the company chooses not to expand:

Probability	0.10	0.30	0.40	0.20
EBIT (in millions)	$1	$1.5	$2.0	$3.5

EBIT if the company expands:

Probability	0.10	0.30	0.40	0.20
EBIT (in millions)	$5	$6	$7	$9

a. Does North Bay face more business risk before or after the acceptance of the project?

b. Determine EPS if: (1) the company does not expand; (2) the company expands using only equity financing; and (3) the company finances the expansion with 12 percent debt. Compare the degrees of financial risk under each scenario.

15.2 National Glass Company has EBIT of $150 million, outstanding equity with a market value of $800 million, and 10 percent coupon perpetual debt worth $200 million.

a. Suppose an MM world existed without taxes. What would be the cost of equity capital, k_s? What would be the WACC?

b. The firm decides to issue an additional $100 million in debt and repurchase $100 million in common stock. How have the k_s and WACC changed?

c. Suppose now that corporations are subject to a tax rate of 30 percent and that k_s for a firm with no debt is equal to the WACC in (a). What is the value of National Glass if it has no debt?

d. Using k_s from (a), determine the market value of equity and the WACC if the firm now issues $200 million in debt.

e. Finally, using k_s from (b), now determine the WACC if the firm has $300 million of debt. What does the difference between WACCs in (d) and (e) suggest about the optimal capital structure?

15.3 Pure Air is an unlevered firm with an equilibrium market value of $9 million. The firm wishes to issue $5 million in 10% coupon, perpetual debt. An analyst has estimated that their marginal stockholder faces a personal tax rate of 25%, and the marginal bondholder faces a personal tax rate of 30%. If Pure Air's tax rate is 40%, what is the value of the levered firm?

(The following information pertains to problems 15.4 through 15.7. These problems integrate concepts taught in Chapters 8 - 14.)

Reynolds Manufacturing has an opportunity to invest in a project with an initial capital cost of $600,000. The project is expected to generate before-tax operating cash flows of $250,000 for five years. Resale value is expected to be zero. Depreciation is figured on a straight-line basis over five years and the firm has a marginal corporate tax rate of 40 percent.

The company's current (market value) capital structure consists of $20 million of equity and $10 million of debt. The firm considers this capital structure to be optimal. The contemplated project has the same risk attributes as the existing firm, so the firm's capital structure and beta will be used to evaluate the project.

15.4 Reynold's debt consists of 12,500 bonds with a par value of $1,000 each, a coupon rate of 8 percent, and a maturity date of 2550. (With this maturity date, the bond can be treated as a perpetuity.)
Calculate the after-tax cost of debt.

15.5 Presently, the expected return on the market is estimated to be 18 percent, while the risk-free rate is 8 percent. The common stock beta is 1.3. What is the firm's weighted average cost of capital?

15.6 Calculate the project's NPV. Should the project be accepted?

15.7 How much debt should be issued for Reynolds to maintain its optimal capital structure?

15.8 Air Utah has decided to purchase two new airplanes to allow it to expand its charter service. In order to finance this $800,000 expenditure, the company is considering three financing plans:

    Plan A Issue common stock at $40 per share. This plan will increase the number of outstanding shares of common stock to 120,000 shares.

    Plan B Issue 12 percent preferred stock only.

    Plan C Issue 12 percent coupon rate bonds only.

The firm presently has no preferred stock but has interest expense of $44,000 per year; its tax rate is 35 percent. What is the crossover EBIT ($EBIT^*$) between plans A and B, and between plans A and C?

15A.1 Tidwell Industries, Ltd., is a manufacturer of housing and furniture located in Haleyville, Montana. According to a recent announcement, its income statement for the nine months ending September 30, 1989 is as follows:

Income Statement
January 1 to September 30, 1990
(units of $1,000)

Sales	$147,477
Less: Variable costs	125,986
Revenues before fixed costs	21,491
Less: Fixed costs	14,400
EBIT	7,091
Less: Interest	1,509
Taxable income	5,582
Less: Taxes	2,395
Net income	$ 3,187
Its EPS is	$ 0.99

Calculate the degrees of operating, financial, and combined leverage.

ANSWERS TO COMPLETION QUESTIONS

15.1 level of business risk
15.2 more
15.3 coefficient of variation
15.4 operating leverage
15.5 the increased variability; financial distress
15.6 increase
15.7 be unaffected
15.8 increase
15.9 increase; increases
15.10 financial distress costs
15.11 decreases; increases
15.12 more
15.13 signalling theory
15.14 flotation costs; market discipline

SOLUTIONS TO PROBLEMS

15.1a

Step 1. If the company chooses not to accept the project:

Expected EBIT = 0.10($1 million) + 0.30($1.5 million) + 0.40($2 million) + 0.20($3.5 million) = $2.05 million

Step 2. Standard deviation = $\sqrt{0.10(\$1 - \$2.05)^2 + 0.30(\$1.5 - \$2.05)^2 + 0.40(\$2.0 - \$2.05)^2 + 0.20(\$3.5 - \$2.05)^2}$

= $\sqrt{\$0.6225}$ = $0.79 million

Coefficient of variation = $0.79/$2.05 = 0.3854

Step 3. If the company expands:

Expected EBIT = 0.10($5 million) + 0.30($6 million) + 0.40($7 million) + 0.20($9 million) = $6.90 million

Step 4. Standard deviation = $\sqrt{0.10(\$5 - \$6.90)^2 + 0.30(\$6 - \$6.90)^2 + 0.40(\$7 - \$6.90)^2 + 0.20(\$9 - \$6.90)^2}$

= $\sqrt{\$1.49}$ = $1.22 million

Coefficient of variation = $1.22/$6.90 = 0.1768

The company will have less business risk if it accepts the expansion project.

15.1b

Step 5. Assuming the company does not expand:

$$\overline{EAT} = \overline{EBIT}(1 - T)$$
$$= \$2.05(1 - 0.30) = \$1.435 \text{ million}$$

$$\overline{EPS} = \overline{EAT}/600,000$$
$$= \$1.435 \text{ million}/600,000 = \$2.392$$

As mentioned in the text, the variability in EPS under all-equity financing is the same as business risk; therefore, the coefficient of variation = 0.3854.

Step 6. Assuming the firm expands using equity financing:

$$\overline{EAT} = \overline{EBIT}(1 - T)$$
$$= \$6.90(1 - 0.30) = \$4.83 \text{ million}$$

$$\overline{EPS} = \overline{EAT}/1,000,000$$
$$= \$4.83 \text{ million}/1,000,000 = \$4.83$$

Again, since the project is still all equity financed, the coefficient of variation of 0.1768 [from (a)] is still relevant.

Step 7. Assuming the project is financed with debt: Interest = ($20 million)(0.12) = $2.4 million.

Probability	0.10	0.30	0.40	0.20
EBIT (in millions)	$5.00	$6.00	$7.00	$9.00
Less: Interest	2.40	2.40	2.40	2.40
EBT	2.60	3.60	4.60	6.60
Less: Tax (at 30%)	0.78	1.08	1.38	1.98
EAT	$1.82	$2.52	$3.22	$4.62
EPS (EAT/600,000)	$3.03	$4.20	$5.37	$7.70

Step 8. Expected EPS = 0.10($3.03) + 0.30($4.20) + 0.40($5.37) + 0.20($7.70)

= $5.25

$$\text{Standard deviation} = \sqrt{\begin{array}{l}0.10(\$3.03 - \$5.25)^2 + 0.30(\$4.20 - \$5.25)^2 \\ + 0.40(\$5.37 - \$5.25)^2 + 0.20(\$7.70 - \$5.25)^2\end{array}}$$

$= \sqrt{\$2.03} = \$1.42$

Coefficient of variation = $1.42/$5.25 = 0.2705

The level of financial risk (as indicated by the coefficient of variation of EPS) is greater if the project is financed with debt rather than equity, but because of the reduction in business risk caused by the expansion, risk is still less than if the firm chose not to expand.

15.2a

Step 1. Cash available to equity holders = EBIT - interest

= $150 - $200(0.10) = $150 - $20 = $130 million

k_s = $130/$800 = 0.1625 = 16.25%

Step 2. WACC = ($800/$1,000)(16.25%) + ($200/$1,000)(10%) = 13% + 2% = 15%

15.2b

Step 3. Cash available to equity holders = EBIT - interest

= $150 - ($300)(0.10) = $120 million

k_s = $120/$700 = 17.14%

Step 4. WACC = ($700/$1,000)(17.14%) + ($300/$1,000)(10%) = 12% + 3% = 15%

Although k_s has increased, the WACC remains constant.

15.2c

Step 5. EAT = EBIT(1 - T) = $150(1 - 0.30) = $105 million

Step 6. Market value = EAT/k_s = $105/0.15 = $700 million

15.2d

Step 7. Market value of equity = $\dfrac{(\text{EBIT} - \text{interest})(1 - T)}{k_s}$

$= \dfrac{[\$150 - 0.10(\$200)](1 - 0.30)}{0.1625} = \dfrac{\$130(0.70)}{0.1625}$

= $560 million

Step 8. WACC = (market value proportion of equity)(k_s) + (market value of debt)(1 - T)(k_b)

$= \left[\dfrac{\$560}{\$560 + \$200}\right](16.25\%) + \left[\dfrac{\$200}{\$560 + \$200}\right](1 - 0.30)(10\%)$

= 11.97% + 1.84% = 13.81%

15.2e

Step 9. Market value of equity = $\dfrac{[\$150 - 0.10(\$300)](1 - 0.30)}{0.1714}$ = $490 million

Step 10. WACC = ($490/$790)(17.14%) + ($300/$790)(10%)(1 - 0.30)

$\qquad$ = 10.63% + 2.66% = 13.29%

The WACC falls as more and more debt is issued. According to MM, the firm should finance itself with virtually 100 percent debt, since that will maximize the value of the firm.

15.3

Step 1. $V_L = V_U + \left[1 - \dfrac{(1 - T)(1 - T_{ps})}{(1 - T_{pb})}\right] B$

$\qquad$ = $9,000,000 + \left[1 - \dfrac{(1 - 0.40)(1 - 0.25)}{(1 - 0.30)}\right]$ $5,000,000

$\qquad$ = $9,000,000 + \left[1 - \dfrac{(0.60)(0.75)}{(0.70)}\right]$ $5,000,000

$\qquad$ = $9,000,000 + [1 - 0.6429]$5,000,000

$\qquad$ = $9,000,000 + $1,785,714 = $10,785,714

15.4

Step 1. Bond price = $10,000,000/12,500 = $800

Step 2. k_b = $80/$800 = 10%

Step 3. $k_i = k_b(1 - T)$ = 10%(1 - 0.40) = 6%

15.5

Step 1. $k_s = k_{RF} + \beta(k_M - k_{RF})$ = 8% + 1.3(18% - 8%) = 21%

Step 2. WACC = $k_i W_{debt} + k_s W_{common\ equity}$ = (6%)(0.333) + (21%)(0.667) = 16%

15.6

Step 1. CF = $250,000(1 - 0.40) + ($600,000/5)(0.40) = $198,000

Step 2. NPV = $CF_t(PVA_{16\%,5yr})$ - $600,000 = $198,000(3.274) - $600,000

$\qquad$ = $48,252

Accept the project since it has a positive NPV.

15.7

Step 1. Note that the amount of debt to be issued should be determined by first examining the increase in the market value that will result from accepting the project. The increase in the market value will be greater than the cost of the project, since the NPV is positive. The increase in market value will be $600,000 + $48,252, the present value of the cash flows associated with the project, assuming the market is efficient.

Step 2. Amount of debt that should be issued equals the change in market value times the targeted amount of debt in the capital structure:
New debt = ($648,252)(0.333) = $215,868

15.8

Step 1. If the new stock is issued, the resulting number of shares will be 120,000. Since the issue increases the number of shares outstanding by $800,000/$40 = 20,000, the present number of shares is 120,000 - 20,000 = 100,000.

Step 2. The crossover EBIT is determined by

$$\frac{(EBIT^* - I_1)(1 - T) - D_{ps1}}{N_1} = \frac{(EBIT^* - I_2)(1 - T) - D_{ps2}}{N_2}$$

Under plan A, $D_{ps1} = 0$
Under plan B, $D_{ps2} = \$800,000(0.12) = \$96,000$

$$\frac{(EBIT^* - \$44,000)(1 - 0.35) - 0}{120,000} = \frac{(EBIT^* - \$44,000)(1 - 0.35) - \$96,000}{100,000}$$

$$\frac{(0.65)(EBIT^*) - \$28,600}{120,000} = \frac{(0.65)(EBIT^*) - \$28,600 - \$96,000}{100,000}$$

$$65,000 \ EBIT^* - \$2,860,000,000 = 78,000 \ EBIT^* - \$14,952,000,000$$

$$13,000 \ EBIT^* = \$12,092,000,000$$

$$EBIT^* = \$12,092,000,000/13,000 = \$930,153.85$$

If EBIT is less than $930,153.85, equity financing will generate a higher EPS.

Step 3. Plans A and C

Plan C will result in an increase in interest expense of ($800,000)(0.12) = $96,000, so interest will be $140,000.

$D_{ps1} = D_{ps2} = 0$

$$\frac{(EBIT^* - \$44,000)(1 - 0.35)}{120,000} = \frac{(EBIT^* - \$140,000)(1 - 0.35)}{100,000}$$

$$\frac{(0.65)(EBIT^*) - \$28,600}{120,000} = \frac{(0.65)(EBIT^*) - \$91,000}{100,000}$$

$$65,000 \; EBIT^* - \$2,860,000,000 = 78,000 \; EBIT^* - \$10,920,000,000$$

$$13,000 \; EBIT^* = \$8,060,000,000$$

$$EBIT^* = \$8,060,000,000/13,000 = \$620,000$$

Equity financing leads to a higher EPS if EBIT is less than $620,000.

15A.1

Step 1. $DOL = \frac{\text{sales - variable costs}}{EBIT} = \frac{\$147,477 - \$125,986}{\$7,091} = \frac{\$21,491}{\$7,091}$

= 3.03 times

Step 2. $DFL = \frac{EBIT}{EBIT - \text{interest}} = \frac{\$7,091}{\$7,091 - \$1,509} = \frac{\$7,091}{\$5,582} = 1.27$ times

Step 3. DCL = (DOL)(DFL) = (3.03)(1.27) = 3.85 times; or

$DCL = \frac{\text{sales - variable costs}}{EBIT - \text{interest}} = \frac{\$147,477 - \$125,986}{\$7,091 - \$1,509} = \frac{\$21,491}{\$5,582}$

= 3.85 times

CHAPTER 16

DIVIDEND POLICY AND INTERNAL FINANCING

HOW THIS CHAPTER RELATES TO THE REST OF THE TEXT

Cash dividends are the basis for common stock valuation (Chapter 6). In this chapter, we examine dividend policy and its link between the capital budget (Chapters 8-11) and the firm's cost of capital (Chapter 14). The chapter also discusses the advantages and disadvantages of changing the dividend policy, stock splits, stock dividends, and stock repurchases, as well as the effects of each on stock prices.

TOPICAL OUTLINE

I. Dividends and financing.
   A. The firm's cash dividend policy results in a decision simultaneously to issue cash dividends and not to reinvest the cash in the firm.
   B. The cash dividend policy affects the firm's cash budget as well as affecting its long-run financing plan.
      1. Firms obtain over two-thirds of their total funds from those generated internally.
      2. Firms that pay cash dividends have less internally generated funds available for other uses.
   C. In both good and bad times, firms in practice pay out a substantial portion of their earnings in the form of cash dividends.
      1. Over the last seven years, business firms have paid out in cash dividends about as much as their net long-term external financing needs.
      2. Firms that do not pay high cash dividends rely substantially less on external financing for their ongoing needs.
      3. Many firms plan to increase cash dividends at a rate which at least equals the rate of inflation.
II. Does dividend policy matter?
   A. The residual theory of dividends.
      1. The firm's optimal capital budget and its cost of capital are determined simultaneously, after the capital structure is determined.

2. Likewise, the firm can determine its cash dividend policy after looking at its optimal cash budget and its capital structure. Dividends are paid only if there is internally generated cash left over.
3. The residual theory of dividends suggests investors are as well or better off when the firm reinvests internally generated funds in opportunities whose returns equal or exceed the investors' returns on alternative investments.
    a. Determine the optimal capital budget, accepting all projects with a positive net present value.
    b. Determine the amount of common equity needed to finance new investments while maintaining the firm's capital structure; if the capital structure is 70 percent equity, the investments will be 70 percent financed with equity.
    c. Use internally generated funds to supply this equity whenever possible, issuing common stock for the shortfall.
    d. Pay cash dividends only after funding capital investments.
4. Residual dividend policy suggests that cash dividends do not affect the value of the firm, and that the value of the firm does not change even though the timing of dividend payments may change.

B. Arguments for relevance of dividend policy.
1. Investors as a whole might prefer high-dividend-payout firms.
    a. Returns from investing in common stock come from cash dividends and capital gains; a high dividend payout may make some of the return more certain.
        i. Investment in a high-payout firm is less risky.
        ii. The required return of the high-payout (less risky) firm is lower and its price is higher than that of the low payout firm.
    b. High dividend payout may signal high future profitability for the firm; the market may bid the price of the stock up.
        i. Evidence suggests that initial dividends and unexpected dividend increases lead to increased

stock prices.
   ii. Dividend initiations are associated with future earnings increases.
  c. Some investors may prefer the certain current income from dividends rather than the less certain capital gains.
  d. Corporations can exclude some dividend income from taxes, lowering the effective tax rate.
 2. Investors as a whole might prefer low-payout firms.
  a. Flotation costs make funding with internally generated funds more attractive than funding with newly issued securities.
  b. Prior to 1986, the lower tax rate on capital gains versus dividend income for taxpaying investors created a bias toward low-payout firms. The Tax Reform Act of 1986 mandated equal tax treatment of dividends and capital gains.
  c. Transactions costs make selling stock to provide current income somewhat costly for the investor.
 3. The clientele effect: Some investors prefer high-payout firms while others prefer low-payout firms.
  a. Investors with low incomes and high current income needs would favor high-payout firms.
  b. Once the dividend policy is established, some investors will buy the stock, and the dividend policy will not affect the market price unless the policy is subsequently changed.
C. Other factors that influence dividend policy.
 1. Stable firms have fewer investment opportunities than newer, fast-growing firms, so they have higher payout policies.
 2. Firms with a shortage of cash will often restrict cash dividends, but firms with a cash surplus will often pay high dividends to avoid being a tempting takeover candidate.
 3. More stable firms are in a better position to pay high cash dividends, since they can plan for the future with more certainty than highly cyclical firms.

4. Firms concerned about maintaining ownership control will prefer to fund new capital investment with internally generated funds rather than issue new common stock.
D. Constraints inhibiting the firm's ability to pay cash dividends.
1. Contractural restrictions require that firms withhold payment of cash dividends until preferred stockholders have received their dividends.
2. Incorporation laws typically prohibit firms from paying cash dividends if the firms' liabilities exceed their assets or if the dividend would be paid from the firms' invested capital.
3. If the level of the firm's cash and marketable securities is beyond that deemed reasonable, the firm must pay dividends or pay a special surtax imposed by the IRS.
E. Where does that leave us?
1. Firms try to maintain stable and increasing cash dividends over time, avoiding a reduction in cash dividends if at all possible.
2. Most firms use the smooth residual dividend policy, setting a target dividend payout ratio after funding the capital budget; they increase the dollar amount if it can be maintained.

III. Dividend policy in practice.
A. Dividend payout policies differ depending on the primary industry in which the firm is located and sometimes vary within the industry.
B. Increases and decreases in cash dividends depend somewhat on the economy and its impact on earnings and internally generated funds.
C. Firms that do not want to increase cash dividends permanently may pay an extra dividend in a good year.

IV. Dividend payment procedures.
A. Cash dividends are normally paid quarterly.
B. Procedures:
1. The board of directors meets and issues a statement declaring the next quarter's dividends (date declared).
2. An arbitrary date, the ex-dividend date (which is the fourth business day preceding the record date), is established to determine who is entitled to the dividend payment.

3. The record date is the date that stockholder books are closed in order to determine the current stockholders.
4. The payment date is the date the firm actually mails the dividend checks to the stockholders.

C. Because the ex-dividend date determines who is entitled to the next cash dividend, the market price of the stock drops, on average, the amount of the quarterly dividend on the ex-dividend date.

D. Dividend reinvestment plans involve reinvesting in additional new or existing shares of the common stock.
1. In buying existing shares, a bank acts as trustee, accumulating funds from all stockholders who take the option, and purchases (for a small transaction cost) shares in the open market.
2. In buying new shares, investors often enjoy a 3 to 5 percent reduction in the stock's current market price, and firms enjoy expanded capital stock; many firms issue additional stock through dividend reinvestment plans.

V. Repurchasing stock.
A. Methods.
1. Tender offer to all the firm's stockholders.
2. Purchase of the stock on the secondary market.
3. Agreement with a small group of the firm's major investors to buy their shares.

B. Effect of repurchasing stock.
1. The EPS should increase and result in a higher market price per share.
2. Stockholders not selling their shares back to the firm will enjoy a capital gain return if the repurchase increases the stock price.

C. Advantages of repurchasing.
1. If the firm has an excess of cash but does not want to increase cash dividends, it can increase the investor's return without creating a trend toward higher dividends.
2. The firm can reduce future cash dividend requirements, or increase cash dividends per share on the remaining shares, without creating a continuing incremental cash drain.

3. Repurchase can be used to effect a large-scale change in the firm's capital structure, perhaps increasing debt usage.
4. Repurchasing can signal information about the firm's future cash flows.

D. Disadvantages of repurchasing.
1. Firms which repurchase substantial amounts of stock rather than invest in capital projects generally have poorer growth and investment opportunities than those which do not repurchase large amounts. The negative impact of this signal appears to have lessened in recent years.
2. The SEC and the IRS may raise questions about the intention of the stock repurchase.

VI. Stock splits and dividends are methods of issuing more shares.
A. Effects of stock split or stock dividend: Increase the number of shares per investor, decreasing each share's value, respectively.
1. No change in firm's total assets, liabilities, stockholders' equity, earnings, cash dividends, or total market value.
2. Drop in per share earnings, cash dividends, and common stock market price, and a corresponding increase in the number of shares outstanding.

B. Difference between stock splits and stock dividends.
1. Stock splits and stock dividends have the same effect from an economic standpoint.
2. For accounting purposes, the NYSE requires all stock dividends of 25 percent or more to be accounted for as a stock split.
3. Accounting treatment of stock splits and stock dividends.
   a. With a stock split, the number of shares is increased and the par value is decreased accordingly.
   b. With a stock dividend, the par value is not reduced.
      i. A transfer is made from the retained earnings account to the common stock and additional paid-in capital accounts.
      ii. The transfer size depends upon the size of the stock dividend and the stock's current market price.

4. Stock splits and stock dividends have no economic effect on the stockholders.
5. Reasons for declaring stock splits and stock dividends.
    a. Some firms view it as an extension of their cash dividend policy.
    b. Many firms believe their shares have an optimal trading range, contrary to the concept of market efficiency.
    c. Firms use stock splits or stock dividends to communicate extra information about their future cash flows.
    d. Firms may "conserve cash" by declaring a stock dividend rather than a cash dividend.

FORMULAS

Notation

P_0 = market price of a share of stock at time 0

k_s = cost of equity capital

g = expected compound percentage growth rate in cash dividends

Basic Valuation Framework

$P_0 = D_1/(k_s - g)$

Effect of a Stock Repurchase

Current EPS = total earnings/number of shares outstanding

Current P/E = market price per share/EPS

EPS after repurchase = total earnings/decreased number of shares

Expected market price after repurchase = (current P/E)(new EPS)

WHAT TO LOOK FOR

In Chapter 15, we examined the firm's capital structure. We decided that in maximizing the value of the firm, we should try to maintain a target capital structure range. In Chapter 16, we look at cash dividend policy and its relationship to capital structure and market value.

Dividend Policy and the Capital Structure

Maintaining the capital structure is not simple. Each time the firm decides to issue cash dividends, it is making a capital structure decision. Any earnings used as dividends are unavailable for reinvestment in the firm in the form of internally generated capital. Therefore, the firm must either curtail capital investments or obtain additional funds through external sources.

Dividend Policy and the Value of the Firm

Residual theory of dividends

The residual theory of dividends states that investors will be as well or better off if the firm invests internally generated funds in capital projects whose returns exceed those available to its common stockholders. The firm would maintain its target capital structure and fund these projects with as much internally generated equity as needed to meet the equity requirements.

The earnings remaining after this investment would be distributed as cash dividends. If the year's earnings fell short of the equity requirement for capital funding, the firm would issue common stock to cover the shortfall. The residual theory suggests that the value of the firm is unaffected by the pattern of cash dividends, as long as the projects yield a higher rate of return than that available to the firm's common stockholders.

Preferences of dividend payout levels

Most empirical testing lends some support to the idea of the clientele effect of dividend payout levels. Investors with low current income and high needs for current income will favor high payout firms. The text discusses other reasons investors may prefer one payout level or another. No consensus exists, however, on whether dividend policy by itself affects the value of the firm's common stock.

Dividend Policy in Practice

In general, firms use a smoothed residual dividend policy. They maintain a stable or increasing dividend, and often attempt to increase it with inflation. Firms are reluctant to decrease the cash dollar dividend per share. In a good year, they sometimes declare extra dividends rather than permanently increase the dividend. Faster-growing firms have more investment opportunities and pay smaller dividends than mature firms. Firms whose managements want to maintain ownership control tend to pay lower dividends, since they use internally generated equity rather than issue more common stock.

Dividends can be an opportunity for the firm to obtain new equity capital. That is, if common stockholders participate in the dividend reinvestment plans which invest in new shares rather than outstanding shares of the firm's stock, the equity capital base of the firm can expand without the cost of underwriting. Such plans are popular with many firms.

Stock Repurchases

In addition to paying dividends, firms occasionally repurchase their stock and either retire it or hold it as treasury stock. From the firm's standpoint, repurchases have several advantages; the firm can provide stockholders with cash without adjusting its dividend policy, reduce future cash dividend requirements, and effect large changes in its capital structure. Repurchasing is also used as a means of attempting to fend off unwanted corporate suitors.

What Are Stock Splits and Stock Dividends?

Stock splits and stock dividends are issuances of additional shares of common stock on a pro rata basis to the existing shareholders. Neither process affects the stockholder's wealth. A stock dividend is an issuance of additional shares which is less than 25 percent of the number of shares outstanding. A stock split is an issuance in excess of 25 percent. The text discusses the accounting of stock splits and stock dividends, as well as reasons why firms declare them.

COMPLETION QUESTIONS

16.1 The cash dividend decision involves a decision simultaneously to pay dividends and not to _____.

16.2 If firms do not pay cash dividends, they would not have to rely as much on _____ to finance their capital expenditures.

16.3 Investors may be as well or better off if the firm _____ _____ internally generated funds, as long as these funds yield a return which _____ the return available to common stockholders on alternative investments.

16.4 In determining how much common equity the firm needs for financing new projects, the firm should maintain its _____.

16.5 If internally generated funds fall short of the equity needed for new projects, the firm will _____.

16.6 The residual theory of dividends suggests that dividend policy _____ _____ the value of the firm.

16.7 The payment of high current dividends can resolve _____.
The current market price for firms with high payout ratios may be _____
_____ as a result of this resolution.

16.8 An increase in the firm's dividend payout ratio may be viewed as an indication of _____ of the firm.

16.9 Prior to 1986, the tax rate on _____ versus ordinary income for taxpaying investors creates a bias toward _____ payout firms.

16.10 According to the clientele effect, the low-income investor needing current income prefers a _____ payout firm. Once the clientele and the dividend policy are established, the dividend policy _____ _____ the value of the firm's stock.

16.11 In practice, firms prefer to pay _____ dividends. They are reluctant to _____ the level of dividends.

16.12 On the ex-dividend date, the market price of the firm's common stock generally _____.

16.13 For accounting purposes, any stock dividend of over 25 percent is accounted for as a stock _____.

16.14 In accounting for a stock_____, the total number of shares is increased by the split ratio times the number of previously outstanding shares. For example, for a firm with 400,000 shares, the result of a 3/2 split is _____ total shares.

PROBLEMS

16.1 Main Line Railroad Company has a target capital structure of 60 percent debt and 40 percent equity. The company currently has available to it $2,000,000 in cash earnings available for cash dividends or reinvestment. It is considering five capital expenditures, each with a 10-year life. The projects are summarized below:

Project	CF_0 (in thousands)	CF_{1-10} (in thousands)
A	$1,000	$254.91
B	2,000	560.07
C	3,000	597.73
D	500	107.32
E	500	115.23

The railroad follows a residual dividend policy. If Main Line's required rate of return is 16 percent, what should be its dividend payout ratio?

16.2 Sandburg Manufacturing has earnings available for distribution to shareholders of $500,000 in cash, which it may pay out or reinvest. The firm is considering two options.

  Alternative 1: A cash dividend. The firm has a 75 percent dividend payout ratio.

  Alternative 2: A 3-for-2 stock split.

The net worth portion of the balance sheet presently looks like this:

Common stock ($3 par)	$ 3,000,000
Additional paid-in capital	6,000,000
Retained earnings	10,000,000
Total net worth	$19,000,000

How would the net portion of the balance sheet look under each of these two alternatives?

16.3 Hamilton Electronics has 1 million shares of common stock outstanding, EPS is $7.50, and its P/E ratio is 12. In order to bring the stock price back into its "optimal trading range," the company declares a 5-for-4 stock split.
- a. How many shares of common stock will be outstanding after the split?
- b. What will be the new EPS?
- c. How far will the share price fall as a result of the split?

16.4 Baron Realty has 100,000 shares of common stock outstanding with a market price of $50 per share. The firm normally distributes 60 percent of its earnings as cash dividends; however, this year, the firm wishes to use its $540,000 in earnings to repurchase 10,000 shares at $54 per share from a dissident stockholder. Assuming that the P/E ratio remains constant, are the remaining stockholders better or worse off after the repurchase? (Ignore any tax effects.)

ANSWERS TO COMPLETION QUESTIONS

16.1 reinvest these funds in the firm
16.2 external financing
16.3 retains and reinvests; equals or exceeds
16.4 target capital structure
16.5 issue new common stock
16.6 does not affect
16.7 investor uncertainty; bid up
16.8 the future profitability
16.9 capital gains; low
16.10 high; does not directly influence
16.11 stable or increasing; reduce
16.12 decreases by the amount of the cash dividend per share
16.13 split
16.14 split; 600,000

SOLUTIONS TO PROBLEMS

16.1

Step 1. Solve for the internal rate of return on each of the projects to determine which ones should be accepted. Since the projects are annuities, the IRR can be solved for by finding k, such that

$$CF_t(PVA_{k\%,10yr}) - CF_0 = 0$$

or $PVA_{k\%,10yr} = (CF_0/CF_t)$

Project A $PVA_{k\%,10yr}$ = $1,000/$254.91 = 3.923   The IRR = 22%

Project B $PVA_{k\%,10yr}$ = $2,000/$560.07 = 3.571   The IRR = 25%

Project C $PVA_{k\%,10yr}$ = $3,000/$597.73 = 5.019   The IRR = 15%

Project D $PVA_{k\%,10yr}$ = $500/$107.32 = 4.659   The IRR = 17%

Project E $PVA_{k\%,10yr}$ = $500/$115.23 = 4.339   The IRR = 19%

Step 2. The firm should choose projects with IRRs greater than WACC. Those projects are A, B, D, and E.

Total CF_0 = $1,000 + $2,000 + $500 + $500 = $4,000 or $4 million

Step 3. Amount financed by equity = (proportion of equity)(total CF_0)
= (0.40)($4,000,000) = $1,600,000. Since the firm has $2,000,000 in earnings, in order to maintain its target capital structure, it should retain $1,600,000 and pay the residual $400,000 ($2,000,000 - $1,600,000) as dividends. The dividend payout ratio is $400,000/$2,000,000 = 0.20.

16.2

Step 1. Alternative 1: The firm would pay total cash dividends of ($500,000)(0.75) = $375,000 and retain $500,000 - $375,000 = $125,000. New retained earnings would be $10,000,000 + $125,000 = $10,125,000. So,

Common stock ($3 par)	$ 3,000,000
Additional paid-in capital	6,000,000
Retained earnings	10,125,000
Total net worth	$19,125,000

Step 2. Alternative 2: Under a stock split, only the par value of common stock is adjusted. The new par value will be ($3)(2/3) = $2.00. If no cash dividends are paid, retained earnings will increase by $500,000, the new net worth portion of the balance sheet will be as follows:

Common stock ($2 par)	$ 3,000,000
Additional paid-in capital	6,000,000
Retained earnings	10,500,000
Total net worth	$19,500,000

16.3a

Step 1. Number of new shares = (number of old shares)(split ratio)
= (1,000,000)(5/4) = 1,250,000 shares

16.3b

Step 2. Total earnings = (1,000,000)($7.50) = $7,500,000

EPS = $7,500,000/1,250,000 = $6 per share

16.3c

Step 3. The old price = (EPS)(P/E)
= ($7.50)(12) = $90 per share

The new price = ($6.00)(12) = $72 per share

The price has fallen by $90 - $72 = $18 per share.

16.4

Step 1 EPS = $540,000/100,000 = $5.40 per share

P/E = $50/5.40 = 9.26

New EPS = $540,000/100,000 - 10,000 = $6 per share

New price = (P/E)(EPS) = (9.26)($6) = $55.56 per share

Investors wil realize an increase in value of $55.56 - $50 = $5.56 per share.

Step 2. The alternative is to receive a cash dividend of

$$\frac{(\$540,000)(0.60)}{100,000} = \$3.24 \text{ per share.}$$

The stockholders will be better off with the repurchase.

CHAPTER 17

LEASING

HOW THIS CHAPTER RELATES TO THE REST OF THE TEXT

To this point, we have assumed that when a firm found a profitable investment (Chapters 8-11), it raised funds either internally or externally (Chapters 12 and 13) and purchased the asset. An alternative method of acquiring the asset is through leasing. Leasing is similar to debt financing (Chapter 13). Cash flow and taxes (Chapter 4) form the basis for lease analysis. Conceptually, the net advantage of leasing (NAL) is similar to the net present value techniques employed in replacement capital budgeting (Chapter 9). The discount rate employed is the after-tax cost of debt.

TOPICAL OUTLINE

I. Leasing and the firm.
   A. Who provides lease financing?
      1. Some manufacturers, such as railway or airplane manufacturers, use leasing as part of their regular sales effort.
      2. Firms such as commercial banks, investment bankers, subsidiaries of other firms, and commercial finance companies also provide lease financing.
   B. Types of leases.
      1. The service lease is short-term and generally cancellable.
         a. Often used with inexpensive assets such as office machines and cars.
         b. The lessor generally services the equipment and pays any insurance and property taxes; this lease is often called a maintenance lease.
         c. Large service leases should undergo in-depth financial analysis before the lessee signs the agreement.
      2. Financial leases are noncancellable long-term contracts between the lessor who owns the asset and the lessee who agrees to lease the asset for a specified period of time.

a. Financial leases are a form of long-term financing similar to borrowing, and the cash flow consequences are also similar to borrowing.
b. The lessee agrees to provide for maintenance, insurance coverage, and property taxes related to the asset leased.
3. Sale and leaseback arrangements occur when an asset owner decides to sell the asset to another party and lease it back.
    a. The firm desires to raise capital by selling an asset, usually real estate, but wishes to maintain use of the asset for some period of time.
    b. The financial analysis of sale and leaseback arrangements versus borrowing resembles the analysis of other finance leases analyzed later.
4. Leveraged leases involve three parties: The lender, the lessor, and the lessee.

C. Tax considerations.
1. Lease payments are a tax deductible-expense for the lessee.
2. The lessor depreciates the asset.
3. The Tax Equity and Fiscal Responsibility Act of 1982 defined financial leases:
    a. The property must be new and eligible for ACRS depreciation.
    b. The transaction must have economic substance apart from the tax benefits.
    c. The lease must be entered into within 90 days after the property is placed into service.
    d. The lessee may be allowed to purchase the asset at the end of the lease if the option price is at least 10 percent of the asset's original cost.
    e. Limited-use property, such as automobile manufacturing tools, may be leased.

D. Accounting for leases.
1. Capital leases exist if the lease:
    a. Transfers ownership of the property to the lessee by the end of the lease term.

b. Gives the lessee the option to purchase the property.

c. Has a lease term equal to 75 percent or more of the estimated life of the property.

2. Capital leases must be capitalized on the firm's financial statements.

   a. The present value of the lease payments must be entered as a liability on the firm's balance sheet.

   b. A corresponding entry to value the asset must be made on the balance sheet.

   c. This asset is amortized over the useful life of the lease, resulting in a reduction in reported income, with corresponding reductions on the liability side each year.

3. Operating leases are those which do not meet the above conditions, and which need not appear on the balance sheet; instead, they show up in footnotes to the financial statements.

II. Selling lease rates.

A. The lessor wants to set a rate that provides it with a satisfactory risk-adjusted return.

B. The lessor focuses on:

1. The after-tax required return on debt-type investments (k_i).

2. The marginal tax rate (T).

3. The cost of the leased asset (CLA_0).

4. Depreciation.

C. To determine the proper lease rate:

1. Determine the tax benefits from owning the asset and depreciation.

2. Calculate the present value of benefits:

$$\text{Present value of benefits} = \sum_{t=1}^{n} \frac{Dep_t(T)}{(1+k_i)^t}$$

3. Determine the amount to be recovered from lease payments.

$$\text{Net recovered from lease payments} = CLA_0 - \text{Present value of benefits}$$

4. The after-tax lease payment (ATL) is found by solving:

$$\text{Net recoverable from lease payments} = ATL(PVA_{k_i\%,n})(1+k_i)$$

5. The required lease payment is:
$$L = ATL/(1 - T)$$
6. Other factors.
   a. Resale value of the asset.
   b. Lessors often know more about the asset than lessees; information asymmetries exist.
   c. Lessors will adjust the payments upward to reflect transactions costs.

III. To lease or not to lease?
   A. Reasons for leasing.
      1. Tax implications.
         a. Lessees may often benefit from leasing if they have a lower marginal tax rate than the lessor, and the lessor passes these savings on to the lessee in the form of reduced lease payments.
         b. The depreciation benefits are worth more to the lessor than the lessee if the lessor has a higher tax rate.
      2. Leases provide flexibility and convenience.
         a. With a service lease, the lessor secures, sets up, and maintains the assets.
         b. It is preferable to lease certain types of assets under a service lease than to buy them.
   B. Dubious reasons for leasing.
      1. Conservation of working capital.
         a. Leases do not provide 100 percent financing, since they require a prepayment.
         b. Although smaller firms might need to rely on leases for financing, larger firms generally can secure about the same amount of financing from leasing as from the capital markets.
      2. Increase the firm's borrowing capacity.
         a. The firm can obtain more long-term funding by combining leasing and borrowing.

b. This assumes that bankers, lenders, and capital markets do not recognize that leasing places a financial obligation on the firm, just as borrowing does.
3. Avoiding restrictions is a weak and perhaps invalid reason to lease.
C. The ultimate test of a lease proposal is to determine whether the value of the firm is maximized by leasing or by borrowing.

IV. Evaluation of financial leases.
A. What decision are we concerned with?
1. Our capital budgeting treatment assumed the asset will be purchased if the NPV is positive.
2. If leasing is a possibility, another step must be added to the capital budgeting analysis to determine whether the asset should be leased or purchased.
a. Calculate the net advantage of leasing (NAL).
b. If the NAL is positive, the firm should acquire the asset by leasing rather than by purchasing.
c. NPV (capital budgeting) and NAL (lease evaluation) decisions interact.
i. If the NPV is negative, the asset might still be leased if favorable lease terms more than completely offset the negative NPV.
ii. If the NPV is negative, the asset should not be leased if the NAL does not offset the negative NPV.
B. Why compare leasing with borrowing?
1. Leasing imposes the same kind of financial commitment that borrowing does.
2. We want to neutralize the risk between the two alternatives.
a. Establish an equivalent borrowing amount that, in terms of the after-tax cash flows, is the same in each future period as the after-tax lease cash flows.
b. Employ the after-tax borrowing rate of the firm as the relevant discount rate to accomplish this.

C. Financial lease evaluation using the NAL approach.
   1. Major elements of the NAL approach.
      a. Lease payments (L) made periodically on an after-tax basis, with the first payment at t_0.
      b. Depreciation tax shields for periods t_1 through t_n, found by multiplying the annual depreciation (Dep) by the lessee's marginal tax rate (T); this tax shield is foregone when leasing.
      c. The cost of the asset (CLA_0) if purchased.
   2. Formula:

   NAL = cost of buying the asset − explicit and opportunity costs of leasing the asset

   $$NAL = CLA_0 - \left[L_0(1-T) + \sum_{t=1}^{n-1} \frac{L_t(1-T)}{(1+k_i)^t} + \sum_{t=1}^{n} \frac{Dep_t(T)}{(1+k_i)^t} \right]$$

      a. NAL = cost of asset − [after-tax cash flow of first lease payment + present value of subsequent lease payments + present value of foregone depreciation tax shield].
      b. If the cost of leasing is less than the cost of purchasing the asset, the firm should lease rather than purchase.

D. The percentage annual cost of the lease can be found by solving the following formula for IRR.

$$CLA_0 - L_0(1-T) = \sum_{t=1}^{n-1} \frac{L_t(1-T)}{(1+IRR)^t} + \sum_{t=1}^{n} \frac{Dep_t(T)}{(1+IRR)^t}$$

FORMULAS

Notation

CLA = Cost of the asset (initial investment) if the asset is purchased

Dep_t = depreciation

$Dep_t(T)$ = depreciation tax shield if the asset is purchased

k_i = after-tax cost of debt

L_0 = lease payment made at time t = 0

L_t = lease payment made for period t

$CFBT_t$ = cash flow before taxes

k_b = before-tax cost of debt

k = weighted average cost of capital (or required rate of return)

Present Value of Depreciation Benefits

$$\text{Present value of depreciation benefits} = \sum_{t=1}^{n} \frac{Dep_t(T)}{(1 + k_i)^t}$$

Net Recoverable from Lease Payments

Net recoverable from lease payments = CLA_0 - present value of benefits

After-Tax Lease Payment

Solve the following for ATL.

$$\text{net recoverable from lease payments} = ATL(PVA_{k_i\%,n})(1 + k_i)$$

Lease Payment

$$L = ATL/(1 - T)$$

Net Advantage of Leasing

$$NAL = CLA_0 - \left[L_0(1 - T) + \sum_{t=1}^{n-1} \frac{L_t(1 - T)}{(1 + k_i)^t} + \sum_{t=1}^{n} \frac{Dep_t(T)}{(1 + k_i)^t} \right]$$

WHAT TO LOOK FOR

Leasing is a debt-like form of financing. It sounds like a good way to finance assets off the balance sheet. The hitch is that capital leases must appear on the firm's balance sheet, and the lease payments are as legal an obligation for the firm as debt payments. In fact, leases have the same cash flow effects on the firm as borrowing.

Perspectives on Leasing

The tax perspective and the accounting perspective on leasing differ somewhat. These differences are reflected in the different terminology the IRS and the accountant use for leases. From the tax perspective two types of leases exist. The first is the financial lease, defined under the Tax Equity and Fiscal Responsibility Act by the five financial lease qualifications listed in the text. For example, the property must be listed under some ACRS category. All other leases from the tax perspective, are the second type, the operating lease.

Accountants view leases as of two types also. The first is the capital lease, defined under FASB No. 13. Capital leases must be capitalized on the firm's balance sheet. That is, the lessee must set up asset and liability accounts on the balance sheet reflecting the present value of the lease payments. The firm amortizes the asset over the asset's useful life, reducing the net income and the liability correspondingly each year. For accountants, the second type of lease is the operating lease, which need not appear on the firm's balance sheet. The important point to remember is that a capital lease for accounting purposes may not be a financial lease for tax purposes, and vice versa.

We can also view leases from the perspective of the lessor and the lessee. From the lessor's point of view, there are sales-type leases, direct financing leases, leveraged leases, and operating leases (shorter-term, generally cancellable leases which do not fit in the other categories). From the lessee's viewpoint, there are two types of leases, financial leases and operating leases (which are all leases other than financial leases). From either perspective, lease valuation employs the net present value techniques discussed in Chapters 8-10.

The Lease-or-Buy Decision

Debt and lease obligations have the same cash flow effects on the firm, but these obligations are valued differently, since taxes, bankruptcy costs, and transactions costs exist. Consider just the effect of depreciation on the lease-or-buy decision. If the firm's marginal tax rate is 34 percent, a purchased asset provides a depreciation tax shield of 34 percent times the annual ACRS depreciation. This tax shield, in effect, reduces the annual cash outflow for the purchase (or borrowing) decision, making purchasing more attractive.

When the firm is operating at a profit, the potential lessee weighs the after-tax cash flows and opportunity costs of leasing against the cost of the asset if purchased. As we noted above, the chief opportunity costs of leasing is the foregone depreciation tax shield. In making this NAL calculation, discount all the value to the present with the firm's after-tax borrowing rate. If the NAL is positive, the firm should lease the asset. Otherwise, the firm should buy the asset (assuming the NPV is positive).

COMPLETION QUESTIONS

17.1 A _____ lease is a lease which is short-term and generally cancellable. The _____ is responsible for the maintenance of the leased asset under this type of lease.

17.2 The cash flow consequences of leasing resemble those of _____.

17.3 Since lease payments are an expense of the lessee in doing business, they are _____.

17.4 If a firm has a _____ lease, the firm must capitalize the lease obligation on its financial statements. _____ leases appear in footnotes to the firm's financial statements.

17.5 In order to decide whether to lease or purchase an asset, the firm calculates the _____.

17.6 To calculate the depreciation tax shield of borrowing, multiply the _____ times the marginal tax rate. When entering into a lease, the lessee incurs an opportunity cost equal to this tax shield. The lower the firm's _____, the lower this opportunity cost.

17.7 The relevant discount rate in the net advantage of leasing calculation is the _____.

17.8 In a _____, the owner of an asset decides to sell it to another party and lease it back.

17.9 Unless a lease is _____ apart from tax consequences it cannot be considered a financial lease.

PROBLEMS

17.1 American Computing has been approached about a five year lease for a new computer. The machine costs $1,500,000. The company intends to depreciate the machine over five years using the ACRS factors. If $k_i = 8\%$, and $T = 30\%$, what lease rate should American set?

17.2 After a capital budgeting process, Amalgamated Plastics Company has decided to acquire a plastic molding machine. If purchased, the firm would be able to depreciate its $350,000 cost over five years to zero. McMillin has offered to lease the same machine to Amalgamated for $80,000 a year for the five years, with the lease payments being made in advance.

　　a. If the firm's marginal tax rate is 40 percent, the before-tax cost of debt is 15 percent, and the firm uses straight-line depreciation, should the molding machine be leased?

　　b. Suppose everything is as above, except the method of depreciation. If the firm intends to depreciate the asset using the five year modified ACRS factors, should it lease or purchase the machine?

17.3 Acme Freightways has recently purchased three forklifts for $450,000. The company intends to depreciate them on a straight-line basis over their five year useful life. The company has the opportunity to sell the forklifts to a leasing company for $450,000 and lease them back for five years with the annual lease payments made in advance. If Acme's tax rate is 25 percent and the before-tax cost of debt is 16 percent, what is the maximum lease payment it would be willing to make?

　　a. Should the project be accepted?

　　b. Suppose the machine could be leased from the supplier for $120,000 per year and the before-tax cost of debt to the firm is 18.33 percent. Should the machine be leased?

ANSWERS TO COMPLETION QUESTIONS

17.1 service; lessor
17.2 borrowing, or debt
17.3 tax deductible
17.4 capital; Operating
17.5 net advantage of leasing
17.6 annual depreciation; marginal tax rate
17.7 after-tax cost of borrowing
17.8 sale and leaseback
17.9 economically justified

SOLUTIONS TO PROBLEMS

17.1

Step 1. Determine the present value of benefits.

Year	Cost	×	Modified ACRS	= Depreciation	$Dep_t(T)$	PV at 8%	Present Value
1	$1,500,000		0.20	$300,000	$ 90,000	0.926	$ 83,340.00
2	1,500,000		0.32	480,000	144,000	0.857	123,408.00
3	1,500,000		0.19	285,000	85,500	0.794	67,887.00
4	1,500,000		0.15	225,000	67,500	0.735	49,612.50
5	1,500,000		0.14	210,000	63,000	0.681	42,903.00

Present value of benefits $367,150.50

Step 2. Amount to be recovered from lease payments:

$1,500,000 - $367,150.50 = $1,132,849.50

Step 3. After-tax lease payment:

$$\text{Amount to be recovered from lease payments} = (ATL)(PVA_{k_i\%,n})(1 + k_i)$$

$$1,132,849.50 = (ATL)(PVA_{8\%,5yr})(1 + k_i)$$

$$= ATL(3.993)(1.08)$$

$$4.312 ATL = \$1,132,849.50$$

$$ATL = \$1,132,849.50/4.312 = \$262,720.20$$

$$L = \frac{ATL}{(1 - T)} = \frac{\$262,720.20}{(1 - 0.30)} = \frac{\$262,720.20}{0.70} = \$375,314.57$$

17.2a

Step 1. $NAL = CLA_0 - \left[L_0(1 - T) + \sum_{t=1}^{n-1} \frac{L_t(1 - T)}{(1 + k_i)^t} + \sum_{t=1}^{n} \frac{Dep_t(T)}{(1 + k_i)^t} \right]$

From the problem, CLA_0 = $350,000

L = $ 80,000

Dep_t = $350,000/5 = $70,000

$Dep(T)$ = $70,000(0.40) = $28,000

k_i = $k_b(1 - T) = 15\%(1 - 0.40) = 9\%$

Step 2. So, NAL = $350,000 - [$80,000(1 - 0.40) + $80,000(1 - 0.40)
$(PVA_{9\%,4yr})$ + $28,000$(PVA_{9\%,5yr})$]

= $350,000 - [$48,000 + $48,000(3.240) + $28,000(3.890)]

= $350,000 - ($48,000 + $155,520 + $108,920)

= $350,000 - $312,440 = $37,560

Since the NAL is greater than zero, the firm should lease the machine.

17.2b

Step 3. The only part of the NAL equation that changes is $\sum_{t=1}^{n} \frac{Dep_t(T)}{(1+k_i)^t}$

Yr	Cost of Asset	×	Modified ACRS	=	Dep	×	T	=	Tax Shield	×	PV of 9%	=	PV of Tax Shield
1	$350,000		0.20		$ 70,000		0.40		$28,000		0.917		$25,676.00
2	350,000		0.32		112,000		0.40		44,800		0.842		37,721.60
3	350,000		0.19		66,500		0.40		26,600		0.772		20,535.20
4	350,000		0.15		52,500		0.40		21,000		0.708		14,868.00
5	350,000		0.14		49,000		0.40		19,600		0.650		12,740.00

$\sum_{t=1}^{5} \frac{Dep(T)}{(1+k_i)^5}$ = $111,540.80

Step 4. NAL = $350,000 - ($48,000 + $155,520 + $111,540.80)

= $350,000 - $315,060.80 = $34,939.20

If the firm uses modified ACRS depreciation, the asset should still be leased, since NAL is positive.

17.3

Step 1. Set the NAL = 0

$$0 = CLA_0 - \left[L_0(1-T) + \sum_{t=1}^{n-1} \frac{L_t(1-T)}{(1+k_i)^t} + \sum_{t=1}^{n} \frac{Dep_t(T)}{(1+k_i)^t}\right]$$

CLA_0 = $450,000

Dep_t = $450,000/5 = $90,000

$Dep_t(T)$ = ($90,000)(0.25) = $22,500

k_i = 16%(1 - 0.25) = 12%

Step 2. So, $0 = \$450{,}000 - [L(1 - 0.25) + L(PVA_{12\%, 4yr})(1 - 0.25)$

$\qquad\qquad\qquad + \$22{,}500\ (PVA_{12\%, 5yr})]$

$\qquad\quad 0 = \$450{,}000 - [0.75L + 0.75L(3.037) + \$22{,}500(3.605)]$

$\qquad\quad 0 = \$450{,}000 - (3.02775L + \$81{,}112.50)$

$\quad 3.02775L = \$368{,}887.50$

$\qquad\quad L = \$368{,}887.50/3.02775 = \$121{,}835.52$ per year

CHAPTER 18

WORKING CAPITAL POLICY

HOW THIS CHAPTER RELATES TO THE REST OF THE TEXT

While the emphasis to this point has been on long-term decisions, much of the manager's time is spent on making decisions that affect day-to-day operations. Chapter 18 begins the discussion of managing current assets and liabilities. The components of working capital--cash and marketable securities (Chapter 19), accounts receivable and inventory (Chapter 18), and short-term financing (Chapter 20)--are analyzed in greater detail in later chapters. As in earlier chapters, the concepts of cash flow (Chapter 4) and risk and return (Chapter 7) are important components in our analysis.

TOPICAL OUTLINE

I. Working capital.
   A. Current assets and current liabilities comprise a large portion of a firm's total assets and total liabilities.
      1. Inventories and accounts receivable are the largest current asset investments; accounts payable are the largest current liability or source of short-term funds.
      2. Current assets and liabilities are volatile within a single year and over business cycles.
   B. Working capital decisions.
      1. Manage the collection of funds from customers and the disbursement of funds to suppliers.
      2. Cash concentration.
      3. Liquidity management.
      4. Bank relations.
      5. Receivables management.
      6. Inventory management.
   C. Why do firms have working capital?
      1. Transactions costs.
      2. Time delays.
      3. Bankruptcy costs.

D. The importance of working capital.
1. The size and volatility of working capital makes working capital management a key function in a manager's day-to-day activities.
2. As sales grow, firms must increase both inventories and accounts payable; accounts receivable will also increase.
3. The health of a firm is apparent from its working capital accounts; liquidity ratios are one way to look at these accounts.
4. Effective working capital management can mean the difference between survival and bankruptcy to smaller firms, since a larger percentage of their assets and liabilities are current.
E. The goal of working capital management: Maximize the value of the firm by effective working capital management that increases the level of future cash flows or decreases their risk.

II. Liquidity and the cash cycle.
A. Ongoing liquidity refers to the inflows and outflows of cash through the firm during the course of the business.
1. Cash conversion cycle is the net time interval between actual cash expenditures on the productive resources and the ultimate recovery of cash: Operating cycle less payable deferral period.
   a. The cash cycle: Increases in purchases, inventories, or receivables serve to decrease liquidity, and vice versa.
      i. As raw materials are purchased, current liabilities increase through accounts payable.
      ii. Firm pays for accounts payable.
      iii. Raw materials are converted into finished goods in production process.
      iv. Finished goods inventory is sold for cash or credit.
      v. Credit sales (accounts receivable) are collected, resulting in cash.
   b. Average collection period is the number of days to collect credit sales.

2. Operating cycle is the sum of the inventory conversion and the average collection period.
3. Payable deferral period = 365/payables turnover.
B. Ratios of the cash conversion cycle.
1. Receivable turnover = sales/accounts receivable.
2. Inventory turnover = cost of goods sold/inventory.
3. Payables turnover = (Cost of goods sold + general, selling, and administrative expenses)/(accounts payable + salaries, benefits, and payroll taxes payable).
4. Conversion periods = 365/the above turnover ratios.
C. Use the above ratios to compute the cash conversion cycle, as in Table 18.1.
1. Cash conversion cycle is useful for analyzing a firm's liquidity over time.
2. This cycle can pick up information hidden by other liquidity measurements.
D. Protective liquidity is the backup liquidity that allows a firm to adjust to unforeseen cash demands.
III. Strategy for current asset and current liability management.
A. Current assets.
1. Factors affecting the level of current assets.
a. Nature of the firm's business.
b. Size of the firm.
c. Rate of increase (decrease) in sales.
d. Stability of the firm's sales.
2. Aggressive versus conservative management.
a. Figure 18.3 shows the difference between aggressive and conservative asset management.
b. Level of current assets: Aggressive--level is lower.
c. Cash conversion cycle: Aggressive--cycle is shorter.
d. Expense and revenue levels: Aggressive--lower expense levels leading to higher EBIT.

e. Risk and return vary together.
   i. Aggressive asset position has greater risks of running out of cash and the possibility of lost sales due to lower inventory.
   ii. Aggressive asset position may lead to greater EBIT.

B. Current liabilities.
1. Factors affecting the level of current liabilities: type of firm and desired flexibility.
2. Aggressive versus conservative management.
   a. Figure 18.4 shows the differences between aggressive and conservative liability management.
   b. Level of current liabilities: Aggressive--level is higher.
   c. Cash conversion cycle: Aggressive--cycle is shorter.
   d. Interest costs.
      i. Term structure of interest rates: Interest costs for various maturities of debt.
      ii. Yield curve: Visualizes the term structure of interest rates. (See Chapter 2, which discusses shifts in yield curves over time.)
      iii. Corporate borrowing costs include a risk premium over the cost of government borrowing.
   e. Risk and return.
      i. Aggressive: There is substantial interest rate risk associated with large amounts of short-term debt, since this debt must be refinanced frequently and short-term rates fluctuate widely.
      ii. Aggressive: Greater returns are possible by reducing the cash conversion cycle and financing at short-term rates, which are generally lower than long-term rates.

C. The management of working capital.
1. The matching principle.
   a. Aggressive: Match a low level of current assets with a high level of current liabilities.

b. Conservative: Match a high level of current assets with a low level of current liabilities.
   c. Moderate: Match an aggressive (conservative, moderate) current asset position with a conservative (aggressive, moderate) current liabilities position.
   d. Generally, a firm should establish a target for its working capital position that takes into account its appropriate current asset and current liabilities positions.
2. Recognizing and dealing with liquidity problems.
   a. Signs of liquidity problems.
      i. Unexpected buildup of inventories.
      ii. Increase in level of outstanding accounts receivable.
      iii. Decline in the daily or weekly cash inflows.
      iv. Increased costs that the firm is unable to pass on to customers.
      v. Decline in the firm's net working capital, or an increase in its debt ratio.
   b. Steps toward the solution of liquidity problems.
      i. Control and reduce inventory investment.
      ii. Reexamine and tighten credit standards.
      iii. Increase the short-term or long-term debt, or issue equity.
      iv. Control overhead and increase concentration on effective asset management.
      v. Lay off employees.
      vi. Reduce planned long-term capital expenditures.
      vii. Reduce cash dividends.
3. Providing for protective liquidity.
   a. Lines of credit.
   b. Marketable securities portfolio.

FORMULAS

Cash conversion cycle = operating cycle − payable deferral period

Operating cycle = inventory conversion period + average collection period

Receivables turnover = sales/accounts receivable

Inventory turnover = cost of goods sold/inventory

Payables turnover = (cost of goods sold + general, selling, and administrative expenses)/(accounts payable + salaries, benefits, and payroll taxes payable)

Average collection period = 365/receivables turnover

Inventory conversion period = 365/inventory turnover

Payables deferral period = 365/payables turnover

Total before-tax interest cost = short-term (ST) interest + long-term (LT) interest

= (ST rate)($ST debt) + (LT rate)($LT debt)

WHAT TO LOOK FOR

In Parts Four and Five we considered long-term investment and financing decisions. While these aspects of financial management are very important, it is equally important to understand the management of current assets and current liabilities--the firm's working capital. This chapter considers the underlying aspects of the firm's working capital levels while later chapters in this section examine the management of each of the components of working capital. Since firms must carefully manage their current assets and current liabilities to insure continued operation, knowledge of these techniques will help managers identify problems and develop appropriate financial plans and strategies as discussed in Part 7.

Working Capital Management

Working capital levels

Chapter 18 focuses on the policies underlying a firm's working capital levels. For example, accounts receivable result from the firm's credit policy. The more lenient the policy, the higher the level of accounts receivable. Accounts payable result from the firm's policy for trade credit financing. If the firm's policy is to take advantage of cash discounts for early payment, its level of accounts payable will be lower than it would be if the firm paid for trade credit on or after the date it is due. If the firm is loose in its inventory management, its inventory levels may be higher than if it used a tighter inventory management policy. The policies themselves are not good or bad. However, the goal of working capital management is that these policies maximize the market price of the stock in order to maximize the value of the firm.

Working capital and the cash cycle

Since the levels of the working capital accounts change daily, there is cash flowing into and out of the firm. The cash cycle involves the investment in inventory, accounts receivable, and the spontaneous financing supporting this investment. The cycle completes itself as a trade credit is paid from sales revenues and credit sales are collected.

Unless the firm is going out of business, this cash cycle is ongoing and the firm is operating simultaneously at many points within the cycle. For example, the credit manager might be collecting accounts receivable while a salesperson is accepting a credit sale. At the same time, the inventory manager is purchasing more inventory on trade credit, and the controller is seeing that the credit is repaid in a timely fashion. This continuous cycle of cash is called ongoing liquidity. The firm may also maintain protective liquidity in order to cover unforeseen circumstances, such as a bulk-ordering bargain or an emergency.

Although the cash cycle is ongoing, we can measure its average length at any point in time. To do this, we calculate the cash conversion cycle, the time from cash investment in productive resources to recovery of the cash:

Cash conversion cycle = operating cycle - payable deferral period

$$= \begin{matrix} \text{inventory} \\ \text{conversion} \\ \text{period} \end{matrix} + \begin{matrix} \text{average} \\ \text{collection} \\ \text{period} \end{matrix} - \begin{matrix} \text{payable} \\ \text{deferral} \\ \text{period} \end{matrix}$$

$$= \frac{365}{(\text{cost of good sold/inventory})} + \frac{365}{(\text{sales/accounts receivable})}$$

$$- \frac{365}{[(\text{cost of goods sold} + \text{general, selling, and administrative expenses})/(\text{accounts payable} + \text{salaries, benefits, and payroll taxes payable})]}$$

The inventory conversion, accounts receivable conversion, and payable deferral (or repayment) are major cash flows in the cash cycle. These measures help pinpoint increases or decreases in a firm's ongoing liquidity. Table 18.1 compares the liquidity ratios and turnover ratios to the cash conversion cycle for J.C. Penney.

Aggressive versus Conservative Policies

A manager can choose from a spectrum of working capital policies that range from conservative to aggressive. It may be appropriate for managers to match conservative short-term asset management policies with aggressive short-term liability management policies and vice versa. The reason for this suggestion is that managers often attempt to match the life of the financing to the life of the assets funded. If a firm has an aggressive current asset position, it will often have a relatively low level of current assets. So it should be funding with mostly long-term rather than short-term financing. This matched approach, however, will give a more moderate return and more moderate risk exposure than that of the firm using both aggressive asset and aggressive liability policies.

Current asset policies

Low current asset levels indicate an aggressive policy. If the managers attempt to shorten the cash conversion cycle, they will reduce their investment in current assets to a minimum. Such a policy will increase the return of the firm, since these current assets work harder and faster to return assets to cash. But this policy will also increase the risk that the firm will have insufficient liquidity in times of emergency. In addition, since inventory and accounts receivable are kept low, those carrying costs are lower, but the firm risks lost sales due to insufficient inventory and unreasonably tight credit management.

Current liability policies

High current liability levels indicate aggressive current liability management. Again, the manager is attempting to shorten the cash conversion cycle. The financing costs of this policy are comparatively lower than those of the conservative policy *if* short-term interest rates are lower than long-term rates. (We can discover whether short-term rates are higher or lower than long-term rates by looking at the term structure of interest rates. Look at the yields on short-term securities versus the yields on long-term securities of equal risk.) Aggressive current liabilities policies, however, are more risky since firms face two possibilities: (1) The short-term lenders might not agree to extend the necessary credit on this ongoing basis; (2) the costs of funds change each time the firm returns for new credit arrangements. With short-term credit, the firm seeks new credit and interest terms more frequently, producing greater uncertainty about financing costs.

Aggressive and conservative policies are neither good nor bad per se. Managers must consider the objective of maximizing the market value of the firm when adopting working capital policies. The policy should be reevaluated if they see unexpected buildups in current assets, declines in cash inflows, increases in costs which cannot be passed on to consumers, or a decline in net working capital.

COMPLETION QUESTIONS

18.1 _____ refers to the firm's current assets minus its current liabilities.

18.2 In the percentage breakdown of retail firms' current assets and current liabilities, the largest current asset investment is in _____ while the largest current liability is _____.

18.3 A firm that maintains _____ can adjust rapidly to unforeseen cash demands and has backup sources for raising cash.

18.4 _____ is the net time interval that elapses between the actual cash investment in productive resources and the ultimate recovery of cash.

18.5 The operating cycle is the time between the purchase of inventory and the receipt for sale of finished goods. It is the sum of the _____ _____ plus the average collection period.

18.6 The payable deferral period measures how long the firm _____ _____.

18.7 As the cash conversion cycle lengthens, the firm's liquidity _____.

18.8 In matching, a firm should match its short-term investments with _____ financing.

18.9 A firm holding low levels of current assets is using an _____ asset management approach, while a firm holding low levels of current liabilities is using a _____ liability management approach.

18.10 An aggressive current asset management _____ a firm's liquidity, since the firm does not have as large a portion of its assets tied up in accounts receivable and inventories.

18.11 An unexpected buildup in inventories, or an increase in the firm's level of outstanding accounts receivable, may be a sign of _____.

18.12 The manager has discovered an increase in the firm's level of accounts receivable. A corrective measure would be to reexamine the firm's _____.

PROBLEMS

18.1 Michaelson's Paint Store has annual sales of $912,500. Michaelson's grants credit on sales, the average accounts receivable balance is $50,000, and the store keeps $139,000 in inventory on hand. Cost of goods sold amounts to 60 percent of sales. General and administrative expenses are $12,000. Accounts payable are $10,000 and salaries, benefits, and payroll taxes due are $50,000. What is Michaelson's cash conversion cycle?

18.2 Gemini Computers, Inc. designs, manufactures, and markets computers for a variety of scientific and engineering applications. The following information is from their 1989 annual report (in units of $1,000):

	1989	1988
Sales	$18,009	$3,400
Cost of goods sold	8,047	2,244
Cost of goods sold + general, selling, and administrative expenses	14,889	5,133
Accounts receivable	4,360	1,680
Inventory	5,692	1,029
Accounts payable + salaries, benefits, and payroll taxes payable	5,039	1,024

How has Gemini's cash conversion cycle changed from 1988 to 1989?

18.3 American Foods Company is a manufacturer of packaged "gourmet" foods. At present, the book value of the stockholders' equity is $50 million. The firm also has $30 million of long-term debt and long-term assets of $70 million. The following are forecasts of the firm's current asset needs for the next two years.

Year 1	Quarter 1	$21
	2	24
	3	35
	4	30
Year 2	Quarter 1	25
	2	29
	3	40
	4	36

Payables and accruals average 40 percent of current assets.

a. Determine the amount of short-term borrowing needed per quarter to complete the financing of current assets.

b. The interest rate on long-term bonds is 12 percent; on short-term borrowing, it is 10 percent. Suppose American Foods reduced long-term debt by $10 million and matched current assets with current liabilities. How much interest would it save over the two years?

18.4 Maylock Cosmetics is considering two working capital management policies, one aggressive and one conservative. Net income is expected to vary under each plan and also is expected to vary with economic conditions. Maylock estimates that there is a 25 percent probability of a growing economy, a 50 percent probability of a normal economy, and a 25 percent probability of a recession. Net income forecasts for each plan are as follows.

	Growing Economy	Normal Economy	Recession
Probability	0.25	0.50	0.25
Net income; aggressive plan	$184,000	$120,000	$92,000
Net income; conservative plan	$120,000	$96,000	$72,000

The firm has 20,000 shares of common stock outstanding. The more aggressive policy is expected to have a P/E ratio of 8 times. The other policy is expected to have a P/E ratio of 12. Which working capital policy should Maylock Cosmetics undertake?

ANSWERS TO COMPLETION QUESTIONS

18.1 Net working capital
18.2 inventories; accounts payable
18.3 protective liquidity
18.4 the cash conversion cycle
18.5 the inventory conversion period
18.6 is receiving credit from others

18.7 worsens
18.8 short-term
18.9 aggressive; conservative
18.10 increases
18.11 deteriorating liquidity
18.12 credit granting policy

SOLUTIONS TO PROBLEMS

18.1
Step 1. Receivables turnover = $912,500/$50,000 = 18.250 times
Step 2. Inventory turnover = $921,600(0.60)/$139,000 = 3.939 times
Step 3. Payables turnover = $\frac{\$912,500(0.60) + \$12,000}{\$10,000 + \$50,000}$ = 9.325 times
Step 4. Average collection period   = 365/18.25 = 20.00 days
        Inventory conversion period = 365/3.939 = 92.66 days
        Payables turnover period   = 365/9.325 = 39.14 days
Step 5. Cash conversion cycle = 20.00 days + 92.66 days - 39.14 days
                              = 73.52 days

18.2

Step 1. Receivables turnover = sales/accounts receivable

Receivables turnover$_{1989}$ = $18,009/$4,360 = 4.131 times

Receivables turnover$_{1988}$ = $3,400/$1,680 = 2.024 times

Step 2. Inventory turnover = cost of goods sold/inventory

Inventory turnover$_{1989}$ = $8,047/$5,692 = 1.414 times

Inventory turnover$_{1988}$ = $2,244/$1,029 = 2.181 times

Step 3. Payables turnover = (cost of goods sold + general, selling, and administrative expenses)/(accounts payable + salaries, benefits, and taxes payable)

Payables turnover$_{1989}$ = $14,889/$5,039 = 2.955 times

Payables turnover$_{1988}$ = $5,133/$1,024 = 5.013 times

Step 4. Operating cycle = inventory conversion period + receivables conversion period

Inventory conversion period = 365 days/inventory turnover

Inventory conversion period$_{1989}$ = 365 days/1.414 = 258.13 days

Inventory conversion period$_{1988}$ = 365 days/2.181 = 167.35 days

Step 5. Average collection period = 365 days/receivables turnover

Average collection period$_{1989}$ = 365 days/4.131 = 88.36 days

Average collection period$_{1988}$ = 365 days/2.024 = 180.34 days

Step 6. Operating cycle 1989 = 258.13 days + 88.36 days = 346.49 days

Operating cycle 1988 = 167.35 days + 180.34 days = 347.69 days

Step 7. Cash conversion cycle = operating cycle - payable deferral period

Payable deferral period = 365 days/payables turnover

Payable deferral period$_{1989}$ = 365 days/2.955 = 123.52 days

Payable deferral period$_{1988}$ = 365 days/5.013 = 72.81 days

Step 8. Cash conversion cycle$_{1989}$ = 346.49 days - 123.52 days = 222.97 days

Cash conversion cycle$_{1988}$ = 347.69 days - 72.81 days = 274.88 days

The cash conversion cycle was shortened by approximately 52 days primarily due to the extension of the payable deferral period.

18.3a

Step 1. The amount of long-term funding available to finance current assets is: Stockholders' equity + long-term debt - long-term assets
= $50 million + $30 million - $70 million = $10 million

Step 2. The cash flow needs are (in millions)

	Current Assets	− Long-term Sources	− Payables + Accruals (40% Of Current Assets)	= Short-Term Borrowing
Year 1 Quarter 1	$21	$10	$ 8.4	$ 2.6
2	24	10	9.6	4.4
3	35	10	14.0	11.0
4	30	10	12.0	8.0
Year 2 Quarter 1	25	10	10.0	5.0
2	29	10	11.6	7.4
3	40	10	16.0	14.0
4	36	10	14.4	11.6

18.3b

Step 3. Under the present scenario, the interest expenses are:

Long-term debt: ($30 million)(0.12)(2 yr) = $7.2 million

Short-term debt:

	Short-Term Borrowing	×	Interest Rate (0.10/4)	=	Interest
Year 1 Quarter 1	$ 2.6		0.025		$0.065
2	4.4		0.025		0.110
3	11.0		0.025		0.275
4	8.0		0.025		0.200
Year 2 Quarter 1	5.0		0.025		0.125
2	7.4		0.025		0.185
3	14.0		0.025		0.350
4	11.6		0.025		0.290

Interest on short-term debt = $1.600 million

Total interest is $8.800 million ($7.2 million + $1.6 million).

Step 4. If the firm reduces long-term debt by $10 million, it will have to borrow an additional $10 million per quarter short-term debt at 10 percent.

Long-term debt: ($20 million)(0.12)(2 yr) = $4.8 million

Short-term debt:

Year 1
Quarter			
1	$12.6	0.025	$0.315
2	14.4	0.025	0.360
3	21.0	0.025	0.525
4	18.0	0.025	0.450

Year 2
Quarter			
1	15.0	0.025	0.375
2	17.4	0.025	0.435
3	24.0	0.025	0.600
4	21.6	0.025	<u>0.540</u>

Interest on short-term debt = $3.600 million

Total interest is $8.4 million ($4.8 million + $3.6 million). Total interest expense has been reduced by $8.8 million − $8.4 million = $0.4 million or $400,000.

Step 5. An alternative short solution is to take the difference in interest rates times the amount borrowed. Thus, 12% − 10% = 2% savings. $10 million reduction in long-term debt × 2% = $200,000 per year, or $400,000 over the two years.

18.4

Step 1. EPS = Net income/number of shares, so

| | EPS | | |
	Growing Economy	Normal Economy	Recession
Probability	0.25	0.50	0.25
Aggressive EPS	$9.20	$6.00	$4.60
Conservative EPS	6.00	4.80	3.60

Step 2. Agressive Policy:

E(EPS) = 0.25($9.20) + 0.50($6.00) + 0.25($4.60)

= $2.30 + $3.00 + $1.15 = $6.45

Step 3. Conservative Policy:

E(EPS) = 0.25($6.00) + 0.50($4.80) + 0.25($3.60)

= $1.50 + $2.40 + $0.90 = $4.80

Step 4. Price = E(EPS)(P/E) ratio, so

Under the aggressive policy, P_0 = ($6.45)(8) = $51.60

Under the conservative policy, P_0 = ($4.80)(12) = $57.60

Maylock should implement the conservative policy since it will yield a higher stock price.

CHAPTER 19

CASH AND MARKETABLE SECURITIES

HOW THIS CHAPTER RELATES TO THE REST OF THE TEXT

Chapter 19 examines the management of cash and marketable securities, an important component of working capital (Chapter 18). Additional components, accounts receivable and inventory (Chapter 20) and short-term financing (Chapter 21), will be discussed later. Cash and marketable security analysis involves the study of cash flows (Chapter 4) and risk and return (Chapter 7). Due to the short time involved, discounting techniques (Chapter 5) are typically ignored. Marketable securities share many features with long-term bonds (Chapter 13).

TOPICAL OUTLINE

I. The cash management function.
   A. Reasons for holding cash.
      1. Transactions purposes: Cash is necessary to meet requirements such as monthly bill payments, tax payments, cash dividend payments, and salaries.
      2. Hedging against uncertainty: Marketable securities and lines of credit provide liquidity for unexpected cash needs.
      3. Cash hoard: Liquidity is useful for weathering bad times when credit is tight and also facilitates making acquisitions.
      4. Compensating balance requirements: Some lines of credit and other bank services require that a compensating balance be left in a checking account.
   B. Risk and return.
      1. Returns earned from holding liquid assets.
         a. Investment in marketable securities results in interest income that makes an important contribution to the firm's profitability.
         b. Liquidity allows firms to take advantage of cash discounts offered by suppliers.
         c. Savings on purchases can result if the firms have the liquidity to take advantage of special sale prices.

d. Their credit rating improves, lowering the risk and thus the associated borrowing costs, if firms increase their liquidity to reasonable levels.
2. Risks from holding too little cash.
a. Problems may occur in paying bills; bill payment may have to be deferred, capital spending curtailed, expensive short-term financing obtained, and opportunities bypassed.
b. In the extreme, firms may be forced to liquidate or file for bankruptcy.
3. The risk-return tradeoff involves firms' holding adequate cash so they can meet their obligations, but that does not then allow them to secure the higher returns provided by investing a greater percentage of their funds in long-term assets.
C. Liquidity policies in practice.
1. Large manufacturing firms tend to hold less liquid assets than do small manufacturing firms.
2. Due to economic conditions and more effective asset control, many firms have tended to reduce their liquid asset holdings.
II. Cash management techniques.
A. The goal of the cash gathering system is to speed collections (to the level at which the increased benefits equal the increased costs of the system).
1. Float is the time which elapses from the writing of a check until the recipient receives the funds and can draw upon them (when it has "good funds").
a. Mail float is the length of time it takes a firm to receive a check after it is mailed by a customer.
b. Processing float is the time that elapses until the selling firm deposits the check; the firm can reduce float here first.
c. Transit float is the time required for the check to clear through the banking system.
2. Decentralized collections in various points in the country can reduce mail float.

a. Local offices of a major firm can collect payments to deposit in a local depository bank to begin clearance.

b. Customers can mail payments to lockboxes--post office boxes in specified cities; a bank picks up the payments several times a day for clearance.

c. Managers must weigh the costs of using these systems versus the benefits of reduced mail float.

3. The banking network is used with collection by lockboxes or local offices.

a. Lockbox: A regional bank maintains the lockbox, forwards the funds to the concentration (or central) bank, and sends the supporting documents to the firm.

b. Local offices: A local depository bank receives the funds from the local office and forwards them to the firm's central bank.

c. Bank transfer mechanisms.

i. Depository transfer checks (DTC), which are nonnegotiable instruments for deposit only to the firm's account.

ii. Electronic DTCs, which send deposit information electronically, cutting the clearing time to one day.

iii. Wire transfers, which can transfer funds within the same day, eliminate transfer float. However, wire transfer is more expensive.

4. Other collection approaches include special couriers and preauthorized checks from customers.

5. Analysis of cash gathering techniques involves weighing the increased benefits (ΔB) of the system against the increased costs (ΔC).

$$\Delta B = (\Delta t)(TS)(I)(1 - T)$$

where Δt = float change time

TS = size of transaction

I = yearly interest rate

T = the firm's marginal tax rate

a. If the change in costs exceeds the change in benefits, the firm should not change the system--$\Delta C > \Delta B$--and vice versa. If the change in benefits equals the change in costs, the firm is indifferent.
b. Lockbox per-day benefits include increased efficiency and reduced float, which can be calculated with the equation above. The costs include the bank fee charged directly or through a compensating balance requirement.
c. To convert per-day figures to per-year figures, convert daily volume to a yearly basis by multiplying TS by 365, or the daily interest rate (I) to a yearly interest rate by multiplying it by 365.
d. To decide between the present method and an alternative, determine the incremental costs, and then determine how much you would have to decrease float time (Δt), the interest rate (I), or the average transaction size (TS) to be indifferent between the two methods.

B. The goal of the cash disbursement system is to control and slow down the outflow of cash without hurting the firm's credit rating.
1. Controlled disbursing takes advantage of transit float, clearing checks through an out-of-the way bank with longer clearance time.
   a. Judge the usefulness of this system with the cost-benefit equation above.
   b. As long as the clearing bank charges less than the breakeven amount per check, the firm should make the change.
2. Zero-balance accounts at the central bank allow all the firm's divisions to draw on individual zero-balance disbursing accounts, creating negative balances that are restored to zero by the firm's positive balance master account at the central bank. Excess cash balances do not build up.
3. Other disbursement approaches include centralized payables, timing of check payments, and sight drafts.

4. Again, the incremental costs and benefits of the disbursement management system should be weighed.
C. Interactions between cash gathering and cash disbursing.
1. Managers must take into account the joint effects and costs of cash disbursement and gathering systems.
2. Firms should select the best mix of disbursement and collection services for them, given the wide variety of cash management techniques offered by the financial services industry.
   a. Electronic data interchange (EDI) affect ordering and manufacturing cycles.
   b. Electronic funds transfer (EFT) systems allow firms to handle payments electronically.
      i. EFTs utilize automated clearing houses (ACH) or corporate trade payment (CTP) systems to speed payments.
D. International aspects include concentration banking, international transfer, international lockboxes, intracompany netting, and timing according to anticipated exchange rate fluctuations.

III. Determining the daily cash balance: How much should be kept?
A. The approach.
1. Prepare cash budget on monthly basis, breaking down inflows and outflows.
2. Identify the timing of the major inflows and outflows for the month so you can estimate when daily transfers into and out of the marketable securities portfolio will be necessary.
3. Use modeling to predict routine inflows and outflows in order to detect cash surpluses and cash needs.
4. Compare the actual outflows and inflows with those predicted to evaluate the planning procedure and to fine-tune it.
5. Evaluate the worth of a change by comparing incremental benefits and incremental costs:
$$\Delta B = (\Delta t)(TS)(I)(1 - T) = \Delta C.$$
B. Short-term investment alternatives include U.S. Treasury bills, federal agency issues, short-term tax exempts, commercial paper,

certificates of deposit, bankers' acceptances, Eurodollars, repurchase agreements, money market mutual funds, and money market preferred stock.
C. Selection criteria for choosing among marketable securities.
   1. General economic conditions change, as do monetary and fiscal policies. These changes affect the level of interest rates.
      a. As market interest rates go up, bond prices go down, providing opportunities to gain through purchasing and to lose through selling at these low prices; this creates uncertainty or risk.
      b. The bank discount yield on U.S. Treasury bills is the investors' expected return as a percent of the face value of the security, based on a 360-day year.

      $$k_{BD} = \left[\frac{P_M - P_0}{P_M}\right]\left[\frac{360}{n}\right]$$

      c. The bond equivalent yield converts the bank discount yield to a 365-day year.

      $$k_{BE} = \frac{(365)(k_{BD})}{360 - (k_{BD})(n)}$$

   2. Inflation increases the required return.
   3. Firm- and issue-specific risk must be taken into consideration when structuring the marketable securities portfolio.
   4. International risk comes into play if the marketable securities portfolio includes Eurodollars.
   5. Some marketable securities are not routinely redeemable before maturity, and some have a limited secondary market.
   6. The expected yield on market securities, balanced by the risk, is the criterion for selection.
D. The marketable securities portfolio.
   1. The firm's risk-return posture determines the specific composition of the marketable securities portfolio after taking into consideration the interaction of risk, liquidity, and yield.
   2. Funds that are not likely to be needed will be invested in longer-term (6 months to 1 year) instruments.

3. Funds which represent very temporary excess cash are invested in repurchase agreements or other short-term investments.
4. Stock and bonds are not part of the marketable securities portfolio.

FORMULAS

Evaluation of Cash Gathering Techniques

ΔB = incremental benefits
ΔC = incremental costs (after tax)
Δt = time in days that float is changed
TS = size of the transaction
I = yearly interest rate
T = tax rate

$\Delta B = (\Delta t)(TS)(I)(1 - T)$

Attempt to find the ΔC that will make $\Delta B = \Delta C$, and thus make the firm indifferent; i.e., where $\Delta C = \Delta B = (t)(TS)(I)(1 - T)$.

Relationship Between Daily and Annual Interest

Daily interest rate = annual interest rate/365

Relationship Between Daily Transaction Size and Annual Transaction Size

Annual TS = (daily TS)(365)
Annual ΔB = (annual TS)(daily interest rate)(1 - T)
   or (daily TS)(annual interest rate)(1 - T)

Bank Discount Yield

$$k_{BD} = \left[\frac{P_M - P_0}{P_M}\right]\left[\frac{360}{n}\right]$$

Bond Equivalent Yield

$$k_{BE} = \frac{(365)(k_{BD})}{360 - (k_{BD})(n)}$$

WHAT TO LOOK FOR

Chapter 19 begins the in-depth study of short-term asset management by focusing on the most liquid assets--cash and marketable securities.

As you recall, the left side (asset side) of the balance sheet shows investment in the firm. The right side (liabilities and stockholders' equity) of the balance sheet shows the funding sources for these investments. As noted in the preceding chapter, we may want to match the maturity of the financing source with the life or recovery period of the asset financed. All financing sources involve a cost. In order to maximize the value of the firm, the return on all assets, including current assets like cash, must exceed their cost.

Why Hold Cash?

If cash itself earns no rate of return, why hold cash? Cash can provide the necessary liquidity for the firm to take advantage of cash discounts by paying for trade credit. This is a roundabout way for cash holding to pay its own way. Keeping cash to take advantage of cash discounts can easily pay for itself. Cash budgeting, discussed in Chapter 4, can help managers fine-tune the cash management system so they can free sufficient cash during the cash conversion cycle to meet such payments.

Cash reserves may also allow managers to purchase items at sale prices. If the sale price is low enough, the savings provide a return in excess of the cost of holding the cash. In emergency situations, cash is often essential to avoid costly delays. This precautionary liquidity can also be served by a line of credit (Chapter 21) or a marketable securities portfolio, which we discuss later. In any case, the return from holding liquid assets should exceed the cost of holding these assets, since the objective of cash management is to maximize the value of the firm.

Cash Management and the Cash Conversion Cycle

In cash management, we meet this value-maximizing objective most efficiently by slowing payments and speeding collections. Recall the discussion of the cash conversion cycle in Chapter 18. In doing business, the firm buys raw materials or inventory with cash or on trade credit. The operating cycle begins at this point. The firm sells its inventory for cash or on credit. As the firm collects on the credit sales, the cash is generated to pay off the trade credit, completing the cash conversion cycle. Thus, the cash conversion cycle is:

$$\begin{matrix}\text{Inventory} \\ \text{conversion} \\ \text{period}\end{matrix} + \begin{matrix}\text{average} \\ \text{collection} \\ \text{period}\end{matrix} - \begin{matrix}\text{payable} \\ \text{deferral} \\ \text{period}\end{matrix}$$

By speeding collections and delaying disbursements, firms attempt to shorten the receivables conversion period and lengthen the payable deferral period. The result is a shorter cash conversion cycle. The goal of cash management techniques, then, is to speed collections and slow payments without hurting the firm's credit rating and without having the incremental costs exceed the incremental benefits.

Methods of Speeding Collections

The text focuses on several methods of speeding cash collections or shortening float time, including lockboxes, local office collection, and bank transfer mechanisms. The analysis of these techniques involves weighing the increased costs versus the increased benefits in terms of reduced float time (Δt), and interest return (I) on the increased liquidity. For example, suppose California Industries has no collections speeding system. It is considering lockboxes at a cost of $35 per day or local office collection at a cost of $30 per day, before taxes.

Assume that the average payment is $780, with 75 check payments a day. If the company uses lockboxes, the reduced float time is 2 days; it is 1.50 days with the local office collection. The firm's marginal tax rate is 40%. To calculate the change in benefits for these two systems, let's use a daily basis. We will adjust our interest by dividing by 365. The total TS is calculated by multiplying the number of transfers or transactions per day times the average size. The incremental benefits are:

ΔB = reduced float time (Δt) × transaction size (TS) × interest rate (I) × (1 - T)

Lockbox: ΔB = (2 days)[($780)(75)](0.12/365 days)(1 - 0.40) = $23.08
The costs are $35(1 - 0.40) = $21.00, so benefits exceed the costs by $23.08 - $21.00 = $2.08.

Local collection: ΔB = (1.50 days)[($780)(75)](0.12/365 days)(1 - 0.40) = $17.31. The costs are $30(1 - 0.40) = $18.00, so costs exceed benefits by $18.00 - $17.31 = $0.69.

The lockbox option is most attractive, since its incremental benefits exceed its incremental costs.

To make the local collection system pay its way, California Industries could increase its number of transactions. Thus:

ΔC = $30(1 - 0.40) = ΔB = (1.50 days)[($780)(W)](0.12/365 days)(1 - 0.40)

$18 = $0.23079W

W = 77.99 or 78 transactions per day.

If the number of transactions increased by three per day, California Industries would be indifferent between its present system and the local collection system.

The Role of the Marketable Securities Portfolio

Once the cash budget and daily forecasting techniques have helped determine the pattern of cash needs and surpluses, the marketable securities portfolio can both provide and absorb liquidity. On days the firm needs cash, the manager can liquidate holdings. On days where there is excess cash, the manager can purchase securities for the portfolio, keeping a minimum balance in demand deposits. The return on the marketable securities portfolio should exceed the costs of purchasing and holding these securities. Otherwise, the value of the firm will be reduced. In selecting among marketable securities for the portfolio, managers will want to layer the maturities of the securities, matching short-term expected cash surpluses with short-term instruments. See Table 19.1 for a description of the various short-term marketable securities and their characteristics.

The manager should also analyze the risk required with respect to the economy, inflation, international conditions, and firm- or issue-specific conditions. As noted in Chapter 7, these risks increase the required return on securities. In choosing among corporate issues, managers must consider the financial ability of the corporation to pay interest and repay principal, since these cash flows are somewhat uncertain. The more uncertain the cash flows, the higher the required return. Managers ultimately should invest in the highest possible return, based on the risk-return posture of the firm that matches the firm's projected liquidity needs.

COMPLETION QUESTIONS

19.1 _____ are short-term securities that the firm can hold temporarily and readily convert into _____.

19.2 Cash management techniques attempt to _____ collection float and _____ disbursement float.

19.3 _____ is the length of time from the writing of a check until the recipient can draw upon the funds. If the firm establishes an efficient internal management system to minimize the delay between payment receipt and payment deposit, the firm reduces _____ _____.

19.4 In an effort to decrease the mail float, firms which do not have local offices can use a _____ arrangement. Customers mail payments to a _____ in a specified city for collection and clearance by a regional concentration bank.

19.5 A commercial collection center can receive deposit information from the firm and transfer that information to a concentration bank. The concentration bank prepares an _____ which is transmitted to the firm' local depository bank. The bank transfer mechanism involves a uniform clearing time of _____ days.

19.6 Under a _____ procedure, customers authorize a firm to draw checks directly on the customer's demand deposit account.

19.7 In order to assess the cost effectiveness of various cash management techniques, compare the incremental _____ with the _____ _____. This technique can be conducted on either a per unit or total basis, on an annual or daily basis. To convert the annual interest rate to a daily interest rate, divide I by _____.

19.8 With _____, divisions write checks on individual disbursement accounts, creating negative balances; these negative balances are restored to zero by the firm's master account.

19.9 Excess cash left idle in a demand deposit account represents an _____ cost for the firm. In order to determine the minimum necessary cash balance, the firm can prepare a _____ budget.

19.10 In a _____ budget, the firm breaks down the major cash inflows and outflows and identifies their _____ during the month. Thus, funds can be transferred at the appropriate times into and out of the _____.

19.11 As economic conditions decline and investors become more risk averse, the market rate of interest tends to _____, and the market price of outstanding debt _____.

19.12 _____ are receipts for time deposits at commercial banks.

19.13 _____ are time drafts issued by a business firm that have been accepted by a bank. Rather than paying interest, they are _____ when issued to yield a stated rate.

19.14 The sale of government securities by a bank or securities dealer with a simultaneous agreement to repurchase them results in a _____ _____.

19.15 If expected inflation increases, the market interest rate will _____ to account for the expected loss in _____.

PROBLEMS

19.1 Stevenson Oil Company allows its customers to purchase gasoline on credit if the balance is paid within 30 days. Presently, all checks are mailed to the central office in Tulsa, Oklahoma. The average bill spends five days in the mail and the Tulsa National Bank, which is the receiver of the checks after processing, requires that Stevenson leave the funds untouched for five days while the checks clear the banking system.

Stevenson is considering a system of eight regional lockboxes, each costing $100 per month. The lockbox system would cut mail float to two days and transit float to three days. Presently, Stevenson receives 500 checks per day, with the average check being written for $45. If the annual interest rate is 14 percent and the firm's marginal tax rate is 35%, what will be the annual gain (or loss) of the lockbox system?

19.2 Harris Industries has set up a controlled disbursing system with two out-of-town banks. The net benefit after taxes (i.e., $\Delta B - \Delta C$) of the system to Harris is $40,000 per year. If Harris writes 300 checks per day with an average amount of $500, how many days of additional float will Harris obtain if the interest rate is 10 percent, the bank charges an additional $0.15 per check cleared, and Harris' tax rate is 40%?

19.3 Marion Francis is interested in purchasing a U.S. Treasury bill for $9,800. The bill has a $10,000 face value and matures in 100 days. Calculate the bank discount and bond equivalent yields for Ms. Francis.

ANSWERS TO COMPLETION QUESTIONS

19.1 Marketable securities; cash
19.2 reduce; increase
19.3 Float; the processing float
19.4 lockbox; post office box
19.5 electronic depository transfer check; one
19.6 preauthorized check
19.7 costs; expected incremental benefits; 365
19.8 zero-balance accounts
19.9 opportunity; cash
19.10 cash; timing; marketable securities portfolio
19.11 increase; decreases
19.12 Negotiable certificates of deposit
19.13 Bankers' acceptances; discounted
19.14 repurchase agreement
19.15 increase; purchasing power

SOLUTIONS TO PROBLEMS

19.1

Step 1. Cost = (number of lockboxes)(monthly rent)(12 months)(1 − T)
$$= (8)(\$100)(12)(1 - 0.35) = \$6,240$$

Step 2. Total float under the present system = mail float + transit float
$$= 5 \text{ days} + 5 \text{ days} = 10 \text{ days}$$
Total float under the lockbox system = 2 days + 3 days = 5 days
Float is reduced by 5 days.

Step 3. ΔB = (days float changed)[(365)(number of checks per day)(average check)](0.14/365)(1 − T)
$$= (5)[(365)(500)(\$45)](0.14/365)(1 - 0.35) = \$10,237.50$$

Step 4. $\Delta B - \Delta C = \$10,237.50 - \$6,240.00 = \$3,997.50$. The lockbox system has incremental benefits of \$3,997.50 per year greater than the incremental costs.

19.2

Step 1. Net benefits = $\Delta B - \Delta C$
$$C = (\text{charge per check})(\text{number of checks})(365)(1 - T)$$
$$= (\$0.15)(300)(365)(1 - 0.40) = \$9,855$$
$\$40,000 = \Delta B - \$9,855$, so $\Delta B = \$30,145$

Step 2. $\Delta B = (\Delta t)[(300)(\$500)(365)](0.10/365)(1 - T)$
$$\$30,145 = (\Delta t)(\$15,000)(1 - 0.40)$$
$$\Delta t = 3.349 \text{ days}$$

19.3

Step 1.
$$k_{BD} = \left[\frac{P_M - P_0}{P_M}\right]\left[\frac{360}{n}\right]$$

$$= \left[\frac{\$10,000 - \$9,800}{\$10,000}\right]\left[\frac{360}{100}\right]$$

$$= \left[\frac{\$200}{\$10,000}\right]\left[\frac{360}{100}\right] = 0.072 \text{ or } 7.20\%$$

Step 2. $k_{BE} = (365)(k_{BD})/360 - (k_{BD})(n)$

$= (365)(0.0720)/360 - (0.0720)(100)$

$= 26.28/360 - 7.2 = 0.0745$ or 7.45%

CHAPTER 20

ACCOUNTS RECEIVABLE AND INVENTORY

HOW THIS CHAPTER RELATES TO THE REST OF THE TEXT

This chapter extends the discussion of working capital management begun in Chapter 18 to accounts receivables and inventory management. As in Chapter 19, this chapter concentrates on the management of current assets. Current liabilities, that is, sources of short-term financing, are discussed in Chapter 21. Decisions based on investments in receivables and inventory employ the concepts of cash flow (Chapter 4), time value of money (Chapter 5), and risk and return (Chapter 7).

TOPICAL OUTLINE

I. Receivables, inventory, and the firm.
   A. A firm which extends trade credit is establishing an account receivable which is eventually paid in cash or becomes a bad debt loss.
   B. The importance of receivables and inventory.
      1. High levels of inventory and accounts receivable may help production and marketing efforts. But, short-term assets must be financed and financing costs may reduce profits.
      2. Large manufacturing and wholesale firms hold 30 percent of total assets in accounts receivable and inventory.
      3. Retail firms hold over 50 percent of total assets in receivables and inventory.
      4. The size and type of the firm as well as its production process help determine the percent of total assets held in accounts receivable and inventory.
   C. Size of accounts receivable also determined by total credit sales.
      1. The state of the economy and aggressiveness of marketing efforts help determine the total sales level.
      2. The credit terms, credit analysis, credit-granting decision, and collection policy help determine the level of credit sales.

II. Credit and collection management.
   A. Terms and conditions of credit sales.
      1. Domestic trade conditions.
         a. Cash before delivery is the typical arrangement of payment for custom-made goods.
         b. Cash on delivery (COD) is typical for risky or irregular deliveries.
         c. Payment periods of 30 to 60 days, plus a discount for early payment, are typical for ordinary trade credit.
         d. Payment agreements themselves include:
            i. An open agreement: The invoice is the bill and contains the terms.
            ii. A draft: The buyer agrees to pay a specified amount at a specific time to the bearer.
            iii. A sight draft: The customer pays the amount on presentation of the draft before receiving title to the goods.
            iv. A time draft: The customer (trade acceptance) or the customer's bank (banker's acceptance) makes payment a certain number of days after accepting the draft; signature on the draft implies acceptance.
      2. International purchases and sales include an order to pay, a bill of lading, and a letter of credit.
   B. Credit analysis determines who will be granted credit and what the credit terms will be.
      1. Sources of credit information.
         a. Financial statements help in judging the financial stability and cash-generating ability of the customer.
         b. Dun & Bradstreet's Reference Book provides credit ratings for 3 million firms.
         c. TRW, Inc., provides a computer-based credit retrieval system.
         d. In addition, banks, trade associations, and firms evaluate the credit worthiness of potential customers.

2. Risk class determination.
   a. Classify potential customers by risk class.
   b. Determine credit policy for each risk class.
   c. Review risk status of customers at least once a year.
   d. Many firms use a credit scoring model to determine the risk of a customer.

C. The credit decision.
   1. The basic model considers the net present value of expected incremental cash inflows and cash outflows from credit sales.
      a. Calculate the after-tax cash flows for credit sales (CF):

         $CF = [(\text{cash inflows}) - (\text{cash outflows})](1 - T)$

      b. Choose a required rate of return appropriate for the riskiness of the cash flows.
      c. Discount the cash flows to their net present value (NPV):

         $$NPV = \sum_{t=1}^{n} \frac{CF_t}{(1+k)^t} - CF_0 = \frac{CF_t}{k} - CF_0 \quad \text{(assuming the cash flows are a perpetuity)}$$

   2. Making the credit decision.
      a. Determine the initial incremental investment in accounts receivable (CF_0):

         $CF_0 = (VC)(S)(ACP/365)$

      b. Determine the incremental cash flows (CF_t):

         $CF_t = [S(1 - VC) - S(BD) - CD](1 - T)$

      c. Determine the NPV. If positive, grant credit.

D. Collection policy.
   1. Managing collections.
      a. Average collection period hides individual differences among customers; changes in both receivables and sales levels change the collection period.
      b. Receivables pattern approach.
         i. The receivables pattern is the percentage of credit sales remaining unpaid in the month of the sale and in following months.
         ii. A key to this approach is to keep each month's credit sales separate for the purpose of analysis.

iii. Exercise control on accounts receivable by focusing on deviations from the projected pattern.
2. Analysis of changes in collection policy.
   a. Determine the incremental initial investment (ΔCF_0):

   $$\Delta CF_0 = \text{initial investment new (N)} - \text{initial investment old (O)}$$

   $$= [(VC_N)(S_N)(ACP_N/365)] - [(VC_O)(S_O)(ACP_O/365)]$$

   b. Evaluate incremental after-tax cash flow (ΔCF_t):

   $$\Delta CF_t = \text{after-tax cash flow new (N)} - \text{after-tax cash flow old (O)}$$

   $$= [S_N(1 - VC_N) - S_N(BD_N) - CD_N](1 - T)$$
   $$- [S_O(1 - VC_O) - S_O(BD_O) - CD_O](1 - T)$$

   c. Calculate NPV:

   $$NPV = \Delta CF_t/k - \Delta CF_0$$

   d. k is the required return given the riskiness of the expected cash flows.
   e. Make a policy change only if NPV is positive, since the goal of accounts receivable management is to maximize the value of the firm.
   f. A similar approach compares the NPV of the new policy with that of the old: if $NPV_{new} > NPV_{old}$, change policies.

III. Inventory management.
   A. Types of inventory include raw materials, work-in-process, and finished goods.
      1. Manufacturers hold all three types of inventory.
      2. Retail and wholesale firms hold finished goods inventory.
      3. Service firms have no inventory except supplies.
   B. Benefits of inventory investment include:
      1. Firms can take advantage of quantity discounts and add to existing inventory.
      2. Firms can avoid stock outages.
      3. Firms can offer a full line of products for marketing purposes.
      4. Inventory speculation is possible during times of inflation; add to existing inventory.

C. Costs of inventory investment.
1. Carrying costs include storage, spoilage, property taxes, and insurance.
2. Ordering costs include clerical and shipping costs.
3. Costs of stock outages are lost sales.

D. Three approaches for inventory management are the "just-in-time" approach, the economic order quantity (EOQ) (see Appendix 20A), and the ABC method.

E. Analysis of inventory investment.
1. An investment in current assets, although it often accompanies a long-term asset investment, also results from a change in policy.
2. Calculate the NPV of the expected incremental cash inflows and cash outflows due to the increased inventory investment, discounting at a rate of return appropriate to the riskiness of the cash flows.
3. Pay attention to the important inventory items while using management-by-exception for other items.

F. Interaction of accounts receivable and inventory decisions.
1. Cost and benefit trade-offs exist between them, with varying consequences for the firm.
2. Develop and evaluate inventory receivables policies on a joint basis.

IV. Appendix 20A: The economic order quantity (EOQ) model. (Located at the end of the text).

A. The basic inventory decision is based on carrying costs (C), ordering costs (O), and annual sales (S).
1. Carrying costs = (average inventory)(carrying costs)
$$= (Q/2)C = QC/2$$
2. Ordering costs = (sales/order size)(ordering costs)
$$= (S/Q)O = SO/Q$$
3. Total costs = carrying costs + ordering costs
$$= QC/2 + SO/Q$$
4. Maximize the firm's value by minimizing the total costs.

B. EOQ model.

$$EOQ = \sqrt{2SO/C}$$

C. Quantity discounts.
1. Savings from quantity discount = (discount per unit)(S
2. Additional carrying costs:

    Additional costs = Q'C/2 - [(EOQ)(C)]/2, where Q' = new order quantity
3. Additional savings in ordering costs:

    Additional savings = SO/EOQ - SO/Q'

D. EOQ assumptions are uniform demand and constant carrying and ordering costs; modify EOQ to deal with variations.

E. Safety stocks should be added only to the point where additional carrying costs equal benefits from avoiding stock outages.

FORMULAS

Notation

CF	= cash flow after taxes
CF_0	= initial investment in accounts receivable or inventory
CF_t	= after-tax cash inflow in each time period
k	= appropriate required rate of return
n	= number of time periods
NPV	= net present value
S	= annual sales in dollars
VC	= variable cash outflow of producing and selling the goods as a percentage of cash inflows
BD	= probability of bad debts as a percentage of sales
CD	= additional collection department outflows
T	= firm's marginal tax rate
ACP	= Average collection period in days
ΔCF_0	= incremental initial investment
ΔCF_t	= incremental after-tax cash inflows
N	= subscript for new cash flows resulting from new collection policy
O	= subscript for old cash flows from old credit policy

The Basic Model

$$CF = [(\text{cash inflows}) - (\text{cash outflows})](1 - T)$$

$$NPV = \sum_{t=1}^{n} \frac{CF_t}{(1 + k)^t} - CF_0 = \frac{CF_t}{k} - CF_0 \quad (\text{assuming cash flows are a perpetuity})$$

Credit Decision Making

$$CF_0 = (VC)(S)(ACP/365)$$

$$CF_t = [S(1 - VC) - S(BD) - CD](1 - T)$$

$$NPV = CF_t/k - CF_0$$

Evaluating a Change in Collection Policy

ΔCF_0 = New initial investment - old initial investment

$$= [(VC_N)(S_N)(ACP_N/365)] - [(VC_O)(S_O)(ACP_O/365)]$$

ΔCF_t = New incremental cash flow - old incremental cash flow

$$= [S_N(1 - VC_N) - S_N(BD_N) - CD_N](1 - T) - [S_O(1 - VC_O) - S_O(BD_O) - CD_O](1 - T)$$

$$NPV = \Delta CF_t/k - \Delta CF_0$$

Appendix 20A (located at the end of the text)

Notation

EOQ = economic order quantity

C = carrying cost in dollars per unit of inventory

O = ordering costs in dollars per order

Q = order quantity expressed in units

S = sales per year in units

Q' = new order size

Carrying costs

$$(Q/2)C = QC/2$$

Ordering costs

$$(S/Q)O = SO/Q$$

Total costs

Carrying costs + ordering costs = $QC/2 + SO/Q$

Economic Order Quantity

$$EOQ = \sqrt{2SO/C}$$

Savings from quantity discounts

$$\text{Savings} = (\text{discount per unit})(S)$$

Additional carrying costs for using quantity discount

$$\text{Additional costs} = Q'C/2 - [(EOQ)(C)]/2$$

Savings in ordering costs

$$\text{Savings in costs} = SO/EOQ - SO/Q'$$

WHAT TO LOOK FOR

Chapter 20 focuses on managing the investment in accounts receivable and inventory. These investments are commonly financed by revolving lines of credit, commercial paper, and trade credit. "Permanent" investments in receivables and inventory are often financed with long-term financing sources. The goal is to earn more on these investments than the firm pays for financing them.

The Cash Conversion Cycle and Current Asset Management

Let's return again to the cash conversion cycle (Chapter 18). The inventory conversion period is the time between the purchase of inventory and its cash or credit sale. The receivables conversion period is the time between the credit sale and the collection of these receivables. To maximize the value of the firm, managers should speed up cash inflows, taking into account the increased costs and risks. Managers want to shorten both the receivables conversion period and the inventory conversion period. In Chapter 19, we discussed shortening the receivables conversion period by reducing float. In Chapter 20, we talk about how to reduce the receivables conversion period and the inventory conversion period by selecting and managing the credit and inventory policies. The optimal credit policy will produce the maximum credit sales net of bad debt losses and collection costs. Achieving such a policy is hard, but it can be done by following the steps outlined below.

Analyzing and Establishing a Credit and Collections Policy

Credit policy

In choosing and implementing a credit policy, the manager should (1) determine the credit-worthiness of potential credit customers; (2) rank customers by credit risk; (3) calculate the expected cash flows of each risk class; and (4) provide credit to those customers for which the net present value of the expected cash flows is positive.

We will demonstrate steps 3 and 4 for two risk classes assuming a corporate tax rate of 30 percent.

Risk Class	Required Rate of Return (k)	Variable Costs As a Percentage of Sales (VC)	Average Collection Period (ACP)	Sales (S)	Bad Debts As a Percentage of Sales (BD)	Additional Collection Department Cash Outflows (CD)
A	16%	82%	60 days	$200,000	3%	$ 8,000
E	28	82	120	240,000	6	12,000

Class A:

$$CF_0 = (VC)(S)(ACP/365)$$
$$= (0.82)(\$200,000)(60/365) = \$26,958.90$$
$$CF_t = [S(1 - VC) - S(BD) - CD](1 - T)$$
$$= [\$200,000(1 - 0.82) - \$200,000(0.03) - \$8,000](1 - 0.30)$$
$$= \$15,400$$
$$NPV = CF_t/k - CF_0 = \$15,400/0.16 - \$26,958.90 = \$69,291.10$$

Since the NPV is positive, credit should be granted to customers in risk class A.

Class E:

$$CF_0 = (0.82)(\$240,000)(120/365) = \$64,701.37$$
$$CF_t = [\$240,000(1 - 0.82) - \$240,000(0.06) - \$12,000](1 - 0.30)$$
$$= \$11,760$$
$$NPV = \$11,760/0.28 - \$64,701.37 = -\$22,701.37$$

Since the NPV is negative, the decision is not to grant credit to customers in risk class E, since it would impair the value of the firm.

Collections policy

The credit policy, projections for bad debts, and total collection costs are only as good as the collections management. Lax collections management can produce collections costs and bad debt losses that far exceed those estimated, and perhaps make all credit-granting activities unprofitable.

The receivables pattern approach to collections management helps track the actual payment pattern experienced by the firm. It relates the accounts receivable to the month in which the sales are made. (Refer to Table 20.3 in the text.) Although 20 percent of the accounts receivable are projected to be outstanding in the third month, 30 percent are still outstanding by this time period. This trend indicates the need to change the collection policy or modify credit risk classes.

In considering a change in collections policy, managers should calculate the net present value of the associated cash flow changes--ΔCF_0 and ΔCF_t. If the net present value is positive, the change will increase the value of the firm. As a manager, you can play with these variables and calculate the net present value under different credit policies. For example, you could considerably tighten up collections and decrease the average collection period. If the new collection policy does not decrease sales excessively, the result will be a positive net present value, indicating the change should be undertaken.

Inventory Management

Inventories, like receivables, need management in order for the firm to meet the objective of value maximization. As we noted earlier, the inventory conversion cycle is the period from inventory purchase to inventory sale. The lower the inventory level, the lower the carrying costs and the shorter the inventory conversion period and cash conversion cycle. Lower inventory levels, however, increase the likelihood that the firm will lose sales through stock outages.

As you can see, the manager again weighs the benefits of inventory management with the carrying costs, ordering costs, and costs of stock outages. The text briefly discusses two inventory management approaches, the just-in-time approach and the economic order quantity model. Production situations like those in Japan can easily be managed by the just-in-time approach, since the distance for transporting inventory is negligible. In the United States, however, some manufacturers may depend upon raw materials suppliers thousands of miles away.

In addition to choosing an inventory management approach, firms often must decide whether an actual increase in the level of inventory is wise. The manager calculates the expected cash flows and their net present value. Suppose Cagney Jeans Shop is considering increasing its inventory investment by $400,000. The expected increase in after-tax cash flows (CF_t) is $60,000 per year, net of storage costs. The inventory investment must return at least 18 percent to be worthwhile. The timeline below shows the cash flows. We will calculate the net present value of this inventory investment.

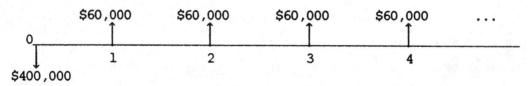

The NPV is $60,000/0.18 - $400,000 = -$66,666.67. Cagney Jeans should not increase the inventory because the return is not satisfactory and will decrease the value of the firm.

COMPLETION QUESTIONS

20.1 As the length of time increases before collection of accounts receivable, the firm's investment in receivables _____.

20.2 As an inducement to encourage early payment of trade credit, many firms offer a _____.

20.3 In international trade, a _____ is the contract for shipment of goods and the title of those goods.

20.4 The backbone of any credit decision is the _____. Information necessary for this process comes from financial statements, credit reports, banks, trade associations, and the company's own experiences.

20.5 In making a credit decision, managers may find it helpful to classify potential credit customers into _____.

20.6 In order to make the credit decision, the manager should find the net present value of the after-tax _____. These flows would be the cash inflows from the credit sales less the incremental _____. Credit should be extended only if the net present value is _____.

20.7 The trouble with using the collection period to monitor collections is that it _____. The _____ _____ approach considers the percent of credit sales paid in the month of the sale, and in each subsequent month.

20.8 The incremental initial investment is the difference between the new initial investment and the _____.

20.9 A tighter collection policy might decrease the average collection period, but it may also _____.

20.10 For a manufacturing firm, the purpose of holding inventory is to _____ the acquisition of goods, the stages of production, and selling activities.

20.11 Costs of inventory investment include carrying costs, ordering costs, and costs of _____. The _____ decides the size of the inventory order to place in order to minimize all three costs.

20.12 Managers should consider the magnitude, _____, and _____ of the cash flows resulting from receivables and inventories investments.

PROBLEMS

20.1 Randleman Furnishings' credit terms are 2/15, net 30. Sales are $4,015,000 per year, half of which are credit. Some of the credit customers pay on the fifteenth day; the remainder pay on an average of the 35th day. If the average collection period is 13.5 days, what proportion of the customers take the discount?

20.2 Norristown Manufacturing presently makes all sales for cash. It is considering the development of a credit sales policy and has classified customers into three credit classes. The appropriate information follows.

Class	Required Rate of Return	ACP	Sales (in thousands)	Bad Debts	Additional Collection Department Cash Outflows (in thousands)
1	14%	30 days	$3,000	2%	$150
2	18	45	4,000	6	150
3	25	150	5,000	15	300

Which, if any, class should be granted credit if the marginal tax rate is 30 percent and variable cash outflows are 70 percent of sales? (Assume a 365-day year.)

20.3 Mayo Medical Supply is considering a $1,000,000 investment in additional inventory to prevent having to turn away customers due to lack of goods. The loss in sales due to the shortage in inventory is estimated at $750,000 per year. Because of difficulty in inventory control, the company expects to lose an additional $50,000 (after-tax) due to theft and spoilage if the new investment is made. Storage expenses are expected to increase by $10,000 per year. If variable cash outflows are 55 percent of sales, and the tax rate is 40 percent, should Mayo increase its inventory if its required return is 16 percent?

20A.1 McMillian Industries has a projected demand for 22,500 units of inventory in the coming year. If the carrying cost is $2 per unit of inventory and the ordering costs are $100 per order, what is the EOQ?

20A.2 Miacom Electronics bases its inventory replenishment decision on an EOQ model. The ordering costs are $50, the storage costs are $0.40 per unit of inventory, and the EOQ is 2,000 units. If Miacom wishes to maintain a safety stock of 1,000 units and it takes 10 days to receive an order, what is the inventory level at which a reorder should be replaced? (Assume a 365-day year.)

ANSWERS TO COMPLETION QUESTIONS

20.1 increases
20.2 cash discount
20.3 bill of lading
20.4 credit analysis
20.5 risk classes
20.6 cash flows; cash outflows; positive
20.7 is affected by the sales level; receivables pattern
20.8 old initial investment
20.9 reduce sales
20.10 uncouple
20.11 running short (or stock outages); economic order quantity model (EOQ)
20.12 timing; riskiness

SOLUTIONS TO PROBLEMS

20.1

Step 1. The average collection period is the weighted average of the time to payment. Remember, for cash sales, there is no time till payment.

Step 2. ACP = 0.5(0 days) + W(15 days) + (0.5 - W)(35 days)

$\qquad$ 13.5 = 0.5(0) + W(15) + (0.5 - W)(35 days)

$\qquad$ 13.5 = 15W + 17.5 - 35W

$\qquad$ 20W = 4

$\qquad\quad$ W = 4/20 = 0.20

20 percent of the customers take the discount.

20.2

Step 1. Class 1

$\qquad$ CF_0 = (VC)(S)(ACP/365 days) = (0.70)($3,000)(30/365) = $172.60

Step 2. CF_t = [S(1 - VC) - S(BD) - CD](1 - T)

$\qquad$ = [$3,000(1 - 0.70) - $3,000(0.02) - $150](1 - 0.30)

$\qquad$ = ($900 - $60 - $150)(0.70) = $483

Step 3. NPV CF_t/k - CF_0 = $483/0.14 - $172.60 = $3,277.40

Since NPV is greater than zero, credit should be granted to class 1.

Step 4. Class 2

$\qquad$ CF_0 = (0.70)($4,000)(45/365) = $345.21

$\qquad$ CF_t = [$4,000(1 - 0.70) - $4,000(0.06) - $150](1 - 0.30)

$\qquad$ = ($1,200 - $240 - $150)(0.70) = $567

NPV = $567/0.18 - $345.21 = $2,804.79

Since NPV is positive, credit should be granted to class 2.

Step 5. Class 3

$\qquad$ CF_0 = (0.70)($5,000)(150/365) = $1,438.36

$\qquad$ CF_t = [$5,000(1 - 0.70) - $5,000(0.15) - $300](1 - 0.30)

$\qquad$ = ($1,500 - $750 - $300)(0.70) = $315

NPV = $315/0.25 - $1,438.36 = -$178.36

Since NPV is negative, do not grant credit to class 3.

20.3

Step 1. CF_t = [Sales(1 - VC) - storage cost](1 - T) - loss due to theft and spoilage

$\qquad$ = [$750,000(1 - 0.55) - $10,000](1 - 0.40) - $50,000

$\qquad$ = ($337,500 - $10,000)(0.60) - $50,000 = $146,500

Step 2. NPV = $\dfrac{CF_t}{k}$ - CF_0 = $\dfrac{\$146,500}{0.16}$ - $1,000,000 = -$84,375

No, the project has a negative NPV.

20A.1 $EOQ = \sqrt{\dfrac{2SO}{C}} = \sqrt{\dfrac{2(22,500)(\$100)}{\$2}} = \sqrt{2,250,000} = 1,500$ units per order

20A.2

Step 1. Find total demand.

$$EOQ = \sqrt{\dfrac{2SO}{C}}$$

$$2,000 = \sqrt{\dfrac{2S(\$50)}{\$0.40}}$$

$4,000,000 = 2S(\$50)/\$0.40$

$S = \$0.40(4,000,000)/2(\$50) = \$16,000$

Step 2. Sales per day = $16,000/365 = 43.8 units per day

Step 3. Reorder entry level = safety stock + (sales per day)(days to fill
                            = 1,000 + (43.8)(10 days) = 1,438 units

CHAPTER 21

SHORT-TERM FINANCING

HOW THIS CHAPTER RELATES TO THE REST OF THE TEXT

Chapter 21 concludes the discussion of working capital management (Chapter 18) by considering current liabilities. The matching principle, which is the basis of current liability management, was discussed in Chapter 15. This chapter also discusses the costs of short-term financing, which are similar to the costs of long-term debt (Chapter 13). Current liabilities account for a substantial portion of total debt for many firms and hence affect the capital structure (Chapter 15).

TOPICAL OUTLINE

I. Sources and importance of short-term financing.
   A. Sources of short-term financing.
      1. Trade credit results spontaneously when a firm purchases goods from another firm and does not pay immediately.
      2. Short-term borrowings are negotiated with commercial banks, finance companies, and the like.
   B. Size of short-term financing.
      1. Accounts payable provide more short-term financing than do short-term borrowings.
      2. Level of accounts payable and short-term borrowing depends upon firms and industries as well as economic conditions, business conditions, and company policy.
   C. Calculation of the after-tax cost of short-term financing (calculated over the same time period).
      1. Effective before-tax annual compound percentage rate (APR)
      $$= \left(1 + \frac{\text{costs} - \text{benefits}}{\text{amount of financing}}\right)^m - 1$$
      2. After-tax cost, $k_i = k_b(1 - T)$
II. Accounts payable or trade credit is a spontaneous form of financing.
   A. Level of accounts payable will increase with increased orders during the busy season, even if you pay accounts by the due date.

B. Calculation of before-tax cost of not taking cash discounts on trade credit.

1.
$$k_b = \left[\frac{\text{discount percent}}{100\% - \text{discount percent}}\right]^{365/(\text{date paid} - \text{discount date})} - 1$$

2. In assessing the desirability of not taking the cash discount, both direct and indirect costs must be considered.

C. Advantages of trade credit: Readily available, free, flexible, not restrictive.

III. Unsecured loans from bank loans or commercial paper are not spontaneous.

A. Bank loans or short-term notes payable have maturities of one year or less, often at a variable rate of interest.

1. Interest rates.
    a. The prime rate is the basic interest charged by banks to their best customers; other customers pay some rate above prime.
    b. The commercial paper rate is typically slightly less than the prime rate.
    c. Short-term rates, such as the prime rate and the commercial paper rate, are volatile, changing with economic and business conditions.

2. Types of bank loans.
    a. Transaction loan is a loan for a specific purpose for which a promissory note is signed and a repayment schedule exists.
    b. Line of credit is an agreement between a firm and a bank for the firm to borrow up to a dollar limit within a specified time period at a specific interest rate on the amounts borrowed.
        i. Repayment must be made by the end of that period and the user is often expected to maintain a compensating balance.
        ii. Can be informal, or can involve a commitment fee.

3. Cost of bank loans depends upon the conditions attached to the agreement.

a. Regular interest is principal and interest paid at end of loan; calculate with a two-step procedure.
   i. Determine interest paid:
   $$\begin{bmatrix} \text{amount} \\ \text{borrowed} \end{bmatrix} \begin{bmatrix} \text{annual} \\ \text{interest rate} \end{bmatrix} \begin{bmatrix} \text{portion of year} \\ \text{borrowed for} \end{bmatrix}$$
   ii. Employ Equation 21.1 to determine k_b:
   $$k_b = \left[1 + \frac{\text{interest}}{\text{principal}}\right]^m - 1$$
b. Discount interest is a loan from which the bank deducts the interest from the loan principal at the beginning of the loan.
   i. The effective interest is greater than the stated interest.
   ii. Use the two-step procedure above to calculate the before-tax rate of interest.
   $$k_b = \left[1 + \frac{\text{interest}}{\text{principal} - \text{interest}}\right]^m - 1$$
c. Installment interest is paid periodically (monthly, etc.) along with principal repayment.
   i. The total amount of interest is calculated and added to the original face value of the loan.
   ii. Principal is repaid along with interest, beginning at the end of the first period, and the borrower has use of about half the principal on average; so the effective interest rate is almost twice as high as the stated rate.
   iii. Calculation of the approximate effective before-tax interest rate:
   Loan = payment($PVA_{k_b,n}$) and solve for k_b
d. Variable-rate loans have interest rates that may change over the life of the loan, and their cost can be calculated only after knowing the rates and the number of days those rates were in effect.
   i. The two-step procedure works well for this calculation.

ii. The APR will be somewhere within the range of the various rates paid.
e. Compensating balances sometimes are required for customers taking out a loan.
   i. If the compensating balance is less than the firm normally keeps in its demand deposit, this requirement does not influence the effective rate of interest on the loan.
   ii. If the compensating balance is more than the amount held in demand deposits by the firm, then the APR is greater than the stated rate, since those dollars otherwise could be invested or held in an interest bearing account.
   iii. Calculation of effective cost on a regular loan with compensating balance that is above the normal balance kept in the bank:

   $$k_b = \left[1 + \frac{\text{interest}}{\text{principal} - \text{compensating balance} + \text{normal balance}}\right]^m - 1$$

   iv. Calculation of effective cost on discounted loan with compensating balance:

   $$k_b = \left[1 + \frac{\text{interest}}{\text{principal} - \text{interest} - \text{compensating balance} + \text{normal balance}}\right]^m - 1$$

f. Line of credit states an interest rate, and often a commitment fee.
   i. Determine commitment fee per loan period:
      (unused portion)(annual commitment fee)(portion of year)
      Do this calculation for each loan period.
   ii. Determine the per period interest cost:
      ($ loan)(annual interest rate)(number of days/365)
   iii. $k_b = \left[1 + \dfrac{\text{total commitment fees} + \text{interest}}{\text{average net amount of financing}}\right]^m - 1$

4. Eurodollar loans are loans of dollars deposited in banks outside the United States.
   a. Rates on Eurodollar loans are not tied to U.S. prime rate, but to the London Interbank Offered Rate (LIBOR).
   b. Rates may be lower than those available in the United States.

B. Commercial paper is a short-term unsecured promissory note sold by large firms to obtain financing.
   1. Nature and use.
      a. Principal issuers include finance companies, bank holding companies, and large industrial firms.
      b. Maturity is 270 days or less.
      c. Sold through dealers or through direct placement.
      d. Vary in riskiness and thus return, depending on issuer's cash flow.
   2. Cost tends to be one or two percentage points below the prime rate, depending upon economic and business conditions.
      a. Sold at a discount to yield the stated rate at maturity.
      b. Calculation of before tax interest cost:
      $$k_b = \left[1 + \frac{\text{discount}}{\text{par value - discount}}\right]^m - 1$$
      c. Commitment fee adds to the cost:
      Fee = ($ loan)(fee percent)(number of days/365)
      d. Calculation of total before-tax cost:
      $$k_b = \left[1 + \frac{\text{discount + commitment fee}}{\text{par value - discount}}\right]^m - 1$$

IV. Secured loans: Backed by accounts receivable and inventory.
   A. Financing with accounts receivable.
      1. Pledging accounts receivable.
         a. Loan is a stated percent of all receivables pledged.
            i. If all receivables are pledged, the lender has no control over quality.
            ii. If lender reviews specific invoices to choose which receivables can be pledged, the process is more costly, but lender can loan a larger amount on these receivables.

iii. Cost is a function of processing fee and annual interest charge.

(a) Interest = $\begin{bmatrix}\text{interest}\\\text{percent}\end{bmatrix}\begin{bmatrix}\text{receivables}\\\text{pledged}\end{bmatrix}\begin{bmatrix}\text{number of}\\\text{days}/365\end{bmatrix}$

(b) Processing fee = $\begin{bmatrix}\text{fee}\\\text{percent}\end{bmatrix}\begin{bmatrix}\text{average}\\\text{credit}\\\text{sales}\end{bmatrix}\begin{bmatrix}\text{number of}\\\text{days}/365\end{bmatrix}$

(c) Annual before-tax cost:

$$k_b = \left[1 + \frac{\text{interest} + \text{processing fee}}{\text{principal}}\right]^m - 1$$

2. Factoring accounts receivable is the sale of accounts receivable to a bank or another firm engaged in factoring; it is often a continuous process.

 a. The amount of the loan is a stated percent of all receivables factored.

 b. Maturity factoring is the purchase of all receivables by the factor who pays the seller once a month for the receivables.

 i. Useful to substitute for credit and collections department.

 ii. Before-tax cost:

$$k_b = \left[1 + \frac{\begin{bmatrix}\text{average}\\\text{receivables}\end{bmatrix}\begin{bmatrix}\text{commission}\end{bmatrix} - \begin{bmatrix}\text{cost}\\\text{savings}\end{bmatrix}}{\text{average receivables}}\right]^m - 1$$

 c. In advance factoring, the factor makes a loan against receivables.

 i. Interest rate is usually 2 to 4 percent above prime; commissions are usually charged also.

 ii. Interest cost:

 (Interest rate)(receivables factored)(number of days/365)

 iii. Factoring commission:

 (Commission rate)(total receivables)

 iv. Before-tax cost:

$$k_b = \left[1 + \frac{\text{interest} + \text{commission fee}}{\text{receivables factored}}\right]^m - 1$$

B. Financing with inventories is common.
   1. The borrowing firm can pledge all its inventories on a blanket lien to the bank.
   2. The trust receipt provides more protection for the lender and is common for larger ticket items like automobiles.
   3. Warehouse financing includes public (or terminal) warehousing on a third party's premises, and field warehousing on the borrower's premises.
      a. Cost consists of the processing fee or storage costs plus the interest costs.
      b. Field warehousing fee = (per diem fee)(number of days)
      c. Interest fee = $\left[\begin{array}{c}\text{interest}\\\text{rate}\end{array}\right]\left[\begin{array}{c}\text{inventory} \times\\\text{pledge percent}\end{array}\right]\left[\begin{array}{c}365/\text{number of}\\\text{days}\end{array}\right]$
      d. Before-tax cost of field warehousing:
      $$k_b = \left[1 + \frac{\text{interest + warehousing fee}}{\text{principal}}\right]^m - 1$$

V. Choosing among short-term financing sources.
   A. Negotiated versus spontaneous.
   B. Match the position of the current assets with current liabilities-- that is, match conservative with aggressive and vice versa.
   C. Consider the direct and indirect costs.
   D. Consider the availability of credit by various means at various times.
   E. Flexibility for the firm to pay off the loan, renew it, or increase it.
   F. Rank sources according to direct costs and then evaluate other factors, including less quantifiable or indirect costs.
   G. Firm should consider multiple sources of short-term financing, due to possible changes in financing needs.

FORMULAS

Basic Equation for Effective Before-Tax Cost, k_b

k_b = before-tax compound annual percentage rate (APR)

m = number of periods per year

$$k_b = \left[1 + \frac{\text{costs - benefits}}{\text{amount of financing}}\right]^m - 1$$

After-tax cost to the firm, $k_i = k_b(1 - T)$

Before-Tax Cost of Trade Credit

$$k_b = \left[1 + \frac{\text{discount percent}}{100\% - \text{discount percent}}\right]^{365/(\text{date paid - discount date})} - 1$$

Before-Tax Cost of Bank Loan with Regular Interest

Interest = (amount borrowed)(annual interest rate)(portion of year borrowed for)

$$k_b = \left[1 + \frac{\text{interest}}{\text{principal}}\right]^m - 1$$

Before-Tax Cost of Discount Interest

$$k_b = \left[1 + \frac{\text{interest}}{\text{principal - interest}}\right]^m - 1$$

Before-Tax Cost of Installment Interest

Loan = Payment($PVA_{k_b, n}$) and solve for k_b

Before-Tax Cost of Variable Rate Loan

Amount Borrowed	× Interest Rate ×	Portion of Year (number of days/365)
$	%	days/365
$	%	days/365

The sum equals the interest cost and so on through the loan period.

$$k_b = \left[1 + \frac{\text{interest}}{\text{principal}}\right]^m - 1$$

Before-Tax Cost of Regular Interest Loan with Compensating Balance

$$k_b = \left[1 + \frac{\text{interest}}{\text{principal - compensating balance + normal balance}}\right]^m - 1$$

Before-Tax Cost of Discount Loan with Compensating Balance

$$k_b = \left[1 + \frac{\text{interest}}{\text{principal - interest - compensating balance + normal balance}}\right]^m - 1$$

Before-Tax Line of Credit

Loan Period	Commitment Fee Percent	× Unused Portion ×	Portion of Year (number of days/365)
1	%	$	days/365
2	%	$	days/365

and so on over the life of the loan.

Interest cost per loan period = (interest percent)($ loan)(number of days per loan period/365)

Add together commitment fee + interest on a period by period basis.

$$k_b = \left[1 + \frac{\text{total commitment fee + interest}}{\text{average amount of financing}}\right]^m - 1$$

Before-Tax Cost of Commercial Paper

$$k_b = \left[1 + \frac{\text{discount + commitment fee}}{\text{par value - discount}}\right]^m - 1$$

Before-Tax Cost of Pledging Receivables

$$k_b = \left[1 + \frac{\text{interest + processing fee}}{\text{principal}}\right]^m - 1$$

Before-Tax Cost of Maturity Factoring Receivables

$$k_b = \left[1 + \frac{(\text{average receivables})(\text{commission}) - \text{cost savings}}{\text{average receivables}}\right]^m - 1$$

Before-Tax Cost of Advance Factoring

$$k_b = \left[1 + \frac{\text{interest + commission fee}}{\text{receivables factored}}\right]^m - 1$$

Before-Tax Cost of Field Warehousing

$$k_b = \left[1 + \frac{\text{interest + warehousing fee}}{\text{principal}}\right]^m - 1$$

WHAT TO LOOK FOR

Chapter 21, the mechanics of short-term financing, completes our study of working capital. Short-term financing, which includes commercial paper, lines of credit, trade credit, and secured loans, covers current liabilities that fund investments in the current assets discussed in Chapters 19 and 20. All short-term financing entails a financing cost such as interest. Here we look at the advantages of and effective interest costs of financing alternatives.

Advantages of Various Short-Term Financing Alternatives

The majority of businesses in the United States are small businesses. The key source of short-term financing for such firms is trade credit. Trade credit's advantages are that it is readily available and grows spontaneously with inventory purchases. In times of tight money, many small businesses cannot get bank loans, and so they rely on trade credit.

Commercial paper is a short-term security that is unsecured. Large firms with impeccable credit ratings can issue commercial paper. This security (1) can often be issued at a lower interest rate than many other short-term loans, and (2) permits a broad distribution of the security.

The terms of bank loans can vary widely, as can the cost. In choosing among financing sources, managers should look at the effective before-tax compound annual percentage rate of interest (APR). In the next section we will calculate the cost of short-term financing. Bank loans such as lines of credit provide flexibility and precautionary liquidity for firms. Therefore, bank loans are essential in the financing package of many firms. Secured loans are loans backed by such assets as accounts receivable and inventory. When a firm cannot obtain unsecured financing, it must seek a secured form.

Factoring of accounts receivable involves selling accounts receivable to the factor for a percentage of their dollar amount. Two key advantages of factoring are that the lender takes on the credit risk of the accounts receivable--that is, the borrower does not need to run a collections or credit department--and as the credit sales grow, the financing grows. Acting as the credit department, the factor can refuse to allow the borrower to grant credit to customers of questionable risk.

Pledging of accounts receivable involves using the receivables as a lien. The lender, however, does not take on the credit risks. The lender can refuse to lend on questionable receivables and has recourse to the borrower (the seller). Again, pledging is flexible since the financing grows with the credit sales. With both pledging and factoring, the manager should be careful to weigh the costs and benefits since the costs can be high.

Inventory financing includes a blanket inventory lien, trust receipts, and field warehousing financing. These methods provide flexible financing that grows with inventories. Field warehousing in particular can save the firm money in personnel and in inventory losses and damage. In addition, it is more convenient than trust receipts, which require receipts to be issued for specific goods, such as sacks of coffee beans. Trust receipts are most appropriate for bulky items like automobiles and trucks.

Cost of Short-Term Financing

Bank Loans

The cost of bank loans varies widely depending upon the terms of the loan. We will work through a series of variations on a $10,000 2-month (60 day) loan to Jack's Sporting Goods with a quoted interest rate of 10 percent. The various loan terms are (1) regular interest; (2) discount interest; (3) installment interest; (4) compensating balance of $3,000, given that Jack's keeps a normal balance of $1,500; and (5) a $10,000 line of credit, in which the commitment fee is 1/2 of 1 percent on the unused portion, and Jack uses $4,000 the first month and $10,000 the second month. A 365-day year is assumed. The basic equation for calculating the effective before-tax interest cost, k_b, is

$$k_b = \left[1 + \frac{\text{costs} - \text{benefits}}{\text{amount of financing}}\right]^m - 1$$

Costs:

Interest = (amount borrowed)(annual rate of interest)(number of days/365)

Fees = (fee percent)(base)

Regular interest:

Cost involved is interest. Amount of financing is $10,000.

Interest = ($10,000)(0.10)(60/365) = $164.38

$$k_b = \left[1 + \frac{\$164.38}{\$10,000}\right]^{365/60} - 1 = 0.1043 \text{ or } 10.43\%$$

Discount interest:

Cost involved is interest = $164.38. Amount of financing is $10,000 - interest = $10,000 - $164.38.

$$k_b = \left[1 + \frac{\$164.38}{\$10,000 - \$164.38}\right]^{365/60} - 1 = 0.1061 \text{ or } 10.61\%$$

Installment loan:

Interest cost = $164.38. The payment is ($10,000 + $164.38)/2 = $5,082. We can estimate k_b because

$$\text{Loan} = \text{payment}(PVA_{k_b, 2mo})$$

$$\$10,000 = \$5,082.19(PVA_{k_b, 2mo})$$

$$PVA_{k_b, 2mo} = \frac{\$10,000}{\$5,082.19} = 1.968$$

From Table F.4, we can see that this is slightly more than 1 percent per month or 12 percent per year. Using a financial calculator, the rate is 13.95 percent per year.

Compensating balance is $3,000 with normal balance of $1,500:

Cost involved is interest. Amount of financing is $10,000 − compensating balance + normal balance.

$$k_b = \left[1 + \frac{\$164.38}{\$10,000 - \$3,000 + \$1,500}\right]^{365/60} - 1 = 0.1236 \text{ or } 12.36\%$$

Line of credit at 10 percent on $10,000 with 1/2 of 1 percent commitment fee on the unused portion:

Jack uses $4,000 in the first month, and $10,000 in the second month. Costs involved are interest and commitment fee. Loan amounts are $4,000 for the first 30 days, and $10,000 for the second 30 days.

Commitment fee:

    1st month: ($10,000 − $4,000)(0.005)(30/365) = $2.47

    2nd month: ($10,000 − $10,000)(0.005)(30/365) = 0

Interest:

    1st month: ($4,000)(0.10)(30/365) = $32.88

    2nd month: ($10,000)(0.10)(30/365) = $82.19

Total costs:

    1st month: $2.47 + $32.88 = $35.35

    2nd month: $ 0 + $82.19 = $82.19

Average amount of financing: $4,000(30/60) + $10,000(30/60) = $7,000

$$k_b = \left[1 + \frac{\$35.35 + \$82.19}{\$7,000}\right]^{365/60} - 1 = 0.1066 \text{ or } 10.66\%$$

As you can see, the effective before-tax financing cost varies widely, depending upon the terms of the loan. We did not show a variable rate loan.

However, if you study the example in the text, you should have little trouble understanding that calculation.

Commercial paper

Rather than paying interest directly, commercial paper is sold at a discount to yield the stated rate. The calculation of the before-tax cost is similar to calculating the cost of a discount interest loan, with a commitment fee. Suppose Pueblo Motors, Inc., issued $200,000 in a 90-day commercial paper, sold at $193,000. The company must keep a matching line of credit, which has a commitment fee of 1/2 of 1 percent a year. Assuming a 365-day year, the yield is found using the following formula:

$$k_b = \left[1 + \frac{\text{discount} + \text{commitment fee}}{\text{par value} - \text{discount}}\right]^m - 1$$

$$= \left[1 + \frac{\$7,000 + [0.005(\$200,000)(90/365)]}{\$200,000 - \$7,000}\right]^{365/90} - 1$$

$$= \left[1 + \frac{\$7,246.575}{\$193,000}\right]^{365/90} - 1 = 0.1612 \text{ or } 16.12\%$$

Secured loans

Secured loans use inventory or accounts receivable as a lien. The calculation of the financing amount or principal depends on how much of the receivables or inventory can be used as a lien. The amount of the loan is stated as a percentage of the inventory or receivables accepted. Secured financing also involves administrative fees. The financing costs are the sum of the interest and the administrative fees. The general formula below is useful for calculating the effective before-tax cost of secured financing:

$$k_b = \left[\frac{\text{interest} + \text{fee or commission}}{(\text{receivables or inventory})(\text{stated percent})}\right]\left[\frac{365}{\text{number of days}}\right]$$

Selection of Short-Term Financing Sources

Costs, risks, flexibility, and availability vary among sources of short-term financing. In selecting short-term financing sources, managers should consider all these factors in order to meet the objective of value maximization.

COMPLETION QUESTIONS

21.1 _____ is a spontaneous form of financing which increases and decreases with the volume of the firm's business.

21.2 To find the relevant financing costs, divide the net costs by the _____ available to the borrower.

21.3 While a firm can employ either the before- or after-tax cost in making short-term financing decisions, its ultimate cost is the _____ _____.

21.4 When firms stretch their payables by not paying on the net date, their before-tax cost of financing _____, but their credit rating might _____, perhaps resulting in curtailment of _____ _____.

21.5 The key advantages of trade credit are its _____, its flexibility, and its lack of _____.

21.6 The basic interest rate charged by banks to their best business customers is the _____.

21.7 A transaction loan is a bank loan for _____. It requires that a _____ be signed by the borrower.

21.8 Lines of credit often involve a _____ paid to the bank whether or not the firm draws on the line of credit.

21.9 Under a discount loan, the borrower receives _____ _____.

21.10 The firm's _____ can reduce the cost of a loan requiring a compensating balance.

21.11 A _____ is a loan whose rate is tied to the London Interbank Offered Rate.

21.12 _____ is an unsecured promissory note issued by large firms to obtain short-term financing. It can be an alternative or complement to short-term bank loans. Its interest cost tends to be _____ the prime rate.

21.13 _____ of accounts receivables involves using receivables as collateral for a loan. If the borrower defaults on the loan, the funds provided when the receivables are collected go to _____ _____.

21.14 _____ is the sale of accounts receivable. The lender takes on the credit-checking responsibilities. With _____, the factor purchases all the receivables, and pays the seller once a month for them. In _____, the factor provides a loan against the receivables.

21.15 In warehouse financing, the inventories are stored on the premises of _____.

PROBLEMS

21.1 Orange County Cooperative purchases vegetables for resale to consumers. It has recently been contacted by two potential suppliers who are willing to offer trade credit. The first, National Vegetable, offers terms of 2/10 net 30. The second, Allied Produce offers terms of 3/15 net 45. If Orange County wishes to minimize the cost of trade credit, which supplier should it choose?

21.2 Fifth Avenue Novelties has secured an $80,000, 90-day loan from a local bank. The total interest charge is $4,000. If Fifth Avenue's after-tax cost of debt is 14.19 percent, what is its tax rate? (Assume a 365-day year.)

21.3 Hebert Candy Company wishes to borrow $300,000, and is in the process of negotiating a 180-day loan from a local bank. The bank has offered the company the following alternatives:

a. A 16 percent annual interest rate, no compensating balance, and interest paid at the end of the loan.

b. A 15 percent annual interest rate with interest discounted and no compensating balance.

c. An installment loan with a 12 percent annual interest rate and six payments one month apart. The bank will use add-on interest.

d. A 10 percent annual interest rate with interest discounted and a 15 percent compensating balance requirement. Hebert presently maintains no balance at this bank.

Which loan offers the lowest before-tax annual percentage cost?
(Assume a 365-day year.)

21.4 McAllistar Chain Saws faces a seasonal demand for its products and hence, has periodic short-term needs for cash. It has arranged for a $750,000 line of credit with the First Massachusetts Bank to enable it to meet these needs. The terms of this line of credit are a 1/2 percent commitment fee on the unused portion of the line, plus 13 percent annual interest rate on the borrowed portion. The following are the expected monthly borrowings from the line of credit:

Month	Days	Borrowing
January	31	$300,000
February	28	600,000
March	31	750,000
April	30	500,000
May	31	250,000
June	30	150,000

a. What are the total costs per month associated with the line of credit?

b. What is the annual percentage cost of funds obtained from the line of credit? (Assume a 365-day year.)

21.5 Bicknell Electronics is considering the issuance of 270-day commercial paper to finance current inventory needs. The firm plans to issue $2.5 million of paper, which will sell for $2.3 million. The firm will, as well, be required to maintain a line of credit with a commitment fee of 3/4 of 1 percent to back the issue. What is the before-tax annual percentage cost of this commercial paper? (Assume a 365-day year.)

21.6 Golden Artwork Jewelry Company is considering pledging its accounts receivable to obtain favorable terms on a loan. The bank has offered two alternatives; both of which are for 50 days and provide the same amount of financing. A traditional loan at 16 percent annual interest rate, or the following loan package: (1) stated rate of interest of 14 percent, which is 2 percent above prime; (2) a 1 percent processing fee; and (3) a loan of 80 percent of the amount pledged. Golden Artwork has average credit sales of $3,000 per day, with an average collection period of 50 days. Which of the two alternatives has the lowest before-tax annual percentage interest cost? (Assume a 365-day year.)

21.7 Martelli Pasta Company averages $350,000 in credit sales per month. By maturity factoring its accounts receivable, it will be able to eliminate the credit and billing department at a monthly savings of $4,000. Martelli cannot accept the factoring arrangement if the cost before taxes exceeds 18 percent. What is the largest percentage factoring commission per month Martelli would be willing to pay? (Assume 12 equal months, not a 365-day year.)

21.8 Dresden Dinnerware Company employs a 180-day field warehouse agreement to finance inventory. The average amount of inventory is $800,000, the bank lends Dresden 80 percent of the value of the inventory, and the field warehousing fee is $100 per day. If the stated rate on the loan is 3 percent over the prime rate of 14 percent per year, what is the before-tax annual percentage cost of the loan?

ANSWERS TO COMPLETION QUESTIONS

21.1 Trade credit

21.2 amount of financing

21.3 after-tax cost

21.4 decreases; suffer; trade credit

21.5 convenience; restrictive terms

21.6 prime rate

21.7 a specific purpose; promissoryt note

21.8 commitment fee

21.9 the amount borrowed less interest

21.10 normal bank balance

21.11 Eurodollar loan

21.12 Commercial paper; below

21.13 Pledging; the lender to repay the loan

21.14 Factoring; maturity factoring; advance factoring;

21.15 a third party

SOLUTIONS TO PROBLEMS

21.1   The cost of trade credit is:

$$k_b = \left[1 + \frac{\text{discount percent}}{100\% - \text{discount percent}}\right]^{365/(\text{date paid} - \text{discount date})} - 1$$

For National Vegetable, the cost is:

$$k_b = \left[1 + \frac{2}{100 - 2}\right]^{365/(30-10)} - 1$$

$$= [1.020408]^{18.25} - 1 = 0.4459 = 44.59\%$$

For Allied Produce, the cost is:

$$k_b = \left[1 + \frac{3}{100 - 3}\right]^{365/(45-15)} - 1$$

$$= [1.030928]^{12.17} - 1 = 0.4486 = 44.86\%$$

National Vegetable's trade credit costs slightly less.

21.2

Step 1. $k_b = \left[1 + \dfrac{\text{costs - benefits}}{\text{amount of financing}}\right]^m - 1$

$$= \left[1 + \frac{\$4,000}{\$80,000}\right]^{365/90} - 1 = 0.2188 \text{ or } 21.88\%$$

Step 2. $\quad k_i = k_b(1 - T)$

$14.19\% = 21.88\%(1 - T)$

$(1 - T) = 0.6485$

$T = 0.3515 = 35.15\%$

21.3a

Step 1. Interest paid = (amount borrowed)(annual rate)(portion of year)

$$= (\$300,000)(0.16)(180/365) = \$23,671.23$$

Step 2. $k_b = \left[1 + \dfrac{\text{costs - benefits}}{\text{amount of financing}}\right]^m - 1$

$$k_b = \left[1 + \frac{\$23,671.23}{\$300,000}\right]^{365/180} - 1 = 0.1665 = 16.65\%$$

21.3b

Step 3. Interest paid = $(\$300,000)(0.15)(180/365) = \$22,191.78$

$$k_b = \left[1 + \frac{\$22,191.78}{\$300,000 - \$22,191.78}\right]^{365/180} - 1$$

$$= \left[1 + \frac{\$22,191.78}{\$277,808.22}\right]^{365/180} - 1 = 0.1686 = 16.86\%$$

21.3c

Step 4. Interest paid = ($300,000)(0.12)(180/365) = $17,753.43

Payment = $\frac{\$300,000 + \$17,753.43}{6 \text{ months}}$ = $52,958.91 per month

Loan = payment($PVA_{k_b, 6mo}$)

$300,000 = $52,958.91($PVA_{k_b, 6mo}$)

$PVA_{k_b, 6mo}$ = $\frac{\$300,000}{\$52,958.91}$ = 5.665%

From Table F.4,

$PVA_{1, 6mo}$ = 5.795%

$PVA_{2, 6mo}$ = 5.601%

Interpolating, k_b = 1% + $\frac{5.795\% - 5.665\%}{5.795\% - 5.601\%}$ = 1.67% per month

or k_b = $(1.0167)^{12} - 1$ = 0.2199 or 21.99% per year

Using a financial calculator k_b is 21.96% per year.

21.3d

Step 6. Interest paid = ($300,000)(0.10)(180/365) = $14,794.52

Compensating balance = ($300,000)(0.15) = $45,000

$k_b = \left[1 + \frac{\$14,794.52}{\$300,000 - \$14,794.52 - \$45,000}\right]^{365/180} - 1$

$= \left[1 + \frac{\$14,794.52}{\$240,205.48}\right]^{365/180} - 1 = 0.1288 = 12.88\%$

Step 7. Alternative d has the lowest before-tax interest cost; hence (other things being equal) it should be chosen.

21.4a

Step 1. Monthly interest charge = (amount borrowed)(interest rate)(proportion of year)

Commitment fee = ($750,000 - amount borrowed)(percent fee)(proportion of year)

<u>January</u>

Interest charge = ($300,000)(0.13)(31/365)   = $3,312.33

Commitment fee = ($750,000 - $300,000)(0.005)(31/365)=   <u>191.10</u>

Total January charges $3,503.43

Step 2. **February**

Interest charge = ($600,000)(0.13)(28/365) = $5,983.56
Commitment fee = ($750,000 - $600,000)(0.005)(28/365) = 57.53
Total February charges $6,041.09

Step 3. **March**

Interest charge = ($750,000)(0.13)(31/365) = $8,280.82
Commitment fee = ($750,000 - $750,000)(0.005)(31/365) = 0
Total March charges $8,280.82

Step 4. **April**

Interest charge = ($500,000)(0.13)(30/365) = $5,342.47
Commitment fee = ($750,000 - $500,000)(0.005)(30/365) = 102.74
Total April charges $5,445.21

Step 5. **May**

Interest charge = ($250,000)(0.13)(31/365) = $2,760.27
Commitment fee = ($750,000 - $250,000)(0.005)(31/365) = 212.33
Total May charges $2,972.60

Step 6. **June**

Interest charge = ($150,000)(0.13)(30/365) = $1,602.74
Commitment fee = ($750,000 - $150,000)(0.005)(30/365) = 246.58
Total June charges $1,849.32

21.4b

Step 7. $k_b = \left[1 + \dfrac{\text{total commitment fees + interest}}{\text{average net amount of financing}}\right]^m - 1$

Total commitment fees plus interest = $3,503.43 + $6,041.09 + $8,280.82 + $5,445.21 + $2,972.60 + $1,849.32 = $28,092.47

Average net amount borrowed per period = $300,000(31/181) + $600,000(28/181) + $750,000(31/181) + $500,000(30/181) + $250,000(31/181) + $150,000(30/181) = $423,204

$k_b = \left[1 + \dfrac{\$28,092.47}{\$423,204}\right]^{365/181} - 1 = 0.1384 = 13.84\%$

21.5

Step 1. Interest cost = $2,500,000 - $2,300,000 = $200,000

Step 2. Commitment fee = $2,500,000(0.0075)(270/365) = $13,869.86

Step 3. $k_b = \left[1 + \dfrac{\$200,000 + \$13,869.86}{\$2,300,000}\right]^{365/270} - 1 = 0.1277 = 12.77\%$

21.6

Step 1. Cost of traditional loan: stated rate, which is 16 percent.

Step 2. Cost of the alternative package:

Processing fee = (0.01)($3,000)(50 days) = $1,500

Step 3. The bank will lend ($3,000)(50 days)(0.80) = $120,000

Interest = ($120,000)(0.14)(50/365) = $2,301.37

Step 4. $k_b = \left[1 + \dfrac{\$1,500 + \$2,301.37}{\$120,000}\right]^{365/50} - 1 = 0.2557 = 25.57\%$

The traditional loan is a much less expensive alternative.

21.7

Step 1. $k_b = \left[1 + \dfrac{\text{factoring commission - savings in expenses}}{\text{accounts receivable/month}}\right]^m - 1$

$0.18 = \{1 + [(\text{commission} - \$4,000)/\$350,000]\}^{12 \text{ months}} - 1$

$[1.18]^{1/12} = \{1 + [(\text{commission} - \$4,000)/\$350,000]\}$

$1.0139 = 1 + [(\text{commission} - \$4,000)/\$350,000]$

$0.0139 = (\text{commission} - \$4,000)/\$350,000$

$\$4,865 = \text{commission} - \$4,000$

Commission = $8,865

Step 2. Martelli could afford to pay a factoring commission of
$8,865/$350,000 = 0.0253 = 2.53 percent per month.

21.8

Step 1. Field warehousing fee = ($100)(180 days)   = $18,000.00

Step 2. Interest = (0.17)($800,000)(0.80)(180/365) = <u>53,654.79</u>

Total fee and interest $71,654.79

Step 3. $k_b = \left[1 + \dfrac{\$71,654.79}{\$640,000}\right]^{365/180} - 1 = 0.2401 = 24.01\%$

CHAPTER 22

MERGERS AND CORPORATE RESTRUCTURING

HOW THIS CHAPTER RELATES TO THE REST OF THE TEXT

In Chapters 8-11, we saw how firms expand through investing in new projects. Another method of growth is through merger with or acquisition of another company. The decision to merge is simply an extension of the capital budgeting process. The firm considers the cash flows associated with the merger (Chapter 4), their timing (Chapter 5), and riskiness (Chapter 7) and calculates a value (Chapter 6). The appropriate required rate of return is the target firm's market-determined cost of capital (Chapter 14). Merger and acquisition possibilities should be considered in financial and strategic planning (Chapter 23). In a corporate restructuring, the firm adds bonds to its capital structure to take advantage of the disciplining role of debt and to make the firm less attractive as a takeover candidate. Additional debt affects the firm's cost of capital (Chapter 14), and capital structure (Chapter 15). Divestiture is the opposite of a merger; the firm sells an asset or division. The divestiture decision is another example of capital budgeting (Chapters 8-10).

TOPICAL OUTLINE

I. Introduction.
   A. Firms can grow not only internally, but also by acquiring other firms.
      1. A firm might acquire a division or part of the assets of another firm.
      2. A firm might acquire an entire firm or all of its assets.
   B. In the market for corporate control, management teams vie for the right to acquire and manage corporate activities and assets.
   C. The focus of the text is the standpoint of the bidding firm rather than the target company.

II. Reasons for merging.
   A. Sensible reasons.
      1. Increased economic performance.
         a. Economies of scale may result when the combined firm has sufficient size to drive down its expenses.
         b. Economies may result from vertical integration by insuring the continous flow from raw material acquisition to production, distribution, and sale.
         c. Merged firms may be able to take advantage of overlapping areas of expertise.
         d. An additional benefit of mergers is market protection.
         e. In achieving economies, the firm attempts to obtain synergistic benefits; the whole is worth more than the parts.
      2. Mergers may create increased economies by removing inefficient management and providing a fresh viewpoint in the management of the acquired firm.
      3. Tax considerations.
         a. The bidding firm with past losses would acquire a profitable target firm.
         b. The profitable bidding firm would acquire a target firm with past losses.
         c. Tax benefits may be due to the write-up of assets to a new tax basis; this increases depreciation for tax purposes, and hence, cash flow.
         d. The combined firm may have a greater debt capacity, increasing interest expense and lowering taxes. Increased debt also provides managerial incentives to create operating efficiency.
   B. Dubious reasons for acquisitions.
      1. Diversification: Diversification does not really benefit the stockholder, since individuals can diversify their own portfolios.
      2. Growth for growth's sake does not produce anything of value unless it is accompanied by economies or tax benefits.

3. Earnings per share increases which result immediately from acquisition do not maximize the value of the firm unless they are accompanied by economies or tax benefits.

III. Deciding whether to merge.
    A. A merger is a capital budgeting decision; use NPVs.
        1. NPV = benefits - costs.
            a. Benefits = change in value + value of the target firm, i.e. Δ value + value$_B$.
        2. Costs = price paid.
        3. For the NPV to be positive, the bidding firm must be able to realize economic or tax benefits not available to the target firm.
    B. Calculating benefits.
        1. Value$_B$ is simply the market value of the target's outstanding securities.
        2. Incremental benefits are the present value of the incremental cash flows, ie.

$$\Delta \text{ value} = \sum_{t=1}^{n} \frac{\Delta CF_t}{(1 + k)^t}$$

            a. Δ after-tax operating cash flows = Δ CFBT$(1 - T)$ + Δ Dep(T).
            b. Include additional outlays for new equipment or working capital.
            c. If a target firm's assets are sold for an amount different than their value as an ongoing concern, Δ CF is affected.
            d. $\Delta CF_t = \Delta$ CFBT$(1 - T)$ + Δ Dep(T) - Δ after-tax investment in long-term assets and net working capital $\pm$ after-tax gains or loss on the disposition of some of the target firm's assets.
    C. Cost equals the value of cash or securities used in the exchange.
        1. In a cash transaction, the value of the combined firm equals the value of the bidding firm + NPV. All net benefits go to the bidding firm's stockholders.

2. When common stock is used, gains are shared since the target firm's stockholders end up owning part of the combined firm.
   a. Proportion of the firm owned by the target firm's stockholders:
   $$W = \frac{\text{shares held by target firm's stockholders}}{\text{total shares}}$$
   b. True cost with stock = $W(\text{value}_{AB})$.

D. Exchange ratio = $\frac{\text{market value of cash and/or securities offered by the bidding firm}}{\text{market value of target firm's stock}}$

   1. Often, a higher exchange ratio is required for cash mergers.

E. How to avoid mistakes in mergers.
   1. Rely on market values; in a reasonably efficient market, the best estimate of the target firm's worth is its market price.
   2. Concentrate on incremental cash flows from the proposed acquisition.
   3. Use a required rate of return appropriate for the riskiness of the incremental cash flows.
   4. Consider transactions costs in your analysis.
   5. Be critical; avoid overpaying, especially in a bidding war. The firm may be better off if it loses.
   6. Consider the form of financing.

F. Who benefits from mergers?
   1. Most mergers involve a premium paid over the target firm's premerger market value, so the target's stockholders benefit.
   2. Empirical evidence does not show that stockholders of the bidding firm receive much benefit.
   3. Investment bankers and others who offer merger valuation services benefit.

IV. Mechanics of a merger.
   A. Form of the acquisition.
      1. Consolidation occurs when two or more firms combine to form a completely new firm, leaving no target or bidding firm.
      2. A merger occurs through the acquisition of the target firm's stock.

3. The bidding firm can acquire the assets of the target firm, and the target firm can dissolve after paying its liabilities and distributing the net proceeds to its stockholders.
4. A holding company can acquire complete or partial control over another company.

B. Tax implications.
1. With a taxable transaction, the target's stockholders must treat the acquisition as a sale for tax purposes, and declare capital gains or losses.
2. If the merger meets the requirement for a tax-free transaction, the target's stockholders experience capital gains or losses only when they sell the new stock at some later date.

C. Accounting treatments.
1. Pooling of interests occurs if the merger meets the four requirements listed in the text.
   a. Balance sheet treatment of a pooling of interests is a simple adding together of the two balance sheets.
   b. Income statement effects.
      i. The pooling of interests is a transfer of assets at their current depreciated book value.
      ii. Earnings per share may or may not change depending on the total earnings and postmerger number of shares outstanding.
2. Purchase.
   a. Balance sheet effects: The assets acquired are revalued to indicate the actual purchase price paid for the target firm, possibly creating goodwill.
   b. Income statement effects.
      i. Assets are revalued to reflect the value of the merger, so more depreciation is often charged off in future years than in pooling of interests, and goodwill is often created.
      ii. As a result, earnings per share tends to decrease.

V. Defensive tactics for fending off takeovers.
   A. Preoffer defenses.
      1. General preoffer defenses.
         a. Private companies are almost invulnerable to takeovers.
         b. Blocking stakes are holdings of more than 50% of the outstanding shares held by an individual or close-knit group.
         c. Some firms are unlikely takeover candidates because of size or political reasons.
         d. Strong stock prices fend off many suitors.
      2. Shark repellant charter amendments.
         a. Staggered board of directors.
         b. Some charters require approval of 62 2/3% to 80% of the stockholders before a merger can be affected.
         c. Fair price amendments prohibit two-tiered bids.
      3. Other pretakeover defenses.
         a. Dual class recapitalization gives one class of stockholders control over the firm.
         b. Poison pills provide stockholders with the right to purchase additional shares or sell existing shares to the target at attractive prices, if a bidder acquires a certain percentage of outstanding shares.
   B. Post-offer defenses.
      1. Litigation.
      2. Asset restructuring involves purchasing other assets, making another merger, or selling off the firm's "crown jewels" to make it unattractive to the bidder.
      3. Liability restructuring involves issuing new shares to a "white squire" or levering up the firm.
      4. In a pacman defense, the target makes a counteroffer to buy the bidder in an attempt to "gobble up" the enemy.
   C. Targeted repurchases (greenmail) involve the repurchase of shares, held by an unfriendly suitor, at a premuim over its current market value.

D. Golden parachutes are supplemental compensation packages for the target firm's management. These packages are paid in the case of takeover and resignation by management.

VI. Corporate restructuring.
   A. There is increased recognition that corporate "fit" and maximizing NPV are the most important aspects of maximizing the value of the firm.
   B. Debt disciplines managers.
      1. With high amounts of debt (and interest expense), managers are forced to concentrate on cash flow instead of accounting earnings.
      2. Because debt is unforgiving, managers must pay closer attention to the firm's operations.
      3. Debt makes the firm less attractive as a takeover candidate.
   C. In a leveraging up operation, the firm issues debt and buys back shares of common stock, drastically increasing its ratio of total debt to total assets.
   D. Many firms are going private; outstanding common stock is purchased by a small group of owners.
      1. In a management buyout, the top management of the firm, typically with an outside partner, buys the firm and turns it into a privately held company.
      2. In a leveraged buyout (LBO), the purchase is financed by borrowing. Often, the borrowing is in the form of junk bonds.
      3. An employee stock ownership plan (ESOP), is an employee trust fund to which the firm can contribute stock or cash at no direct cost to the employee.
         a. The firm buys stock using a bank loan, and gives it to the ESOP.
         b. The employees buy the stock and the proceeds are used to pay off the loan.
   E. Restructuring can also involve changing the legal structure of the business from a corporation to a limited partnership.

VII. Deciding to divest.
    A. Estimate the operating after-tax cash flows associated with the decision including any complementary or substitute effects with other aspects of the firm.
    B. Determine k, the division's required rate of return.
    C. Calculate the present value of the CFs.
    D. Determine the NPV of keeping the division by subtracting the market value of the division's associated liabilities from the present value of the CFs:

$$NPV = \sum_{t=1}^{n} \frac{CF_t}{(1+k)^t} - B$$

    E. If the NPV is less than the after-tax divestiture proceeds (DP), sell the division.
    F. The divestiture proceeds (DP) may vary.
        1. If the bidding firm also acquires both the assets and the liabilities of the division, the after-tax amount received by the seller is DP.
        2. If the seller retains the liabilities of the division, DP = after-tax diviestiture proceeds - B_0. must meet the division's obligations if it keeps the divisions in question.
    G. The divestiture decision is the opposite of capital budgeting and merger decisions; the firm divests if the benefits do not exceed the forgone divestiture opportunity.
    H. This analysis is useful for any kind of asset divestiture decision, but is typically used only for fairly large projects or divisions.

FORMULAS

Notation

$Value_A$ = value of the bidding firm
$Value_B$ = value of the target firm
$Value_{AB}$ = value of the combined firm
ΔCF_t = change in cash flows
B   = current market value of debt associated with the assets
DP   = after-tax divestiture proceeds
k   = required rate of return

Net Present Value of a Merger

NPV = benefits - costs

Benefits = Δ value + value$_B$

Costs = price paid in cash or stock

Incremental Gains

$$\Delta \text{ value} = \sum_{t=1}^{n} \frac{\Delta CF_t}{(1+k)^t}$$

Incremental Cash Flows

$\Delta CF_t = \Delta CFBT(1 - T) + \Delta Dep(T) - \Delta$ after-tax investment in long-term assets and net working capital $\pm$ after-tax gains or loss on the disposition of some of the target firm's assets

Proportion of the Combined Firm Held by the Target Firm's Stockholders

W = shares held by B/total shares

True Cost of a Merger Involving Stock

True cost with stock = W(value$_{AB}$).

Exchange Ratio

$$\text{Exchange ratio} = \frac{\text{market value of cash and/or securities offered by the bidding firm}}{\text{market value of target firm's stock}}$$

Divestiture

Net present value of keeping assets:

$$NPV = \sum_{t=1}^{n} \frac{CF_t}{(1+k)^t} - B$$

Divestiture proceeds when the seller retains the liabilities:

DP = after-tax divestiture proceeds - B

WHAT TO LOOK FOR

During the long-range planning process, the firm discovers its strengths and weaknesses. The firm plans to build on its strengths through growth. Any kind of growth the firm pursues should maximize the value of the firm. This rule applies not only to internal growth in capital budgeting projects, but also to external growth through mergers. The text discusses how firms evaluate merger proposals from the bidding firm's point of view.

Good and Poor Motives for Merging

Merger decisions should make stockholders better off. Wise merger decisions are those made to pursue an increase in the firm's value through synergistic effects. Such synergistic mergers produce a merged firm whose value is greater than the sum of the two individual firm's values. Synergism can occur only when the bidding firm obtains either economies or tax benefits unavailable except through the merger. Economies can result from vertical or horizontal integration, and through economies of scale. Tax savings can result if either the target firm or the bidding firm has unused tax losses that the other can use to offset taxable income.

Some firms choose poor reasons to merge. They might merge in order to diversify and reduce risk. However, there is no evidence that this increases the value of the firm for its stockholders. In efficient capital markets, stockholders can diversify more cheaply and efficiently on their own. In addition, firms merge in order to keep growing. But if the merger is not accompanied by economies or tax benefits, it does not increase the value of the firm. A nonsynergistic merger sometimes produces the illusion of an immediate earnings per share increase. But this increase is a mathematical phenomenon and does not reflect increased value, since such a merger does not involve tax benefits or economies. Thus, an increase in EPS is not, in and of itself, a good reason to pursue a merger.

Pricing the Target Firm

Merger decisions are like capital budgeting decisions. The only difference is that the growth is from acquiring an external project or firm rather than developing an entity within the firm. In deciding whether to proceed with a merger proposal, the bidding firm weighs the value of the merger after taking account of the cost of acquisition. The gain from the proposed acquisition is the maximum price the bidding firm should offer to pay for the target firm. In this net present value calculation, the bidding firm takes into account expected cash inflows and outflows from the merger.

The least the bidding firm can offer for the target firm is the target firm's premerger market value. Usually, the bidding firm offers the target firm some premium over market value. The greater the synergism the bidding firm expects to experience with the merger, the higher the premium it is willing to pay. If several firms are competing for a single target firm, their different offering prices somewhat reflect the synergism each expects to experience, or how much the merger is worth to them. The bidding firm should remember, however, that the expected synergism might not occur if the firm has trouble integrating the new firm (or division) into its ongoing operations.

Who Benefits from Mergers?

The premium offered over the target firm's premerger value makes the target stockholders better off with the merger than without it. The economy and the stockholders of the bidding firm may or may not benefit from mergers, however. No new products or services are produced. They just change hands. If the merger eliminates inefficient management, then the economy as a whole might gain.

The Basics of Mergers

Mergers can occur in any of four ways: (1) the consolidation or combination of two or more firms; (2) the acquisition of the target firm's stock, perhaps through a tender offer; (3) the acquisition of only the assets of the target firm; (4) the gain of partial control of the firm by a holding company.

The second type of merger, the acquisition, can be a tax-free or taxable transaction for the target firm's stockholders. If the transaction results in an exchange of stock for cash, the stockholders must declare capital gains or losses. If the target's stockholders receive voting preferred or common stock in exchange for their shares, the transaction is tax-free. They report capital gains or losses only when they sell the new stock later on and pay taxes at that time.

Not every merger attempt is friendly. If a target firm wants to ward off an unfriendly tender offer, the target might try to find a friendly merger partner (a "white squire") or give its chief executives "golden parachutes." In any defensive tactic, the target firm should keep the stockholders' interests in mind. Sometimes merger tactics and golden parachutes can harm rather than help the target firm and its stockholders.

Divestiture

The firm's goal is to maximize the value of the firm. Sometimes it is best if the firm sells a division or some assets which either do not fit or have a low profitability. In contrast to the acquisition decision, the divestiture decision requires the firm to decide how much to ask for the assets or division. The firm should not divest if the after-tax proceeds from the divestiture will not exceed the NPV of the expected cash flows from the assets if retained.

As noted in Chapter 10, the appropriate discount rate for the NPV calculation depends upon the riskiness of the asset's cash flows. The riskier the cash flows, the higher the discount rate and the lower the NPV. Note that the divestiture decision is exactly the opposite of the capital budgeting decision. The firm divests the assets if the discounted cash flows do not exceed the expected after-tax proceeds from the divestment.

Financial distress, or the inability to meet current financial obligations, can force firms to involuntarily divest assets. For example, during the oil glut of the early 1980s, many firms producing oil exploration equipment experienced financial distress. Some of these firms auctioned off assets to raise the necessary cash.

COMPLETION QUESTIONS

22.1 Waves of merger activity typically are related to _____ and general economic activity.

22.2 Increased _____ may result from a merger. In firms with large fixed costs, these economies would be _____. In firms hoping to achieve a continuous flow from acquisition of raw materials through ultimate sale, the economies would be the result of _____ _____.

22.3 _____ refers to the idea that the sum of two firms is worth more than the individual firms.

22.4 When a profitable firm acquires a target firm having tax losses, the rationale for the merger is to receive the _____ benefit.

22.5 From the bidding firm's point of view, the decision to acquire a target firm is a _____ decision.

22.6 For a positive net present value to exist, the bidding firm must achieve _____ or _____ not available to the target firm.

22.7 Postmerger EPS is _____ to the merger decision. When the focus is on postmerger EPS rather than NPV, the decision can be _____.

22.8 A _____ is an offer by the bidding firm directly to the target firm's stockholders.

22.9 A _____ occurs when two or more firms combine to form a completely new firm.

22.10 If a merger transaction qualifies as a tax-free transaction, the target firm's stockholders realize their capital gains or loss _____ _____.

22.11 When firms account for the merger as a _____, the individual balance sheet accounts are simply added together. When it is a _____, the assets are revalued and goodwill may be recorded.

22.12 A _____ is a special employment package that protects certain key executives if their firm is acquired in a merger.

22.13 The issue involved in divestiture is the opposite of the issue involved in _____.

22.14 If the net present value of keeping the assets exceeds the net proceeds expected from the divestiture, the firm should _____ the assets.

PROBLEMS

22.1 Cougar Aluminum is considering a potential merger with Anderson Mining Company. Anderson presently has 1,000,000 shares of common stock outstanding trading at $10 per share. Cougar has estimated the following incremental cash flows from the merger:

Year	Δ CFBT	Δ Dep	Δ Investment
1	$100,000	$100,000	$300,000
2	200,000	100,000	100,000
3	300,000	100,000	
4	400,000	100,000	
5	500,000	100,000	
6-10	600,000	100,000	

Anderson has agreed to sell the shares for $11.00 per share. If Cougar's tax rate is 40%, and k = 16%, should they merge?

22.2 Benson Industries is thinking of acquiring Vantage Corporation via an all stock sweep. Information for both firm's is as follows.

Firm	Stock Price	Shares
Benson	$50	5,000,000
Vantage	$10	2,000,000

Δ Value is estimated to be $5,000,000. Benson intends to exchange one share of Benson for each five shares of Vantage. What will be the price per share of Benson after the merger?

22.3 Millhouse Manufacturing recently acquired Spencer Industries by exchanging four shares of Millhouse for five shares of Spencer. Information on the two firms prior to the merger is listed below:

	Millhouse	Spencer
Total earnings	$200,000	$600,000
Number of shares	100,000	150,000
Price	$15	$12

What is the EPS for Millhouse before and after the merger?

22.4 Portland Industries is considering a merger with Jarvis Corporation and wishes to determine the accounting effects of such an action. The premerger financial statements for both firms follow.

Balance Sheet
(In thousands)

	Portland	Jarvis
Current assets	$ 50	$ 10
Net long-term assets	300	80
Total	$ 350	$ 90
Debt	$ 100	$ 40
Equity	250	50
Total	$ 350	$ 90

	Income Statement (In thousands)	
Sales	$1,000	$400
Less: Cash expense	600	300
Less: Depreciation	100	20
EBIT	300	80
Less: Interest	50	20
EBT	250	60
Less: Taxes (40%)	100	24
EAT	$ 150	$ 36
Number of shares	100,000	10,000

Portland Industries paid $150,000 for Jarvis Corporation by issuing 10,000 shares at $15 each. If purchase accounting is used, net long-term assets for Jarvis will be valued at $120,000 and goodwill at $20,000. Debt will be listed at book value. Both additional depreciation and goodwill will be written off on a 5-year straight-line basis. Assuming that the number of shares in the combined firm is 110,000, calculate the balance sheet, income statement, and EPS under both pooling of interests and purchase accounting.

22.5 The president of Mervin Toy Company has suggested the divestiture of the company's plastic model division. Next year's CFs are expected to be $2 million, and because of the new mature nature of the business, these cash flows are expected to grow at only 1 percent per year. The appropriate required rate of return is 11 percent, and the division now has $12 million in debt. What is the minimum divestiture price the firm would be willing to accept?

22.6 Jacobson Luggage Company is unhappy with the performance of its designer luggage division. Full capacity has been reached, which means that the firm can only expect CFs of $600,000 per year, with no growth prospects. A proposal to expand the plant has been put forth. The expansion will require investments of $2.5 million per year for the next two years, during which time the CFs will remain as above. After that (starting in year 3), CFs will be able to grow at a rate of 10 percent per year. The division presently has $2 million in debt, and no new debt will be added should the company expand. A competitor has offered to pay Jacobson $5 million (after-tax) for the division. If the discount rate is 15 percent, what should Jacobson do?

ANSWERS TO COMPLETION QUESTIONS

22.1 stock market prices
22.2 economies; economies of scale; vertical integration
22.3 Synergism
22.4 tax
22.5 capital budgeting
22.6 increased economies; tax benefits
22.7 irrelevant; wrong
22.8 tender offer
22.9 consolidation
22.10 at a later date when they sell the new stock
22.11 pooling of interest; purchase
22.12 golden parachute
22.13 capital budgeting (or mergers)
22.14 retain

SOLUTIONS TO PROBLEMS

22.1
Step 1. Calculate ΔCF_t (units of $1,000)

Year	Δ CFBT	Δ Dep	Δ CFBT(1 - T)	+ Dep(T)	- Inv	= ΔCF_t
1	100	100	60	40	300	-200
2	200	100	120	40	100	60
3	300	100	180	40		220
4	400	100	240	40		280
5	500	100	300	40		340
6-10	600	100	360	40		400

Step 2. Calculate Δ Value

$$\Delta \text{ value} = \sum_{t=1}^{n} \frac{CF_t}{(1 + k)^t}$$

$= -\$200(PV_{16\%,1yr}) + \$60(PV_{16\%,2yr}) + \$220(PV_{16\%,3yr})$

$\quad + \$280(PV_{16\%,4yr}) + \$340(PV_{16\%,5yr})$

$\quad + \$400(PVA_{16\%,5yr})(PV_{16\%,5yr})$

$= -\$200(0.862) + \$60(0.743) + \$220(0.641) + \$280(0.552)$

$\quad + \$340(0.476) + \$400(3.274)(0.476)$

$= -\$172.40 + \$44.58 + \$141.02 + \$154.56 + \$161.84 + \$623.37$

$= \$952.97$ or $\$952,970$

Step 3. Benefits = $value_B + \Delta$ value

$$= \$10(1,000,000) + \$952,970$$

$$= \$10,952,970$$

Step 4. NPV = benefits - costs

$$= \$10,952,970 - \$11(1,000,000)$$

$$= -\$47,030$$

Since the NPV is negative, the firms should not merge.

22.2

Step 1. Number of new shares required = $\dfrac{2,000,000}{5}$ = 400,000

Step 2. Shares in combined firm = 5,000,000 + 400,000 = 5,400,000

Step 3. $Value_{AB} = value_A + value_B + \Delta$ value

$$= \$50(5,000,000) + \$10(2,000,000) + \$5,000,000$$

$$= \$250,000,000 + \$20,000,000 + \$5,000,000 = \$275,000,000$$

Step 4. Price = $\dfrac{value_{AB}}{shares} = \dfrac{\$275,000,000}{5,400,000}$ = \$50.92

22.3

Step 1. EPS before = $\dfrac{\text{total earnings}}{\text{number of shares}} = \dfrac{\$200,000}{100,000}$ = \$2 per share

Step 2. Total new shares = 100,000 + 4/5(150,000) = 220,000

Step 3. Postmerger EPS = $200,000 + $600,000/220,000 = $3.64

22.4

Step 1. Under pooling of interest, the balance sheet and income statement are just the sum of the premerger amounts.

Balance Sheet
(In thousands of dollars)

Current assets	$ 60
Net long-term assets	380
Total	$440
Debt	$140
Equity	300
Total	$440

Step 2.
Income Statement
(In thousands of dollars)

Sales	$1,400
Less: Cash expense	900
Less: Depreciation	120
EBIT	380
Less: Interest	70
EBT	310
Less: Taxes (40%)	124
EAT	$ 186

EPS = $186,000/110,000 = $1.69 per share

Step 3. Under purchase accounting, the figures in the problem are used in place of the Jarvis balance sheet entries.

Balance Sheet
(In thousands of dollars)

Current assets	$ 60
Net long-term assets	420
Goodwill	20
Total	$500
Debt	$140
Equity	360
Total	$500

Step 4. On the income statement, depreciation will increase by ($120 - $80)/5 = $8 and goodwill will be amortized at $20/5 = $4 per year.

Income Statement
(In thousands of dollars)

Sales	$1,400.0
Less: Cash expense	900.0
Less: Depreciation	128.0
EBIT	372.0
Less: Interest	70.0
EBT	302.0
Less: Taxes (40%)	120.8
EAT	181.2
Less: Writeoff of goodwill	4.0
Net income	$ 177.2

EPS = $177,200/110,000 = $1.61 per share

22.5

Step 1. The firm is indifferent if DP = NPV.

$$DP = \sum_{t=1}^{n} \frac{CF_t}{(1+k)^t} - B = \frac{\$2,000,000}{0.11 - 0.01} - \$12,000,000 = \$8,000,000$$

Step 2. If Mervin Toy Company can get $8,000,000 or more (after taxes) for the division, it should divest.

22.6

Step 1. No expansion:

NPV = $600,000/0.15 − $2,000,000 = $2,000,000. The net proceeds from divesting would be $5 million − $2 million in debt = $3 million. Without the possibility of expanding the division, the decision would be to divest it since the net divestiture proceeds of $3 million exceed the net present value of continuing to operate of $2 million.

Step 2. With expansion:

$$NPV = (\$600,000 - \$2,500,000)(PV_{15\%,1yr})$$
$$+ (\$600,000 - \$2,500,000)(PV_{15\%,2yr})$$
$$+ [\$600,000(1.10)/(0.15 - 0.10)](PV_{15\%,2yr}) - \$2,000,000$$
$$= -\$1,900,000(0.870) - \$1,900,000(0.756) + \$13,200,000(0.756)$$
$$- \$2,000,000 = \$4,889,800$$

Jacobson should proceed with the expansion since its value is greater than the net proceeds from divesting. The stockholders would receive only $3 million from divestment since the $2 million in debt must be paid off.

CHAPTER 23

FINANCIAL PLANNING AND STRATEGY

HOW THIS CHAPTER RELATES TO THE REST OF THE TEXT

Effective financial and strategic planning contributes to the continual success of the firm. Financial and strategic planning incorporates decisions made relative to working capital budgeting (Chapters 18-21), capital budgeting (Chapters 8-11), and long-term financial decisions (Chapters 14-16). Long-term financing sources (Chapters 12 and 13) must be considered in the planning process. Both short- and long-term financial and strategic planning requires the use of cash budgets (Chapter 4).

TOPICAL OUTLINE

I. Introduction: Essentials of financial planning.
   A. Bring all previous decisions of the firm into a coherent, workable package.
   B. Assess the tradeoffs between risk and required return.
   C. Continuously monitor the firm's liquidity and flexibility.
II. Impact of financial and strategic factors on the firm.
   A. Factors affecting the value of the firm.
      1. General economic factors that affect the firm's value.
         a. The robustness of the economy, and the cyclical nature of the firm.
         b. The tone of the administration in Washington.
         c. The cost of money in the economy, which affects the cost of financing.
         d. The level of taxes, which affects both the taxes paid and the tax shields enjoyed by the firm.
      2. Inflation and disinflation.
         a. Increases in inflation cause the cost of capital to increase, decreasing the number of positive NPV investments.
         b. If cash outflows increase more than cash inflows, the firm's free cash declines, reducing the value of the firm.

3. Firm- and issue-specific risk.
   a. Business risk.
      i. The firm's position in its industry is a function of past investment decisions.
      ii. The firm's future investment decisions are a function of the firm's current investment opportunities.
      iii. The major business of the firm determines its investment in short-term assets; the firm might have too little or too much investment in short-term assets.
      iv. The firm's cash dividend policy is a function of both its industry and its investment opportunities.
   b. Financial risk, which depends on the financing strategy, affects the required rate of return.
      i. An aggressive strategy involves using few current assets, but more current liabilities, and is considered risky.
      ii. A moderate strategy involves matching high (low) current liabilities with high (low) current assets.
      iii. A conservative strategy involves using few long-term assets, and more long-term liabilities.
      iv. The firm's capital structure will limit the amount of debt the firm uses; judicious use of debt appears to reduce the firm's cost of capital.
   c. Issue-specific risk involves the type of financing and the types of restrictive provisions.
4. International factors affecting firm's market value.
   a. The currency exchange rates and social and political structures.
   b. The effect on cost of capital due to excess demand for international capital.
   c. Cost differentials, which may shift market share to foreign-based firms.

B. The basic valuation model.
   1. Definitions.
      a. Free cash flows = cash inflow - cash outflow - investment.
         i. Cash inflows = cash revenues + financing inflows.
         ii. Cash outflows = cash expenses + repayments.
         iii. Investments = investments in short- and long-term assets.
         iv. Free cash flows that are not reinvested in the firm are paid out in cash dividends.
      b. Value = $P_0 = \dfrac{\text{cash inflow}_1 - \text{cash outflow}_1 - \text{investment}_1}{k_s - g}$
   2. Effects on value due to changes in free cash flow.
      a. Increase in expected cash inflow results in increased value.
      b. Increase in expected cash outflow results in decreased value.
      c. Increase in expected investment.
         i. If the investments are good and have positive NPVs, g increases and the value of the firm increases.
         ii. If the investments have a negative NPV, the firm makes these investments with no incremental benefits and the value of the firm decreases.
      d. Increase in required rate of return due to increased inflation, increased risk aversion, or increased firm-specific risk will decrease the value of the firm.
      e. Increase in expected growth in cash dividends will increase the value of the firm.

III. Financial and strategic planning.
   A. What is financial planning?
      1. Analyzing the interactions of the firm's decisions to find the best plan.
      2. Projecting the consequences of decisions to avoid surprises.
      3. Determining which alternative to take.
      4. Measuring the performance against the financial plan.

B. What is emphasized?
   1. Cash flows form the basis for successful financial plans since we can see the interactions among liquidity, flexibility, risk, and the firm's value.
   2. Large firms break down planning on the basis of divisional units or strategic business units.
   3. Estimate the probability of various states of the world in order to determine the possible effects of various outcomes (scenario analysis).
   4. Financial planning considers both short-run cash considerations and long-run risk-return considerations.
C. Accounting statements are not very useful for financial planning, since they do not consider cash flows.
D. What is assumed?
   1. The firm has made some decisions.
      a. The firm has taken a conservative, moderate, or aggressive stance toward its working capital strategy.
      b. The firm has established its cash gathering system.
      c. The firm has established its collection and sales terms and policies.
      d. The firm has made its investment in inventory.
      e. The firm has used capital budgeting procedures, based upon its cost of capital and its capital structure.
   2. The firm's corporate strategy is the result of the financial planning process; NPV determines the strategy.
E. What is the outcome?
   1. Project cash flows for both the short- and long-term.
   2. Articulate the firm's corporate strategy.
   3. Develop the firm's short-run and long-run capital budgets.
   4. Identify the amount and approximate timing of necessary financing.

IV. Developing financial and strategic plans.
   A. Short-run financial planning can be on monthly or quarterly basis.
      1. Firm calculates expected cash inflow or outflow per period and the amount of short-term financing needed.

2. Determine the best manner for securing the needed short-term financing, net of excess cash and marketable securities.
   a. Alternative 1 in Table 23.3 is a line of credit at 12 percent plus an inventory loan at 15 percent.
      i. Draw on the line of credit until it is used up, then take out the inventory loan.
      ii. Pay off the inventory loan first since it is more costly.
      iii. Evaluate this alternative in terms of the firm's future financial health.
   b. Alternative 2 (Table 23.4) is an accounts receivable loan at 11 percent and a commercial paper issue at 9 percent.
   c. To choose among financing plans, compare both the financing costs and the effects on the firm's future financial health.

B. Long-run planning considers the firm's longer-term financing requirements.
   1. Long-term financing requirements also include the firm's short-term spontaneous financing, and its short-term borrowing.
   2. Steps toward long-run planning.
      a. Make a cash budget for longer time periods and in less detail.
         i. Consider internally generated equity funds.
         ii. Consider any needed investment in current assets.
         iii. Consider the timing and magnitude of projected capital expenditures, liquidation of assets, or acquisitions.
         iv. Consider repayment of principal.
         v. Consider short-term financing costs incurred.
         vi. Consider the firm's cash dividend policy.

b. Evaluate financing alternatives to meet the long-term needs.
   i. First alternative (Table 23.6) involves increasing long-term debt and issuing common stock.
      (a) The firm's current ratio remains constant, while its debt increases.
      (b) The value of the firm's stock rises to $52.73.
   ii. Second alternative (Table 23.7) finances with both short- and long-term debt.
      (a) The firm's current ratio falls and the debt ratio increases.
      (b) The firm's value will increase and the stock price rises to $54.17.
   iii. The firm selects among alternatives by looking at the effects of the alternative upon the firm and its value.
   iv. If the firm expects markets to be tight, the firm might prefinance by obtaining funds 6 to 12 months before they are needed, and roll these funds over in short-term money market securities until needed.

FORMULAS

Notation

P_0 = market price of the firm at time zero
D_t = cash dividends expected to be received in time t
g = expected compound rate of growth in the cash dividend
k_s = required rate of return on stock, based on the risk-free rate and a risk premium appropriate to the firm in question
β_j = nondiversifiable risk of stock j
k_M = return expected on the market
k_{RF} = risk-free rate of return

Basic Valuation Model

Market value = $P_0 = D_1/(k_s - g)$

Capital Asset Pricing Model

$k_s = k_{RF} + \beta_j(k_M - k_{RF})$

Redefined Valuation Equation

$$P_0 = \frac{\text{cash inflow}_1 - \text{cash outflow}_1 - \text{investment}_1}{k_s - g}$$

WHAT TO LOOK FOR

Financial Planning as a Discipline of Integration

Financial planning and strategy is a discipline of integration; Chapter 23's discussion of financial planning integrates the material of previous chapters. Planning brings together into a coherent package all the previous decisions the firm has made concerning financing and investing.

Working capital policy

The firm chooses its working capital policy (Chapter 18), deciding what level of short-term assets to maintain (Chapters 19 and 20), and how to finance them (Chapter 21). The firm's working capital policy will help to determine its short- and long-term financing needs. If the firm uses an aggressive working capital strategy, it has relatively few short-term assets and relatively more short-term liabilities. Thus, the firm has a greater need for short-term financing. With a conservative strategy, the firm has relatively more short-term assets funded with more long-term debt. The conservatively financed firm would have greater long-term financing needs. With the moderate or matched approach, the firm funds short-term assets with short-term liabilities, and long-term assets with long-term financing. The eventual financial plan, which we will discuss later, must take into account these short- and long-term requirements.

Capital structure, capital budgeting, and long-term financing policies

In addition to choosing its working capital policy, the firm chooses its capital structure (Chapter 15). Maintaining this capital structure and using its estimated cost of capital (Chapter 14), the firm can do its capital budgeting (Chapters 8 - 11). Any project with a positive net present value (NPV) will enhance the value of the firm. That is, if the present value of the project's inflows exceeds the outflows, the value of the firm will increase (Chapter 6). The manager must remember, however, that all projections involve some uncertainty and that the discount rate used in the NPV calculations should reflect this uncertainty (Chapter 7). The firm chooses all positive NPV projects, subject to any financing limitations.

It is these projects which help define the firm's future long-term and short-term financing needs, and which produce the firm's future growth in earnings and dividends. Other things being equal, the greater the firm's current investment opportunities, the lower its current cash dividends, since cash flows are retained for reinvestment in the firm (Chapter 16).

The firm funds the projects according to the capital structure. To achieve the equity funding requirement, the firm uses internally generated funds first. In choosing among the other sources of long-term financing, the firm considers its capital structure, the costs of each funding type, and the effects of these funding types upon the riskiness and return of its future cash flow (Chapters 12, 13, and 17).

Risk, return, and valuation

The firm's financial management decisions help determine both the riskiness and the return (Chapter 7) of the firm's cash flows (Chapter 4). We can use the redefined equation of the firm's constant growth valuation model to see the potential impact on the firm of cash flows, risk, expected growth, and required return. If the cash inflows increase, or cash outflows decrease, or the expected growth of cash dividends increases, or the riskiness and required rate of return decrease, then the value of the firm increases. If the opposite occurs, the firm's value declines.

An aggressive working capital management policy is risky, since it relies on continual refinancing with short-term sources to fund long-term assets. Its potential return is higher, however, since the cash cycle is shortened. The opposite is true with a conservative working capital management policy. Working capital policy is one source of financial risk. The other is the firm's capital structure.

Business risk and issue-specific risk also exist. The firm that has a relatively small market share, few future investment opportunities, or an inappropriate investment in short-term assets will have more business risk than a well-managed market leader in a growing industry. The different types of financing available to a firm each have their own specific risks and costs. The risk of the firm helps determine its required rate of return and its value.

In addition, external economic and governmental factors affect the value of the firm. These factors include inflation, the robustness of the economy, the monetary-fiscal posture, government regulation of business, and the required return by investors.

The Financial and Strategic Planning Process

Once the firm has made its financing and investment decisions, it is ready to integrate these decisions through financial planning. In this way, the firm can assess the risk-return tradeoffs, maintain liquidity and flexibility, establish concrete goals, provide standards for performance, and avoid unexpected surprises.

A good analogy for business financial planning is the planning of the home buyer. The new homeowner has not only the fixed costs of home ownership in the form of a mortgage, but the associated monthly bills, the potential home improvements, and the costs of unexpected repairs. If the homeowner's policy is to pay for all improvements and repairs in cash, he or she cannot spread out the payments for any one investment. The financial plan would be to space out any investments in home improvement and repairs in order to maintain the policy of cash payment. However, suppose the homeowner uses credit and pays for major remodeling and for major appliances over several years' time. In this case, the financing plan allows the homeowner to make more appliance purchases and home improvements during a shorter period of time.

Each financing plan has an impact on the homeowner's liquidity, flexibility, financing costs, and risk exposure. Each financing plan has an array of possible financing implications. The homeowner chooses that plan which maximizes satisfaction while maintaining sufficient liquidity and flexibility. As time passes, the homeowner should review the financial plan and evaluate these effects.

Similarly, the manager of the firm conducts financial planning. Managers analyze the investment and financing policies and decisions of the firm, and look for a plan that maximizes the value of the stockholder claims on the firm, provides sufficient liquidity to meet unexpected needs, and effectively handles risk. In studying each potential plan, the managers project the consequences of each plan in terms of financing costs, liquidity, flexibility, and value maximization. The manager then selects the plan that best meets the firm's goals and objectives. Financial planning is, of course, an ongoing process, since today's investments and financial decisions affect tomorrow's growth, investment opportunities, and plans.

COMPLETION QUESTIONS

23.1 _____ forces the firm to bring together all investment and financing decisions into a coherent and workable package.

23.2 The firm cannot evaluate various alternatives, options, and strategies without considering how they will affect the _____.

23.3 When only expected cash inflows increase, the value of the firm _____; when only expected cash outflows increase, the value of the firm _____.

23.4 For planning purposes, GAAP-based accounting rules are not very useful, since they are not based upon _____.

23.5 The firm's required rate of return will increase if: (a) the risk-free rate _____; (b) investors' risk aversion _____; or (c) if its beta and firm-specific risk _____.

23.6 A _____ stock pays small or no cash dividends since it has temporary superior investment opportunities. The _____ valuation model may not work well with such a stock.

23.7 As the economy declines, investors become _____ risk averse, and their required rate of return _____. This causes the cost of the firm's financing to _____.

23.8 If the firm maintains few current assets, but more current liabilities, the working capital policy is _____.

23.9 Due to uncertainties involved in the firm's internal and external environment, its financial and strategic plans should allow for some _____.

23.10 The performance of the firm, its managers, and its employees should be evaluated relative to the firm's _____.

23.11 In short-run, the emphasis is on how to meet the _____ most efficiently while maintaining flexibility. In long-term financial planning, the emphasis is to _____.

23.12 The process results in the projection of the firm's _____, articulation of its _____, development of its short- and long-run _____, and identification of the amount and timing of the firm's financing needs.

23.13 In addition to spontaneous short-term financing, the firm uses _____ and _____ to meet its financing needs.

23.14 To estimate the firm's cash needs, the firm should take into account internally generated _____, increases in the investment in current assets, the timing and magnitude of the firm's projected _____ _____, repayment of principal, and short-term financing costs. The free internally generated funds available for reinvestment depend upon the firm's _____ policy.

PROBLEMS

23.1 Briggs Machinery Company has ordinary expected cash outflows of $100,000, inflows of $300,000, and investment of $75,000.
  a. If k_{RF} is 8 percent, k_M = 17 percent, and the beta for Briggs is 1.25, what is the firm's value if cash dividends are growing at 3.25 percent per year?
  b. Suppose the firm could undertake an additional investment for $25,000. The new investment would increase Brigg's beta to 1.5, but allow dividends to grow at a rate of 6.5 percent in the future. Should Briggs undertake the investment?

23.2 Tucker Frozen Foods is expected to pay a dividend next year of $5.00 per share. The required return on the stock is 18 percent and dividends are expected to grow at a constant rate of 4 percent in perpetuity. The company has available to it investment opportunities that would require a reduction of dividend growth to two percent per year for the next five years (that is, the last year of 2 percent dividend growth is year 4 to year 5). These investments would enable Tucker's to increase dividend growth after year 5 to 7 percent per year in perpetuity and would result in an increase in the required return on the stock to 20 percent (starting today). Is it in the firm's best interest for Tucker to undertake these investments?

23.3 Sonora Mountain Vintners has determined its short-term cumulative financing needs as follows:

	Quarter 1	Quarter 2	Quarter 3	Quarter 4
Net cash inflow (+) or outflow (−)	−$60	−$20	+$40	+$50
Calculated short-term financing needed:				
Cash at start of period	$25	−$35	−$55	−$15
Net cash inflow or outflow	− 60	− 20	+ 40	+ 50
Cash at end of period	−$35	−$55	−$15	+$35
Minimum balance required	− 15	− 15	− 15	− 15
Cumulative short-term financing needed (−) or surplus (+)	−$50	−$70	−$30	+$20

Sonora plans to borrow the principal plus interest. If interest is paid every quarter, the tax rate is 40 percent, and interest is 3 percent per quarter, what balance is owed at the end of the year? (Note: In contrast to the text, where there is a one-period lag in interest payments, in this problem interest is paid in the quarter it is incurred.)

23.4 Buckeye Corn Products has forecast the following long-term capital needs for the next four years.

	1	2	3	4
Long-term financing needed per year	$25	$15	$30	$50
Internal funds	− 15	− 17	− 20	− 20
External needed (+) or surplus (−)	$10	−$ 2	$10	$30

The firm at present has a capital structure of $100 equity and $100 debt but would like to reduce its debt ratio to 40 percent. Either long-term debt or equity can be issued in $5 increments. Indicate year-by-year whether long-term debt or equity or both should be issued. (Any surplus will be used to reduce the firm's debt.)

ANSWERS TO COMPLETION QUESTIONS

23.1 Financial and strategic planning
23.2 value of the firm
23.3 increases; decreases
23.4 cash flows
23.5 increases; increases; increases
23.6 growth; constant growth
23.7 more; increases; increase
23.8 aggressive
23.9 flexibility
23.10 stated goals
23.11 cash needs; maximize the value of the firm
23.12 cash flows; corporate strategy; capital budgets
23.13 short-term borrowing; long-term financing
23.14 funds; capital expenditures; cash dividend

SOLUTIONS TO PROBLEMS

23.1a

Step 1. $k_s = k_{RF} + \beta_j(k_M - k_{RF}) = 8\% + 1.25(17\% - 8\%) = 8\% + 11.25\% = 19.25\%$

Step 2. $P_0 = \dfrac{\text{cash inflow}_t - \text{cash outflow}_t - \text{investment}_t}{k_s - g}$

$= \dfrac{\$300,000 - \$100,000 - \$75,000}{0.1925 - 0.0325} = \dfrac{\$125,000}{0.16} = \$781,250$

23.1b

Step 3. $k_s = 8\% + 1.5(17\% - 8\%) = 21.5\%$

$P_0 = \dfrac{\$300,000 - \$100,000 - \$75,000 - \$25,000}{0.215 - 0.065} = \dfrac{\$100,000}{0.15} = \$666,666.67$

No, firm value will fall if the investment is undertaken.

23.2

Step 1. Under the current investment plan:

$P_0 = \dfrac{D_1}{k_s - g} = \dfrac{\$5.00}{0.18 - 0.04} = \$35.71$

Step 2. To calculate the stock price under the new investment plan, calculate the dividend stream.

$D_1 = \$5.000$

$D_2 = \$5.000(1.02) = \$5.100$

$D_3 = \$5.100(1.02) = \$5.202$

$D_4 = \$5.202(1.02) = \$5.306$

$D_5 = \$5.306(1.02) = \$5.412$

$D_6 = \$5.412(1.07) = \$5.791$

Since the growth after year 6 is constant,

$$P_5 = \frac{D_6}{k_s - g} = \frac{\$5.791}{0.20 - 0.07} = \$44.546$$

Step 3. $P_0 = \$5.000(PV_{20\%,1yr}) + \$5.100(PV_{20\%,2yr}) + \$5.202(PV_{20\%,3yr})$

$+ \$5.306(PV_{20\%,4yr}) + \$5.412(PV_{20\%,5yr})$

$+ \$44.546(PV_{20\%, 5\ yr})$

$= \$5.000(0.833) + \$5.100(0.694) + \$5.202(0.578)$

$+ \$5.306(0.482) + \$5.412(0.402) + \$44.546(0.402)$

$= \$4.165 + \$3.539 + \$3.011 + \$2.557 + \$2.176 + \$17.907$

$= \$33.355$ or $\$33.36$

Since the stock price is lower under the new plan, the firm should stay with its current plan.

23.3

Step 1. From the cumulative cash needed, Sonora needs after interest

$50 in Quarter 1

$20 in Quarter 2

-$40 in Quarter 3

-$50 in Quarter 4

Step 2. Let P = the amount needed after interest and B = the amount borrowed. The after-tax cost of borrowing is 3%(1 - 0.40) = 1.8%

$$B = P + 0.018B$$
$$B = P/1 - 0.018$$

First quarter borrowing, B_1 = $50/1 - 0.018 = $50.916
Second quarter borrowing, B_2 = $50.916 + $20/1 - 0.018 = $72.216
Third quarter borrowing, B_3 = $72.216 - $40/1 - 0.018 = $32.807
Fourth quarter borrowing, B_4 = $32.807 - $50 = -$17.193
Since there is a surplus of $17.193, all funds are repaid.

23.4

Step 1. 1st year issue all equity, total capitalization = $200 + $25 = $225
$100 debt/$225; total capitalization = 44.4%

Step 2. 2nd year: Total capitalization = $225 + $15 = $240. No debt or equity needs be issued since internally generated equity is in excess of requirement. Therefore, debt decreases by $2 to $98. ($98/$240) = 40.8% debt.

Step 3. 3rd year: Total capitalization = $240 + $30 = $270.
(40% debt)($270) = $108 in debt. Debt is currently 98, so issue $10 in debt; $120 in equity is internally generated. The issuance of $10 in debt will yield exactly a 40 percent debt/total capitalization ratio.

Step 4. 4th year: Total capitalization = $270 + $50 = $320. (40% debt)(320) = $128 in debt. Debt is currently at $108; the firm should issue the required $20 in debt to maintain exactly a 40 percent debt ratio. Since the firm has $20 in internally generated equity, an additional $10 must be raised in the capital market.

CHAPTER 24

INTERNATIONAL FINANCIAL MANAGEMENT

HOW THIS CHAPTER RELATES TO THE REST OF THE TEXT

To this point, we have concentrated on financial management within the United States. When operating internationally, our primary goal remains the same; maximize the value of the firm by focusing on cash flows (Chapter 4), risk (Chapter 6), and required returns. But, international operation carries with it several complications that affect capital budgeting (Chapters 8 to 10). The foreign markets also provide additional sources of short-term (Chapter 21) and long-term capital (Chapter 12).

TOPICAL OUTLINE

I. Foreign exchange.
   A. International transactions are conducted in more than one currency. Foreign exchange rates are the conversion rates between various currencies.
      1. International markets operate under a "managed" floating exchange rate system. Rates float freely with market sources, but central banks intervene to smooth out some fluctuations.
   B. Spot rates vs. forward rates.
      1. The spot rate is the price paid for delivery of a currency today.
         a. A spot rate for the British pound of $0.5650 means it takes a dollar to buy 0.5650 pounds today.
      2. A forward rate is a price agreed upon today for delivery of a currency in the future.
         a. A 30-day forward rate for the British pound of 0.5682 means that the purchaser agrees to exchange 0.5682 pounds per dollar thirty days from now.
      3. When the forward rate is above the spot rate, the forward rate is at a premium; if below, it is at a discount.
         a. Forward rates will increase at a percentage rate approximately equal to the difference between the U.S. inflation rate and the foreign country's inflation rate.

C. Hedging is the use of the foreign exchange market or some other market to eliminate foreign exchange risk.
   1. If hedged, the exchange risk is said to be covered; if unhedged, it is said to be open.
   2. To hedge a future receipt of funds, sell a forward contract for the same date as the future receipt.
   3. Hedging in the currency options market can eliminate downside risk.
   4. Other hedging methods.
      a. Bill in U.S. dollars.
      b. Sell the receivable.
      c. Pay earlier or later, depending on the strength or weakness of the two currencies.
      d. Coordinate transactions in numerous countries and hedge the net exposure.
      e. Borrow abroad.

II. International capital budgeting.
   A. The basic steps of capital budgeting remain the same; identify the incremental after-tax cash flows, discount at an appropriate required rate of return, and accept projects with positive net present values.
   B. Calculating net present values.
      1. Calculate NPVs in terms of the foreign currency, using an appropriate local required rate of return.
         a. 1 + required return = (1 + risk-free rate)(1 + risk premium).
         b. Using the U.S. required return and risk-free rate, calculate the required rate of return.
         c. Using the risk premium and the local risk-free rate, calculate the required rate of return.
         d. Convert the NPV to dollars using the spot rate. Accept all projects with positive NPVs.
      2. An alternative method is to convert cash flows to dollars and discount at a U.S. based discount rate.
         a. Use the spot rate to convert time 0 cash flows.

b. Calculate expected spot rates to convert future cash flows.

i. expected spot rate at the end of year t = $[\text{spot rate}][\text{inflation rate differential}]$

c. Discount at a dollar denominated required rate of return.
d. Both methods of calculating net present values should provide the same NPV in terms of dollars.

3. Most U.S. firms convert cash flows to dollars to calculate NPVs.

C. Problems in international capital budgeting.
1. Remittance: It may be difficult for parent companies to bring back funds from foreign subsidiaries.
    a. Many countries are sensitive to exploitation and limit the ability of international firms to take funds out of host countries.
    b. Taxes must be paid in foreign countries, and many countries additionally tax remitted funds.
    c. Taxes also must be paid in the United States, but firms receive a foreign tax credit.
2. Additional considerations in calculating required rates of return.
    a. There is evidence that international financial markets are segmented and U.S. firms may be able to raise capital more cheaply overseas, lowering required rates of return.
    b. International firms also face expropriation risk, raising required rates of return.
    c. Bankruptcy laws differ across countries. In many countries, creditors face more risk than in the U.S. and should demand a higher required return.
    d. It is impossible to state that foreign required returns should be higher than, lower than, or equal to domestic required returns. Firms need to know the territory and to evaluate all possible legal, tax, and political factors to calculate required returns.

III. International financing and operating decisions.
   A. The host company typically invests a small amount of equity and raises the remainder of the funds.
      1. Raise funds by borrowing in the U.S.
         a. The borrower is exposed to exchange risk.
      2. Raise funds by borrowing in the country where the project is located.
         a. This procedure provides a direct hedge against exchange risk.
      3. Raise funds where interest rates are most favorable.
   B. Operating and accounting for foreign subsidiaries are important since they have a direct impact on the U.S. parent's accounting statements.

FORMULAS

Required Rate of Return

$1 + \text{required return} = (1 + \text{risk-free rate})(1 + \text{risk premium})$

Expected Spot Rate

$\text{expected spot rate at the end of year } t = (\text{spot rate})(\text{inflation rate differential})$

Net Present Value

$$NPV = \sum_{t=1}^{n} \frac{CF_t}{(1 + k^t)} - CF_0$$

WHAT TO LOOK FOR

In the past 30 years, economies of various countries have become more and more integrated. Japanese automobile manufacturers, either alone or in concert with U.S. companies, own and operate manufacturing facilities in the U. S. United States corporations now own or operate facilities in virtually all corners of the globe. Many of the financial decisionmaking tools we have discussed are applicable to international situations, but additional factors must be discussed.

International financial management is complicated by the fact that transactions are conducted in more than one currency. American companies doing business in Malaysia are likely to be paid in ringgits, in India, rupees, or in Denmark, krone. Like any commodity, foreign currencies trade, and their prices, relative to the U.S. dollar, fluctuate. This fluctuation, called exchange rate risk, can be eliminated by good financial management.

Spot Rates and Forward Rates

A foreign exchange rate is the rate of conversion between currencies. Spot rates, or today's exchange rates, are quoted in either dollars needed to buy one unit of currency, or in units of currency needed to buy one dollar. For instance, on June 21, 1989, you could buy 38.65 Venezuelan bolivars with one dollar, or 0.02587 dollars with one bolivar. Using exchange rates found in the Wall Street Journal, you can calculate exchange rates between any two currencies. For instance, if the spot rate for Uruguay's new pesos was 577.00 per dollar, the exchange rate between bolivars and new pesos should be 577.00/38.65 = 14.93 new pesos per bolivar.

If you wish to take delivery of a currency at some point in time in the future you can buy a forward contract. A forward rate is an exchange rate agreed upon today for delivery of foreign currency at some time in the future. Forward rates are also listed daily in the Wall Street Journal. For example, a quote such as the following may appear:

Rate	Dollars required to buy one West German mark
Spot	0.5105
30-day forward	0.5118
90-day forward	0.5139
180-day forward	0.5167

The purchaser of a 90-day forward contract agrees to take delivery of marks at an exchange rate of $0.5139 per mark ninety days from now. Note that the forward rates are all above the spot rate. The primary reason for this is the difference in the expected rate of inflation between the two countries. If the U.S. inflation rate is expected to be higher than that of West Germany, the spot rate will be at a discount and the forward rates will increase.

Hedging

Because of the presence of forward currency contracts, it is possible for firms to eliminate exchange rate risk through hedging. The buyer of a forward currency contract agrees to trade dollars for a foreign currency at a rate decided upon today while the seller agrees to trade the currency for dollars. For example, suppose Consolidated Manufacturing agrees to sell equipment to Knessel Industries. Knessel agrees to pay 3.5 million marks for the equipment in 90 days. Consolidated is exposed to exchange risk; if exchange rates vary, Consolidated could receive fewer dollars than expected. They can eliminate this risk by selling a 90-day forward contract on 3.5 million marks. This will insure that they can trade marks at a rate of $0.5139 per mark and receive 3,500,000($0.5139) = $1,798,650 in the transaction, irrespective of spot rates 90 days from now.

There are other methods by which firms can construct at least partial hedges against exchange rate risk. For instance, a firm may hedge downside risk in the currency options market by buying and selling calls and puts. The company may also require payment in dollars or sell the receivable to shift exchange rate risk to other parties.

International Capital Budgeting

Traditional capital budgeting approaches can be used to make capital budgeting decisions, so long as we consider the additional risk associated with international operations. Suppose that Westfall Corporation is considering a capital budgeting project for their British subsidiary, York Industries Limited. If the project was undertaken in the U.S., Westfall would use a required return of 16%. The cash flows from the project (in pounds) are as follows:

Year	CF
0	-45,000
1	10,000
2	12,000
3	15,000
4	18,000
5	20,000

We can calculate the NPV in two ways. First, let's leave the cash flows in the local currency (in this case, pounds). A question immediately arises; is the 16% required return appropriate for this project? To answer this, we need to determine what the risk premium on this project is. Recall that the required return to the project must satisfy the equation:

1 + required return = (1 + risk-free rate)(1 + risk premium)

If the risk-free rate in the United States is 7.5%, the risk premium is:

$$1 + \text{risk premium} = 1.16/1.075$$
$$= 1.07907$$
$$\text{risk premium} = 0.07907 \text{ or } 7.907\%$$

Using this risk premium, we can solve for the required return in Britain. If the British risk-free rate is 9.5%, the required return is:

$$1 + \text{required return} = (1.095)(1.07907)$$
$$= 1.1816$$
$$\text{required return} = 0.1816 \text{ or } 18.16\%$$

Using this required return, we can calculate the NPV of the project.

$$\text{NPV} = \frac{10{,}000}{(1.1816)^1} + \frac{12{,}000}{(1.1816)^2} + \frac{15{,}000}{(1.1816)^3} + \frac{18{,}000}{(1.1816)^4} + \frac{20{,}000}{(1.1816)^5} - 45{,}000$$
$$= -932.41 \text{ pounds}$$

Given an exchange rate of 0.6425 pounds per dollar, the NPV in dollars is -932.41/0.6425 = -$1,451.22. The project is unacceptable. You should note that if you had not adjusted the required rate of return, and used 16% as the discount rate, the net present value is 1,612.01 pounds ($2,508.96) and you would have made the wrong decision.

A second approach is to convert cash flows to dollars and use a domestic discount rate to calculate net present value. To do so, we must forecast expected spot rates. The expected spot rate is simply the current spot rate times the inflation rate differential. If we assume that the real rate of interest is 2% in both Great Britain and the U.S., using the risk-free rates, the rate of inflation in the U.S. is 7.5% - 2% = 5.5%, and in Great Britain, 9.5% - 2% = 7.5%. The expected spot rate at the end of year 1 is $(0.6425)(1.075^1/1.055^1) = 0.6547$. At the end of year 2, the expected spot rate is $(0.6425)(1.075^2/1.055^2) = 0.6671$, and so on. Given all of the expected spot rates, we can convert the cash flows from pounds to dollars.

		Year					
		0	1	2	3	4	5
1.	Cash flow in pounds	-45,000	10,000	12,000	15,000	18,000	20,000
2.	Expected spot rates	0.6425	0.6547	0.6671	0.6797	0.6926	0.7058
3.	Cash flows in dollars (1/2)	-$70,039	$15,274	$17,988	$22,069	$25,989	$28,337

At 16%, the NPV of the above cash flows is -$1,519.96. Theoretically, it should be identical to that of the first method; the $68.74 difference is due to rounding. Most American companies convert cash flows to dollars before calculating present values.

Problems in International Capital Budgeting

A discussion of international capital budgeting would not be complete without mention of two problems. To this point, we have assumed that the U.S. firm can bring back (remit) the cash flows to the United States. Many nations provide barriers to such a remittance. These barriers include controls on exchange or taxes on remittance. Firms must also pay taxes in both the foreign countries and the United States, although foreign taxes result in a tax credit. Taxes, of course, reduce cash flows and make projects less attractive.

A second problem is risk. Not all economies and governments are as stable as the United States'. Firms venturing into less developed countries face expropriation risk; the host country may take over or demand part of the enterprise, resulting in a loss to the parent company. This risk is real, and must be accounted for in determining the required rate of return. Bankruptcy laws also differ across countries and need to be considered in reaching appropriate decisions. There is no substitute for understanding the economic and political climate in which the foreign subsidiary operates.

Financing and Operating an International Enterprise

Typically, the parent company invests only a part of the proceeds (in the form of equity) in a foreign operation and finances the rest of it by borrowing. There are three general approaches to financing. First, the firm can borrow in the United States and export the funds. Since the debt is denominated in dollars, the borrower is exposed to considerable exchange rate risk. The second approach is to borrow in the country where the project is located; this shifts exchange rate risk to the lender. The third alternative is to find the cheapest source of financing. In this approach, the parent should consider exchange rate risk.

Operating a foreign enterprise is complex; you must consider local customs, the local economy, and take into account various sources of international risk. There are also accounting complications that arise from foreign operations. Managers need to consider all of these facets before deciding whether or not to engage in an international project.

COMPLETION QUESTIONS

24.1 The _____ rate is the rate of exchange between currencies today.

24.2 The _____ rate is a rate of exchange between currencies, agreed upon today, for delivery in the future.

24.3 _____ is the risk that exchange rates will fluctuate and adversely affect cash flows.

24.4 Managers can eliminate some or all exchange rate risk by _____.

24.5 A firm expecting a payment in a foreign currency in the future can hedge by _____ a forward contract.

24.6 _____ risk is the risk that a host country will take over all or part of an enterprise.

24.7 The spot rate will be at a _____ if the U.S. rate of inflation is higher than that of the foreign country.

24.8 Bankruptcy laws differ across countries, exposing U.S. borrowers in foreign countries to _____ risk.

24.9 Some countries restrict _____ of funds and make it difficult for U.S. firms to bring profits back to America.

24.10 The expected spot rate is equal to the current spot rate times the _____.

PROBLEMS

24.1 If the exchange rate for Kuwaiti dinars is 0.2972 per U.S. dollar, and for the Saudi Arabian riyal is 3.7500 per dollar, what is the exchange rate between dinars and riyals?

24.2 National Watch has agreed to sell quartz watch movements to Zantar, Limited, a Swiss manufacturing firm. Zantar has agreed to pay 1.5 million Swiss francs in 30 days. The 30 day forward rate is 1.6855 Swiss francs per dollar. How should National construct a hedge to eliminate exchange rate risk? How much will they receive (in dollars) in 30 days?

24.3 The spot rate for Israel shekels is 1.816 per dollar. The inflation rate in Israel is expected to be 13% per year while in the U.S., it is expected to be 6% per year. Calculate expected spot rates for the next five years.

24.4 Georgia Gardeners is considering a joint venture with Netherlands Tulip Co. The cost of the project is 100,000 Dutch guilders and cash flows (after taxes) are forecasted to be:

Year	Cash Flows (in guilders)
0	-100,000
1	30,000
2	35,000
3	40,000
4	40,000

Georgia Gardeners would use a discount rate of 19% if this project were located in the United States. The U.S. risk-free rate is 9.5% while the risk-free rate in the Netherlands is 5.4%. Should the above project be accepted?

24.5 New York Fashions is considering a joint venture with Paris Designs. The venture will cost New York Fashions 68,000 francs and promises the following cash flows (before all taxes):

	Year			
	1	2	3	4
CF (in francs)	15,000	20,000	30,000	50,000

The corporate tax rate in France is 45%, and remittances are subject to a withholding tax of 12%. The U.S. tax rate is 40%. The current spot rate is 6.35 francs per dollar, the French inflation rate is expected to be 5%, and the U.S. rate is expected to be 7%. New York fashions believes that domestically, this project should have a required return of 15%. Should New York Fashions participate in the joint venture? (Hint: Use Table 24.2 as a guide to calculating cash flows.)

ANSWERS TO COMPLETION QUESTIONS

24.1 spot
24.2 forward
24.3 Exchange rate risk
24.4 hedging
24.5 selling

24.6 Expropriation
24.7 discount
24.8 creditor
24.9 remittance
24.10 inflation rate differential

SOLUTIONS TO PROBLEMS

24.1

Step 1. $\dfrac{3.7500 \text{ riyals per dollar}}{0.2972 \text{ dinars per dollar}} = 12.6178$ riyals per dinar

Step 2. or,

$\dfrac{0.2972 \text{ dinars per dollar}}{3.7500 \text{ riyals per dollar}} = 0.07925$ dinars per riyal

24.2

Step 1. National should sell a hedge for 1.5 million Swiss francs in the forward market. They will receive:

$$\frac{1,500,000}{1.6855} = \$889,943.64 \text{ in 30 days}$$

24.3

Step 1. Expected spot rate = (current spot rate)(inflation rate differential)

Year 1: expected spot rate = $1.816 \left[\dfrac{1.13^1}{1.06^1} \right] = 1.936$

Year 2: expected spot rate = $1.816 \left[\dfrac{1.13^2}{1.06^2} \right] = 2.064$

Year 3: expected spot rate = $1.816 \left[\dfrac{1.13^3}{1.06^3} \right] = 2.200$

Year 4: expected spot rate = $1.816 \left[\dfrac{1.13^4}{1.06^4} \right] = 2.345$

Year 5: expected spot rate = $1.816 \left[\dfrac{1.13^5}{1.06^5} \right] = 2.500$

24.4

Step 1. Solve for the risk premium in the U.S.

1 + required return = (1 + risk-free rate)(1 + risk premium)

1 + risk premium = 1 + required return/ 1 + risk-free rate

= 1.19/1.095 = 1.0868

risk premium = 0.0868 or 8.68%

Step 2. Solve for the required return in the Netherlands

1 + required return = (1 + risk-free rate)(1 + risk premium)

= (1.054)(1.0868) = 1.1455

required return = 0.1455

Step 3. $\text{NPV} = \sum_{t=1}^{n} \frac{CF_t}{(1+k^t)} - CF_0$

$= \frac{30{,}000}{(1.1455)^1} + \frac{35{,}000}{(1.1455)^2} + \frac{40{,}000}{(1.1455)^3} + \frac{40{,}000}{(1.1455)^4} - 100{,}000$

$= 26{,}189.44 + 26{,}673.37 + 26{,}611.83 + 23{,}231.63 - 100{,}000$

$= 102{,}706.27 - 100{,}000 = 2{,}206.27 \text{ guilders}$

24.5

Step 1. Calculate the expected spot rates.

$$\text{Expected spot rate} = \begin{bmatrix} \text{current} \\ \text{spot rate} \end{bmatrix} \begin{bmatrix} \text{expected} \\ \text{inflation differential} \end{bmatrix}$$

Year 1 expected spot rate $= 6.35 \left[\dfrac{1.05^1}{1.07^1}\right] = 6.231$

Year 2 expected spot rate $= 6.35 \left[\dfrac{1.05^2}{1.07^2}\right] = 6.115$

Year 3 expected spot rate $= 6.35 \left[\dfrac{1.05^3}{1.07^3}\right] = 6.001$

Year 4 expected spot rate $= 6.35 \left[\dfrac{1.05^4}{1.07^4}\right] = 5.888$

Step 2. Following Table 24.2:

		Year			
	0	1	2	3	4
1. Cash flow before taxes, in francs	-68,000	15,000	20,000	30,000	50,000
2. French corporate tax (1 × 0.45)		- 6,750	- 9,000	-13,500	-22,500
3. Cash flow available for remittance to parent (1 - 2)		8,250	11,000	16,500	27,500
4. Tax withheld at 12% (3 × 0.12)		-990	- 1,320	- 1,980	- 3,300
5. Remittance after French taxes, in francs (3 - 4)		7,260	9,680	14,520	24,200
6. Forecasted spot rate (from step 1)	6.350	6.231	6.115	6.001	5.888
7. Remittance received by parent in dollars (5/6)	-10,709	1,165	1,583	2,420	4,110
8. U.S. corporate tax (7 × 0.40)		-466	-633	-968	-1,644
9. Foreign tax credit [(2 + 4)/6]		1,242	1,688	2,580	4,382
10. Cash flow in dollars, CF (7 + 8 + 9)	-10,709	1,941	2,638	4,032	6,848

Step 3. Calculate NPV.

$$NPV = \sum_{t=1}^{n} \frac{CF_t}{(1+k^t)} - CF_0$$

$$= \frac{1,941}{(1.15)^1} + \frac{2,638}{(1.15)^2} + \frac{4,032}{(1.15)^3} + \frac{6,848}{(1.15)^4} - 10,709$$

$$= 1,687.83 + 1,994.71 + 2,651.11 + 3,915.37 - 10,709$$

$$= 10,249.02 - 10,709$$

$$= -459.98$$

Since the NPV is negative, the project should not be accepted.